THE IDEA OF ANCIENT
LITERARY CRITICISM

The Idea of Ancient Literary Criticism

*

Yun Lee Too

CLARENDON PRESS · OXFORD
1998

Oxford University Press, Great Clarendon Street, Oxford OX2 6DP
Oxford New York
Athens Auckland Bangkok Bogotá Buenos Aires Calcutta
Cape Town Chennai Dar es Salaam Delhi Florence Hong Kong Istanbul
Karachi Kuala Lumpur Madrid Melbourne Mexico City Mumbai
Nairobi Paris São Paolo Singapore Taipei Tokyo Toronto Warsaw
and associated companies in
Berlin Ibadan

Oxford is a registered trade mark of Oxford University Press

Published in the United States
by Oxford University Press Inc., New York

PA
3001
.T66
1998

British Library Cataloguing in Publication Data
Data available

Library of Congress Cataloging in Publication Data
The idea of ancient literary criticism / Yun Lee Too.
Includes bibliographical references and index.
1. Classical literature—History and criticism—Theory, etc.
2. Criticism—Greece—History. 3. Criticism—Rome—History.
I. Title.
PA3001.T66 1998 801'.95'0938—dc21 98–8001
ISBN 0–19–815076–8

1 3 5 7 9 10 8 6 4 2

Typeset by Hope Services (Abingdon) Ltd.
Printed in Great Britain on acid-free paper by
Biddles Ltd., Guildford & King's Lynn

PREFACE

By this book I have variously been enthralled, puzzled, driven to distraction, and absorbed over a number of years. This project had its germ during my time as an undergraduate in Classics and English at the University of Toronto, attempting to reconcile the different demands of philology and literary theory. At this point I was thinking about issues of how antiquity read and wrote as 'ancient literary theory', working on the assumption that there must have been an historical precedent for the forms of analysis we now term 'modern literary theory'. In the course of graduate school, I had my interests redirected to rhetorical discourse, and the diversion was an important one because it demanded attention to cultural context and specificity, and shifted my attention to 'criticism'. It is for this reason that this book encounters the 'idea' of literary criticism as a plurality of 'ideas': as a possible interpretive tool, perhaps more for literary history than the Greek and Latin texts themselves; as an obstacle to literary interpretation; and, latterly, as a discourse with a pragmatic function, the making and ordering of the community.

Because it has accompanied me, as idea and as material project, for such a long time, this study owes much to many people. At Toronto, I must acknowledge the teaching of W. David Shaw at Victoria College for showing me what close attention to a text might involve; I also owe debts to Alexander Dalzell, Elaine Fantham, and Brad Inwood for supporting my early forays into literary and rhetorical theory. At Cornell, I wish to thank Pietro Pucci, Fred Ahl, and Thomas Hubbard for challenging me to read in other and plural ways, and above all, 'against the grain'. More recently, I would like to acknowledge the support of the exceptionally stimulating and lively community in Classics at Cambridge, amongst others, Jamie Masters, Jas Elsner, Sam Evans, John Henderson, Simon Goldhill, Robert Wardy, Cathy Atherton, Malcolm Schofield, Myles Burnyeat, who provided early encouragement for the project; Richard Hunter, who read and commented on early drafts of chapters, and Paul Cartledge, who discussed with me in various contexts the state of 'classics'. A Research Fellowship at Gonville and Caius College, Cambridge provided the crucial time during which I was able to begin work on this manuscript. At the University of Liverpool, I would like to thank Christopher Tuplin; Henry Blumenthal for his support, collegiality, and discussions of Plato; Nick Davis, who discussed literary criticism and theory over many pleasurable lunches; and Bernard Beatty, who dispensed his invaluable wisdom in Staff House. I wish to acknowledge in addition the encouragement and support given by Don Fowler and by Jim Porter.

To the anonymous readers for Oxford University Press I am grateful for many valuable suggestions on how the different versions of the manuscript were to be improved and for their confidence that ancient criticism was a topic worth exploring. Hilary O'Shea has been a supportive and helpful editor; Jenny Wagstaffe has been an important source of advice. I must of course pay tribute to Donald Russell whose own scholarship has established ancient literary criticism as an important topic for classicists and who has provided support and valuable advice in recent years. My students at Cambridge and at Liverpool have proved the interest and engagement to be had from the study of ancient literary criticism.

For encouragement, moral support, and friendship, heartfelt thanks to Clare Brant, Paul Cartledge, Ewen Green, Jonathan Burt, Edward Burns, and my family.

Y.L.T.

Washington, DC
Autumn 1997

CONTENTS

ABBREVIATIONS

AJP	*American Journal of Philology*
ANRW	*Aufstieg und Niedergang der römischen Welt (Festschrift J. Vogt)*, ed. H. Temporini and W. Haase (Berlin and New York, 1972–)
CA	*Classical Antiquity*
CHCL i	*The Cambridge History of Literary Criticism*, i, ed. G. Kennedy (Cambridge, 1989)
CP	*Classical Philology*
CQ	*Classical Quarterly*
Crawford	M. H. Crawford (ed.), *Roman Statutes*, ii (*Bulletin of the Institute of Classical Studies*, Suppl. 64; London, 1996)
CW	*Classical World*
DCD	Augustine, *De civitate Dei*
DK	H. Diels and W. Kranz (eds.), *Die Fragmente der Vorsokratiker*, i and ii (Berlin, 1952)
ELH	*English Literary History*
GR	*Greece and Rome*
GRBS	*Greek, Roman, and Byzantine Studies*
H–G	F. W. Hall and W. M. Geldart (eds.), *Aristophanis Comoediae*, ii (Oxford, 1901)
HSCP	*Harvard Studies in Classical Philology*
ICS	*Illinois Classical Studies*
Jahn	O. Jahn (ed.), *Satirarum Liber* (Leipzig, 1843)
JHI	*Journal of the History of Ideas*
JHS	*Journal of Hellenic Studies*
JRS	*Journal of Roman Studies*
Kühn	C. G. Kühn (ed.), *Medicorum Graecorum Opera*, xvii (Leipzig, 1828)
Lindsay	W. M. Lindsay (ed.), *Sexti Pompeii Festi de Verborum Significatu* (Leipzig, 1913)
L–P	E. Lobel and D. Page (eds.), *Poetarum Lesbiorum Fragmenta* (Oxford, 1955)
MH	*Museum Helveticum*

MPhil	*Modern Philology*
NLH	*New Literary History*
PCPS	*Proceedings of the Cambridge Philological Society*
Pf.	R. Pfeiffer (ed.), *Callimachus*, 2 vols. (Oxford, 1949–53)
PMLA	*Proceedings of the Modern Language Association*
Proc. Arist. Soc.	*Proceedings of the Aristotelian Society*
QUCC	*Quaderni Urbinati di Cultura Classica*
REG	*Revue des Études Grecques*
REL	*Revue des Études Latines*
RhM	*Rheinisches Museum*
Rose	V. Rose (ed.), *Aristotelis qui Ferebantur Librorum Fragmenta* (Leipzig, 1886)
Stud. in Phil.	*Studies in Philology*
TAPA	*Transactions and Proceedings of the American Philological Association*
Usener– Radermacher	H. Usener and L. Radermacher (eds.), *Dionysii Halicarnasei Opuscula*, ii (Leipzig, 1904–29)
Warmington	E. H. Warmington (ed. and tr.), *Remains of Old Latin*, 3 vols. (Cambridge, Mass. and London, 1935–8; vol. i rev., 1956)
WD	Hesiod, *Works and Days*
West	M. L. West (ed.), *Delectus ex Iambis et Elegis Graecis* (Oxford, 1980)
WS	*Wiener Studien*
ZPE	*Zeitschrift für Papyrologie und Epigraphik*

Except for *WD* and *DCD* (see above), abbreviations of ancient authors and their works are those used in the *Oxford Classical Dictionary*, 3rd edn. (1996) and/or Liddell, Scott, and Jones, *A Greek–English Lexicon*, 9th edn. with Suppl. (1968).

Introduction

... the forces of censorship do not invariably operate by crude prohibitions, and ... oppression may adopt the demeanour of rationality, even of cooperation.

Frank Kermode in Johnson (1993), 46

I

The Idea of Ancient Literary Criticism is a book about an important episode in critical history stretching from the archaic Greek period to late antiquity. It is a study of literary criticism in antiquity as the collected, edited, anthologized, translated, historicized, and explicated body of ancient texts that supposedly helps us in understanding what the ancients thought art and literature were and that assists us consequently, as seems reasonable, in reading this literature.[1]

But it is also the case that a book entitled *The Idea of Ancient Literary Criticism* indicates that ancient literary criticism is not a discourse to be taken for granted; nor is it a self-obvious or self-evident discipline. It must be borne in mind that literary history is always to a degree an anachronistic construction. It is a narrative produced after the fact, and in the case of ancient literary criticism, long after the fact. As modern readers, we might be deceived into assuming that the texts constituting ancient criticism have always served the purposes that we now perceive them to fulfil—amongst these, attesting to and presenting an origin for a tradition of writing about how to produce and evaluate literary texts. This becomes clear from one mainstream history of criticism which emphatically distinguishes 'modern' criticism from 'ancient' criticism, so that a

---

[1] Major books and studies include Saintsbury (1908); Atkins (1934); Wimsatt and Brooks (1957); Gilbert (1962); Warry (1962); Grube (1965); Beardsley (1966); Harriott (1969); Russell and Winterbottom (1972); Trimpi (1983); Kennedy (1989).

temporal boundary is erected between the 'old' and the 'new', the 'ancient/classical' and the 'modern'. (Logically, of course, it is the case that *contemporary* literary criticism can exist only when scholars assert its departure from a prior, an 'ancient' literary tradition, and vice versa, so that to define itself as such the ancient tradition requires the 'moderns'.) René Wellek, one of the most important figures for criticism in the twentieth century, locates the *terminus post quem* for his encyclopaedic history of European criticism, *A History of Modern Criticism*, properly in the mid-1750s. He writes:

> Our sense of the continuity of critical tradition can be increased if we realize that the problems we discuss today have a long history and that we need not start thinking about them from scratch. The fact that modern criticism does not realise this . . . is the most serious obstacle to the propagation, establishment and final victory of an excellent cause.[2]

Writing in response to what he perceives to be New Criticism's disregard for history as a strategy of interpretation, Wellek proposes to reinstate history, and specifically the history of criticism itself. For him, critical tradition assists the contemporary reader in understanding contemporary critical issues, and economizes in the writing of critical history. But the economy comes at an expense. Wellek sees in pre-enlightenment criticism a seamless continuity, noting that prior to the seventeenth century, Greece and Rome were considered to be on the same plane as France and England, and ancient authors were regarded as virtual contemporaries.[3] A largely fixed and authoritative body of texts, Aristotle's *Poetics*, Horace's *Ars Poetica*, Quintilian, and Longinus, were invoked, read, and reread.[4] This history ironically instates its own form of historical unconsciousness, producing a rupture in the late eighteenth century by regarding this as the origin of questions and problems that the twentieth century might recognize as its own.

No less do classicists incorporate texts within our own literary-critical histories in ways that fix and settle their original intentionalities before allowing them to be questioned. Temporal distance enables us to forget or to fail to notice that this discourse and its texts are no less the result of often arbitrary authorizations which manifest themselves as debates, quarrels, or serious questionings.[5] By approaching 'ancient criticism' as an *idea*, this study acknow-

---

[2] Wellek (1955), 5.   [3] Ibid. 27.   [4] Ibid. 1 and 5.
[5] See Perkins (1992), 72.

ledges that to at least some degree a history of literary criticism is a reflection and indication of what we now think, imagine, and conceive criticism might have been.[6] A literary history is only one of many possible constructions, some more valid than others, contingent on any variety of factors. This book takes this understanding as a justification for attempting to offer an alternative account of the episode of critical history which belongs to Greek and Roman antiquity. This view of literary history becomes my invitation to interrogate the conventional understandings, the familiar perceptions, and contextualizations of 'ancient literary criticism' as a discourse *about* literature, perhaps as a metaliterary language. Where, for some individuals, a history of ancient criticism might centre its concerns on *what* to read as the privileged critical canon, the pressing issue for me is rather the question of *how* to read what we determine to be the canon.

This study argues for a radical reassessment of its role and place in cultural and literary history, and it adopts as a central premiss the position that ancient literary criticism is *readable*, understanding criticism as requiring the same forms of attention that a literary text is deemed to merit. The book is in part a response to the tendency of scholars to overlook or to fail to consider the possibilities of approaching ancient literary criticism as a discourse which itself requires reading and rereading. They have missed opportunities for considering how the texts may enact some of the problematics of writing and reception,[7] and ironically so in light of the perception that the amalgam of texts and discourses forming our idea of 'ancient literary criticism' supposedly highlights various key issues about reading and writing. Responsible for such an oversight is the hypostasizing and objectifying treatment which the academy both deliberately and undeliberately gives to matters unfamiliar and distant (in whatever sense). An account of such treatment is given by Frank Lentricchia when he perceptively paints the following unflattering portrait of the psychology of 'tradition': 'The literary intellectual, for example, feels an *esprit de corps* with the activities, however diverse, of literary critics since Aristotle—they are all in disinterested pursuit of that elusive essence, Literature; they are all

---

[6] For the view that literary history says as much about the present as about the past, see Starobinski (1975), 83, and Perkins (1992), 182.

[7] On the importance of 'rereading' as opposed to 'just reading', see A. Patterson (1993), 29; also La Capra (1985) 113; Graff (1993), 72–4.

united by the connective tissue of a common conceptual nomencla-
ture.'[8] The naïve faith in the continuity and community necessarily calls into question the historicity of such a literary intellectual's
project, his responsibility and sensitivity to the texts he reads.
When scholars work with such a perspective, hardly ever is the
notion of the 'classics' open to scrutiny with the result that modern
quarrels are conducted in isolation from other levels of textuality
which may have much to contribute to the latter-day debates.

Moreover, where ancient literary criticism is concerned, such an
intellectual must ignore the political and social agendas present in
the works over which we may be currently conducting battles
focused on questions of what we should read and study in schools
and institutions of higher education.[9] My emphasis on *how* to read
criticism enables us to engage more fully with these discussions,
and it is one which proceeds simply by asking such basic questions
as 'what' exactly ancient literary criticism was and for what pur-
pose(s) it might have been produced. After all, not everyone has
been oblivious to the difficulties of writing literary history where
antiquity is concerned. Closing his review of Donald Russell and
Michael Winterbottom's anthology of texts, *Ancient Literary
Criticism*, Marsh McCall provocatively observes, 'The standards of
ancient criticism . . . remain puzzling'.[10] That the standards of
ancient criticism should seem 'puzzling' to McCall is provoking as
a response to a collection of texts purporting to be ancient literary
criticism and thus should prompt the reader to consider a number
of questions, namely, whether we have correctly identified ancient
criticism, whether ancient criticism is similar to or different from
our own discourse(s) of criticism, or more radically, if there is after
all a coherent body of discourse, a system of texts sharing an intention and function, that we can recognize as a critical language.

A further justification for writing a different kind of history
comes from the recognition of the current 'crisis' in criticism. The
struggles between various camps—philologists, new critics, historicists, new historicists, post-structuralists and so on—interrogate the idea that criticism is anything but a neutral body of
statements about how to read and write texts. Criticism is now most
evidently a fluid and hardly self-obvious discourse; it is accordingly
one which indicates that it might always be other than what it is

[8] Lentricchia (1983), 125–6.   [9] e.g. Bromwich (1992); Graff (1993).
[10] McCall (1975), 85

constituted to be at any one point. Dominic La Capra incisively observes: 'The very constitution of literary criticism as a discipline depended upon a network of inclusions and exclusions (generally conceived in terms of the establishment of a 'canon') and the insertion of the discipline into an institutional matrix.'[11] This remark recognizes that literary criticism is never anything other than a construction, by drawing attention to its status as a product of various canonizations, of selections, which include certain texts and omit others and which value some texts more than others in its corpus. La Capra's statement about the formation of literary criticism as a discipline may also be read as a statement about ancient criticism itself. Likewise, where the latter discourse is concerned, we never simply read its texts; rather, we are always preferring certain discourses at the expense of others, and certain questions or issues to the neglect of still other equally valid ones. We allow our readings, inadvertently or not, to be shaped by presuppositions about what it ought to be and about what its function and role in society might be.

II

To see criticism as an activity detached or somehow set apart from the larger cultural and political life of society is to offer a basis for a narrative and an analysis very different from one which regards criticism as a central activity of and within society. If 'ancient criticism' has been responsible for casting ancient authors in the sort of roles that we currently have of them as disinterested, scholarly, critical, and theoretically informed readers who can guide us in our reception of works from Greek and Roman antiquity, it is because it has been assigned an aesthetic function, that is a socially disinterested role in judging the artistic merit and value of ancient literature. This study provides the opportunity to rethink and relocate the discourse of literary criticism by recognizing that it is an element of the cultural and political life and structure of a community. It rejects the description of criticism as an 'aesthetic' process, as one concerned with the regulation of taste or the appreciation of beauty, because 'taste' and 'beauty' tend to operate as uncontextualized/-able terms.

---

[11] La Capra (1985), 111.

Criticism is always to some extent a social language: it cannot be without its various and plural contexts, as the individuals who produce this discourse are to some degree formed by and within their environments, however we choose to understand 'environment'.[12]

But, if ancient criticism is not simplistically a discourse *about* literature, it is not for that reason also simplistically one *about* the world. In making this point, my study interrogates what Eric Auerbach established in 1953 as one of the privileged themes of contemporary literary theory, the understanding of literature as a *mimēsis*, as an imitation or a representation, of some sort of reality.[13] Where the discourse about *mimēsis* suggests that literature should be perceived most obviously as a product, an image, of its particular ideological or historical context, and while I propose the need to take 'environment' into account in the reading of criticism, I resist the notion that literary art and its poetics should be read as a literal or uncomplicated account of reality, and at its logical extreme that art should be treated as historical document. After all, Plato's *Republic*, which to all intents and purposes has become the *fons et origo* for the discourse on art as 'imitation', is a work whose concern explicitly is the *construction* of the ideal state. (As we shall see, it is also a problematic text, given what appears to be the expulsion of literature from the ideal state.) Recently, the value of new historicism has been to deny the reading of literary texts in any naïve or simplistic historicist fashion, and to show that life and community always also have the capacity to imitate and to be formed by literary discourse.[14] In contrast, the sort of approach I reject implicitly understands a text as wholly determined by the historical conditions and circumstances in which it was produced, and thus regards study of these conditions and circumstances as the meaning of the text. As David Perkins makes us aware, it inevitably produces a literary history which relies on textual authorities which are not necessarily reliable representations of the past.[15]

---

[12] Lentricchia (1980), 140.

[13] See Auerbach (1953). The privilege of μίμησις in literary theory and history may explain why there has been such considerable interest in Aristotle's *Poetics*, the work which discusses the status of tragedy as 'representation' and which, as Cave (1988) has shown, had until recently been an extremely marginal text in literary history.

[14] As President, Ronald Reagan plagiarized dialogue from his films, which suggests either that the movies do have an effect on real life, or else that Reagan was unable to distinguish between fantasy and reality; cf. Greenblatt (1987), 263–5; see also Eco (1987), esp. 3–58 and 213–14.   [15] Perkins (1992), 73.

Criticism participates in the process of social and political construction as a discourse bearing a close relationship to power and its structures.[16] This is a point that historians of post-antique criticism, and in particular of criticism as a 'modern' phenomenon, have variously highlighted. In the preface to *Culture and Society* Raymond Williams observes that key terms, such as 'industry', 'democracy', 'class', 'art', and 'culture', underwent a dramatic transformation in their usage at the end of the eighteenth century and that 'culture' in particular came to denote a distinct body of moral and intellectual activities.[17] In an article entitled 'From Classicist to Classical Literary Criticism, 1730–1806' Klaus Berghahn suggests that the eighteenth century produced a criticism which regarded itself as offering a liberation from ancient authorities.[18] Criticism became a bourgeois discourse which affirmed the values of the group who created it and was a key factor in the formation of the new bourgeois identity.[19] Likewise, Peter Hohendahl regards the eighteenth century as the point of origin for literary criticism as a language that creates rules for the reception and perception of literary texts within the public sphere.[20] Criticism is now a discourse of protest produced by the new middle classes against the authority of the aristocrat and the ancient authorities (i.e. the classics), with which he was identified and identified himself.[21] Literature and art began to have a broader-based audience and with this, what presented itself as a broader-based aesthetics. In English criticism, the most prominent proponent of this position is Terry Eagleton. Like Berghahn and Hohendahl, Eagleton perceives the 1700s to be the period when, through newspapers such as the *Spectator* and the *Tatler* and the salon culture in England, criticism becomes a discourse that provides instruction in a public taste and morality to be distinguished from that of the aristocratic élite. For this Marxist scholar, criticism is *cultural* criticism, a significant political catalyst in the struggle against absolutism, a programme which he perceives much of contemporary criticism to have abandoned.[22]

Literary historians may be right to see the eighteenth century as marking a significant point of transformation in that it is at this

[16] Mitchell (1982), 1.
[17] R. Williams (1958), pp. xiii–xviii.
[18] K. Berghahn in Hohendahl (1988), 15.
[19] Ibid. 21.
[20] Hohendahl (1989), 38.
[21] Hohendahl (1988), 14.
[22] Eagleton (1984), esp. 10–22.

point that the emergent middle class gains a voice and begins to articulate its own necessarily ideological discriminations regarding literature, art, and society. None the less, because 'criticism' is inflected with the social agenda 'to criticize' and so 'to protest', *ancient* literary criticism is produced only as an implicit, and generally unwanted, by-product. Criticism is specifically a middle-class discourse which seeks to and does make culture and cultural intervention more broadly based in society by protesting against a particular élitist authority. So where Wellek disregards antiquity as uniform and thus to be taken for granted, scholars working with a left perspective ostensibly largely exclude ancient texts from inclusion in this category of discourse. They reject classical antiquity and its texts as tainted with an élite authority and as the product of the socially and politically empowered élite, which their particular model of criticism seeks to oppose. Politicized criticism since the eighteenth century and the writing of its history in the later twentieth century have constituted a liberation of literary criticism from the courtly society of the early modern period and from the ancient rules of rhetoric and taste prescribed by Aristotle, Cicero, and Horace.[23]

Yet not all politically situated accounts of criticism require the exclusion of antiquity. For some non-classical scholars, criticism is to be regarded specifically as a process which undoes and neutralizes the effects of censorship. Chris Baldick observes that criticism does not operate in an open society, declaring, 'Criticism from Plato onwards has, on the contrary, presupposed censorship, banishment, and official persecution in the very language of its "judgements" and in its images of its own authority'.[24] A very different sort of critic, Leo Strauss, no less proposes the influence of repression upon modes of literary production and reception. In his *Persecution and the Art of Writing* he suggests that ancient rhetoric, often identified with or as an aspect of literary criticism, provides guidelines for subversive 'writing between the lines', and ancient criticism is its antidote. The latter discourse is concerned with the recovery of the hidden and esoteric meanings produced by rhetoric.[25] In her study of textuality in the early modern period, Annabel Patterson analyses the ways in which early modern

---

[23] Hohendahl (1988), 15, 28.   [24] Baldick (1983), 9.
[25] L. Strauss (1952), 24; for the view that rhetoric masks and dissembles meaning, see Ahl (1984a), esp. 204.

authors produce literary discourse and methods of reading by negotiating formal constraints placed upon what could be said, and offers her analyses as a general model for our notion of 'literature'.[26] For Patterson, the silencing of discourse is the impetus for literary language. As she admits, her approach to early modern writing constitutes an analysis derived from Foucault, who has argued that power in the early modern state and later is constituted by prohibitions, exclusions, and limits set upon what is, by contrast, deemed to be freedom, and whose work has generally sought to uncover the constraints and repressions, the systems, and the institutional structures, of such authoritarianism.[27] This legacy of constraint is acknowledged to some degree by Stanley Fish, who has argued that constraint is not necessarily to be equated with repression; rather he makes the point that we require constraints—rules and regulations—to make meaning out of language.[28]

While advocating the political dimensions of criticism, I offer an account of ancient criticism which differs on one significant point in maintaining that ancient criticism *qua* political process does not simply presuppose a background of, or is simply to be located in, repression. I want to suggest that ancient criticism is itself the frame of 'inclusions and exclusions'—and certainly, Straussian 'writing between the lines' is as much a form of censorship in seeking to control access to philosophical knowledge and wisdom. It is helpful to recall that the English word 'criticism' derives from the Greek verb *krinein*, which has a common sense in antiquity of 'judge', 'separate', 'pick out'. The Greek and Roman texts I read characterize criticism in antiquity as a discourse of distinctions.[29] In its legal context, *krinein* denotes the discrimination by the jury of two possible sides of a case presented by two opposing litigants (e.g. Aesch. *Eum.* 683). By judgement and discrimination, however arbitrary or however rationalized, criticism declares what sorts of discourse, literary or otherwise, may be uttered, written, and/or published, what sorts of language, again literary or otherwise, may be received and by what sorts of people and implicitly, in turn,

---

[26] See A. Patterson (1984), esp. 4.   [27] Ibid. 17; Lentricchia (1980), 349.
[28] Fish (1980) proposes that the 'interpretive community' and its interpretive conventions serve as a limit on what language can mean; in a later work (1994) he considers more formal, including legal, constraints on language.
[29] See in contrast Trimpi (1983: pp. x ff.), who has argued that in antiquity literary language itself resists distinctions of subject-matter and discipline which modern scholars have been too ready to impose upon it.

what may not, all in the service of social and/or political order.[30] It is significant that where the Greek verb *krinein* denotes a legal issue to be judged and resolved, the matter of legal discrimination is often presented as one on which the welfare of the state or city rests. But *krinein* also expresses the idea of selecting and discriminating between different discourses or explanations in non-legal contexts. The capacity and authority to make such selections is the basis for determining what will be heard and read—in contemporary terms, it is a strategy for 'canon formation'—and so a means of controlling what people may utter, write, and, in turn, hear and know.[31]

This book traces the origins and development of 'criticism' as a process of 'discrimination' and 'judgement' between various types of language, literary and non-literary: discourses are good/just/useful/truthful/utterable or, conversely, bad/unjust/useless/false/unspeakable and so on in the context of the communities in which they are produced, are circulated, and are received. Criticism is involved in authorizing and/or excluding discourses from society. Ancient criticism works on the assumption that the specific social and political circumstances which produce it are also in turn shaped and produced by language: language thus in some sense explains language. So the poet or rhetorician of antiquity might shape language, but poetic and rhetorical language were in their turn responsible for creating and shaping the world. The philosopher Democritus wrote of Homer constructing 'a structure (*kosmos*) of every sort of verse' under divine influence or inspiration,[32] while Solon says, 'I myself have come as a herald from lovely Salamis, having composed a structure of verse (*kosmon epeōn*) instead of an oration (*anti' agorēs*)' (Plut. *Sol.* 8. 2). Rosemary Harriott understands these texts to articulate praise for the *structure* of the epic poet's work.[33] Bruno Gentili, while also emphasizing the compositional aspects of early Greek poetry, goes further in his reading of

---

[30] At *Histories* 7. 54. 3 Herodotus employs the verb διακρῖναι when he admits that he cannot decide why the Persian leader Xerxes made offerings to the Hellespont: either Xerxes wanted to make an offering to the sun or he regretted lashing the Hellespont or he simply wished to offer a gift to the sea.

[31] Most (1990: 44) proposes that we recognize canonization as a form of censorship which governs textual reception rather than textual production.

[32] Ὅμηρος φύσεως λαχὼν θεαζούσης ἐπέων κόσμον ἐτεκτήνατο παντοίων (DK 68 B 21).

[33] Harriott (1969: 87, 137) cites as support for this interpretation of the Democritus passage *Od.* 8.170, θεὸς μορφὴν ἔπεσι στέφεν, 'the god crowned the form with words'.

these passages when he writes that 'every piece of poetry constituted a linguistic universe (*kosmos epeōn*) carefully worked out and
fitted together'.[34] The Greek word *kosmos* highlights the sense in
which the literary text is a self-contained entity. It suggests, moreover, an implicit analogy between the order of words and the order
of the world or cosmos, which this word also denotes, and in the
case of a materialist poetics, a synonymity between word and
world.[35] Certainly, the Solonic verse draws attention to the way in
which the poet-lawgiver created democratic Athens in part by writing laws and poetry. In later rhetorical culture, language plays a
central role in the creation of social identities. As the practitioners
of sophistic culture at Athens emphatically claimed, learning how
to use and manipulate words and their structures enabled one to
become a significant social and political agent. Choosing to say one
thing rather than something else, or to speak in a certain way rather
than another way is to select one way of being rather than another,
and in turn to influence the community to which one belongs and
which surrounds one.

Criticism assumes that language, oral or written, is the basis of
power because it is in turn the material from which political identities are formed. In discriminating between forms of discourse in
the community, it includes and excludes these discourses in ways
which inevitably mirror the configurations of power within the
society in question. The discourse about the creation and reception
of literary texts is coterminous and often identical with the construction of individuals as members of the political élite or, conversely, as the politically dispossessed. By pronouncing legitimate
certain types of discourse rather than others, criticism authorizes
the individuals who produce this discourse; by forbidding other
types of discourse, it excludes from power the individuals who
might lay claim to them. Literary discrimination serves to manufacture and maintain various political communities, and may do so
quite arbitrarily even when it serves to establish democratic discourses (as we shall see in the case of Aristotle, for example) or to
counter non-democratic ones (as we shall see in the case of
[Longinus]). Critical discourse is also one that, while reflecting the
state and its structures, may also seek to transform them, redefining the role and perception of discourse in society, and with this to

[34] Gentili (1988), 50.
[35] See, for example, Clay (1995), 10; Armstrong (1995), 210–32.

change society itself. If the constant of 'criticism' is its selective and discriminating processes, the discriminated categories are subject to constant redefinition and renegotiation as society redefines itself and its various ideals. Criticism is a discourse which may signify an ideal society, a perfect community perhaps to be found nowhere but in the text which produces the discourse, and thus can be said to exhibit a melioristic programme. So if in pronouncing about literary texts, critical languages are discourses of community, they are such in the very particular sense that they participate in the manufacture and then in the preservation of political communities.

The account I offer may explain why crisis is a central element of contemporary criticism, one that is perhaps overdetermined by ancient criticism: and *krinein* connotes, in addition to 'discrimination' and 'judgement', 'dispute' and 'conflict'.[36] Literary criticism in antiquity is either about preventing confrontations and hostilities by silencing the 'other' unwanted discourse(s), or else it is itself the scenario of these confrontations and hostilities. Ancient literary criticism articulates crisis in the sense that its discriminations are necessary for the good of the state and its citizens, but also in the sense that it engages in negotiation and struggle with alternative sets of discriminations established by prior and contemporary authors and institutions. Criticism is crisis (*krisis*) precisely because it advocates an ideal of community and citizen against the background or in competition with other alternative ideals of community and citizen.

III

No narrative can ever lay an authoritative claim to being complete; still less can it profess objectivity.[37]

To seek to locate ancient literary criticism in a set of texts previously unnamed and unrecognized as such may serve to open up the canon. Perhaps, what one needs to recognize in such a revision is the lure and comfort of marginality, a revision which is, none the less, a move that only sidesteps the historically authoritative texts and does little or nothing to interrogate with a view to unsettling the conventional 'idea' of literary criticism.[38] Since there are

---

[36] The middle voice κρίνομαι can mean 'contend'.
[37] See Perkins (1992), 13.   [38] See Bové (1986), 11.

necessary limitations—of length, of time, of comprehensiveness, and so on—to any literary history, I declare the status of this study as metanarrative, that is as an account that is constructed on the basis of a prior authoritative narrative in order to elucidate and to reinterpret the latter. While an objection could be raised that this book merely reinstates what it purports to be dislodging and is therefore rather more conservative than it would claim to be, I would offer in its further defence the more pressing need for a project which rehistoricizes and re-evaluates criticism in antiquity exactly by engaging with the traditionally privileged sites of the discourse.

The 'idea' of ancient criticism needs to be (re)considered on the textual terrain already accorded to it, in order to demonstrate how its functions, its significations, its boundaries, and even its disciplinarities may be other than previously recognized. This is regardless of whether or not canon revision is the explicit project of this book, although this may offer another way into the project of canon revision. Because choices are to be made amongst the available texts of this canon, I select texts which seem at first sight to challenge the notion that criticism is a political activity. My selections are those which seek to invite a rethinking as to whether 'literary' is distinct from political or from social, and conversely, as to whether 'political' stands in contradistinction to 'aesthetic', 'poetic', 'sublime', and so on. The reconsideration is in part set up by a narrative in which texts that might initially appear unpromising for such an enquiry are juxtaposed with other texts, where 'literary' is quite clearly 'political' or 'interested' in its concerns. I look at works (e.g. Plato, *Republic*; Augustine, *Confessions*) which reject a role for the literary or poetic in the political sphere to the extent that criticism, and still less *literary* criticism, appears not to be an issue, or else at works (e.g. Aristotle, *Poetics*; Hellenistic scholarship; *On the Sublime*) which seem to insist upon the distinctiveness of the literary and political in order to invite a reconsideration of the ways in which literary and the political concerns may be aligned. At other times, I deal with texts which are widely regarded as supporting a political criticism (e.g. Aristophanic comedy, Tacitus' *Dialogus*, and Lucan) in order to qualify and to locate within a larger context what is conventionally regarded as their political aspects.

As a recognition that the history of criticism is one of many possible narratives with one of many possible points of origin, I suggest here that I might have located the beginnings of ancient criticism in the eighteenth century, in the late nineteenth, or else in the twentieth century. This literally preposterous move would acknowledge the critical discourse of antiquity as the retrospective construction that serves to authorize 'modern' criticism.[39] Instead, taking as its point of departure several available accounts of ancient criticism, my narrative is organized chronologically to make apparent the historical and contextual specificities of the critical process. Chapter 1 reads the poetry of Hesiod as a 'beginning' of literary criticism. It considers the myth of Typhon, first as it appears in Hesiod's *Theogony* and then in its subsequent evocations in the comedies of Aristophanes—as an originary narrative for literary criticism as a process which discriminates between discourses for the good of the community. With his multiple and plural voices and the capacity they allow him for representation, Typhon is the mythical or metaphorical figure who threatens the stability of the community he inhabits. The Hesiodic and Aristophanic portraits of Typhon treat him as the figure who most prominently offers the justification for the selection of certain languages at the expense of others through legal judgement (*krisis*) or poetic contest.

Chapters 2, 3, and 4 revisit conventionally privileged sites of Greek criticism and poetics: Plato's *Republic*, Aristotle's *Poetics*, and the Alexandrian Mouseion-Library. Chapter 2 reconsiders the treatment of literature in Plato's ideal state within the context for reading criticism as established by Hesiod. It suggests that the banishment of the poet and his poetry is less the result of a 'quarrel between poetry and philosophy' than of the requirements of a stable community.[40] If the concept of justice (*dikaiosunē*) requires that each citizen has only one proper role and identity in the city, it is the case that the discourse of poetry threatens to disrupt the identity of the just citizen with its multiple and variegated roles and identities. Chapter 3 reads the *Poetics* of Aristotle on the understanding that there is a much closer affinity between the discussions of poetry in Plato's writing and in this work than is generally admitted. Where the *Poetics* has often been regarded as a non-political, because an aestheticizing, theory of tragedy, this chapter proposes a social contextualization for the Aristotelian discussion of literary art, arguing for the continuities between it and the *Politics*, where

---

[39] Cf. Perkins (1992), 36; also Bové (1986), 3.   [40] See S. Rosen (1988).

the philosopher considers the role of literature in the formation of the young citizen's identity. The *Republic*, Hesiod, and Aristophanes insist on the need for discrimination of literature, and Chapter 3 goes on to show how in the *Poetics* the identity of the ideal and socially privileged (Athenian) citizen is defined through its preference for tragedy and its pleasure at the expense of all other genres. Chapter 4 calls into question another topos of critical disinterest, Hellenistic literary study in the Alexandrian Mouseion-Library. It considers the way in which the professionalized and institutionalized activities of the scholar-critics actually construct an image of a political community predicated on a glorious Hellenic past. The editing of texts, the canonization of texts as authentically Greek, the translation of others so that they become Greek are all processes which allow Hellenistic culture and society to lay claim to what are appropriated origins.

The following two chapters examine Roman criticism in the republic and in the empire. Where the previous chapters consider criticism as a discourse and political strategy of the empowered élite, Chapters 5 and 6 show how the critical process and the sites of power in the community become disassociated and move apart, beginning with the empire. The authors I consider in Chapter 5— Horace, Ovid, Tacitus, and Lucan—retrospectively produce liberty of expression, and sometimes licence, as a condition of the past, whether this is constituted by classical Greece or the Roman republic, in order to signal or else to complain about the external repressions on discourse which are precisely not for the good of the community. My concern here is also to draw attention to how this body of critical discourse qualifies the ideal of *libertas*. While nostalgically idealizing freedom of expression, these authors none the less insist upon alternative constraints, engaging in self-criticism and in modes of oblique expression as a response to external regulation. Chapter 6 considers the self-critical dimensions of Roman rhetoric as represented by Quintilian and [Longinus] in *On the Sublime*. In particular, I offer a reading of *On the Sublime* which may appear to be iconoclastic; rather than interpreting the sublime as a strategy for writers to transcend the contemporary restraints placed on discourse and contemporary society, this chapter suggests that this work offers a cultural, but not necessarily a political, élite the opportunity to impose a set of discursive constraints in the interests of the creation of an alternative world.

The final two chapters of the study, 7 and 8, consider the transferability of the models of criticism enacted in the ancient Greek and classical Roman community to very different kinds of community. Chapter 7 argues that Augustine's discussions of literature and art in the *Confessions* and the *City of God* continue to insist upon the need to discriminate and regulate literature for the good of society, this time the Christian 'city'. Where Roman imperial authors complain about the lost freedom of speech (*libertas*), Augustine presents a view of a world which is created precisely by discriminations—following the biblical account of Creation—and he justifies the imposition of discursive constraints by invoking literary and legal material, which attest to the deficiencies of discrimination in pagan antiquity. If Augustine's critical programme shares a common overall purpose with those of Plato, Aristotle, and [Longinus], his specific model of a spiritual community and citizen leads him to reinterpret, displace, and reject prior critical discourses, both Greek and Latin. The last chapter, 8, interrogates the historicization which produces an 'ancient' and a 'modern' literary criticism. It argues that the discrimination of discourse is still with us and is still justified as being for the good of the community and its inhabitants. It looks at the analogies between ancient sites of criticism and modern ones, especially as concerns obscene material, pornography, and the contemporary curriculum. This final chapter examines contemporary North American and British cultural debate as the most influential critical sites for the phenomena that we might term a 'modern criticism'. It suggests that, while discriminations between materials being good or bad for society and anxieties about the plurality remain a constant of criticism, the agents of criticism are now more diverse in that they comprise both empowered and disempowered minorities. Criticism, it argues, continues to exist amongst us and should be recognized as a serious medium for contemporary cultural and political debate and transformation.

In offering a narrative of 'ancient literary criticism' as a narrative of textual models of political identity, this book produces a picture of criticism which questions, disappoints, revises, or even contradicts some of our assumptions about what criticism, past, present, and future, might or should be. To accept the arguments and readings this book offers, then, is to take a risk. It is to venture losing a familiar disciplinarity, namely 'criticism', and a model for what one does as a literary critic or interpreter of literary texts. In doing so, however, it simultaneously offers the opportunity to displace a particular model of criticism by a variety of other models which claim the social and political importance of critical activity, and to relocate these within the sphere of social and political discourse.

I

Krisis and *Agōn*: The Etymology of Criticism

In love with Tartarus through golden Aphrodite monstrous
Gaia bore Typhon, her youngest [or 'most capable of bearing
arms'] child. The powerful god's hands have works of
strength and his feet are tireless; from his shoulders descend a
hundred heads of a snake, of a terrible serpent, flashing with
dark tongues; from the eyes of his wondrous heads fire flashes
forth under his brow; from all of his heads fire burned as he
looked around. In all his terrible heads were voices producing
every manner of wonderous utterance. Sometimes they spoke
as to be understood by the gods; at other times [they uttered]
the voice of a bellowing, proud bull irrepressible in strength;
at other times, of a lion which possesses an unabashed heart; at
still other times, utterances like those of puppies, wondrous to
hear; or sometimes he whistled and the long mountains rang
out.

Now he would have posed an intractable task on that day,
and he would have ruled mortals and immortals if the father of
men and gods had not been quick to perceive it. . .*

Hesiod, *Theogony* 821–38

I

Histories have discursive beginnings. As the earliest Greek author
to treat poetry self-consciously through depictions of the poets
Demodocus and Phemius, and through his invocations of the
Muses, Homer is the logical starting-point for a history of *ancient
poetics*. As the earliest author to provide an explicit example of criticism as a discourse of discrimination, Hesiod is the paradigmatic
author for this history of *ancient criticism*. The originative scene of

* All translations are my own, unless otherwise noted.

criticism is the 'Typhonomachy', the story of Zeus' defeat of Typhon, the many-mouthed and many-tongued monster.[1] In the first part of this chapter (§§ II–V), I argue that Hesiod presents the first justification for silencing multiple discourses, as the voices of Typhon are associated with chaos and disorder. In the second part of this chapter (§§ VI–VII), I go on to examine how the meaning of this text for the history of criticism is established and confirmed by Aristophanes, who subsequently invokes the monster's utterances as a metaphor for oratorical excess in the classical democratic city.

I I

At *Theogony* 821 and following, Hesiod provides a narrative of the birth of Typhon, a description of this extraordinary creature, and an account of his defeat at the hands of Zeus. According to the poet's account Typhon is either the youngest or the most capable of bearings arms (cf. *hoplotaton*) of the offspring of Zeus and Gaia. From his shoulders hang a hundred heads of serpents; from under his eyes and from all his heads flashes forth fire. Also in all his terrible heads there are voices which utter sounds of every imaginable kind (cf. *pantoïēn*). Sometimes the voices are those which the gods can understand; at other times, they resemble the bellowing of a mighty bull, the roaring of a brave lion, or the yelping of puppies wondrous to hear; at still other times, the voices whistle and shriek. The high mountains echo with the voices of Typhon. The narrator closes his description of the monster by observing that the creature would have been an unmanageable problem and that he would have ruled over both mortals and immortals if Zeus, the father of men and gods, had not been quick to perceive the danger and act upon it. In the following section of the narrative Zeus selects his weapons, the thunderbolt and the flashing lightning rod, and with them cuts through the monster's fantastical heads (854–6). He lashes the monster so that the earth groans and is set alight. Finally,

---

[1] On the issue of the authenticity of the 'Typhonomachy', see Van der Valk (1953); for a commentary on the 'Typhonomachy', see M. L. West (1966), 379 ff. My argument implies that to exclude the Typhon-passage from the *Theogony* paradoxically deprives the poem of a justification for exclusion as a strategy for regulating the reception of the language in the community. It removes the argument for the removal of Typhon and his voices from the community, depriving subsequent authors of a critical paradigm which they might take up and negotiate.

the god casts Typhon into the depths of Tartarus to ensure that he, Zeus, holds absolute and unassailable power.

Typhon is the last of several monstrous beings who are subdued and constrained so as to ensure the stability and order of the community in the *Theogony*. Just as the god defeated Typhon, so his deputies Heracles and Bellerophon respectively defeat and destroy fifty-headed Cerberus (312) and the three-headed Chimaera (321) for the sake of preserving order in the community. What these beings have in common is the potential to upset the order of things, and this is especially the case with Typhon, whom Jean-Paul Vernant and Marcel Détienne have perceptively described as 'a power of confusion and disorder, an agent of chaos'.[2] Earlier in the *Theogony*, Hesiod describes the many-headed monster as hubristic and lawless (307), depicting him as a figure who transgresses social justice and order, literally *kosmos*. In the *Homeric Hymn to Apollo* Typhon is specifically described as a trouble to mortal men (352) and as afflicting the tribes of men with numerous evils (355). The *Theogony*'s Typhon is so threatening that even after his defeat he continues to endanger mortals. Zeus' metamorphosis of the monster merely transforms his power, changing the myriad, imitative voices—of which we hear no more—into the swelling winds which scatter ships and destroy the lives of sailors upon the sea, and upon the land ruin the labour of men (875–80). The Typhonic winds are 'other (*allai*)' (872) than and far apart from Notos, Boreas, Argesteos, and Zephyrus, the winds who are the offspring of the gods and a great boon to mortals (870–1).

The specific reason as to why the monster should ever have been a threat to the gods is less immediately apparent from the *Theogony*'s narrative. But the one feature that is central to the Hesiodic and subsequent depictions of Typhon is his vocality. Elsewhere, the *Homeric Hymn to Apollo* makes explicit Typhon's capabilities, declaring that, while the monster is like neither the gods nor human beings,[3] his voices (*phōnai*) resemble utterances and sounds including those made by the gods and by a variety of creatures: bulls, lions, puppies. In the *Prometheus Bound* Aeschylus presents Zeus as the brutal tyrant who has recently defeated the

---

[2] Vernant and Détienne (1974), 115–16; see also Ford (1992) 190.

[3] ἣ δ' ἔτεκ' οὔτε θεοῖς ἐναλίγκιον οὔτε βροτοῖσι (*h. Hom. Ap.* 351), which may be a confusion with the description of the Echidna, which neither resembles mortal men nor immortal gods and which mates with Typhon (*Theog.* 295–307).

Titans, amongst them Typhon. What the dramatist singles out for attention in his abbreviated Typhonomachy is the fact that the monster made boasts against the god (*PV* 351–72, esp. 360). He identifies the danger posed to the gods by Typhon as one specifically attributable to his utterances, and in this, I suggest, he invokes and rehearses the danger posed to the Olympian gods in the Hesiodic story. The boasting of the Aeschylean Titan alludes to the Hesiodic Typhon's ability to replicate the sounds of all sorts of beings, mortal and divine, so that those hearing these voices are deceived into thinking these beings are actually present.

Aristotle speaks of the voice (*phōnē*) as the human attribute most able to imitate.[4] Typhon's voices, like human ones, have imitative power as they enable him to seem any number of things he is not. Through his myriad voices, the creature has in effect a limitless capacity to lie and deceive, to be mistaken for other than what he really is.[5] The problem of mistaken identity perhaps may be what his many heads signify. At line 229 lies are said to be, like ambivalent speeches, the offspring of detestable Strife (Eris) and they stand in marked and significant opposition to unlying and truthful Nereus, the offspring of Pontus, who does not disregard laws and knows just counsels and whose speech is unfailing and innocent (233–6). Pandora, the woman created by gods to be a bane to mankind, wears a veil on which her creators have placed representations which 'resemble (cf. *eoikota*) living creatures with voices' (*Theog.* 584).

Lies and falsehoods mislead. By appearing to be what they are not, they confuse the perception of the order of things. But Typhon does not simply lie. The particular problem is that, because Typhon can speak in a manner comprehensible to the gods, he can also speak as the gods: his voices can offer a simulacrum, an imitation, of divinity. It is this quality which explains why he is disruptive as far as the order of things is concerned. As a creature who can speak like the gods and is not subordinate to them, he possesses a facility which potentially puts him in competition with the king of

---

[4] καὶ ἡ φωνὴ πάντων μιμητικώτατον τῶν μορίων ἡμῖν (*Rh.* 1404ᵃ22). So Orestes and Pylades pretend to be Phocians by imitating their accent (γλώσσῃ) (Aesch. *Cho.* 564). See Halliwell (1986: 114), for further references to vocal imitation, and Else (1958: 78), for ancient Greek actors imitating animal voices.

[5] Walsh (1984), 99.

gods and men.[6] The monster's plethora of mimetic voices thus has
the potential to disseminate, proliferate, and to confuse the origins
and sites of power. His voices have the capacity to articulate the
genealogies of authority which (as we shall see) are important to the
politics of the *Theogony*. Hence Zeus disposes of Typhon's numerous metamorphosing voices; he transforms them into inarticulate
winds and in this way he removes their mimetic capacity. Pindar
later presents Zeus' victory as a narrative of more literal containment of the monster and his discourse. Typhon, here specifically
described as the enemy of the gods, is imprisoned under the sea in
a Cilician cave, fastened down by the snowy volcano Etna (*Pyth.*
1.16–20). The cave, described as 'many-named' (*poluōnumon*), 17),
contains the discourse of the Pindaric monster.

III

In a famous epigram attributed to Simonides, painting is described
as silent poetry and poetry as a voiced painting. This statement,
often identified as one of the earliest self-conscious poetic statements and as one conventionally described as literary criticism,[7]
treats voice as the defining feature of poetry by its presence, and by
corollary, of painting by its absence. In early Greek poetry, multiple voices and the ability to produce all kinds of voices are regarded
as characteristic of superlative poetry.[8] In *Pythian* 12 Pindar
describes a melody produced by Athena which has the voice of
every flute, and the goddess's song is furthermore characterized as
having many heads which can imitate the groaning of the monster
Euryale.[9] In the *Homeric Hymn to Apollo* the Delian maidens are
said to 'know how to imitate the voices and clattering speech of all

---

[6] Vian (1952: 15 n. 1 and 17), observes that in the 4th cent. BCE Typhon is
depicted as the leader of the giants in accounts of the Gigantomachy.

[7] See Harriott (1969), 143 n. 5, and Plut. *De glor. Ath.* 3. 346 f.

[8] Polyphony is distinct from providing a full account or from telling everything,
which Aristotle refers to by the noun πολύμυθον, 'epic mass'; see Young (1983),
157–60, 164 ff. For an example of multiple tongues denoting πολύμυθον in the sense
that Aristotle ascribes to it, see *Il.* 2. 487–9, where the narrator wishes for 'ten
tongues, tens mouths, and an unbreakable voice', which would enable him to produce a better narrative in so far as it is more complete. The commonplace appears in
later epic, cf. e.g. Enn. *Ann.* 547–8; Ov. *Met.* 8. 533; *Fast.* 2. 119; *Tr.* 1. 5. 53; Sil.
Pun. 4. 525 ff.; Verg. *Ae.* 6. 625.

[9] ἐρρύσατο παρθένος αὐλῶν τεῦχε πάμφωνον μέλος, . . . | ὠνύμασεν κεφαλάν
πολλᾶν νόμον, | εὐκλεᾶ λαοσσόων μναστῆρ᾽ ἀγώνων (Pind. *Pyth.* 12. 19–24).

men', so that everyone thinks that he himself is producing the
utterances that he hears. The song of the maidens deceives
the audience into thinking itself the author of what is uttered.[10]
The maidens are fittingly the servants of Apollo, the god who possesses a whole range of song.[11] The idea of a plenitude of voice is
apparent elsewhere as signifying poetic excellence. It seems to
underlie Phemius' declaration that the gods put 'all kinds of paths
of song' (*oimas pantoias*) into his mind as a defence of his poetic skill
(*Od.* 22. 347–8), and Pindar's description of Apollo, god of the lyre
and song, as having control over 'all melodies' (*pantoiōn nomōn*)
(*Nem.* 5. 23–5). Bacchylides similarly makes reference to the 'myriad paths of immortal song' which are the gift of the Muses (19. 1).
It is interesting to note that plenitude is also a merit of artistic skills
other than poetry. In *Olympian* 7 Pindar praises the Rhodian artists
to whom the goddess Athena granted 'every skill' (*technan pasan*)
belonging to humans to fashion with their hands: so exceptional is
their artwork that what they produce resembles living and 'moving
beings' (*zōoisin herpontessi*) and their fame is vast (50–3).

These texts propose that the *Theogony* is an eccentric text in
expressing anxieties about Typhonic polyphony. As well, they
would seem to suggest that conventional early Greek poetics is
incommensurate with a political perspective inasmuch as Hesiod's
account of the defeat of Typhon is most obviously a narrative about
the origins of Zeus' ascendancy. But this is only to read the discourse of pre-classical poetics and the Typhonomachy in the most
superficial manner. Andrew Ford points out that a voice with
divine properties—and he thinks in particular of a limitless one
(*athespatos audō*)—is not in itself a good thing.[12] So each of the
non-Hesiodic descriptions of literary excellence specifically attributes plurality or variety of voice to supernatural beings, either the
gods themselves or their mediators, whether the Delian maidens,
the bard Phemius, the poet of the *Iliad*, or the Rhodian artists.
Following this logic, multiple voices are legitimate and praisewor-
thy when, and only when, they are authorized by a divine figure
such as Zeus or Apollo.

---

[10] πάντων δ' ἀνθρώπων φωνὰς καὶ κρεμβαλιαστὺν | μιμεῖσθ' ἴσασιν· φαίη δέ
κεν αὐτὸς ἕκαστος | φθέγγεσθ' οὕτω σφιν καλὴ συνάρηρεν ἀοιδή (*h. Hom. Ap.*
162–4). See also L. H. Pratt (1993), 78.

[11] πάντη γάρ τοι, Φοῖβε, νόμοι βεβλήατ' ᾠδῆς (*h. Hom. Ap.* 20).

[12] Ford (1992), 189.

The discursive politics of early Greek poetry is one which requires language to be divinely legitimated because language is in turn responsible for shaping perceptions of the world and ultimately, the world itself. The *Theogony* draws attention to the intimate link between poetic language and reality—that there are plural realities will become apparent—through its numerous etymological puns and wordplays: e.g. *Kuklōpes*, 'Cyclopes', from *kukloterēs*, 'round', describing their single eye (144–5); *Aphroditē*, 'Aphrodite', from *aphros*, denoting the 'foam' from which the goddess was born (195–8); *Titēnas*, 'Titans', from *titainontas*, expressing the 'striving' which characterizes the ambition of these deities (207–9). Poetic language evocatively names the Muses, following the narrative of their birth in such a way as to establish the propriety of their naming: *en thaliēis* ('in festivities') for Thaleia (= 'abundance', 'good cheer'; (65), *melpontai* ('they celebrate with song and dance') for Melpomene (66), *kleiousin* ('they celebrate/make famous/tell of') for Clio (67), *opi kalēi* ('with fine voice') for Calliope (68), *eratēn* and *eratos* ('lovely') for Erato (65 and 70), *humneusais* ('for/by those hymning') for Polymnia (70), *ouranôi* ('heaven') for Urania (71). Hesiodic language is homonymous and to some degree coterminous with the world that it signifies. Sometimes language plurally denotes reality. So gods and men may call the goddess of love 'Aphrodite', to refer to the foam (*aphros*) from which she emerged (191), 'Cytherian' because she came to Cytherians (198), and also 'Cyprus-born' because of her association with Cyprus (199).

Hesiod's Typhon-narrative is one which emphatically recognizes the need for language, and particularly extraordinary language, to be authorized by those who govern the order of things. Typhon's voices are peculiar as far as the *Theogony* is concerned in being the only ones to be 'heard' in the poem that are without the validation of the Olympian ruler. And thus they are silenced because they are not subordinated to Zeus' control but rather compete with the god's authority by potentially assuming the divinity's identity. Poignantly, the poem legitimates its own discourse and that of its world as poetry, most immediately as the language of Muses, and less immediately as the voice of Zeus. Although initially identified with Mount Helicon (1–2), the Muses also sing, dance, and live on the heights of Olympus, the home of the ruling gods, and they thus merit the epithet 'Olympian' (*Olumpiades*) (25;

cf. 51, 62, 68). It is not surprising that what these goddesses utter is in the service and the furtherance of divine authority. They are said to sing of the laws or conventions (*nomoi*) and the customs (*ēthea*) of all the immortals (66), but in particular they honour Zeus (81): so they sing hymns to delight the mind of father Zeus (36–7). When they hymn the generation of the gods, they utter a discourse above all about this god's origins and power (105). 'Hymn' is above all the language of praise (*kleos*) (cf. the verb *kleoioimi*, 32, and *kleiete*, 105). In providing its account of how the divine and mortal worlds came into their present condition, the song of the Muses attempts to naturalize the order of things, and in implying that the order of things can be no other way, their utterance is deeply conservative. Hesiodic genealogy is on one level a narrative about how words acquire their meaning and significances; but on another level it is also a narrative about how certain gods acquire the authority they have and why they are justified in holding it.

As a narrator of cosmogony, the poet is no less implicated in the production of discourses which establish and reinforce the position and authority of Zeus as leader of mortals and gods. The poet, as he depicts himself in the *Theogony*, is initiated into song by the Muses and granted by the goddesses a sceptre (*skeptron*), which signifies both poetic and political authority (30). As Robert Mondi points out, the sceptre is often associated with mortal kings and is linked with the poet's function in establishing what is right.[13] Several significant things occur in the initiation of the poet to suggest that this figure has surrendered any autonomy that he may have had as the uncultured shepherd. At line 22 the poet refers to himself by name, 'Hesiod', and he recalls that the Muses taught him fine song while he was tending his flock on Helicon.[14] Following his instruction by the goddesses, the poet no longer names himself but only refers to himself with the first-person pronoun *me* (24). The speaking voice gives up his name when he assumes his new role as *aoidos*. Between lines 22 and 24, the 'I' has been transformed from 'Hesiod', the uncultured shepherd who might stand for all such persons (cf. the goddess's invocation to him as 'shepherds' (*poimenes*)), into the pupil of the Muses and the poet of the *Theogony*.

Richard Martin observes that the *Theogony* is the recompense that the poet gives to Zeus in return for the gift of the sceptre,

---

[13] Mondi (1980), 207.   [14] Cf. M. Griffith (1983), 39.

elsewhere a mark of the king's authority.[15] In the *Works and Days* the poet identifies himself with the ruler of the gods and the latter's intentions when he declares that he speaks the mind of aegis-bearing Zeus and has been taught to sing an immortal song by the Muses (662). But the exchange described in the *Theogony* is one which requires the poet's discourse to surrender its status as an authorial text, one which the poet had a role in creating, to become an overdetermined script, which locates its authorship with someone other than the poet, namely the Muses (cf. 36) and, again, ultimately Zeus. The poet is ordered by the Muses to hymn the generation of the immortal gods (33), including Zeus, as the strongest and most powerful of the gods (49).

But the poet makes his audience aware that poetic language such as the present text is anything but disinterested. If and because the Muses, named the maidens of aegis-bearing Zeus at line 52 and the 'children (*tekna*) of Zeus' (76, 104), are the agents of the divinity who rules over the gods and mortals (cf. 71), they do not necessarily sing the truth, or inspire others to utter the truth. The poet of the *Theogony* reports that while the goddesses order him to make known the future and the past (32), they also declare to him that 'they know how to say many lies which resemble true things (*pseudea . . . etumoisin homoia*), and when they wish, to utter many truths (*alēthea*)' (27–8). The discourse authorized and inspired by the goddess involves truth, and falsehoods which appear to be true but are not so—in other words, verisimilitudes. (Perhaps, by their naming of 'falsehoods which resemble truths', they also imply the existence of a third category of discourse—falsehoods which do not resemble truths (cf. Odysseus, *Od.* 19. 203; Plut. *Mor.* 346 f. and ff.).[16]) Not surprisingly, scholars give lines 27–8 of the poem special attention because they exhibit awareness of what it might mean to produce poetry either in the abstract or in the context of an archaic community.[17] But the poet's description of lies (*pseudea*) '*like* (*homoia*) true things' (27–8) itself poses an interpretive prob-

---

[15] Martin (1984), 35; and see Duban (1980: 7 n. 1), for a list of passages where sceptres appear in the possession of kings.

[16] The author of the *Dissoi logoi*, which may be dated to the 5th cent. BCE, observes that the best tragedians and painters produce deceptions which resemble the truth and implies that poets write not to teach but for pleasure (3. 10). See also Halliwell (1986), 14.

[17] Russell and Winterbottom (1972: 2–3) anthologize these lines as one of the inceptive texts in their narrative of criticism in antiquity.

lem for its reader. It presents an epistemological problem, as Derridean readings of the lines in particular highlight. Pietro Pucci reads these verses as inviting us to collapse the categories of truth and falsehood and in so doing, to abolish a category of absolute Truth: because the Muses' falsehoods resemble truths, the mortal poet and his audience have no criterion by which to establish what *is* and what is not true.[18] Accordingly, poetry leaves its audience unenlightened, for the unknowing poet is bound to mediate the message with which the goddesses inspire him and to present this to other similarly unknowing and undistinguishing mortals. In response to the Derridean perspective, Giovanni Ferrari prefers to restrict the reference of Hesiod's lines, so that they are to be read as a description of how lies function and not as a statement about (poetic) language in general.[19] This scholar suggests that the pre-occupation with truth and its disruption by followers of Derrida is mistaken, as archaic poetics does not necessarily regard language as an imitation of a fixed reality.

Ferrari is quite right to distinguish between falsehood and truth on the basis that the former is an imitation (of truth) and the latter is a non-imitation. He is mistaken, however, in wanting to limit the significance of what the Muses say, for their own description of what their language might be has far-reaching implications for discourse in the *Theogony* as a whole. The goddesses' account of their own discourse draws attention to the importance of political authorization in the categorizations of language in terms of value-laden dichotomies, e.g. true/false, just/unjust, and so on. As a mimetic discourse which deceives by appearing to be what it is not, the Muses' own language has affinities with the voices of Typhon, which appear to suggest actual beings and objects that they are not. To put it another way that makes the analogy apparent, the many-headed monster no less utters 'lies resembling true things'. Where the *Theogony* is specifically concerned, G. B. Walsh proposes that while true poetry is destined for Zeus and the gods, plausible poetry is intended above all for humans.[20] The poetry that the Muses inspire functions in part deceptively to preserve the reputation of the gods as the benevolent 'bestowers of blessings', as the poet describes them at 46 and 111. Thus even the relatively unimportant Hecate is portrayed as the deity who assists Zeus' critical

---

[18] Pucci (1977) 16; see also Arthur (1983), 105.
[19] G. Ferrari in Benjamin (1988), esp. 47, 53.   [20] Walsh (1984), 26.

project: she bestows honour on mortals and assists revered kings in their judgements and the people in their public gathering places, much as Zeus and the Muses are said to (429–38).[21]

The Muses deceive in still another and larger way. They have the capacity to make their audiences forget the truth. The poetry they inspire shields its audience from the less pleasant side of their existence and of the status quo. Poetry operates as a panacea for the divine king's mortal subjects, keeping the community ruled over by Zeus content and, accordingly, well ordered.[22] Hesiod describes the goddesses as a 'forgetting (*lēsmosunē*) of evils and a cessation of cares' (55), and he later speaks of the Muses' attendant, the singer-poet, as forgetting his own worries and cares (102). The Muses are paradoxically the offspring of Memory (*Mnemosunē*), but it is also the case that they undermine the status of Memory as recollection of actuality. As a means by which mortals forget their sorrows and recall the beneficences performed by the gods, poetry attributes the responsibility for human woes to figures other than the Olympian gods and their agents. Thus the poet attributes the woes of sailors to the winds of Typhon (874) and he ascribes the miserable state of mankind above all to Pandora, literally 'the all-giver', who stands as the archetype of all women (590). While the gods play their part in making Pandora, poignantly described as humanity's 'unmanageable (*amēchanon*) problem' (589) in anticipation of the description of the many-headed sea monster as the gods' unmanageable problem (also *ergon amēchanon*, 836), the narrative is insistent that they do so only as a response to Prometheus' theft of fire.

In inducing forgetfulness, the Muses are engaging in further lies. As Thomas Cole reminds us, truth, *a-lētheia*, is etymologically conceived as 'un-forgetting' or remembering.[23] Hesiod calls into question the view that early Greek poetry, especially epic, authorizes itself as a medium of truth in reference to its function as a record of 'historical truth' and of a past glorious world through the

---

[21] Of this passage M. L. West (1988: 69) writes: 'He [Hesiod] sounds like an evangelist for Hecate, who is not mentioned by Homer and seems to have been a relatively new goddess. She has not yet developed the sinister associations that she comes to have in later centuries.' M. Griffith (1983: 51–5) sees the extravagance of the account as a sign that it is motivated by Hecate's proximity to Zeus. By later authors such as Euripides (cf. *Med.* 394 ff.) Hecate is characterized as a goddess who assists sinister actions

[22] See Duban (1980); Walsh (1984: 34) notes the similarities between the deceptive παράφασις of kings and Pandora.

[23] Cole (1983) 7.

Muses.[24] Questioning the view of poetry as society's truthful discourse and as a mnemonic which maintains the identity and stability of the community in which it circulates, Ewen Bowie significantly argues that epic and archaic poetry nowhere lay claim to access to a universal truth and calls for recognition of poetry's role in giving pleasure (cf. *Od.* 8. 43–5).[25] Bowie's observations have support from Aristotle who attributes to *the* epic poet Homer responsibility for teaching other poets how they are to lie (*pseudē legein*) (*Poet.* 1460ᵃ19).

IV

Zeus' treatment of Typhon in the *Theogony* dramatizes the exclusion from the community of discourses which are not sanctioned by the beings who hold power. It is the text which provides the most explicit paradigm and justification for other critical scenarios in Hesiod's poetry. The defeat of Typhon is rehearsed, for instance, amongst mortals in the discourse of human kings. Kings are the human representatives and analogues of Zeus. They appropriately derive their authority from the ruling god, as the phrase 'from Zeus' (*ek Dios*, 96) and the epithet *diotrepheoi*, literally 'nurtured by Zeus' (82), suggest. In addition to denoting the god's concern for kings, the epithet *diotrepheos/diotrephēs* also carries the sense of divine authorization and legitimacy. In the *Homeric Hymn to Hermes* the prophecy of the Delian bee maidens is described as 'Zeus-nurtured prophecy' (*manteiēn . . . diotrephes*, 533); the epithet indicates that the god has specially granted the maidens the capacity for such song. Apollo makes explicit the authorization entailed in being described as, and in being, *diotrephēs*. The god declares that while Hermes has been granted a sceptre signifying his prerogative to control words and deeds, Zeus refused the gift of prophecy to other immortals including Hermes (*h. Hom. Merc.* 534). Elsewhere, in book 2 of the *Iliad* the Greeks gather to listen to their leaders, described as 'Zeus-nurtured kings' (*diotrepheōn basilēōn*, 98). The adjective occurs precisely at a point when the authority of the leaders and their discourse is highlighted. Nine heralds ensure that the council will attend to its leaders. They set

---

[24] Rösler (1980); Macleod (1983), 4–6; Halliwell (1986), 11.

[25] Bowie (1993), 12.

the gathering in order. They silence and constrain the crowd which
is producing a din (*klangē*), denoted in the Greek by a word which
may also denote the scream of birds, the hissing of snakes, or the
baying of dogs (95–8). Perhaps Thersites, who utters his disorderly
and vile abuse as a challenge to the authority of Agamemnon,
makes apparent the insubordination potentially entailed in such a
hubbub (*Il.* 2. 212–16).

Significantly, Zeus' nurturing of the Hesiodic kings involves
attention from the Muses. The goddesses pour sweet dew upon the
tongues of kings so that from their mouths proceed words which
are variously described as 'sweet', 'flattering', and 'gentle' (*Theog.*
83–93) and which in turn recall the Muses' 'sweet utterance'
(39–40) and 'lovely voice' (*eratēn . . . ossan*, 65; cf. *epēraton ossan*,
67).[26] Appropriately, the most powerful of the Muses (79),
Calliope, serves kings: she transmits to them a discourse which
operates in the service of the community.[27] Martin has shed additional light on what might constitute royal language. This scholar
observes verbal affinities between the description of the kings' language at *Theogony* 86–93 and Odysseus' description of the man
whom the gods are said to bless at *Odyssey* 8. 166–77.[28] He suggests
that both passages share a common genre, namely that of the
'instruction of princes'. This genre, which Martin West shows to
have a notable subsequent tradition, is concerned to transmit the
rules and norms of proper social and political behaviour.[29]

As far as Hesiod's poetry is concerned, the instruction of princes
must ostensibly be above all concerned with the transmission of
knowledge of justice, for the kings of the *Theogony* distinguish
between what is right and wrong, straight and crooked. Hesiod's
kings have the prerogative to judge (cf. *diakrinonta*) what is just in
disputes between members of the community (85–6). The participle *diakrinonta* specifically denotes an act of discrimination and
selection. They are described as entering a public space, either the
market-place (*agorē*) or lawcourt (*agōn*), to end a great dispute or
strife and to accomplish deeds which bring restitution or recom-

---

[26] See Arthur (1983), 109.   [27] Duban (1980), 10, 16.

[28] Martin notes the common phrases: 'he speaks firmly' (ὁ δ' ἀσφαλέως
ἀγορεύει, *Theog.* 86; cf. *Od.* 8. 171), 'with/by gracious dignity' (αἰδοῖ μειλιχίῃ,
Theog. 92 and *Od.* 8. 172), and 'he is distinguished amongst the assembled' (μετὰ δὲ
πρέπει ἀγρομένοισι(ν), *Theog.* 92 and *Od.* 8. 172); cf. also *h. Hom.* 25. 2–5. See
Martin (1984), 29–48; also Duban (1980), 11–12, and Braswell (1981), 237–9.

[29] M. L. West (1978), 14–18; Martin (1984), 32–3.

pense by means of their placatory and knowing judgements (87–90). Poignantly, Hesiod declares that the people placate the king who comes into their midst 'as if he were a god' (91). This comparison of the mortal leader to a god is significant because it underscores the status of kings as the human counterparts to Zeus. Just as Zeus orders the overall community by excluding the multiple voices of Typhon, the human king chooses between the discourses of his subjects and in this way sets his community in order. By divine right the king regulates public discourse for the good of his people, dismissing the account of the unsuccessful litigant as 'unjust'.[30]

The legal scenario is precisely and essentially a critical one. In the forensic judgement represented on the Shield of Achilles in book 18 of the *Iliad*, the leader of the community selects and favours the account of the party who spoke more justly or more straightly in a case regarding compensation for a homicide, and he rejects the competing accounts (cf. *Il.* 18. 507–8). The designation of the legal argument as a *dikē* (cf. *Il.* 18. 508) offers an etymology of such a judgement as a *discrimination*, a criticism, of discourses. Scholars have noted that the word *dikē*, either 'justice' or 'legal case' or 'dispute', is derived from 'boundary' or 'dividing line'.[31] To signal his recognition of this etymology, Hesiod juxtaposes the verb *diakrinōmetha*, literally 'let us distinguish between', with the phrase 'with straight judgements (*itheīēsi dikēis*)', when he prescribes how quarrels are to be resolved at *Works and Days* 35–6. The importance of the leader's ability to discriminate between discourses as just or unjust is made apparent elsewhere in this poem. Here the poet declares that when judgement is just, the city and her people flourish (*WD* 227), but when judgement is corrupted and crooked, then trouble comes upon the people (223). In the society depicted in this text the problem is that discernment has gone astray and its poet implicitly assumes the responsibility of re-establishing it.

Martin understands the dignity (*aidōs*) (cf. *aidoi meilichiei*) which graces the leader's speech described in the *Theogony* and the *Odyssey* as implying 'proper speech', that is undeceptive language,

---

[30] Mondi (1980), 203; also Benveniste (1969), ii. 15.
[31] For the Muses as the arbiters of justice in society, see Gagarin (1973), 82–3; Roth (1976), 333, 338.

and timely discourse.[32] Yet, just as the poetry of the Muses is not simply 'true', the discourses which critical activity in the *Theogony* authorizes as being 'just' (where the kings are concerned) are not simply absolutely just or true. They are, rather, interested constructions of justice and truth by the individuals who have the power, however justified or however arbitrary, to discriminate between speeches which may themselves be neither straightforwardly true nor false. Epic poetry reveals the arbitrariness of divinely authorized judgement when it presents the 'instruction of princes' and the king's enactment of this instruction as being concerned above all with the question of how to rule in an orderly and authoritative fashion, perhaps as Zeus does in the Hesiodic cosmogony.

The *Odyssey* is a poem which portrays its hero, Odysseus, as a master of disguises, deceptions, and indirections; and Homer's representation of the education of the prince, Telemachus, by Athena in book 1 of the *Odyssey* suggests that this genre may serve as a training in manipulation and deception in the service of political authority. At the beginning of the epic Athena arrives at the palace of Odysseus to prepare the way for the hero's return and to oversee the initiation of the prince into manhood (1. 295–305). The goddess fills the role of father-surrogate and teacher to Telemachus (cf. 308); however, the pedagogy which she provides is one that engages in concealments and misrepresentations of the whole truth. She arrives in disguise as Mentes, an ancestral guest-friend (179 ff.), and spurs Telemachus to action by telling him that savage men, and not Calypso, hold Odysseus captive on an island (196–9). Athena's re-representation of facts is deliberate. To appear as a contemporary of Odysseus, she constructs herself in a fatherly role, and in not speaking of Calypso's capture of the hero, she does not compromise the latter's heroic status and all-important identity as husband of Penelope. The goddess's instruction of the prince through the models of heroism she offers in herself and in his father succeeds, for in the following book Telemachus assumes his father's seat in the assembly (2. 14) and delivers a speech which stirs its audience to pity for the royal household (2. 80–3). Telemachus has learned how to conceal his true intentions and actions for his own advantage. He assures Athena that he has only

---

[32] Martin (1984), 38–41.

told the nurse Eurycleia about his expedition to learn of his father's fate and no one else, not even his mother (412–3).

Elsewhere in the *Odyssey*, there are clear indications that speech will be guided by social and political exigency. In book 2 Mentor begins his speech to the assembled Ithacans by urging that the sceptred king can no longer afford to be well disposed, kind, or just in his thoughts but must now be harsh and severe in his actions in light of the problem of the suitors (2. 229–40). Later, in book 4 of the *Odyssey*, Penelope observes that although Odysseus never did or spoke anything which might be regarded as 'transgressive' (*exaision*), it is nevertheless the right (*dikē*) of divine kings to act or speak in such a manner, especially where enemies are concerned (4. 689–93).

V

If the *Theogony* reveals the constraints on its discourse through its genealogy of poetry, the poet's initiation, and, of course, the defeat of Typhon, then the *Works and Days* depicts the human world as a critical scenario where language is discriminated and legitimated as true, just, or beneficial. The *Works and Days* takes it as a given that public discourses need to be regulated if the orderly community, now the 'just community', is to exist. The poem presents its audience with a series of authoritative, but none the less arbitrary, discriminations and categorizations of language. Hesiod inaugurates the work with an invocation to Zeus as the figure who has determined what is acceptable and unacceptable discourse in the community. The god establishes what is utterable (*phatoi*) and unutterable (*aphatoi*) and, furthermore, he determines which members of the mortal community are to be spoken of, or commemorated (cf. *phatoi/rhētoi*), or, conversely, not spoken of (cf. *aphatoi/arrhētoi*) (3–4). The utterable and unutterable appear to correspond to categories of just and unjust discourse respectively, as the poet commands his addressee, most immediately his wayward brother Perses, to 'make straight ordinances' or 'laws' through justice (9–10).

As in the *Theogony*, Zeus has the power to define and to redefine at whim the acceptable and unacceptable categories of discourse. The god can easily (cf. *rhea/rheia*) make heavy what is light, diminish what is pre-eminent, increase what is unremarkable, and straighten the crooked (5–8). The adverb *rhea/rheia* is emphatically repeated in these lines to suggest that these categories are after all fluid and that their given designations are constructed rather than natural. In this respect, the prologue of the *Works and Days* perhaps anticipates the fifth- and fourth-century definitions of rhetoric as a skill which enables the speaker to make small things seem great, great things seem small, old things new, new things old, and so on.[33] The mortal society of the *Works and Days* is one which needs not only to defer to Zeus' judgements if it is to flourish but perhaps also to forget that justice and the language associated with it are arbitrary authorizations. Between the initiation narrated in the *Theogony* and this passage, Hesiod engages in a strategic amnesia. Thus the present poem naturalizes the categories of language, effacing the etymological consciousness of the *Theogony*. The poet concludes his proem by declaring that he now speaks what *is* (cf. *etētuma*) to the addressee, Perses (10). He conveniently elides any potential distinctions between what resembles what *is* (*etētuma*) namely plausible falsehoods (cf. *pseudea . . . etumoisin homoia*, *Theog.* 27–8), and the truth itself as far as his poetry is concerned.

Hesiod's exclusion of categories of discourse other than the truth as a description for his poetry is a strategy for strengthening the authority of the current text. This authorization of the poetic text is elsewhere reinforced by the poet's attempt to silence other possible poetic voices, by locating them, as it were, outside the epic's fictive community. The narrative of the 'Ages of Man' realigns kings with Zeus, recalling their close association in the community depicted in the *Theogony*. Robert Lamberton notes that, unlike Homeric kings, who are always mortal, these Hesiodic kings may be men *or* gods, and so mediate between the divine and human spheres.[34] The poet observes that the inhabitants of the Golden Age are knowledgeable through the plans of Zeus (*WD* 120) and have now gained possession of kingly honour (*geras basilēion*) (126). Frederic Solmsen (OCT), following ancient critics, brackets lines 124–5 for the reason that they recur as lines 254–5. These lines tell us that the kings preserve justice (*dikas*) [against] wicked deeds. Whether these lines appear twice or only once in the text, they are important because they suggest that the ruling mortals of the

---

[33] e.g. Pl. *Phdr.* 267a–b; Isoc. *Paneg.* 8, and Demetr. *Eloc.* 120.
[34] Lamberton (1988), 65.

Golden Age preserve the categories of justice and injustice as they have been established by the gods, and especially Zeus, in the proem. In lines 249 ff., which precede the description of kings as preservers of justice, the poet appears to recall the privileged inhabitants of the Golden Age. He refers to the thirty thousand individuals whose task it is to take note of those who do injustice (*skolieisi dikeisin*) to others and who ignore the vengeance of the gods. These beings are described as guardians (*phulakes*) of mortal men, because they watch for (cf. *phulassousin*) justice and wicked deeds, and receive the assistance of the goddess Justice (253–5).

In stark contrast to the inhabitants of the Golden Age are the poet's own contemporaries, the inhabitants of the corrupt Fifth Age. These mortals speak with 'harsh words (*chalepois* . . . *epessi*), ignorant of the gods' voices' (186–7), and with 'crooked speeches (*muthoisi skoliois*), forswearing their oaths' (194; cf. 190–1). They judge (*krinosi*) the laws with 'crooked cases' (*skolieis* . . . *dikeis*), as do their kings, who utter crooked judgements (cf. *dikas skolios enepontes*) and receive bribes (cf. *dorophagoi*, 221). The poet provides an aetiology of the Fifth Age both in the narrative of decline that is presented in the myth of the Ages of Man and indirectly in the Pandora-narrative in this poem. Here, Pandora is said to utter lies (*pseudea*) and beguiling words and to possess a deceitful character (78). She is created and adorned by the gods at the command of Zeus, and, like the *Theogony*'s Pandora and Typhon, is a source of man's woes, an 'intractable grief' (*dolon* . . . *amechanon*, *WD* 83; cf. *Theog.* 836). As Zeus' spokesperson, and as with the story of Typhon, the poet is careful to continue to propagate the myth of the gods as the bestowers of blessings and benefits upon humankind. He insists that Pandora constitutes the punishment that Zeus' subjects deserve and her creation is thus not to be conceived of as maliciousness on the god's part. Described emphatically as a gift or *doron* (lines 82 and 85; cf. 86), Pandora demonstrates the negative consequences of receiving unmerited gifts, i.e. bribes, an action that emblematizes injustice in the human community elsewhere, and especially where the corrupt kings of the Fifth Age are concerned (cf. also 220–1 and 263).

But if the poet classifies the language of his contemporaries in a way to suggest that it constitutes the unspeakables (*aphata* and *arrheta*) mentioned in the proem, at the same time he attempts to reassimilate their discourse into his ideal community by inviting it

to conform to the ideal of the Golden Age justice. Hesiod attempts
to distance unjust discourse and injustice from the orderly community that the *Works and Days* aspires to bring into being to the
extent that Mark Griffith is prepared to regard him as a 'junior
partner to Zeus'.[35] The poet characterizes himself in the myth of
the Ages of Man, and elsewhere in the poem, as a lone figure striving to maintain 'justice' (*dikē*) and good speech (e.g. 213, 275, 286).
He tells his audience to 'straighten their words' (262–4), and commands in particular his fictional or actual brother Perses, a notable
example of the depravity and corruption of the current age, to
maintain the laws and customs with justice (9; cf. 213, 274–5).[36]
Hesiodic poetry occupies a favoured position as a language which
celebrates the idealized community and articulates the ideal of justice ordained for it. Unbeneficial discourses are those which have
the capacity to appropriate authority or the appearance of authority, as in the case of Typhon's divine voices, or which do not conform to the model of just speech established by the community's
rulers, and these are severely constrained or excluded from the
community.

In the *Works and Days* and the *Theogony*, Hesiod offers the criticism of language—most obviously where the voices of Typhon are
concerned and then where the binarisms of just/unjust, true/false,
straight/crooked speech are involved—as a means of maintaining
order and control in the community, which is ultimately figured as
'order' (= *kosmos*). The poet is an implicit judge/ critic; he locates
himself and his poetry *outside* the critical scenario as a figure who
already has the support of the judge/critic *par excellence*, Zeus. A
later work, the so-called *Contest Between Homer and Hesiod*, sometimes dated to the reign of Hadrian, makes explicit and confirms
the identification of 'Hesiod' with the critical scene and locates him
within it.[37] The anonymous author of the *Contest* begins by observing that all people try to claim the two great poets Homer and
Hesiod as their own citizens (313), and he proceeds to offer two
judgements on the relative merits of Homer and Hesiod. The first
of these is given by the people of Calchis in Euboea who deem
Homer to be the winner of the poetic contest on the basis of the

---

[35] M. Griffith (1983), 59.   [36] See ibid. 57.
[37] See the reference to Hadrian in section 314 of the work; also Evelyn-White
(1914), p. xli, and Lamberton (1988), 5–6. Harriott (1969: 135) thinks that the work
may be dated to the 5th cent. BCE; see also Kirk (1950), 149–50.

pleasure provided by his poetry (321–2). The second judgement is the authoritative one, given by King Paneides, who declares it right that Hesiod should win because he is the poet who concerns himself with farming and peace, that is the things which benefit society. In contrast, Homer writes about war and slaughter, which concern the destruction of the community (322). Hesiod is, moreover, the poet who has declared the right priorities. He has asked his opponent to establish a 'measure' (*metron*) which prescribes what is best and worst for mortals, and then he questions the latter as to how men would live best in cities and with what sort of customs (320). Paneides grants the crown of victory to Hesiod in order that he will later have the greatest fame among men who have participated in a test of wisdom.[38] The *Contest* provides an indirect aetiology for the process of discrimination, depicting a site of judgement which includes one sort of discourse—the useful poetry of Hesiod—at the expense of another—the merely pleasurable poetry of Homer.[39] In so doing, it draws attention to the critical authority of Hesiod, whose work the wise king Paneides prefers for the community of Calchis.

VI

The *Contest* is perhaps one of the more evident references to the Hesiodic project of criticism by later authors. The role of the poet as critic is rehearsed elsewhere on numerous other occasions. I might, for instance, note that early Greek poets reproduce a series of inclusions and exclusions within their own poetry, distinguishing between what is acceptable and unacceptable discourse, between what is just and unjust, true and false. As with Hesiod, these discriminations are not abstract or absolute but are defined in terms of what is beneficial or not within the context of their own public spheres, generally as established by divine or political authority.[40]

---

[38] Ἡσιόδου, τοῦ πλεῖστον ἐν ἀνθρώποις κλέος ἐστὶν | ἀνδρῶν κρινομένων ἐν βασάνῳ σοφίης (323).

[39] For the *Contest* as an affirmation of the socially determined aim of literary judgement and for the view that the scene of literary *krisis* presented in the work is a means for constructing and institutionalizing a canon (*kanōn*), that is a strategy for including and authorizing literary texts, see G. Nagy in *CHLC* i. 7.

[40] See e.g. Xenophanes, DK 21 B 1. 19–23; B 11 (on poetic representations of the gods as sexual miscreants); B 15 (on anthropomorphism in depictions of the gods).

But my particular concern here is to see how the poetry of a later community, democratic Athens, accommodates the critical imperative. In the remainder of this chapter, I shall examine the way in which Aristophanes presents the return of 'Typhon', who is now associated with anxieties about the limits of acceptable discourse at classical Athens, as a pretext for re-establishing criticism in the city-state.

The interest lies in the qualification poetry offers to the right to public expression in the classical Attic state. Historians conventionally characterize classical and democratic Athens as a phonocentric community, one where the opportunity for public speech is available to all citizens (*isēgoria*). A variety of sources inform us that in the Assembly the herald (*kērux*) invited those assembled to voice their views and opinions with the formula, '. . . who wishes to speak' (. . . *tis agoreuein bouletai*) (e.g. Aeschin. 3. 4; Dem. 18. 170; Ar. *Ach.* 45).[41] Barry Strauss notes that citizenship in classical Athens is figured in terms of 'sharing' in the city and in the courts, suggesting that citizenship specifically entails participation in public oratory as speaker or audience.[42] The opportunity for public speech is thus entrenched in the city's political process, and so taken for granted that in the 'Funeral Oration' Thucydides' Pericles faults the citizen who neglects to exercize his right to public speech for the good of the community. The general suggests that the individual who fails to partake in political, that is oratorical, activity is not a 'quietist' (*apragmōn*) but is rather useless (Thuc. 2. 40. 2).

The poetry of Old Comedy is conventionally associated with the outspokenness of Athenian democracy. In the *Poetics* Aristotle reports that the Megarians trace the origins of comedy to a time when their state was democratic (1448ᵃ31–2), perhaps marking what the Old Oligarch saw as the assumption of pre-classical literary institutions by democracy.[43] This Aristotelian etymology associates the comic genre with the freedoms, particularly of

---

[41] G. T. Griffith (1966), 115; Woodhead (1967), 127. Hansen proposes that ὁ βουλόμενος, the individual who takes advantage of the herald's invitation to engage in oratorical activity and who is named again and again in literary sources as an initiator of legislative process, should be seen as a significant political actor. ὁ βουλόμενος is not to be thought of as a specific official; see Hansen (1991), 266–7.

[42] For references to 'sharing' in the city and for 'sharing in the courts', see B. Strauss (1993), 41–2.

[43] J. Henderson in Winkler and Zeitlin (1990), 279.

expression, that characterize this type of constitution. Other fourth-century sources characterize comedy as a genre which tests and which on occasion transgresses the limits of democratic expression. The speaker of Demosthenes 2.19 refers to Callias and others like him as imitators of laughter and as poets of base song. He poignantly characterizes himself as a moderate when he declares his unwillingness to mention the drunken behaviour of these individuals in the preceding sentence and so to engage in accusation. The speaker of Isocrates' *Peace* associates rash outspokenness (*parrhēsia*) with reckless orators, who are one of the main targets of the work, and comic poets (14). In the *Politics* Aristotle suggests that the young should not be exposed to *iambos* or to comedy (1336^b20), and that everything base should be made alien to them (1336^b34–5), an idea that is also expressed in the *Poetics* (as we shall see in Chapter 3). In the *Athenian Constitution* pseudo-Xenophon observes that curbs existed to prevent poets from making the common people the subject of comedy or defamatory statement: the rich, noble, or powerful were fair game for comic portrayal or slander. The oligarchical author regards comedy as a means of keeping the more privileged members of society in check, by deflating public opinion of them. He notes that few individuals from the poorer and less privileged segments of society were the victims of comic poets except where there was an agenda of personal self-aggrandizement or public meddling (*polupragmosunē*) on the part of the writer (2.18). Here the function of comedy resembles that of ostracism, which copes with disruptive, because over-powerful, individuals by temporarily removing them from the city.[44]

In modern scholarship, one convention has been to present comedy as an asocial space and occasion in an otherwise conservative democracy. Following C. L. Barber's study of Shakespearian comedy, scholars cast Attic comedy as a 'holiday'; after Cornford's ritualistic interpretation, as a static ritual; and after Mikhail Bakhtin, as a space of carnivalesque disorder and topsy-turviness enacted in its licence of expression.[45] In a series of articles written in the mid–late 1980s, Stephen Halliwell seeks to preserve the comic state as an institution which tolerated complete freedom of expression; similarly Simon Goldhill interprets Aristophanes' *Acharnians* in particular as carefully renegotiating and affirming comic freedom

---

[44] See e.g. Rosivach (1987).
[45] J. Henderson in Winkler and Zeitlin (1990), 285.

such that speaking ill is the benefit which the poet performs for his city.[46] Goldhill points to the parabasis of the *Acharnians* (esp. 641-51) as a passage where the chorus portrays the best poet, implicitly Aristophanes himself, as one who speaks out what is just (*ta dikaia*) despite any repercussions to himself.[47]

But these readings seem to assume, somewhat misleadingly, that comedy is an all-or-nothing discourse as far as freedom is concerned. Jeffrey Henderson has suggested—and quite rightly, I shall argue—that it is mistaken to regard comedy, even if it appears to take liberties, as standing outside civic rule and order. For him, comedy operates as a space parallel to the Assembly or lawcourts, a sphere in which discourse was public in the sense of being open to the citizens and in the more particular sense of being concerned with the welfare of the democratic city-state. If comic licence is characterized above all by the practice of criticizing victims by name (*onomasti kōmōdein*),[48] then ancient sources show that legislation recognized the significance of comic speech when it sought to place constraints upon it. Ancient writers provide us with reason to think that comedy and its personal satire are subject to the same considerations as other public language. Evidence exists for a law which forbids *onomasti kōmōdein* so as to limit the freedom of comic satire. A scholiast on the *Birds* mentions an Athenian politician, Syracosius, who is credited with carrying a decree to limit slander in comedy.[49] Scholars, perhaps as a result of being committed to preserving ideals of comic licence and anarchy, have been eager to qualify this evidence. Alan Sommerstein believes with Droysen that Syracosius' decree is a far more limited law which specifically prohibited the naming of persons condemned for the notorious mutilation of the Hermai or for parodying the Mysteries. He suggests that the function of this legislation was not to ban *onomasti kōmōdein per se* but to prevent comic writers from continuing to publicize the name of the exiled general Alcibiades.[50] While Halliwell believes that the decree of Syracosius is an invention by

---

[46] Goldhill (1991), 199 ff.

[47] S. Goldhill in Winkler and Zeitlin (1990), 103.

[48] Radin (1927), 217; Halliwell (1984*b*), 7; Goldhill (1991), 185.

[49] Cf. δοκεῖ δὲ καὶ ψήφιομα τεθεικέναι μὴ κωμῳδεῖσθαι ὀνομαστί τινα, ὡς Φρόνιχος ἐν Μονοτρόπῳ φησί, 'They decided to vote against making fun of anyone by name, as Phronichus says in the *Monotropos*' (schol. ad *Birds* 1297); Sommerstein (1986), 101.

[50] Sommerstein (1986), 107.

the commentator,[51] Max Radin and Malcolm MacDowell propose that it is identical with the law of Antimachus, passed before 427 BCE, forbidding the use of names in comedy and under which Theomnestus is prosecuted in Lysias 10, namely the law of *aporrhēta*.[52] Plato may refer to this law in the *Symposium* when he has the fictional Aristophanes ask Eryximachus to allow what he has spoken to stand as *arrhēta* (189b4). Dover suggests that we translate this word as 'unsaid' but also notes that elsewhere it has the sense of 'what is unspeakable' or 'shocking'.[53] Perhaps *arrhēta* invokes the Hesiodic adjective *arrhētoi*, which describes individuals who are unspeakable (*WD* 4): after all, Eryximachus remarks that the comic poet is forcing him to be the 'guard (*phulaka*) of his speech', possibly alluding to the semi-divine guardians of justice from the *Theogony* (*Symp.* 189a8–b2).

If the evidence for legislated constraints on comic speech is uncertain, there is other material which suggests that comedy does not enjoy complete licence precisely because it is a genre integrated into the *polis*, enjoying an institutional status and participating in political debate so that it operates as a parallel space to the Assembly or lawcourts.[54] But I also want to move beyond this position to venture a stronger thesis. I would like to propose that comic discourse itself is part of the regulative or critical structure of classical democracy. If conservative writers express anxieties about comic authors, they focus their worries even more upon the 'new politicians', individuals like Cleon, Cleophon, and Hyperbolus, and upon their political meddling (*polypragmosunē*). These individuals destabilize and threaten the well-being of fifth-century Athens through their relentless litigations and sycophancies in the lawcourts and through their demagogic rhetoric in the Assembly; they produce discourses that engage, more often than not, in the blame of their fellow citizens, uttering slanders and defamations which Athenian law to a degree curtailed. It is by counter-definition with these individuals and through a prior critical imagery that comedy establishes itself as moderate and as moderating. The comedy of Aristophanes invokes a Hesiodic characterization and, with it, a rhetoric of *krisis* in the portrayal of these notorious figures.

[51] Halliwell (1991), 61–3.   [52] Radin (1927), 220; MacDowell (1978), 128–9.
[53] Dover (1980), 112.
[54] J. Henderson in Winkler and Zeitlin (1990), 271–313.

The dramatist's *bête noire* is above all Cleon, the sycophant and demagogue *par excellence*, and he is figured as a Typhonic mouth. In the *Acharnians* Dicaeopolis, whose very name ('Just-city') conjures up an implicit dichotomy between just and unjust speech, describes himself as the victim of Cleon. The latter is described as roaring like a Cycloborus, a powerful and destructive wind, uttering lies in the *bouleutērion* (379–81; cf. *Knights* 137; fr. 636 H–G). In the *Wasps* the politician is said to go forth shouting, bawling, and blustering (596). Aristophanes presents us with a more extended representation of Cleon in the *Knights*. Here he presents himself, in his capacity as comic poet, as the individual who alone dares to speak what is just and to oppose Cleon, whom he compares to a Typhonic wind (cf. *pros ton tuphō*) and to a hurricane (510–11). Cleon is nothing but a mouth. In this same play his dramatic *alter ego*, Paphlagon, chatters away endlessly; he shouts alike just and unjust things in the lawcourts; and he possesses the voice of the Cycloborus, a raging wind that is not unlike the winds of the Hesiodic Typhon. Aristophanes seizes the opportunity to suggest that the sort of discourse produced by Paphlagon-Cleon is motivated by greed: the mouth of Paphlagon-Cleon is one that both spews out and consumes. Paphlagon hungrily licks down quantities of cakes (103) and ravenously gobbles sausages (256, 312, 487).

In the parabasis of the *Wasps*, a play which offers a critique of the political meddler (*polupragmōn*), the comic poet becomes the figure who combats the discourse of 'monsters' like Cleon and Hyperbolus (cf. 1007). (In the *Wealth* Aristophanes provides us with an interview between a sycophant and a just citizen, who indicates to the former that his meddling (*polupragonein*) might not benefit the city (913).) The chorus of the *Wasps* credits the poet with the anger and courage of Heracles, and portrays him as taking on single-handedly a sharp-fanged creature with flashing eyes and a hundred flickering heads and the voice of a torrent (1031–4). If the rhythm of the following line, which attributes to the creature the odour of a seal, the filthy dances of the ogress Lamia, and the genitals of a camel, recalls the description of the Chimera at *Iliad* 6. 181,[55] the preceding lines once more conjure up the caricatured Cleon and the Hesiodic subtext that underlies this portrait. The hundred heads are those of Typhon, the monster who emblema-

---

[55] MacDowell (1971), 266.

tizes the politician in the *Knights*, while the reference to the torrent
at 1034 recalls the comparison of Cleon to a hurricane and the
Hesiodic Typhon's metamorphosis into storm winds. It is significant that the chorus later speaks of the barbarian Persians who
invade Greece as blowing down (cf. *tuphōn*) and setting fire to
Athens (1079). This figuring of the barbarian as a typhonic wind
recasts Cleon, the latter-day enemy who must be resisted. In the
terms of the mythological discourse evoked in the parabasis,
Aristophanes becomes the heroic individual who will rid the land
of the monstrous threat to it through his comedies and win the
approval of those who are wise (*sophoi*, 1046–9): he is the subduer
of monstrous discourse in the city.

Aristophanes' comparison of Cleon and Hyperbolus to both
Typhon and Cycloborus and his identification with Paphlagon in
the *Knights* suggest that the orator, like the Hesiodic Typhon, is a
versatile master when it comes to producing discourse *and* identity.
It also proposes that Cleon in particular is a figure who threatens the
well-being of the contemporary democratic state, which can only
tolerate equality of opportunity for citizens to speak in public to the
point that it is not the licentious discourse constituted by the slanders, libels, and abuse that feature in the lawcourts. The implication
is that, just as Zeus transforms the voices of Typhon into the inarticulate sound of the winds, so Aristophanes will neutralize the discourse of Cleon and the new politicians with his re-representation of
their speech as the blustering winds of Typhon, as the hurricane
Cycloborus, or as the greedy feeding of a Paphlagon. The invective
of the comic theatre takes the sting out of the invective discourse of
the lawcourt, as Aristophanes reinforces the Hesiodic reinscription
of the 'voice' and its authority. Elsewhere, the Aristophanic image
of Typhon identifies and discredits the discourse which is undesirable for the depicted community. Thus, in the *Clouds* the Unjust
Speech uses the metaphor of blustering winds and hurricane to criticize the Just Speech. It labels the *Dikaios Logos* as an 'inflated old
man' (cf. *tuphogerōn*) and disharmonious (908). The Unjust Speech
ironically brings the charge of injustice and social threat against its
opponent by allusion to Typhon's voices (1068 ff.), and, in doing
so, it uncovers the hypocrisy of his antagonist, the speech which
relishes too much in the sexuality of young boys, despite protesting
that their training must be strictly constrained and disciplined
(972 ff.). In the *Lysistrata* the chorus of women refer to the

aggressive old men who harass them as *tuphogerontas* (335–6). They
go on to observe that these men utter the most terrible, threatening
words (339); the discourse of the men is that of destabilizing invective. But again the critique is not so easy to locate, as the women can
be seen to challenge the well-being of society by calling for an end
to war and by withholding sex from their husbands.

VII

It is also the case that Aristophanic comedy both negotiates and
might be seen to produce anxieties about licence of literary expression from within its own discourse with the return of 'Typhon'.
When Aristophanes takes up the figure of 'Typhon' from Hesiod,
he distinguishes this image from that produced by the earlier poet
in drawing attention to the instability of his critique and accordingly of the categories of acceptable and unacceptable discourse.
The Hesiodic constraints of language which circulate in the public
and political sphere are recalled in ways which necessarily point up
their arbitrariness. The comic poet queries the constraints placed
on social language in several of his plays. While he criticizes Cleon
for the sycophancies and invectives he produces in the lawcourts,
he himself, however, no less engages in slanderous name-calling,
which by its very nature is potentially disruptive of social hierarchy. Phillip Harding has suggested that comic invective may
have its origins in the figure of Thersites, the Homeric hero who
oversteps the social boundaries to challenge the leadership of
Agamemnon in the *Iliad*.[56] If invective is generally destabilizing, it
is the case that Aristophanic invective seeks specifically to disrupt
above all what is to be perceived as the challenge to the élite monopoly on public discourse posed by the self-made 'new politicians'
and their oratorical meddling.

    In particular, Aristophanes himself extends comic licence to per-
mit what would otherwise constitute the *aporrhēta*, the category of
terms which Athenian law prohibited as detrimental to the city and
its inhabitants and which comes to characterize the language of the
sycophants. In Lysias 10 the litigant cites the law against defamation (*aporrhēta*) which limits the possibility for one citizen to

---

[56] Harding in Worthington (1994), 197–8.

accuse another of particular crimes and actions. That the law concerns wrongs which specifically call into doubt the defendant's
membership in the community becomes evident at 10. 8–9, where
the speaker reminds the jury that it was unlawful to accuse a citizen
of being a murderer (*androphonos*), a deserter of ranks (literally a
'shield-thrower' (*rhipsaspis*)), a parricide (*patraloias*), or matricide
(*mētraloias*). Interestingly, the speaker of Lysias 10 negotiates the
law on unsayables in such a way as to silence his opponent but also
to enable himself to utter the prohibited vocabulary without legal
repercussions for himself. Not dissimilarly does Aristophanes
problematize what you cannot say, for it is precisely these proscribed terms that the poet notably invokes in his comedies.[57] On
several occasions, Aristophanes refers to Cleonymus as 'shield-
thrower' (*rhipsaspis*), using one of the legally proscribed terms
(*Peace* 678; *Clouds* 353; cf. *Peace* 1298–9; *Wasps* 19, 592).
Elsewhere, in the *Birds*, the chorus announces a comic programme
of licence when it gives its audience sanction to engage in actions
considered shameful (*aischron*) by law, such as beating one's father
(755–60), while in the *Clouds* the son, Phidippides, influenced by
his reading of the dramatist Euripides, who occupies the role of
subversive influence, beats his father Strepsiades in return for the
punishment he received as a child (1323 ff.). On the one hand, the
presence of libel in the plays may support the idea that there is a
separation between comic discourse and political discourse, especially that of the lawcourts, as they depict what would be *aporrhēta*
or else forbidden by law. On the other hand, and as the interpretation I prefer, it points to the ways in which the regulation of discourse is artificially constructed and enacted.

---

[57] See Todd (1993: 258 ff.) for discussion of Lysias 10. Clay (1982) has shown
how Greek tragedy enacts and respects within its own discourse the legal prohibition on certain words and terms as ἀπόρρητα, the libellous terms proscribed in
Athenian law (cf. Lysias 10 and 11). He observes how the awareness that some labels
may not be uttered is marked in *Oedipus Tyrannus* by Oedipus' refusal to refer
directly to the as yet unknown 'murderer' as such (line 238) and by his subsequent
invocation of Tiresias as the individual who controls 'all that is to be taught and is
not to be said, both in the heavens and on the earth' (300–1; cf. Soph. *OC* 1000–3).
Clay examines the manner in which the play's various characters negotiate the forbidden term 'murderer' and, even worse, the word 'parricide' by evasive plurals,
circumlocutionary compounds, and hypertactic syntax: φονέας . . . κἄνδρας (*OT*
362); τοῦ πατρὸς . . . φονεύς (459–60); φονέα . . . πατρός (721); φονεύς . . . τοῦ
φυτεύσαντος πατρός (793); πατρὸς . . . φονεύς (1001).

There are certain aspects of Typhonic discourse which Aristophanes admits may be recuperated in his comedies and in the city that his comedies depict. While using the image of multiple discourses as a critique of contemporary political figures, Aristophanic comedy recuperates particularly the identification of versatility in voice and imitation with poetic discourse and representation. In the parabasis of the *Knights*, the speaker cites the case of the poet Magnes, who was able to represent 'all [kinds of] voices' (*pasas . . . phōnas*, 522). Where in archaic poetry polyphony is a quality of the divinely inspired poet or the divine poet, the problem here, as the poet identifies it, is that the inhabitants of the Aristophanic city do not necessarily recognize it as such. The comic poet shows that possession of all (kinds of) voices (*pasai phōnai*) does not in itself guarantee a poet anything more than ephemeral recognition since he has to depend on an audience which does not always perceive or understand true poetic talent. Aristophanes appears to regret the failure of the audience to value the poet's voices. The chorus-leader remarks that Magnes wrote to the great acclaim and pleasure of the crowd in his youth but he later lost the favour of his audience and died a ridiculous old man (*Knights* 520–5). It becomes apparent that rather than assisting his community through the constraint and regulation of poetry as one of the city's political discourses, Aristophanes now expresses disapproval at the community's failure to admit a poetic discourse that is many-voiced.

In the *Clouds* the simplistic proscription of polyphonic language is more evidently called into question. The Cloud-chorus are presented as clever imitators *par excellence*, most immediately emblematizing the shifting identities and roles of contemporary sophistic and rhetorical culture. The Clouds have the capacity to assimilate their identities to that of the creatures and individuals around them: when they see the thief Simon, they take on the form of rapacious wolves; when they see the cowardly deserter Cleonymus, they come to resemble timid deer; and when they view the effeminate Cleisthenes, they take on the form of women (348–55). In addition, they produce many different noises and sounds (383 ff.). Emphasis is placed on their vocal aspect when Socrates invokes them along with Tongue (*Glōtta*) at line 423. That they are patrons of poets amongst others suggests an identification between them and Aristophanes (331–4). After all, the chorus provides the *ego*-voice of the parabasis, which we are to identify as the authorial voice even if we are inclined to distinguish between it and the historical Aristophanes. This is the *ego*-voice which claims to be *sophos*, and which thus takes responsibility for the present play's *sophia* (520). It is the voice which also says it has created the play's 'new forms' (*kainas ideas*), which do not resemble one another (cf. *ouden allēlaisin homoias*) and are all artful (*dexiai*) (547–8). The speaker of the parabasis attributes to the poet a versatility and breadth of imitation which recalls the ideal of poetic excellence as a plethora of voices and discourses. Nevertheless, there is again the suggestion that this Typhonic polyphony cannot be accommodated within the *polis*, not because it is disruptive but because the audience does not honour the Clouds, despite the benefits they bring to the city (577–8). It is the case that the *polis* unjustly voted down a previous play, *The Banqueters*, upon which the poet exercised his wisdom and labour.

Aristophanes also evokes the Hesiodic Typhonomachy in such a way as to interrogate the earlier poet's negative valorization of multiple and shifting identities. At the first appearance of the Clouds Aristophanes makes Socrates, ostensibly in reference to the philosopher's atheism, deny the existence of Zeus—'what sort of Zeus?' . . . 'Zeus doesn't exist' (366–7)—in favour of Dinus and the Clouds as the causes of meteorological phenomena. Strepsiades later denies the existence of Zeus when confronted by his creditor Pasias (1228–41), while Phidippides rejects Zeus in favour of Dinus in the final argument with his father (1469–70). These lines in the *Clouds* refer most immediately to the concern that intellectuals, particularly philosophers, are responsible for casting doubt on the existence of the gods. More significantly, however, they recall that Hesiod traces the origins of critical activity to the protection of the interests of the gods and the community that they rule over. Poignantly, the Hesiodic narrative of the *Theogony* is recalled later in the play as the Oedipal struggle in the contest between the Stronger and Weaker speeches is mapped on to the mythological defeat of Cronus by Zeus. In the father–son conflict Strepsiades tells his son not to call him 'Iapetus', the brother of Cronus (cf. 698–9), and Barry Strauss suggests that this reference together with the derogatory use of *archaios*-words (cf. 821, 915, 984, 1357, 1469) may as well evoke Cronos himself.[58] But where Hesiod's poem

[58] See B. Strauss (1993), 159. The father–son conflict may also enact an *aporrhēton*; father-beating, which Phidippides inflicts upon Strepsiades 'was a comic substitute for parricide'; see Reckford (1976), 109.

reinforces divine authority, presenting poetry as the voice of Zeus and the rejection of competing discourses, Aristophanes implicitly characterizes poetry as the language that threatens to displace Zeus with the whirlwind Dinos and the metamorphosing Clouds. While recognizing that this interpretation is possible, it would be too naïve to suggest that the comic poet simply inverts the function of poetic discourse by proposing that the function of the latter is now to undermine political authority and the language that it produces to safeguard its own concerns. Socrates may be an unsavoury figure in the *Clouds* but there are no definite or clear-cut indications that the Clouds themselves are to be unproblematically assimilated to or identified with the voice(s) of Aristophanes. The Clouds are after all associated with the sophists, the class of individuals with whom Socrates and Chaerephon are identified.

The uncertainties of how to valorize polyphony and discursive contraint are also supported by the *Frogs*, a play that is sometimes seen as providing us with one of the earliest texts of literary criticism.[59] In this comedy Dionysus, the god of comedy and tragedy, arrives in the underworld to stage and then to 'judge' (*krinai*) a contest between the dramatists Aeschylus and Euripides (873–4; cf. *krisis*, 1467). Dionysus, a god whose authority is undermined in the course of the play through cross-dressing and through role reversal with his slave Xanthias, sends up the idea that literary judgement is based on reliable criteria. As the judge of the 'contest of wisdom' or *agōn sophias*, he pronounces that one (*ho men*) of the contestants has spoken 'wisely' (*sophōs*), while the other one (*ho d' heteros*) has spoken 'clearly' (*saphôs*). As numerous commentators have observed, his statement leaves it notoriously uncertain as to who spoke 'wisely' and who spoke 'clearly'. The judgement in favour of Aeschylus further complicates the issue. Dionysus declares the poet the winner with part of a line he cites from Euripides' *Hippolytus* (612), 'my tongue has sworn'. The Euripidean text itself notoriously announces a perjury, a dichotomy between what is said and what is actually thought or intended, and Aristophanes employs the phrase with this sense earlier in the *Frogs* at line 102 and, elsewhere, in the *Thesmophorizusae* at 275–6.

After the contest, Dionysus explains that the purpose of the contest is to ensure that the city may be 'saved' by the poet, since he is

---

[59] For Russell and Winterbottom (1972: 15–38), *Frogs* 830–1481 is one of the texts which constitutes the 'beginnings' of ancient literary criticism.

implicitly constructed as the figure who benefits the *polis* through beneficial teachings (cf. 1434–6). He states that the poet will praise what is 'useful' (*chrēston*) for the city, reaffirming the utilitarian ideal of ancient poetics, and will show that he can do so by offering his opinion on Alcibiades (1419–21; cf. 1458–9). W. B. Stanford (1958, ad loc.) comments at this point that the god's mission has been converted from a poetic and artistic one to a political one. Yet throughout the contest Euripides and Aeschylus have uttered statements which call into question Stanford's view of the poetic contest as one which is at any point non-political. Aristophanes affirms the utilitarian ideal of discourse for the classical city depicted in the *Frogs*, although he calls into question the criteria for determining what is useful for the *polis*. In response to Aeschylus' demand that he justify the awe accorded to the poet, Euripides explains that poets make men better in their cities.[60] Aeschylus responds that his opponent, however, depicts the dregs of society, making out of good and noble characters those who are most troublesome (1011), while he in contrast depicts men who are brave in war (1020–7). He allies himself with Orpheus, Mousaeos, Hesiod, and Homer, whom he describes as 'useful poets' (1031 ff.). Both Aeschylus and Euripides affirm the social role and function of the poet when they depict themselves as teaching the citizens of Athens through their poetry; they affirm that one of the poet's responsibilities is to be a teacher (*didaskalos*) (cf. 954–5, 964, 1009–10, 1054–5, 1420).[61] None the less, Dionysus' description of Aeschylus as a Typhonic wind (*tuphōs*) at line 848, reinforced by the chorus's depiction of the tragedian's language as 'an earth-born puffing' (*gēgenei phusēmati*, 825), should cause some consternation or, at the very least, discomfort, for it calls into question his choice of winner. The comic poet characterizes Aeschlyus through the very image which he uses to discredit Cleon-Paphlagon in the *Knights*, for instance, and which has a poetic history associating it with a discourse that, even when it is transformed, must be contained and repressed for the well-being of society as a whole, lest it continue to cause harm.

---

[60] δεξιότητος καὶ νουθεσίας, ὅτι βελτίους τε ποιοῦμεν | τοὺς ἀνθρώπους ἐν ταῖς πόλεσιν (*Frogs* 1009–10).
[61] Havelock (1982), 261 ff.

VIII

This chapter has traced the fate of Typhon from his initial defeat at the hands of Zeus to his reappearance as the *alter ego* of Aristophanes' troublesome Cleon, in order to demonstrate the initiation of criticism in the Hesiodic world and its subsequent development in classical Athens. I suggest that the respective fates of Typhon highlight the containment of undesirable voices to ensure the pre-eminence of the voices that do the containing and constraining, namely those of Zeus, of kings, of judges, and of poets. Typhon's defeats also demonstrate the arbitrariness and specificities of the staging and performance of the discrimination and categorization of discourse as variously positive or negative. In subsequent chapters of this study we shall see re-enactments of the critical scene—of judgement, the privileged manifestation of criticism—in other communities both historical and literary, some in ways that deliberately recuperate the Hesiodic scene, others in ways that evolve criticism in very particular and specific manners.

2

Criticism in Plato's *Republic*: Writing the Just City/Just Writing the City

I do not consider these things but myself, whether I am a creature more complex and lustful than Typhon or one gentler and more uncomplicated, sharing in some divine and un-Typhonic lot by nature.

                                        Plato, *Phaedrus* 230a3–7[1]

I

George Grube has characterized Plato as the first writer 'to develop a theory of literature and of its place in society'.[2] If this is so, it is a theory of literature which must raise some anxieties. In the *Republic*, one of the traditionally privileged texts in the history of criticism, if not the most privileged, Plato would appear to banish poetry from the ideal state, and accordingly, to propose that (literary) art and philosophy are distinct categories of discourse and practice. Scholars draw attention to the discussion of art and *mimēsis* in Book 10, where the philosopher rejects imitation for the reason that it is an ontologically and epistemologically deficient copy of the object that it attempts to represent. Despite apparently contradicting the stance of books 2 and 3, where the work's interlocutors admit the role of poetry in the education of the young citizen, the final book of the *Republic* has become the authorized and privileged Platonic position on literary art.[3]

The unease caused by the tension between books 2, 3, and 10 has produced numerous responses. Some readers have gone on to

---

[1] σκοπῶ οὐ ταῦτα ἀλλ᾽ ἐμαυτόν, εἴτε τι θηρίον ὂν τυγχάνω Τυφῶνος πολυπλοκώτερον καὶ μᾶλλον ἐπιτεθυμμένον, εἴτε ἡμερώτερόν τε καὶ ἁπλούστερον ζῷον. θείας τινὸς καὶ ἀτύφου μοίρας φύσει μετέχον. For later Stoic treatments of this passage, see Vian (1952), 26, 33.

[2] Grube (1965), 47.   [3] Cf. Gadamer (1980), 39.

disassociate the concluding discussion of literature from the prior dialogue, regarding it as a later addition to the dialogue,[4] or as Plato's political vision finally getting the better of his love for poetry.[5] Alexander Nehemas, on the other hand, accounts for the discrepancy between the two discussions of art in terms of the dialogue's narrative of education. According to him, imitative poetry is one of the tools used in the education of the guardians-to-be and thus features significantly in the earlier book—which deals with the early years of the citizens of the ideal city—but is strongly censured in the final book as something that might disturb and unsettle the completely formed identity of the state's adult citizen.[6]

Others have dealt with the work's discussion of literature by drastically removing it from the realm of political *praxis*. They have dislocated the treatment of art as imitation from its immediate social framework—namely the society constructed within and by the text. Depoliticizing and hypostasizing the treatment of literature and imitation, they characterize it as a disembodied aesthetics or callistics, regardless of the work's main concern—the construction of the ideal city.[7] Symptomatic of this tendency are the anthologies and historical surveys of literary criticism which cite the discussion of imitation from the *Republic* with little or no attention to the larger issues raised in the surrounding text.[8] Karl Popper offers an extreme version of this last approach, proposing to see Platonic art as a self-sufficient and self-contained entity without any bearing upon reality, whether understood as the empirical world or as a higher metaphysical reality. In this interpretation, the *Republic, qua* ideal art, becomes an autonomous heterocosm:

> Politics, to Plato, is the Royal Art. It is an art—not in a metaphorical sense in which we may speak about the art of handling men, or the art of getting things done, but in a more literal sense of the word. It is an art of composition, like music, painting, or architecture. The Platonic politician composes cities, for beauty's sake.[9]

Popper's understanding of Plato's politics dispenses with the need for a textual or practical supplement for the discourse of the

    [4] See Else (1972).
    [5] Gould (1964), 74; on the other hand, Annas (1982: 9) faults Plato's argument on the basis that the painter, whom the author uses as the poet's analogue in book 10, is not a good counterpart, since the painter and poet imitate in quite different ways.
    [6] Nehemas (1982), 53.   [7] See Warry (1962).
    [8] Wimsatt and Brooks (1957), 57–76; Grube (1965), 46–65.
    [9] Popper (1962), 165.

Republic. For him, the dialogue and its politics can be self-contained and self-sufficient because they are now assimilated to an anachronistic Romantic ideal of art. Popper offers the reader a politics which consists of a language that stands aloof from temporal society and owes its allegiance to the aesthetic ideal of Beauty. He gives us a suspended, disinterested art, and for this reason, an apolitical one. Yet Popper's aesthetic state cannot ultimately escape politics, for it is a totalitarian, closed society, permitted no movement or change, and protected from questioning.[10]

Against the grain of earlier prior scholarship, I intend to argue that Plato's unsympathetic attitudes towards literature and art are not as problematic for the historian of criticism as has previously been thought, because they are precisely constitutive of ancient criticism. In the reading I venture, the *Republic* achieves its identity as criticism by being the most familiar instance of silencing and exclusion, as the author banishes poetry in favour of philosophy from the ideal state. The philosopher, I shall argue, rehearses and refines precisely the same anxieties articulated both by archaic and by his contemporary authors about the need to regulate and constrain multiple languages for the benefit of his model society. Where Plato makes his significant contribution to the whole critical agenda is in the specific and complex ways he understands literary discourses to shape political identity. Where we have seen how the censoring of particular types of language seeks to protect the identity of the state by protecting the reputation of its citizens and its rulers, we now observe how Plato curtails certain forms of language to achieve the more ambitious project of creating the identity of the citizen and, through this, the identity of the state as a whole, before any undesirable identities from literature establish themselves.

II

I seek to repoliticize art and the discussion of *mimēsis* by turning to the dialogue's discourse on justice (*dikaiosunē*). This I offer less as an initial move away from literary concerns and more as a relocation of the critical sphere, for the legal contest and the establishment of justice constitute after all the privileged scenario for the

[10] Popper (1962), 174; Ophir (1991: 151) speaks of a 'dialogue of suspension'; also Eagleton (1984), 107, and (1990), 378 f.

discrimination of language in Hesiod. In book 1 of the *Republic*, Socrates offers a paraphrase of the definition of justice given by one of the interlocutors, Cephalos:

Do we say that justice is simply this, [telling] the truth and giving back what one has taken from someone else? Is this sometimes just, and sometimes not? What I mean is this sort of thing. Everyone would agree that if you borrowed weapons from someone who was in his right mind but who demanded back his weapons when he had gone insane, you would not be just to return them, nor to tell him the whole truth.[11]

According to this definition which, the reader is told, originates with the archaic poet Simonides (331d5), justice consists in returning (cf. *apodidonai*) to an individual what has been taken from him. The definition is then generalized by Socrates at 331e3–4 so that justice comes to mean rendering what is owed to each person (cf. *to ta opheilomena hekastōi apodidonai*, cf. 332a7–8, 332d2–3). Socrates makes an important qualification: rendering (*apodosis*) must not involve or lead to potential harm—so you would not return a mad person's weapon to him lest he injure himself or others.

This account of justice proposes some of the key terms for the dialogue, and certainly the vocabulary of justice recurs in the text particularly and appropriately in the discussion of what the just community might be. At the level of the microcosm, of the individual citizen, Socrates establishes that the just community is one in which the citizens are in a just condition, and this entails that their appropriate roles are assigned to them (435b). The individual who belongs to such a community is required to do *his* or *her own* task (cf. 394e, 397d–e, 400e, 406e, 433b1–2, and *Alc.* 1. 127c5), namely what his or her nature has most suited that individual to do (433a), especially with regard to ruling or being ruled (443b1–2). The premiss is that an individual's role and identity is established at least in part by the particular job or jobs that s/he does. Making an individual's actions a basis for defining social identity implies that this individual's social identity can conversely and in turn be expressed in terms of the task(s) and labour(s) s/he performs. So a

---

[11] τοῦτο δ' αὐτό, τὴν δικαιοσύνην, πότερα τὴν ἀλήθειαν αὐτὸ φήσομεν εἶναι ἁπλῶς οὕτως καὶ τὸ ἀποδιδόναι ἄν τίς τι παρά του λάβῃ, ἢ καὶ αὐτὰ ταῦτα ἔστιν ἐνίοτε μὲν δικαίως, ἐνίοτε δὲ ἀδίκως ποιεῖν; οἷον τοιόνδε λέγω· πᾶς ἄν που εἴποι, εἴ τις λάβοι παρὰ φίλου ἀνδρὸς σωφρονοῦντος ὅπλα, εἰ μανεὶς ἀπαιτοῖ, ὅτι οὔτε χρὴ τὰ τοιαῦτα ἀποδιδόναι, οὔτε δίκαιος ἄν εἴη ὁ ἀποδιδούς, οὐδ' αὖ πρὸς τὸν οὕτως ἔχοντα πάντα ἐθέλων τἀληθῆ λέγειν (*Resp.* 331c).

doctor is someone who heals the sick and a pilot is someone who controls a ship. Furthermore, designating someone's social identity or role thus implies a discourse about that person's actions. Because justice (*dikaiosunē*) consists in an individual performing his or her own labour (433a), only when someone does the task of citizen X and is X, is s/he a just citizen. To describe an individual as X *or* Y, or as X *and* Y is to say implicitly that s/he does what X *or* Y should do, or what X *and* Y together do. Furthermore, in establishing a relationship between social identity and task, Socrates endows this whole discourse with a judgement of propriety. The discussion of who does what conveys a secondary sense that because someone is X, s/he is ideally doing *only* his/her task as X, that is his or her own proper work; or conversely because s/he does the tasks of citizens X, Y, and Z, in spite of being citizen X, s/he has assumed improper identities.

The exclusivity of role is one necessitated by Socrates' emphatic argument that the individual's nature will make him or her fit to engage in only *one, single* activity (cf. 'each person does one thing', *hekastos hen prattei*, 397e2). Each person's nature determines what is his or her proper place in the community, if s/he is to avoid the condition of being 'double' (*diplous*) or 'multiple' (*pollaplous*). The microcosm, the individual citizen, is intricately related to the macrocosm, the city, in the *Republic*.[12] So in the ideal city a strict division of labour exists such that each individual has a particular task to perform for the benefit of the whole society. The guardian must learn his or her proper role in society, that is, to do only one thing so that s/he does not fail when s/he tries his/her hand at many things (394e1–5). The guardians are not to assume any role other than the specific role of ruling that they have been trained to take up in the ideal state. On the analogy of a fine animal, Socrates defines the fine city as one in which every part has been assigned its proper place, 'we make the whole beautiful, rendering (*apodidontes*) what is suited to each element' (420d4–5). The idea that the discussants are planning the city by assigning tasks and roles properly is reiterated later in the dialogue with regard to the education of the young citizens and the distribution of roles according to the sex of the citizens. Socrates invokes the language of 'rendering' at 451d2 when he asks his companions to consider if in assigning

---

[12] See Lear (1992).

(*apodidontes*) the birth and upbringing of the citizens in the ideal
city, they have done so in a manner that is fitting (cf. 451e4). The
philosopher elaborates his account, declaring that it is 'necessary to
render' (*apodoteon*) to women matters regarding both children and
war (452a4–5). Slightly later, he insists that it is important to
'assign (*apodidonai*)' the same roles to both male and female
citizens, except for particular roles, such as childbirth, which
depend on biological qualities peculiar to women alone (454d–e and
456b).

Socrates presents the just state as one which excludes, or, at the
least, carefully constrains, plural and complex activities, which he
now denotes by the term *polypragmosunē*. As the word that otherwise and conventionally denotes meddling political behaviour,
namely litigious activity or self-interested demagoguery in the
Assembly, *polypragmosunē* here connotes injustice. It now specifically refers to the condition of engaging in tasks that should properly
be performed by another person or persons in the community.
Socrates uses 'to do one's own thing' (*to ta hautou prattein*), the citizen's ideal and just condition, as a synonym for 'not to meddle' (*mē
polupragmonein*, 433a8–9), while he employs the phrase 'to do the
things of others' (*tallotria prattein*), namely a job or plurality of jobs
which should be performed by others, as a way of articulating
polupragmonein (443d). The citizen who diversifies activity is
accordingly the city's *polypragmōn*, the busybody or meddler. For
the community as a whole, the implications of the poor distribution
of roles and tasks to the individual citizen become clear later in the
dialogue, where Plato characterizes a series of actual, historical
types of state. In the less than ideal constitutions distribution goes
awry. In the oligarchical city described in book 8 the various labour
roles are improperly distributed among its citizens, so that the
community is an unjust city. Jobs and tasks are concentrated
amongst a privileged minority so that the *same* people (*tous autous*)
farm, make money, and go to war, even though their natures do not
suit them to all of these activities (551e–2a). The vocabulary of justice reappears to mark the impropriety of this type of constitution
and its disorderly and flawed distribution of wealth. The verb *apodidonai* now denotes the unfortunate redistributions which follow
the state's original misallocation of persons and roles. Oligarchy
finds a citizen selling, literally 'giving away' (*apodosthai*), all his
own goods to another person. When he has done this (cf.

apodomenon), he lives in the city, poor and destitute and without a part to play, whether as a businessman, craftsman, knight, or hoplite (552a).

But it is the account of democracy which above all makes apparent the continuity between the distribution of tasks and political identity. A democratic constitution is a plural, multiple, and variegated state, where the many (*hoi polloi*) rule. Plato declares that the many, always presented as an indiscriminate plural and so figured here as the democratic mob, are bad (*kakoi*), and bad in every sort of badness (490d3–5). They explicitly engage in and support *polupragmosunē*, which is in one sense to be understood in its conventional form as the meddling politics associated with the new politicians, the orators and sycophants, such as Cleon, Hyperbolus, and Dinarchus. They also involve themselves in *polupragmosunē* in the particular sense that the dialogue indicates, so that, if oligarchy concentrates activities among the few, democracy disseminates them indiscriminately. Socrates says that democratic citizens prefer '*all other things*' (*panta talla*) to the single true 'Beauty' (*to kalon*) and to the Good (cf. 493e2–3). Accordingly, they go to every length and say everything (cf. *pan d' epos legontas te kai prattontas*) to prevent others from engaging in philosophical activity and to exclude the philosopher from their midst (494d9–e7; cf. 500b), just as the sailors of the ship of state refuse to listen to the experienced captain, tossing him overboard (488c–d). The unjust distribution of roles and behaviours in the democratic state is denoted by the phrase 'going to every length and saying everything' (*pan d' epos legontas te kai prattontas*).

Accordingly, the democratic citizen's psychological constitution is one which Socrates describes as anarchic and variegated (*poikilos*): it admits equal status to alternative lifestyles and characters (558c3–6). The democratic citizen, like his or her state of which (s)he is the microcosm, is the one who possesses the paradigm for various, or very many, different characters and lifestyles. Like his or her city, the citizen is diverse (*pantodapon*) and 'full of most character types' (*pleistōn ēthōn meston*). The democratic citizen leads the life that many men and women would envy and desire because he has at his disposal the greatest choice of states and of *tropoi*, a word that may denote either the characters of these states or of individuals (561e). Furthermore, the democratic citizens have souls which sustain all manner and types of pleasures (cf.

559d9–10[13]). The democratic citizen's soul is complex and desirous; perhaps it is one to which the adjective 'Typhonic' may be applied (cf. *Phdr.* 230a4–6).

If democracy continually threatens to appear other than itself, it eventually actually becomes other than itself. According to Socrates, the democratic state and citizen contain models of all the other constitutions and characters which form them (561e). It follows that they contain the paradigms of aristocracy, oligarchy, democracy, tyranny, and, one must assume, of the ideal state as well. This is because democracy is a state in which the masses hold sway but also in which individuality and variety is tolerated such that no one individual or individual character enjoys special privilege. Because such variety leads to a lack of coherence and unity and makes a state extremely unstable and prone to change, democracy creates the circumstances for its own decline into a tyranny, a state in which an individual with the least integrated and least informed soul possesses power.[14] At 575c5–d1 Socrates affirms that it is the multitude (cf. *polloi*) who create the tyrant because they have no firm or stable norms by which they can determine justice or injustice. Socrates' description of this individual once more invokes the vocabulary and concept of *dikaiosunē*. When he is a youth, a tyrannical person characteristically spends enormous sums of money satisfying his greed. He exhausts his income and then he has to turn to loans and borrowing (573e ff.). Borrowing ought to entail repayment (*apodosis*) if justice is to result; however, in Socrates' account, the pay-off comes in the negative qualities that the philosopher attributes to the result of such actions. The philosopher declares that he will attribute (*apodōsomen*) to this figure greed, faithlessness, injustice, unholiness, and an openness to all vice. The tyrant is someone who is full of *many and all sorts* of fears and desires.[15] The language of multiplicity and multitude figures in the psychological portrait of the tyrant, an individual who arrogates and appropriates an excess of wealth, power, and roles.

---

[13] παντοδαπὰς ἡδονὰς καὶ ποικίλας καὶ παντοίως ἐχούσας δυναμένοις σκευάζειν (559d9–10).

[14] Arendt (1951: 10–15) observes that democratic freedom creates the circumstances—namely a highly 'atomised' society—which give rise to the masses and in turn make totalitarian control more possible.

[15] Cf. ὁ τύραννος . . . πολλῶν καὶ παντοδαπῶν φόβων καὶ ἐρώτων πεστός (579b4–5).

Only the final myth of Er offers a greater variety of lifestyles and characters than democracy. It is here that the mythical narrator, Er, observes that the souls which he views provide him with a view of all manner (*pantodapa*) of lives (618a3), not only of human beings but also of all different animals in all different material and psychological states and circumstances (618a). Beyond this, the myth presents the paradigms (*paradeigmata*) of different constitutions. The important difference between the eschatological world visited by Er and the democratic state is that, while choice and variety is available in the latter, the soul who visits the former is bound to choose only one life for himself and this choice is to a large degree determined by the soul's experiences in his or her former life and by the fate Lachesis. Furthermore, if in democracy all lives are supposed to be equivalent, Plato makes it clear that some of the lives on offer are better than others. The myth which concludes the *Republic* offers the possibility of variety, from which each soul is allotted only one life specific to itself—such that the misogynistic Orpheus becomes a swan; Ajax, traumatized by the quarrel over arms with Odysseus, refuses a human life; and Epeius, the maker of the Trojan Horse, becomes a craftswoman (620a–d). These lives mirror and enact the identities appropriate to these souls, unlike Aristophanes' Cloud-chorus, which merely produces a series of fluid, shifting images which characterize Athens' notorious citizens (see pp. 46–7 above).

III

The argument about the nature of civic identity and role in the ideal state, and in turn about the identity of constitutions, provides, as I earlier suggested, a crucial frame for understanding the discussion of literature, especially poetry, in the *Republic*. Poetry has a crucial role to play in the creation of the ideal state and its citizen, making a deceptively cautious entrance into the dialogue in book 2 (and this may be what suggests to Carnes Lord the implausible view that literature and the arts are 'impotent', being unable to affect political life for good or ill).[16] As far as the creators of the ideal state are concerned, poetry is one of the arts which

[16] Lord (1982), 20.

distinguishes a society from the simple, primitive community in which only the bare necessities of the inhabitants are met and which Glaucon dismisses as a 'city of pigs' (372d4). Society requires some of the comforts of everyday life and once it begins to admit a few of these, it is bound to admit the various forms of art and imitation (372e–3c). The city will now include painters, musicians, poets, rhapsodes, actors, chorus-dancers, and all manner of craftsmen (373b5–c1). Although Socrates begins by suggesting that these are non-essential roles in the city and are what cause sickness in what we are implicitly to regard as the body politic, it soon becomes clear that art and its practitioners are an integral element of the political structure. To invoke the terminology of contemporary material-ism, it might be said that the artist provides the city with a certain 'cultural capital' which is no less valuable than the economic capital of goods produced by non-artistic craftsmen (*dēmiourgoi*)—hence the designation of both artisans and this latter group by the same term, *dēmiourgoi*.

Once admitted, literary art has to be an important part of the author's politics because, like the citizen's proper task and role in society, it establishes and provides the citizen with his or her iden-tity. If the Muses instruct Hesiod in fine song (*Theog.* 22) and the Parnassian maidens in the *Homeric Hymn to Hermes* are described by the poet as teachers of divination (556), mortal poets are for Plato, as for his contemporaries, typically the teachers of men.[17] They instruct their audiences in their civic identities and in the identities of their communities. In the *Protagoras* Protagoras implies that, together with the sophist, the poet is society's privi-leged teacher (*didaskalos*).[18] The sophist Protagoras relates how young pupils are made to read and learn poetic works which praise and recount the lives of noble individuals whom they will take as models for imitation (cf. *mimeisthai*, 326a). In *Republic* 10 Socrates states that those who praise Homer do so because he has educated Greece: Homer is the 'first teacher' of all the tragedians (595c1–2) and the 'leader (*hēgemēn*) of Greek culture (*paideias*)' (600a9; cf. 598d8). As a term that in fourth-century political language denotes a democratic leader of the city, like Pericles, the noun *hegemôn*

---

[17] Gentili (1988), 55.
[18] Havelock (1982), 261 ff. See Harriott (1969: 145 ff.), who suggests that *Pr.* 343d–344d exemplifies the linguistic, historical, and nationalistic concerns of sophistic literary interpretation.

significantly suggests that where Homer is concerned poetic authority is synonymous with political authority. Elsewhere, Socrates uses *epistatēs* ('leader') to refer to imitators, whether the painter, the carpenter, the creative god, or their counterparts (cf. 597b13).

Socrates specifically draws attention to the role of literature in establishing itself in the character and nature of its audience and in determining the way in which a citizen will behave and act in society (cf. 395d, 396b–c). The education of the guardians involves the cultivation of both soul and body, with music being important in the development of the former, and gymnastics in the development of the latter (376e). Giving priority to the formation of the soul, and thus to the role of music in education, Socrates declares that even before they begin physical training, the young citizens must be told stories, since their souls are most malleable and receptive at this point (esp. 377b5–9). The education of children through literature is implicitly compared to the stamping of a plastic material (cf. Isoc. *C. Soph.* 14–18). Literary texts literally offer impressions (*tupoi*) which children receive into their malleable and accepting souls (*Resp.* 377–9); or else, they present them with paradigms which they are to take as models for their own behaviour (395c ff.). It is precisely because of its central role in the creation of civic identity that poetry is subject to the constraints of criticism. In the *Laws*, where (choral) music is assumed to be both an imitation of and an influence on character (cf. 655d), the Athenian Stranger demands that the good legislator oversee and enforce the production of literature and songs because they reproduce the character of virtuous citizens (660a, 660e). Above all the legislator must ensure that the poets do not write anything in contradiction of the laws (719b).[19]

In the *Republic* Plato rehearses this imperative. He defers to the widespread idea, stressed for instance and albeit somewhat ironically in Aristophanes' *Frogs*, that the poet and his work must be watched over because of the poet's political position in society. It is important to recognize, however, that the anxieties about art in the

---

[19] It is the task of the legislator to see that hymns are composed for the weddings of the leaders (*Resp.* 459e–460a). The function of these and other such legislated songs is to preserve the power of the leaders. Marriage songs are part of the process which regulates the number of leaders in the city, while encomia of the leaders ensure that their subjects continue to respect them even in times of adversity (460a8).

state in books 2–3 and 10 are not about imitation *per se*, which is the basis of the pedagogy that Socrates envisages even for the young guardian; rather, the anxiety is about *what* and more specifically *how many* things are imitated. A number of the *Republic*'s readers have argued that there might be a taxonomy of imitation along the dichotomy of 'good' and 'bad' imitation. So on the question of *what* is imitated, J. Tate suggests that Plato admits 'good imitation', which knowledgeably represents things as they really are, but rejects 'bad imitation', which fails to employ a good, i.e. divine, paradigm.[20] On the question of *how many* things are imitated, Elizabeth Belfiore suggests that an important distinction should be made between the *mimētikos*, somone who claims to be an expert in the art of imitation, and the *mimētēs*, an individual who does not purport to know and be able to imitate everything. According to her, the former is a 'versatile imitator' and responsible for bad imitation, on the principle that each individual should do one type of work, while the latter is the proponent of good and discriminating imitation, which is also truthful imitation.[21] Likewise, Diskin Clay reinforces the importance of *how many* things are imitated when he observes that in *Republic* 10 Plato casts the discussion of art in the same terms that he employs in speaking of *polypragmosunē* (which he also glosses as 'meddling' and 'interference' where an individual has no legitimate business). For Clay, the ultimate artistic *polupragmōn* is the artistic imitator portrayed in book 10. This is an individual who represents everything indiscriminately.[22]

The final book provides us with several images of the versatile imitator. There is the divine demiurge who fashions all things in the cosmos (cf. 596c) and is said to be a marvellous sophist (596d). There are painters and poets who engage in modes of imitation which, in the case of painting, enable the painter to fashion *all* things (*panta apergazetai*, 598b) and, in the case of poetry, allow the poet to appear to demonstrate knowledge of all skills, of all things regarding good and evil, and even of divine matters (598e). At 598d7 ff. the philosopher observes that tragic poets, in particular taking their lead from Homer, are said to know *all* skills, *all* human things regarding human virtue and lack of virtue, and also divine things.[23] Yet the principle that one person can only do one

---

[20] J. Tate (1928); (1929–30); (1932).   [21] Belfiore (1984), 126–8.
[22] See D. Clay in Griswold (1988), 19–33, and 269–72 at 271 n. 20.
[23] Cf. Xen. *Symp.* 4. 6.

thing well is not to be disregarded: both painter and poet dabble in too many things and in nothing well. The painter's lack of special-ization—he does not always paint the same sort of work or thing—means that he can convey only a limited aspect of each thing he does represent (595b). Inevitably, he produces an image (*eidolon*) which Socrates declares to be at a third remove from reality and therefore to be deficient as a representation of reality. According to the exam-ple given by the philosopher and frequently cited in secondary literature, a painting of a bed is just a copy of an actual bed which is in turn no more than a copy of the Form of Bed (597b–d). There is a damning suggestion that the versatile imitator may resemble an apparently all-wise (*passophos*) and bewitching (cf. 'sorcerer', *goētēs*) sophist (596d). Historically, sophists such as Protagoras and Prodicus originated the study both of language—prescribing cor-rect usage—and of what we might conventionally understand to be 'literary criticism' (cf. *Phdr.* 266b ff.). As far as Plato is concerned, the sophist is, however, a linguistic transgressor and therefore must be silenced. He is the individual who is able through his wisdom to appear in different guises (*pantodapon gignesthai*) and to imitate all things (*mimeisthai panta chrēmata*) (398a; cf. *Hp. mi.* 368c–d).[24] He will come to the city and will wish to make a display of his poetic compositions. Socrates observes that the citizens of the ideal city will worship this changeable individual as a holy man, but the philosopher also insists that such a person can and must have no place in the perfect city, because he has no role or identity that is properly his.

Lear concludes his excellent article on the *Republic* by asking whether poetry might ever make a return to Plato's city, and I would stress that on the basis of the foregoing argument book 10 is not a rejection of imitative art *in toto*.[25] Instead it is a qualified rejection of imitative art when such art has negative implications for society, because it involves *polupragmosunē* and therefore injus-tice. It is, moreover a rejection of imitative art that stands less in contrast to the discussion of literature in earlier books of the *Republic* than as one which takes this discussion to its logical devel-opment and conclusion. To ensure that the citizen of the ideal city

---

[24] In his discussion of *Republic* 392c–398b ff. Else (1958: 84) gives the adjective παντοδαπαί the sense of 'indiscriminate' and observes that 'we want only the sim-plest and most uniform kind of imitation, that of a good man'.

[25] Lear (1992), 215.

does his or her own proper task, the regulation of art has in turn as its aim the regulation of the identities with which it can endow the state's citizens. What the earlier books of the *Republic* enact is criticism, understood in the sense of discrimination and distinction, which serves as a specific strategy for expelling *polupragmosunē* from the state. So in book 3 Socrates forbids the future guardians from practising the various arts and crafts, precisely because these activities will involve them in diverse roles (395b9–c1), and will expose them to a bewitchment which might hinder them from doing what is best for society (412e). The bewitched individual is one who has become fearful or pleasure-seeking (cf. 413d7 ff.) through exposure to the multitude of images that are made available through conventional education, i.e. through poetry, theatre, and music. Socrates compares the false pleasures derived from these activities to images painted on a screen (583b5). The philosopher denigrates the enjoyment to be derived from dramatic performance as being analogous to that derived from one of the modes of imitation rejected in book 10. Ideally the good guardian is 'hard to charm' (*dusgoēteutos*) and not susceptible to the sorcery (*goēteia*) which makes him or her think that anything other than the pleasure of the soul is a true pleasure (584a10). S/he maintains watch over her- or himself and remains faithful to the guardian's strict upbringing. Socrates declares that such an individual will give up all other crafts in order to be 'demiurges of the free city' (395c1–2). For the guardian to engage in artistic activities or in crafts would be for them to surrender their political class identity and to become the third and lowest artisan class in the state, the group of citizenry that Socrates describes as being iron or bronze in his Noble Lie (cf. 415a6–7).

I want to emphasize that the role of art in the guardian's education is not so much excluded as rigorously constrained, as it is for the other citizens. In books 2 and 3 Socrates considers the power of texts to determine and shape the character of the child, the future adult citizen of the ideal state, and he sets out legislation to regulate the content of mythical narratives which nurses and mothers may tell to children in the course of their musical education. Where myths of gods are concerned, the philosopher prohibits accounts of the many (*pollas*) and diverse (*pantodapas*) divine hostilities lest they provide the young citizens with an impetus towards civil unrest (378c–e). Allegory, which can make the unacceptable

acceptable, offers such myths no defence. Socrates also forbids older citizens and teachers to relate stories which depict the same gods appearing in all sorts of different forms or shapes at different times.[26] He observes initially that such stories of divine metamorphosis may frighten young children and make them cowardly (381e) but, beyond this, he also objects to the fact that they falsify divine nature. According to the philosopher, a god is a being who is least likely to change, that is become other than (*alloioun*) himself, and who remains as far as possible always and simply (*haplōs*) in his own form (381c); divine nature is simple (*haplous*) (382e, 380d). For a god to change form, as traditional poetic narratives depict, is for him to engage in a lie, not just in speech (*en logōi*) but also in deed (*en ergōi*) (382a, 383a). Plato here insists on the gap between truth and falsehood, observing that both men and gods detest lying in deed (382a–c), although the Noble Lie is subsequently tolerated because it encourages all the citizens and especially the leaders of the ideal city to act for the benefit of the whole community by persuading them that they are 'brothers' (415a3, 7).[27] The goal of education as the formation of political identity warrants an implicit analogy between the metamorphosing god and the less than ideal mortal citizen. Multiple transformations would turn a god into a divine *polupragmōn*, a being who assumes roles and tasks which are not properly his own. The true divine nature, which is the best because it resists all forms of change, is the model for the character of a just, responsible citizen.

The discussion of mythical narrative may enable the reader to defend the illusion that art is distinct from political *praxis*. One might argue that Socrates' critique of theological discourse only shows how literary texts may provide the citizens with a negative model for civic behaviour but do not, however, directly involve their producers and recipients in such behaviour by actually requiring them to become other than they are.[28] Nevertheless,

[26] Cf. ἐξ ἐπιβουλῆς φαντάζεσθαι ἄλλοτε ἐν ἄλλαις ἰδέαις, 'to appear at will at different times in different forms' (380d); πολλοῖς ξένοις καὶ παντοδαποῖς ἰνδαλλόμενοι, 'appearing like many strangers of all different sorts' (381e); παντοδαποὺς φαίνεσθαι, 'to appear in many different forms' (381e).

[27] Note that the definition of justice at 331c already offers pragmatism as a rationalization of lies. According to the scenario sketched by Socrates, one would lie in order to avoid giving weapons back to their insane owner.

[28] Yet the *Ion* suggests the power of poetry to affect those who produce and receive, offering as an analogy for poetic inspiration the image of a magnetic stone

Socrates' treatment of mimetic narratives in *Republic* 3 specifically reveals how the very use of poetry in education may in itself contribute to the presence of *polupragmosunē* and of the unjust, meddling citizen in the city. In book 3 the philosopher distinguishes between simple narrative (*haplē diēgēsis*), where the poet relates a narrative in his own person, and mimetic narrative (cf. *dia mimēseōs*), where the poet dramatizes the speech of another person, namely one of his characters. He also identifies a third kind of narrative, which combines both simple and mimetic modes (392d). This narratological taxonomy, which Aristotle later adopts at *Poetics* 1448ª19 ff., is also implicitly but significantly predicated upon the earlier discussion of the citizen's duties and responsibilities, namely to do his or her own thing and so to fulfil his or her social role. Because simple narrative does not attempt to create the impression that anyone other than the poet is speaking (393a), it does not require the poet to be anyone other than himself: that is to say, the poet is not required to conceal the fact that the speaking voice belongs to him. In contrast, the poet who engages in mimetic narrative, as the comic or tragic poet does, impersonates and dramatizes the utterance of someone other than himself (*hōs tis allos ōn,* 393c). He becomes another person—perhaps a Chryses, an Achilles, or an Odysseus—in his speech and appearance (cf. 393a–b), despite the fact that he should be only himself and perform his proper role as poet to the extent that this is legitimate (394e). It is in this way that Homer, as teacher of tragedians (cf. 595c1–2, 600b, 606e2), is understood to provide society with multiple discourses and identities and to construct the identity of those who read, recite, and enact them—whether the pupil in the school or the rhapsode, like Ion in the dialogue named for him—and in this way, to control the character of society.

(the Muses) which attracts to itself a series of concentric rings (the poet, his rhapsodes, and then the audience) (*Ion* 535d). As the inspired interpreter of the Homeric epics (cf. 534e), the rhapsode claims to know all of Homer's poetry, even when it appears to articulate specialized knowledge such as that known best to charioteers or doctors (539e ff.). Socrates thus declares Ion a 'manifold Proteus' (541e). That this is an implicitly unflattering description of the rhapsode where the *Ion* is concerned becomes clear from the philosopher's conclusion that the rhapsode must be either 'unjust' or else divine, in the sense of divinely inspired (542a). The unjust person does not know his own proper knowledge, role, and place in the community, as the *Republic* establishes, while the divine person is, as the earlier discussion in the *Ion* has revealed, not in complete control of himself and in fact 'outside of himself' (cf. *Ion* 535b). Socrates' treatment of mimetic narrative in *Republic* 3 goes further than the *Ion* in offering a more detailed analysis of poetic performance and reception.

Mimetic narratives involve others apart from the poet and professional performer in impersonation inasmuch as children do not just listen to stories and myths. They also eventually dramatize and enact the characters presented in them in the course of their education and thereby become *mimētikoi* (cf. 394e). So if the pupil recites mimetic texts, such as tragedies and comedies, he will assume the identity and emotions of the characters who speak in them. The description of the frenzy which grips the soul of the rhapsode in the *Ion* makes evident the powerful effect that recitation can have on the emotions: in particular, the reciter of poetry becomes a corybant, no longer in control of his mind (534a2 ff.). Mimetic narratives provide an opportunity for an individual to imitate 'many things' (*polla*), 395a), and yet because each individual can only do one thing well (cf. 394e), they also reveal his incompetence in many things (cf. 394e–395a). Socrates draws an analogy between acting theatrical roles and performing (*prattein*) the roles which are represented in the play (395b3–6). Plato stresses the consistency and continuity between art and political life: the verb *prattein* is one which may also denote political action in the state.

Although the sorts of dramatic narratives examined in book 3 support political meddling (*polupragmosunē*) and invite it into the city, Socrates' rejection of them is qualified. He does not prohibit them in themselves. Rather, he proposes stringent regulations which ensure that those who may be exposed to them, and especially the future guardians, who must do nothing other than rule well (395b–d), maintain their integrity, where 'integrity' entails unity of identity as defined through action. The philosopher ensures that mimetic narratives will represent only virtuous individuals, such as the citizens themselves must be (395c). At 395d ff. Socrates proceeds to catalogue the various *other* characters that must not be permitted to enter the ideal city through dramatic poetry: women railing at husbands, women quarelling with the gods, women in distress, pain, or lamentation, in love or labour, slaves, male or female, men who are cowardly, abusive, drunk, and so on. Clearly the male citizen is the privileged model of identity. Socrates also legislates against a variety of different 'discourses' which an actor or reciter of mimetic narratives would have to dramatize: horses neighing, bulls lowing, rivers gurgling, the sea crashing (396b). Not only does Socrates propose to ban all such sound effects (*panta . . . ta toiauta*) as those exemplifed by this list

(396b) but also all (*panta*) other animate and artificial noises like those mentioned at 397a. By conventionally requiring their actors to produce so many different sounds for the young citizen to imitate (cf. *mimēsontai*, 396b7), poets form souls of the kind which Socrates attributes to the unjust citizen. Such souls resemble mythological creatures—the philosopher names Chimaera, Scylla, and Cerberus—who are multiheaded and are able to transform themselves at will (588c7–10). Socrates observes that such many-headed beasts (cf. *tou polukephalou thremmatos*, 589a–b) can be tamed only by justice. By this account of dramatic narrative as producing among other things many voices and sounds (e.g. 396b) Plato alludes to and expands upon the Hesiodic and Aristophanic discourses about the political nature of voice.

If drama is part of the pupil's education—again the future guardian is envisaged—it is important for him to learn to impersonate virtuous men, those who are courageous, pious, moderate, and unslavish (395c3–7).[29] His literary model is to be the good man (*anēr agathos*, 395d6, 396d1). The only discourse that can remain in an ideal state is a human speech, whose style (*lexis*) can have only slight variations and not a great range of variations.[30] Such a consistent *lexis* is the mark of someone who is truly *kalos kagathos*, 'a fine gentleman' (396b), while a divergent style denotes his opposite number, in this dialogue, the *polupragmōn*. It is worth noting that the following discussion of music reveals the same privileging of simplicity and uniformity. According to Aristotle (cf. *Pol.* 1340[b]18–19), the Pythagoreans believed that there was an affinity between music and the soul.[31] Plato exhibits Pythagorean influence in this respect. At 399c f. Socrates prohibits polyphonous instru-

[29] Euben (1986: 23) observes that the verb διδάσκειν means both 'to teach' and 'to put on plays'.

[30] οὐκοῦν αὐτοῖν τὸ μὲν σμικρὰς τὰς μεταβολὰς ἔχει, καὶ ἐάν τις ἀποδιδῷ πρέπουσαν ἁρμονίαν καὶ ῥυθμὸν τῇ λέξει, ὀλίγου πρὸς τὴν αὐτὴν γίγνεται λέγειν τῷ ὀρθῶς λέγοντι καὶ ἐν μιᾷ ἁρμονίᾳ—σμικραὶ γὰρ αἱ μεταβολαί—καὶ δὴ καὶ ἐν ῥυθμῷ ὡσαύτως παραπλησίῳ; 'Thus of these two types, doesn't one involve *small changes*, and if someone ascribes a harmony and rhythm that suits the style, doesn't it happen that he nearly speaks like one who does so correctly and in a single harmony—*for the changes are minor*, and in a similarly consistent rhythm?' (397b); also τί δὲ τὸ τοῦ ἑτέρου εἶδος; οὐ τῶν ἐναντίων δεῖται, πασῶν μὲν ἁρμονιῶν, πάντων δὲ ῥυθμῶν, εἰ μέλλει αὖ οἰκείως λέγεσθαι, διὰ τὸ παντοδαπὰς μορφὰς τῶν μεταβολῶν ἔχειν; 'What about the other type? Doesn't it require the opposite—all harmonies and all rhythms—if one is to speak in keeping with it, *since it has all manner of forms of change?*' (397c).

[31] Else (1958) 87.

ments—e.g. trigones, lyres, flutes—as well their craftsmen, while favouring monodic ones, such as zithers and syrinx flutes. He also prefers rhythms which are neither complex (*poikiloi*) nor variegated (*pantodapoi*) as being those characteristic of the orderly and courageous citizen (399e).

IV

The criticism of literature and artistic imitation in *Republic* 2, 3, and 10 makes the point that literature has the capacity to involve the citizen in *polupragmosunē*, which is not only antithetical to the ideal of civic behaviour in the philosopher's *polis* and to the ideal city itself, but also potentially threatens their existence. Exposure to or involvement in variegated art is one of the factors responsible for the various imperfect and thus unjust types of constitution. Again, art *per se* is not an obstacle in the creation of the ideal state; the obstacle is rather art when it is a diverse and diversifying activity involving its producers and recipients in plural behaviours and identities. Indeed, Plato requires the architects of of the ideal state to exercise caution and establish constraints not just where drama might be involved in education but also where public performance of drama is concerned. At 492b Socrates identifies attendance at the theatre as one of the occasions on which 'the many' (*hoi polloi*) of democracy gather and respond irrationally to what they see and hear. He comments that the artist who has discerned the emotions and pleasures of the numerous and varied (*pantodapōn*) group with regard to painting, music, or politics could make the many (*tous pollous*) powerful masters (493d5). Art empowers its audience, enabling it to function as the democratic mob. Significantly, the citizens of the unjust state inform and influence the content of versatile imitation. At 601e ff. Socrates states that the poet will not have a 'correct belief' (*pistin orthên*), knowledge, or even a 'correct opinion' (*doxan orthēn*) about his subject, in this case the beautiful and evil (601e–602a). He will have only the tastes and pleasures of *hoi polloi*, who have no real knowledge, to guide him (602b). Thus he imitates what *hoi polloi* think they know since he cannot know everything that his variegated and superficial art deals with (602b3–5).

Plato offers here a critique of contemporary drama at Athens as a democratic and civic institution. If art can create and control the civic and constitutional character of the ideal state in books 2 and 3, it can also create the identity of the citizens and government in the less desirable city-states. It is the case that the versatile art of tragedy is particularly suited to creating and reinforcing a constitution which encourages a citizen to be similarly versatile. In book 8 the philosopher observes that the poets are hired by tyrannies and sometimes by democracies to praise these forms of government and to draw their citizens into approving of them (568b–c). Such governments gather crowds and hire actors who produce fine, loud, and persuasive voices such as those we might associate with the public orator and sophist (568c2–5). Thus it is appropriate for Socrates to speak of the tyrant engaging as it were in artistic activity: the tyrant fashions (cf. *apergazesthai*) others in his own image (580a5–6). The many-mouthed, -tongued, and -voiced Typhon of Hesiod's *Theogony*, who can threaten the authority of Zeus and the well-being of mortal men, is now replaced by the magician-like poets and their texts, which can destabilize a constitution and pave the way for the tyrant.

Socrates presents a psychology of artistic reception which explains how such versatile art actually effects such political decline. For Plato, the constitution of the soul is a miniature of the constitution of the state and determines the nature of the latter; however, it is the case that art can effect the constitution of the soul and in turn that of the state. The work of tragedians nurtures desire (*erôs*), which in turn becomes the 'public leader' (*prostatēs*) of lazy and desirous individuals (572e6–573a1), and perhaps ultimately of the despot whose soul allows desire to be a metaphorical tyrant (573d4).[32] Socrates also warns that the sort of false or boastful words (*logoi*) and opinions (*doxai*) produced by artistic imitators can enter into the audience's soul and take hold of its 'acropolis', particularly if the soul is devoid of learning and true words (560b5–c), and thus the poet who owes his origin to Homer endangers the constitution within the soul of his audience (608b1). (The metaphor of the soul's acropolis and Socrates' references to learning and truth as the 'best defenders (*phrouroi*) and guardians (*phulakes*)' (560b9–10) insist upon the parallelism between soul and city.[33]) The poetry usurps any truth present in the soul, undermin-

---

[32] On προστάτης as part of the political vocabulary of classical Athenian democracy, see Connor (1971), 116.

[33] On this analogy, see Lear (1992).

ing the 'monarchy of truth' with versatile imitation, which stands
at a third remove from it (597e7). It establishes a monarchy of pleasure and grief in place of one governed by the law and the best reason (607a6–7). Earlier on, Socrates had spoken about the
presidency of wisdom[34] and proclaimed knowledge the most powerful faculty (477d9).

The recognition that literary art is a potent force in the shaping
of both individual and state political identities poses the large and
important question as to the relationship of art and imitation to the
discussion that is dramatized within the *Republic* itself: in other
words, where does the dialogue (either as a *literary* text or even just
as a text) stand with regard to its own discussion of literary art?
Earlier in this chapter, I pointed out that Socrates characterizes the
ideal state as one that exists only in words—so Popper's view of
Plato's 'republic' as a self-contained aesthetic state. But where
Popper aestheticizes, that is disembodies, politics, I want to
emphasize its integral role of art in the political project of the dialogue. Richard McKeon notes that for Plato 'all discourse is an imitation, and the interlocutors of the dialogues are constantly using,
discussing, and complaining of images, likenesses, metaphors, and
copies.'[35] Socrates frequently invokes artistic metaphors, statuary,
painting, drama, and poetry, which liken the interlocutors' conversation to artistic activity and the discussants themselves to craftsmen or demiurges—in fact, Glaucon is the only other interlocutor
to use an artistic metaphor when he likens the political discussion
to the burnishing of a statue in book 2. The philosopher is also the
individual who introduces the discussion and critique of the various conventional forms of art, e.g. poetry and tragedy, into the dialogue, especially in books 2, 3, and 10. It is particularly significant
that Socrates, the philosopher, is the individual who initiates and
uses the language of art in the dialogue. He deliberately displaces
the conventional comparison of poetry to a craft, and, moreover,
as the philosopher, he takes control over art and its vocabulary,
thereby assuming the position of authority in the construction of
a city which ideally sees the philosopher as its leader (cf.
499b2–3).[36]

[34] σοφίαν δὲ τὴν ἐπιστατοῦσαν ταύτῃ τῇ πράξει ἐπιστήμην . . . (443e6–7).
[35] McKeon (1936), 13–14.
[36] Harriott (1969: 92–104) and Gentili (1988: 50–1) draw attention to the depiction of poetry and poetic composition in terms of artistic and craft metaphors.

The *Republic* enacts a taxonomy of just art. One of the first artistic metaphors is introduced into the dialogue at 361d4–6 when Socrates speaks of Glaucon scrutinizing the just and unjust man as if he were scrubbing and cleaning statues of men (cf. *hosper andrianta*). An analogy is drawn between the types of citizens being described and examined and plastic representations of men. At 420b–c the philosopher imagines that someone might criticize himself and his colleagues for not 'drawing statues' (*andrianta graphontas*) with the best possible adornments and colours when they describe an ideal state in which all classes of citizens are equally happy rather than one in which a particular class enjoyed privileges kept from the others (cf. 420d2). Glaucon picks up the philosopher's imagery when at 540c3–4 he compliments him for fashioning (cf. *apeirgasai*) the finest rulers just as a statue-maker would (cf. *hosper andriantopoios*). The comparison is poignant and particularly appropriate, as the philosopher has just said that the citizens of the ideal state will revere their leaders as blessed men and gods, and construct monuments, i.e. statues, to them (540b7–c2).

The verbs 'to fashion' (*apergazein*)/'to work' (*ergazein*) are also specifically employed to describe, through various educational regimes, the creation of civic identity and character both of the citizen and of the city as a whole (cf. 381e6, 420e1, 433c5, 457a1). At 464c5–6 Socrates depicts the earlier and current discussion as involving the 'fashioning' of the true guardians of the state in such a way that they share the same ideas of ownership (cf. *apergazetai*; also *apergazomenoi*, 501b1). The idea of education as a mode of artistic fashioning is also expressed by the verb *plattein*. Myths 'form' (*plattein*) the souls of children in the discussion of the young citizen's education in book 2 (377c3). Elsewhere, at 374a5, Socrates observes that he and his companions are 'forming and shaping' (cf. *eplattomen*) their city; at 420c2, they are 'forming' the blessed city (cf. *plattomen*; also 466a6). In the Noble Lie the god fashions (cf. *plattōn*) the golden race of men (415a4); however, the dialogue's participants must also engage in self-fashioning. The philosopher is obliged by necessity both to fashion himself (cf. *heauton plattein*) and also to set in order the characters of others privately and publicly if he is to avoid being a bad craftsman (*dēmiourgon*) of public virtue (500d). This implies that by fashioning other citizens and himself he becomes a good craftsman (*dēmiourgos*) of virtue. At 588b10 Socrates states that the discussants are 'forming' an image of the soul in language (cf. *eikona plasantes tēs psuchēs logoi*). Words are the material of the political artist, and they are more pliable than wax, as Socrates says at 588d1–2.

The creation of the ideal city is also figured as a painting. Socrates introduces the metaphor of painting at 373a6–8, when he compares the addition of citizens who perform roles and tasks beyond the essential ones to the adorning of the city with variety and decorating it with gold and ivory. Later the interlocutors depict themselves as painters who paint an object which does not exist in the physical world according to the image of 472d ff. They are painting a picture which will be a paradigm of a good city (cf. *paradeigma . . . agathēs poleōs*) rather than a graphic imitation of any existing city. Socrates embellishes the metaphor when he claims that a city can only be happy when philosophers draw (cf. *diagrapseian*) it using a divine paradigm, like painters (500e2–3). If they are given a pre-existing city together with its citizens, they will regard it as a canvas to be made clean and then reinscribed with their own laws (501a2–7). The philosophers will produce their painting, mixing and combining 'colours', namely different characters, erasing, and painting over until they make their citizens as divine as possible (501b ff.). Socrates goes on to say that the comparison of the philosopher to the painter of living creatures (*zōographos*) is necessary if the public is to accept the leaders of what will be the ideal state (501c). In another passage, Socrates speaks of the need to get beyond the mere outline of the guardians' education to the perfect artefact (cf. *tēn teleōtatēn apergasian*, 504d6–7), but when he discusses the oligarchical state in book 8, he says that there is no need to get beyond the outline of the constitution (cf. *schēma politeias hupograpsanta*) to produce a detailed work of art. Socrates assures his audience that in this case it is possible to see what the most just and unjust men are like from the outline alone (548c9–d4).

Above all, the enactment of the philosophical state is a dramatic production, which seeks in turn to invalidate and silence the voices of the traditional, civic drama and its creators.[37] The dialogue's reader observes the progress of the dialogue as she would observe a theatrical performance; she follows the production of the discussion, which is a play within our larger play. The *Republic* opens with Socrates and his companions going down to the Piraeus to

[37] Chytry (1989: p. xlii) observes that Plato banishes the tragedians and dislodges their 'theatocracy' to establish the city's life as itself a 'tragedy' in the *Laws* (817b).

watch (*theasasthai*, 327a3; cf. *theōrēsantes*, 327b1) a festival and the arrival of a Thracian cult in the city of Athens. The friends will watch (cf. *theasasthai*, *theasometha*) the passing of the torches in the ceremony (328a7–8). The centre of attraction shifts, however, from this festival to the dialogue about the ideal city and the verb 'to watch' (*theasasthai*) emblematizes the role of Socrates and his friends in observing the political discussion. Thus at 369a5 the philosopher speaks of himself and his companions watching (cf. *theasaimetha*) the city coming into being through word. First, they must be spectators of the development and education of the citizen as a child. Socrates commands his interlocutors to consider (cf. *theaton*) the response of the hypothetical pupil to various emotional stimuli at 413d7 f., and then to watch over (cf. *theaton*) the development of the whole state at 421b6. Later, Socrates recalls that they are trying to observe (*theasasthai*) justice by looking at it on a larger scale, namely in the city as a whole (434d8). The task of spectating shifts from the interlocutors of the *Republic* to the citizens that inhabit their ideal state. At 415d8–9 it is the responsibility of the leaders to watch out for (cf. *theasasthōn*) the best site for military manœuvres to take place. The military class in the ideal state is taught to ride early on, so that it will be able to perceive (*theasontai*) its responsibilities readily (467e5–6).

At 451c2 Socrates makes explicit the analogy which the verb *theaomai* suggests between the current political dialogue and a drama or play. Before turning to consider the role of women in the ideal state, he speaks of the foregoing discussion of men's roles as a masculine performance (*andreion drama*). At 506c11 visual vocabulary stresses the status of the Divided Line metaphor as spectacle when Socrates asks his interlocutors if they wish to see (*theasasthai*) what is base, blind, and crooked when they can hear what is clear and fine. Above all, the participants in the dialogue are to be understood as watching a theatre of the soul, as spectators of the 'chorus (*choron*) of the philosopher's nature' (490c8) rather than of the 'chorus (*choron*) of ills' that accompanies the soul in which truth does not take the leading role—truth is implicitly the 'chorusleader' in this image (490c2–3). Indeed, when they observe the tyrant's whole soul, they see (cf. *theasasthai*) that it is in fact the most needy and poor of all souls rather than the richest and is full of all sorts of grief and pains (579e3–5). The drama of the soul reaches its climax in the final book with the myth of Er, a narrative concerning the process by which souls select different lives for themselves. At 611c Socrates explains that to appreciate the soul as immortal, one needs to consider (*theasasthai*) it as a pure entity and not, as we now do (cf. *hōsper nun hēmeis theōmetha*), when it is marred and damaged by its association with the body and its ills. The language of the theatre returns slightly later when the fictional narrator, Er, refers to the punishment of a tyrant named Ardiaeus as a 'terrible spectacle' (*ta deina theamata*) (615d4). Er sums up his experiences by referring to the whole sight of souls selecting their lives as a 'spectacle' (*thea*) at 619e6.

V

Plato's literary art is a just politics in a more direct sense. The characters in the dialogue engage in good imitation as they enact the ideal, philosophical politics through their discussion. If the ideal city rests on the just distribution of elements within the community, then the discourse of the *Republic* produces justice in its just attribution of elements within the ideal it offers and the process that creates it. In the initial exchange between Socrates and Thrasymachus, the sophist accuses the philosopher of refusing to answer questions when they are put to him but, when someone else answers, of taking up the account (*logos*) and of refuting his interlocutor (337e). The word *logos* is significant because it can denote both 'word/speech' and '(financial) account', and Glaucon's talk of rendering payment for a good definition of justice at 337d lends support to the monetary connotations of *logos*. Thrasymachus' *double entendre* suggests that not only is the philosopher failing to give his own definition of justice, he is also unfairly, perhaps unjustly, gaining from the verbal exchange. Thrasymachus implicitly accuses Socrates of injustice but, because he is the individual who perversely defines justice as the advantage of the stronger (338c), his accusation is inevitably rejected in the ensuing discussion.

In subsequent books of the *Republic*, Plato's language indicates that Socrates is acting justly as far as explaining his account of the ideal city goes. At 457e the philosopher ironically declares that he had hoped to escape the obligation to discuss women and children as common property in the ideal state and how such an arrangement is possible. Picking up Socrates' language, Glaucon says that the philosopher will be noticed if he escapes and commands him to give an account (cf. *didou logon*) of both these points. Socrates offers the rejoinder, 'it is necessary to pay the penalty' (*huphekteon . . . dikēn*, 457e7). In this passage Socrates and Glaucon briefly assume the roles of defendant (conventionally designated as the person who 'flees') and prosecutor (conventionally the 'pursuer') respectively. The philosopher allows himself to be put on the defensive so that he can explain further the need for the family to be abolished in the ideal city. In a later part of this book Socrates again characterizes himself as the just speaker. At 466b4 ff. he uses the following phraseology, 'However, as I said there, it is just (*dikaion*) to say here also . . .',[38] before declaring that the guardian who departs from his proper role in the state in seeking personal happiness should be declared less than wise. At 474a4 Glaucon warns the philosopher that unless he can defend his case for making the philosopher the ruler of the state, he will be mocked and have to pay the penalty (cf. *dōseis dikēn*). Socrates reinforces the legal imagery by asking his interlocutor if he is responsible for, that is guilty (*aitios*) of, these things (474a5).

In book 10 the philosopher returns to the language of just discourse and invokes the definition of justice given in book 1 when he asks Glaucon to render (*apodounai*) to justice and virtue the rewards (*tous misthous*) that the just soul possesses both in life and after life, following the discussion contained in the previous books (612b7–c3). To settle the account properly Socrates also demands that he is paid back (cf. *apodōsete*) the interest owed to him by Glaucon.[39] What he requires is that his interlocutor recant the statement that the just man can appear unjust and the unjust man just. This financial terminology forms a leitmotif in the dialogue as a whole. In the central books Socrates had presented his epistemological narrative as a fair financial transaction between himself and the interlocutors. When Glaucon urges him on to offer a narrative as recompense (cf. *apoteiseis tēn diēgēsin*, 506e5–6), the philosopher responds that he is willing to 'render' (*apodounai*) this and in addition to pay interest—*tokos* means both 'child' and 'interest'—on the Good. Socrates plays with the financial metaphor as he warns Glaucon to be on the lookout lest he renders (cf. *apodidous*) a false account (*logon*) for the interest (507a). The speaker pays up his

---

[38] ἀλλὰ μέντοι, ὅ γε καὶ ἐκεῖ ἔλεγον, δίκαιον καὶ ἐνταῦθα εἰπεῖν (466b4–5).

[39] ἆρ᾽ οὖν ἀποδώσετέ μοι ἃ ἐδανείσασθε ἐν τῷ λόγῳ; (612c5).

'account' with his description of the Divided Line, an explanation of human knowledge and opinion which attributes (cf. *apodidon*, 508e2) different forms of perception to the proper sensory and intellectual faculties. This explanation is proportional (*analogon*, cf. 511e2) and, according to his definition of *dikaiosunē*, just. Hence Socrates has 'rendered' (*apodos*) the intellectual faculty (*noēsis*) to the highest part of the soul, thinking (*dianoia*) to the second, belief (*pistis*) to the third, and imagining to the fourth and lowest.

The reader is subsequently invited to follow the lead offered by Socrates in the allocation of terms to their significances where metaphor is concerned. Metaphors have their proper and appropriate place in the dialogue. They are an importants element of Plato's philosophical art, as a form of image which represents or imitates the truth (510b4–9), and necessary to the whole process of comprehension of the truth. In the Cave metaphor, Socrates explains that the inhabitants of the cave are able to emerge and to look up at the sun, a symbol for the Good itself, without being blinded and hurt only after they have gradually accustomed themselves to gazing at its reflection in the water (515c–516b). The reader has to recognize that the reflections of the sun in the water are the counterpart to the images in water in the Divided Line passage (cf. 510a1 and 510e2–3), which individuals employ in their pursuit of understanding reality itself. On the Line, this corresponds to *eikasia*, the lowest mode of cognition (511e1–2). Other parts of the dialogue which are described as an *eikōn* or image— 375d5, 487e (the ship of state metaphor); 517a8 (the Cave metaphor); 588b10 (*eikona plasantes tēs psuchēs logoi*; cf. 588d10)— fulfil their pedagogical function of helping the reader to come gradually to terms with reality once s/he makes the appropriate attributions of text to meaning.

By requiring the enactment of justice and then by dramatizing its enactment, the dialogue's discussion has the significant effect of distinguishing the *Republic* as a literary work from conventional art and its failings. Normal drama and poetry pluralize the distribution of roles and identities within the community, but they also inadequately allocate meaning and being to their discourses such that the copy is always an epistemologically and ontologically insufficient image of what it represents. In contrast, Plato's philosophical literary art engages in a just distribution of elements within the hypothetical city, a proceeding which also breaks down the distance

between art as a mode of imitation and art as reality. Hans Georg
Gadamer and André Laks, who still work within a model of art as
necessarily mimetic, insist that the ideal city presented in the dialogue is not self-sufficient. It is a state removed from the empirical
world of *praxis* or deed, and thus needs another text—an oral dialogue, as Gadamer would have it. This scholar proposes that as a
literary dialogue the *Republic* functions as a proemium to the true
laws.[40] For him, the language of the written dialogue is not the
privileged philosophical discourse, the true poetry, which is the
basis for power in the state.[41] Regarding the written dialogues as an
introduction to a more advanced oral teaching, he sees the dialogue
as propaideutic, and as setting the human soul in order as a first step
towards ordering the true state. Alternatively, the *Republic* needs a
later written text, the *Laws*, as Laks would have it, which is the possible enactment of the otherwise impossible ideal articulated in the
Republic.[42] But philosophical art represents itself as invalidating
the hierarchical gap between copy and original that determines the
deficiencies of the former and the superiority of the latter with
respect to knowledge and reality as proposed in book 10. Socrates
says that the ideal city exists only in words (*logoi*) (472d9–e1,
592a10–11) but he is also careful to deny that it is a mimetic text.
Further, he proposes that this literary city is to be a paradigm of the
good city, a model for philosophical politics. The suggestion is that
we view the dialogue's discussion of the ideal *polis* as simultaneously the copy and the original, the paradigm and the enactment
of the paradigm itself. The author presents us with a radical notion
of art in which the artefact is simultaneously the object it depicts,
and so in which the ontological and epistemological chasm between
imitation and imitated disappears.

The gap between image and reality is closed precisely because
metaphors in the dialogue denote discursive acts or roles that cannot be distinguished from the language which designates political
activity and its actors in the state. In book 1 Thrasymachus introduces the idea that the current discussion is civic action. The orator ironically accuses Socrates of being a 'sycophant (*sukophantēs*)
. . . in words' (340d1; cf. 341a5) and of doing dastardly deeds (*kak-
ourgounta*, 341a7) when he has just proposed an inequitable defin-

---

[40] Gadamer (1980), 48, 72. For the idea of 'proem' in the dialogue, cf. 357c2,
432e8, 531d8, 532d7.
[41] Gadamer (1980), 67.   [42] Laks (1990), 213.

ition of justice as the advantage of the stronger (340c). Socrates
reinforces the idea that the present discourse is a political activity
when he proposes that if they attempt to gain agreement from one
another and examine the strength of their arguments, they will be
'judges' (*dikastai*) and 'orators' (*rhetores*) (348b4). He goes on to
charge his opponent with demagoguery, the rousing of the democratic mob through speech (350e1). In book 6 the interlocutors
depict themselves as the guardian-class that is so vital in overseeing
the preservation of civic ideology and structure. At 499d Socrates
claims that he and his interlocutors are prepared to defend with
their speech the idea that the ideal city will come into being once it
is ruled by the Muse.[43] The phrase 'to defend with speech' (*tōi logōi
diamachesthai*) characterizes the discussants as the verbal counterparts of the guardians, who defend their city with their military
skill as well as with their surveillance of the state's education.
Socrates, in particular, is called upon by Glaucon to 'defend' verbally (cf. *amunē tōi logōi*) his suggestion that philosophy is a political force. Glaucon says that he envisages many people throwing off
their cloaks and seizing weapons in preparation for an attack on
Socrates' daring claim (474a).

Other passages in the dialogue show that explanation of an action
may constitute that very action itself. Later, Glaucon observes that
the dialogue's participants are founding (*oikizontes*) a city in words,
while Socrates and Adeimantus say that they prefer to be known as
founders of the city (*oikistai poleōs*) rather than as makers of the city
(*poiētai . . . poleōs*) (378e7–379a1; cf. also 592a10). The philosopher
insists that they are not merely poets, despite the fact that he and
his companions frequently describe their discursive activity with
the verb that is also used to denote poetic creation and composition,
poiein (cf. 358b7, 369c9; also 401b1–2). Socrates explains that the
dialogue's participants must be known as the city's founders
because it is their task to establish the guidelines (*tupous*) for the
writing of myths and poetry rather than to produce the literature
themselves. The dialogue's participants have assumed the responsibilities of the state's legislators for the establishment of festivals
(see above and e.g. 459e), and they name themselves as 'legislators'

---

[43] περὶ τούτου ἕτοιμοι τῷ λόγῳ διαμάχεσθαι, ὡς γέγονεν ἡ εἰρημένη πολιτεία
καὶ ἔστιν καὶ γενήσεταί γε, ὅταν αὕτη ἡ Μοῦσα πόλεως ἐκρατὴς γένηται, 'On this
matter, we are ready to take up the cause with an argument that the aforesaid state
has been, is, and will be when the Muse is in charge of the city' (499d).

at 497d1–2. Similarly, explanation of the ideal education *is* this pedagogy itself. Socrates assumes the role of 'a curious and not entirely evident teacher' (*geloios . . . eoika didaskalos einai kai asaphēs*) at 392d8 when he explains to his companions the education of the guardians in an attempt to displace the position and authority of Homer as society's teacher (cf. 407a11).

The slippage between political vocabulary and the language used to describe discursive and artistic activity in the dialogue suggests that to speak about the just state, or to engage in philosophy as Socrates describes it, is to enact the just state. Thus, the philosopher can speak about philosophy as a political power (cf. *dunamis te politikē*) at 473d3 when he explains why philosophers should rule cities and then, at 499d, speak of philosophy as the Muse which controls the ideal city. This description of philosophy indicates that it is an inspired activity, like the writing of poetry, and reminds us that the dialogue's speakers are to be viewed as producing a political poetry. In calling into question the idea that the dialogue is a mere copy, that it is a representation, of political activity, Plato proposes that the dialogue is itself the ideal political activity and so its own paradigm and its own self-representation. So the city that is constructed in the dialogue is compared not to the images of letters (*eikonas grammatōn*), which provide the model for the copy, but to the letters themselves, which, Socrates states, one must know first and which signify the original (402b). The philosopher insists that the dialogue is analogous to the original letters when he declares that the discussants will consider justice in the context of the whole city rather than only where the individual citizen is concerned (368e2–3). He explains that they will proceed with their investigation by considering letters, not small ones (*grammata smikra*), which are hard to see, but the very same letters (*ta auta grammata*) on a larger scale (cf. 368d). The *Laws*, which is concerned with the second-best state (739a and 807b),[44] perhaps offers an analogy for the dialogue of the *Republic* as the letter/original, since this work is presented as a paradigm for imitation. At *Laws* 811c the Athenian Stranger observes that the present discussion may be just the sort of *paradeigma* that could be used in the education of young citizens in their hypothetical city. The *Laws* is the Platonic dialogue which demonstrates how the *Republic*'s ideal

[44] See e.g. Greene (1918), 63 ff.

state might be instantiated through rigorous and comprehensive legislation, for Annabel Patterson offers a reading of the *Laws* which views its society as one in which censorship and surveillance are ubiquitous and unrelenting, and so in which a crucial aspect of the ideal state of the *Republic* is put into practice.[45]

VI

The *Republic* is a work that depicts the nightmare scenario of multiplicity in the community, only to repress it severely through criticism. The work refigures Typhon's myriad voices as the voices, identities, and superficial knowledge of the fourth-century intellectual, the poet and the sophist. These are individuals who through their discourses offer the inhabitants of the ideal city alternative, and thus competing, identities and roles which threaten the stability of a state in which each citizen has only one proper identity and role to enact if it is to achieve its ideal, just condition. Plato's discourse, the dialogue he places in the mouths of Socrates and the latter's interlocutors, presents itself as a space of self-privileging. It offers a critique of imitative art which serves to repress these differing voices, each of which has the capacity to construct an alternative state or states, and which operates as the basis of power in the ideal state. The repression of voices becomes an instrument of authority for the philosopher-king, as the voices of the poets and sophists are transformed into and displaced by epistemology and the whole language of justice.

45 For this reading of the *Laws*, see A. Patterson (1993), 12–14.

3

Discriminating Pleasures: Aristotle's *Poetics* and the Civic Spectator

> Mimesis, we recall, as an activity, the mimetic activity, does
> not reach its intended term through the dynamism of the
> poetic text alone. It also requires a spectator or reader.
>
> Paul Ricoeur (1983), 46

I

Chapter 3 remains with the fourth century in offering a reading of
Aristotle's contribution to ancient criticism. What justifies the current study giving this attention to Plato's close contemporary is the
way in which scholars have constructed chronologies of literary
history which attribute significance to this author and his work,
even, on occasion, to the disregard of Plato. Aristotle fills an important gap between classical Greek discussions of literature and the
Hellenistic period. His and Theophrastus' works apart, no substantial works of criticism exist from Plato until the first century
BCE so that we must rely on fragments and testimonia preserved in
later authors for the intervening period. Aristotle is a reference
point, and precisely a *terminus post quem*, for the narrative of 'criticism', which ancient and modern scholars understand as a discourse *about* literature. In antiquity, Dio Chrysostom attributed
the beginnings of the arts of criticism (*kritikē*) and of grammar
(*grammatikē*) to the philosopher (*Or.* 36. 1). He also referred to the
numerous other writings in which the philosopher discussed the
works of Homer, the non-extant *On Poets*, and the *Homeric
Problems*—the latter text is summarized in chapter 25 of the
Poetics.[1] In the twentieth century, George Grube ensures that
Aristotle's importance does not go unnoticed when he insists that

---

[1] See Halliwell in *CHLC* i. 149; also Blum (1991), 21–3.

Theophrastus is entirely Aristotelian in his outlook, and thereby diminishes this individual's importance, so that Plato and Aristotle remain the focus of literary criticism in classical Greece.[2]

One of the large questions in Aristotelian scholarship is the relationship between the thought of Aristotle and that of Plato. Where literature is concerned, Aristotle enjoys the privileged position in literary history as the thinker who offers an alternative and an antidote to the admittedly disturbing Platonic treatment of literature. If Plato attempted to exclude contemporary poetry and drama from the ideal society of the philosopher-king in the *Republic* as 'unjust', then, in its treatment of drama, the *Poetics* seems to offer the response to Plato's challenge to produce a defence of poetry against philosophy at *Republic* 607d.[3] Because it puts dramatic poetry back on the (philosophical) agenda, the *Poetics* has come to occupy a central position in the modern literary-critical canon. By way of introduction to the section containing his work in Russell and Winterbottom's *Ancient Literary Criticism*, Margaret Hubbard comments, 'Aristotle's *Poetics* is probably the most important single book that has ever been written about poetry, both for what it says and for what it has been taken to say.'[4] Numerous modern works bear out the truth of Hubbard's observation, as studies are devoted exclusively to analysis of the *Poetics* (Stephen Halliwell[5]), to its tradition and influence on subsequent tragic composition (e.g. Terence Cave[6]), or to making Aristotle's work on tragedy the basis of a contemporary poetic theory (e.g. Elder Olson[7]). So important is the *Poetics* that Umberto Eco (see pp. 95–6 below) and Richard Janko have suggested in very different ways that the recovery of the work's missing book 2 would be one of the most important events for Western literary scholarship.[8]

This chapter is interested in a different form of recovery and reconstruction where Aristotelian poetics is concerned. It defers consideration of the *Poetics* until it has attempted to understand how Aristotle responds to the Platonic critique of poetry in a broader context. To this end, it draws attention to the larger social

---

[2] Grube (1952).

[3] Halliwell (1986), 1; Halliwell in *CHLC* i. 150; Gould (1964), 73.

[4] Russell and Winterbottom (1972), 85.   [5] Halliwell (1986).

[6] Cave (1988).

[7] Olson (1965). Most (1990: 49) sees Aristotle as the first individual to formulate criteria for determining authorial identity and property.

[8] See Janko (1984).

and political framework provided for the discussion of literature, and in this way endeavours to recontextualize Aristotle's treatment of literature within the history of criticism.

II

I want to begin by considering the *Politics* as the text which significantly inflects any response that we might perceive Aristotle to be offering to Plato. As a work which presents a taxonomy of states as they actually are, or could or ought to be, and describes the structures and the processess that actually constitute them rather than a model for an ideal state, its agenda differs conspicuously from that of Plato's *Republic*. Where its agenda coincides with that of the earlier work is in recognizing the importance of education for the construction and stability of political identity. Education (*paideia*) endows both the ruler and his subject with their respective identities and roles (1277ª25–31). At 1287ª25–7 Aristotle speaks of the law educating the city's rulers to judge and to govern justly; at 1287ᵇ25–6 he observes that each ruler has the capacity to judge when he has been well educated by the law; while at 1288ᵇ1–2 he affirms that when education (*paideia*) operates together with character, it may produce an individual who is serious (*spoudaios*), politically engaged as a citizen (*politikos*), and noble (*basilikos*). The identity of the citizen created by this education is one who in turn characterizes the aristocratic or monarchical state (cf. 1288ª41). In book 4 the author emphasizes that particular types of education are responsible for the identity of particular types of constitutions, noting how some states are defined as aristocratic because they embrace an education and ideal of good breeding which is suited to those who are wealthy (cf. 1293ᵇ34–8; 1296ᵇ18–19). Following Plato (*Resp.* 425b), he observes that, to ensure the stability of constitutions, it is crucial to educate citizens, instructing them in and accustoming them to the particular laws of the state lest the laws have no effect (1310ª12–18).

The final two books of the *Politics*, which address at some length the issue of what an ideal *paideia* should consist in, explicitly reiterate the function of education to socialize individuals as citizens, whether they are rulers or subjects. At 1332ᵇ12–16 the philosopher writes that, since a state consists of rulers and ruled, who must be different from each other, their educations must differ accordingly. What this statement does is reassert the function of education to establish and to fix the social roles of the citizen in a state. The task of overseeing education falls to the legislator (*nomothetēs*) (1337ᵃ11–12). His obligation is to ensure that individuals are educated to be good (*agathoi*) (1333ᵃ14–16). The 'good' citizen is not 'good' in the abstract but good in the sense that he fulfils the goals of the state, whether they involve war or peace. To accomplish this is to perform what is necessary, useful, and fine (1333ᵇ1–5).

The discussion of the goals and aims of education in the *Politics* as a whole and particularly in its final two books provides a framework for Aristotle's prescriptive statements on what sort of literature and art should or should not be made available to the city's citizens. In book 7 the author states that education should not be illiberal—that is, unsuited to the citizen—laborious, or over-slack (1336ᵃ28–9). He goes on then to stipulate that those in charge of the state's children, namely the *paidonomoi*, should concern themselves with determining and establishing the sort of discourses (*logoi*) and stories (*muthoi*) that children of various ages may hear with a view to them becoming serious and respectable (*spoudaioi*) citizens (1336ᵃ30–4). In a clear rebuttal of Plato, Aristotle criticizes those who legislate against the dispositions of children (1336ᵃ34–5); however, he follows his predecessor in excluding certain forms of discourse from the state. He envisages that it is necessary for the legislator to forbid in his city *aischrologia*, the discourse which is shameful (*aischra*) because it is about shameful things (1336ᵇ4–5). This is to ensure that the young themselves neither hear nor say what is shameful (1336ᵇ7–8). Anyone who appears to utter or to do what he is not permitted to utter (cf. *apēgoreumena*) is to be deprived of rights through certain penalities (i.e. *atimiai*). Such a citizen is to be beaten, if he has not yet fully come of age, or if he has, then he is to be deprived of his free status. Aristotle continues his account of the restrictions in the child's education, suggesting that since the legislator prohibits 'ugly' discourses in his city, he will also ban ugly images, whether they are statues or paintings, unless they involve those gods whom it is permissible to mock (1336ᵇ15–17). Like Plato, he is aware that children are most impressionable and places further constraints on what they may be exposed to. To protect them from the effects of *iamboi* and

comedies, the younger citizens are forbidden to be spectators of
these literary genres until they are old enough to participate in public messes and symposia ($1336^{b}20-3$). Underlying the prohibition
on these genres for the young is the assumption that, even if *iamboi*
and comedy do not constitute the forbidden category of *aischrolo-*
gia, they nevertheless produce base 'images' and/or discourses
which may adversely affect their audience, and thus must be carefully regulated (cf. Plato *Ion* 534c and *Laws* 935d–e).

Aristotle stresses the social and political teleology of *paideia* in
book 8, cf. 'it is necessary for education to be in accordance with
each [constitution]' ($1337^{a}14$). Here he sets out a 'curriculum' of a
hypothetical state's pedagogy. The utilitarian function of pedagogy
as a process of socialization, as a means of making the citizen and
his identity and, through him, the state and its identity, governs
what the student must learn. Thus the philosopher observes that,
while *paideia* must teach 'the necessary useful things' (*ta anagkaia*
. . . *tōn chrēsimōn*), it should not, however, attempt to teach 'all
things' (*ou panta*); it must discriminate between free and unfree
deeds ($1337^{b}4-6$).

If Plato's anxiety is about an indiscriminate pedagogy producing
an unstable and complex identity, Aristotle's is particularly about a
pedagogy that fails to make the correct *class* distinctions in a state
which depends upon a clear distinction between ruler and ruled.
Having covered the teleology of *paideia* as a whole, Aristotle proceeds to differentiate the various parts of the curriculum according
to their function. For an individual to act and learn for his own sake
and that of his friends, and to do so through virtue, would establish
him as free (*eleutheros*), while to act *through* others frequently
would make him appear to do what is appropriate to a bondsman or
slave ($1337^{b}18-21$). Of the four common subjects of study—writing, gymnastics, music, and drawing or painting—he observes that
writing and drawing/painting have numerous uses. In making this
observation he implies that they are less 'liberal' subjects. When he
glosses gymnastics as being for the purpose of courage, he suggests
that it is for a virtue and thus 'liberal' ($1337^{b}24-8$; cf. $1338^{a}15-21$,
$1338^{a}37-^{b}3$). When he comes to music, the philosopher notes that
there is some doubt as to its function. Some people engage in it for
the sake of pleasure (*hēdonēs charin*), even and although it was used
from the beginning in education: music thus has uses for leisure
and non-leisure activities ($1337^{b}27-32$). He goes on to declare that

if both functions must be admitted, then music's leisurely purpose must be the preferred one.

The important point to understand is that leisure is not to be understood as the sort of 'play' (*paidia*) that one engages in as a respite from work, labour, and toil. To understand leisure in this way would be to make it serve a particular function predicated on work, and thus would be to qualify its function as leisure. True leisure exists in a state of leisure and does not need to be defined in opposition to a state of work (1337^{b}33–1338^{a}8, 1339^{a}15 ff.): it must be for its own sake, as all the activities of the citizen must be. Because music is for the enjoyment of individuals who are already free (*eleutheroi*) and not in a state of labour (the philosopher cites Homer as the proof text for regarding the poet as someone who provides pleasure) it is a subject of study which is not 'functional' (*chrēsimēn*) or 'necessary' (*anagkaian*)—one must understand, 'for anything external to it'—but properly 'free' (*eleutherion*) and 'fine' (*kalēn*) (1338^{a}30–2). The aristocratic ideology of the wealthy democratic citizen (*kalos kagathos*, 'a fine gentleman'), who does not work for his keep because he does not need to, serves as the subtext of the *Politics*. The work sets leisure (*scholazein*) and the pleasure derived from leisure above occupation (*ascholazein*) (1337^{b}28–1338^{a}3). The pleasure which is produced by such leisure is one of the things that distinguishes a noble and liberal education from one which is merely functional and therefore banausic. Aristotle notes that leisure (*scholazein*) itself has pleasure (*hēdonē*), happiness (*eudaimonia*), and a blessed lifestyle (*to zēn makariōs*) (1338^{a}1–2), while happiness, one of the outcomes of leisure, is accompanied by pleasure too (1338^{a}6)—at *Nicomachean Ethics* 1177^{a}23 Aristotle observes that pleasure is mixed in with happiness (*eudaimonia*). A pleasurable pastime, which may consist in musical education, is specified as the pastime (*diagōgē*) of free citizens and as beautiful (*Pol.* 1338^{a}23 and 32).

This discussion might appear to suggest a notion of music as something removed from all other spheres of social activity and confined to a disinterested aesthetic realm. Carnes Lord, however, rightly cautions the reader not to see in this a step in the direction of an 'aesthetic modernism', although I shall argue later on that even Lord underestimates the social context of music.[9] It is the case

---

[9] Lord (1982), 85.

that even when Aristotle speaks of music, which includes poetry, as being 'fine' or 'beautiful' and as 'one of the sweetest things' (1339^{b}20, 1340^{a}14), he is not applying exclusively aesthetic criteria of judgement to it. Rather, 'fine' and 'beautiful' are to be understood in the context of how they may contribute to the social ideal of a 'fine' citizen, namely one who is 'free' and aristocratic, perhaps the *kalos kagathos* of classical Athens. Beyond these categorizations of *mousikē*, there is also the realization that music and poetry determine what sort of people their audiences become. The realization is one which recalls but also constructively addresses the Platonic anxieties about the capacity of a text or a melody to transform the identity of its audience. Aristotle is prepared to accept that all those who listen to imitations sympathize with them (1340^{a}12–13). So, for instance, victory poems or epinikia make the souls of their listeners enthusiastic, inasmuch as enthusiasm is a condition (*pathos*) of the soul's character (1340^{a}10–12), while likenesses of various characteristics—e.g. anger, gentleness, courage, moderation, and so on— in rhythms and melodies will produce a change in the souls of those who listen to them (1340^{a}18–23). If Aristotle stresses the effects of aural music on its audience, he observes, nevertheless, that it is not visual images which are likenesses (*homoiōmata*) of characters; rather, the shapes and colours which occur are signs of character. So while he bans young people from watching the works of Pauson, he does not prohibit them from viewing the work of ethical painters and statue makers, like Polygnotus, because their works constitute imitations of character (1340^{a}33–8).

Aristotle develops the discussion of *mousikē* by going on to discriminate between the sorts of music that different age groups should be exposed to. He observes that it is not a difficult task to 'define' (i.e. *diorisai*, literally, 'delimit') what is fitting and not fitting for different ages and declares that it is necessary to be able to judge (*krinein*) what is fine (*ta kala*) for the education of youths (1340^{b}33 ff.). As for the instruments which may be employed in musical education, Aristotle forbids use of flutes, lyres, and other such instruments, since they do not help in making the pupil a good recipient of education (1341^{a}17–21). The flute in particular is not ethical but is orgiastic (*orgiastikon*) (1341^{a}21–2). He goes on to offer a history of the role of the flute in conventional education, attributing its initial use to a failure to discriminate between what is and what is not suitable for free citizens. He states that the Greek ancestors adopted every form of teaching (cf. *pasēs . . . mathēseōs*) and failed to distinguish (cf. *diakrinontes*) one from another, with the result that the chorus-leader at Sparta played the flute to his chorus and many free citizens at Athens also made use of this instrument. He proceeds to inform his reader that the flute, along with other ancient instruments such as the lyre, was later rejected, once people were able to 'judge' (*krinein*) what was conducive or not to virtue. Divine authority is depicted as underlying the judgement. Aristotle recalls the myth in which Athena rejected this instrument because playing it distorted her face (1341^b3-6). The philosopher reinforces his identity as the authoritative and knowledgeable arbiter of music when he states that he judges (cf. *krinomen*) flute-playing to be a labour (*ergasian*) not of free citizens (*eleutherōn*) but of serfs (1341^b13-15).[10] To conclude the section, he raises the question as to whether one should employ 'all harmonies' (*pasais . . . tais harmoniai*) and 'all rhythms' (*pasai tois rhuthmois*) in education, or choose between them (cf. *diaireteon*) (1341^b20-2). He proceeds to identify the ethical harmonies and rhythms as being suitable for education, and states that those which are practical or enthusiastic are functional and therefore not in keeping with his ideal of liberal education and citizenship (1342^a2-4; cf. 1342^a28-9).

The explicit contextualization of *mousikē* in a larger discourse of pedagogy in the *Politics* confirms the nature and purpose of the critical pronouncements on literary discourse beginning with Hesiod. Aristotle presents a literature institutionalized through and in *paideia* as a strategy for fashioning and reinforcing an ideal identity for the citizen and his state. Beyond this, he establishes pedagogy's critical function in privileging desirable discourses and in excluding unproductive or disruptive ones as far as the state is concerned. That Aristotle is offering a deliberate response to the Platonic programme for the creation of an ideal state becomes apparent at the end of book 8. Here the author invokes the language that his predecessor uses to denote the distribution of roles and identities within the state in the *Republic*: the philosopher declares the need to apportion (cf. *apodoteon*) contests and shows, where the recreation of the city's mass populace is concerned (1342^a21).

If the pedagogical process involves a discriminated 'curriculum', a body of material which has been selected by a legislator or by an

---

[10] Halliwell (1992: 243) glosses ἐργασία as 'finish', i.e. of an artistic work.

analogous figure, the pedagogical 'curriculum' in turn gives the pupil the ability to discern (*to krinein orthōs*) and to judge correctly the ideal qualities and actions and their representations (1340ª15–18). Lord argues that the 'good judge' should not be understood to be a 'good literary critic', given that the pupil is exposed only to the Dorian mode rather than a whole variety of musical kinds and rhythms; the 'good judge' makes a moral judgement as to whether music is banausic or not (1340ᵇ40–1341ª9).[11] Yet Lord jeopardizes his own claim for the social function of music. His argument reinstates the rift between the socially valuable and the aesthetic. It fails to recognize that the good judge must be a good literary critic precisely because being able to discern the appropriate forms of culture for society and its citizens is one of the bases of the good society. If nothing else, the properly educated citizen is one who reinstates society's privileged body—perhaps its 'canon'—of knowledge and art.

III

It would appear from the secondary scholarship that the *Poetics* responds to Plato's critique of conventional art in the *Republic* by denuding poetry of its political impact. Discussions frequently draw attention to the claim that the standards of correctness (*orthotēs*) in poetry should be seen to be quite distinct from those in other disciplines, such as morality, politics, and so on (*Poet.* 1460ᵇ13–15). Previous readers have regarded the philosopher as offering a theory of 'fine art' (Butcher), a pure aesthetics which assumes the status of art as disinterested and distinct from all other activities. Influenced by German aestheticism and idealism, Butcher insists that Aristotle's ideal art is one which has no function or end apart from the creation of pleasure,[12] while the Chicago neo-Aristotelians, contemporary with and influenced by New Criticism and its decontextualizing imperative, regard the *Poetics* as presenting a purely formalist theory of tragedy.[13] It is in this respect that the *Poetics* seems to present itself as the originative point of a disinterested or liberal view of culture, namely one which holds that art and literature exist independently and for their own

---

[11] Lord (1982), 99–100.   [12] Butcher (1951), 115, 198 f.
[13] Halliwell (1986), 317.

sake without the need to perform a social function.[14] The work appears to offer a case for why society should maintain literary culture even if it serves no obvious economic or political function, reintegrating it as a non-essential element in the political structure.

Certainly, against the larger backdrop of fourth-century Greek writing about the role of poetry in society, the *Poetics* is conspicuous in neglecting to treat at length the most obviously politicizing element of dramatic art, namely the treatment of the chorus as a representative of the civic structure. Halliwell points to what might be regarded as an egregious lack of emphasis on the chorus in the *Poetics*, for the Greek lyric voice, almost more explicitly than any other poetic voice apart from the epic one, ought to be the voice of the community. In the case of the epinician poem, this voice recalls the past through myths, eulogizes the present through the praise of the athletic victor and his patron, and offers a vision of what the state might become when it has been morally instructed.

Plato, Xenophon, and Aristotle make obvious the political and sociological meaning of archaic choral poetry as a whole when they present the choral process as a more general representation and reinforcement of social structure.[15] Choral lyric recuperates poetry as a didactic discourse. At Plato, *Laws* 672e5–6, the Athenian Stranger proposes that the whole choral process, the choral rhythms and harmonies, should be viewed as a form of instruction (*paideusis*); if choral process is a mode of pedagogy, it logically follows that the uneducated citizen should be described as one who is 'unchorused' (*achoreutos*) (654a9). In book 7 of the *Laws*, the Athenian Stranger elaborates this idea. In the context of a discussion of musical education, he describes the role of the choral activity—singing and dancing—in establishing the character and identity of a citizen.[16]

Following on from the idea that education is a strategy of socialization, choral language and action are also perceived to be an enactment of the *polis* and its order.[17] Classical authors characterize the ordered chorus as a paradigm for the harmonious and well-governed city; in particular, they portray the proficient

---

[14] Lord (1982), 23; see also Harriott (1969), 1.   [15] Nagy (1990), 142, 339.

[16] See discussion of the role of music in the educational programme of the *Laws* by Morrow (1960), 297 ff.

[17] An interesting analogy might be drawn with the exhaustive description by an anonymous 18th-cent. bourgeois of a *procéssion générale* as an event which displays the city, its segmentations, and hierarchies; see Darnton (1984), 107–43.

chorus-leader (*chorēgos*) as a model for the good leader. The narrator in Xenophon's *Hiero* effects the translation of the chorus into
political metaphor when he asks what prevents the training and
ordering of a chorus by its leader (*chorēgos*) from being carried over
into other political matters (9. 4–5). In a later work Xenophon uses
the choir's obedience to its teacher as an image to illustrate the
inherent orderliness of Athens and her citizens to his interlocutor,
Pericles (*Mem.* 3. 5. 17–19). At *Politics* 1288ᵇ37–89a5, Aristotle
portrays Sparta as an ideal chorus when he holds up the
Lacedaemonian state as a model practical constitution.[18] At *Politics*
1325ᵇ37–8 he declares that the ideal state cannot exist without a
chorēgia which is moderate in character: he presents the training
and ordering of the chorus as an image for the good leader.

Recognizing that the discussion of the chorus in the *Poetics* is
uncharacteristic, Halliwell seeks to rationalize it. He proposes that
the chorus's lyric voice is largely non-dramatic and subjective, and
that its function is an ornamental one with regard to the core of the
drama, the plot.[19] But this is a rather defensive reading as far as it
concerns what Aristotle seeks to do with the chorus. I suggest that
the philosopher seeks to subordinate the chorus to plot (*muthos*),
which he describes as the tragedy's beginning and soul at
1450a37–8, and then to character, which he declares the second
most important element of a tragedy (1450a38). When he refers
briefly to the role of the chorus at the end of chapter 20, he declares
that it should be regarded as one of the actors and then that it
should be an element of the whole (1456a25–9). In chapter 12 he
locates choric song and ode in the overall structure of the tragedy,
and he rejects any tendency to grant the chorus and its song any
special status apart from the rest of the tragedy. The author's criticism of Euripidean and Sophoclean choruses as elements of the
tragedy which are not sufficiently tied to the rest of the play, and
therefore stand apart as interludes, makes apparent his concern to
integrate the choral ode and its speakers into the whole work
(1456a27–32).

But merely to cite the foregoing scholarly views is to risk a reading which sets the *Poetics* and the *Politics* at odds with one another

---

[18] For the order of the chorus as a metaphor for military or political order, see
Xen. *Oec.* 8. 3; *Mem.* 3. 3. 12, 3. 4. 4, 3. 5. 6; *Cyr.* 1. 6. 18. Pausanias (3. 11. 9) later
depicts the chorus as a microcosm of Spartan society in particular.

[19] Halliwell (1986), 239 ff., 250.

in light of the admittedly contentious characterization of the former text as an aesthetics,[20] and in view of the latter text's discussion of literature as a tool for defining social identity in education. Even if we attribute to Aristotle a concept of 'art for art's sake' in the *Poetics*, it is hardly obvious that social and political issues and contexts are absent from this text. Accordingly, some readers have attempted to reconcile the apparently politically disinterested and interested perspectives in the two works, on the basis that Aristotle himself prompts such an undertaking. In book 8 of the *Politics* the philosopher states that music serves the functions of education (*paideia*) and catharsis (*katharsis*), but he then declines to expand on what he means by catharsis for the reason that he intends to discuss this later, 'in his discussion of poetry' (*en tois peri poiētikēs*) (1341^{b}39–40). The phrase *en tois peri poiētikēs* might be understood to anticipate further discussion on poetry in the *Politics* that is now lost or that Aristotle never managed to complete. This view tends to be favoured by those who think that any links between the treatment of *katharsis* in the *Politics* and the *Poetics* have been, as David Depew phrases it, 'conclusively discredited'.[21]

But by understanding the word *poiētikēs* as a reference internal to the *Politics*, one by no means subscribes to the view that the discourses on music (in the larger sense of 'music' as an activity that encompasses poetry) in the two works are necessarily mutually exclusive in their views of literature and its place in society. Stephen Halliwell proposes that, while Aristotle does not locate the discussion of poetry in the *Poetics* in the larger perspectives of education and politics as he does in the *Politics*, for instance, the reader should not assume that these perspectives are irrelevant or, conversely, that they should be transferred into the treatise on tragedy.[22] Other readers have also been more assertive about seeing the phrase *en tois peri poiētikēs* as a deliberate reference to the *Poetics*.[23] One might understand it to indicate that Aristotle did not intend his audience to read the two works in isolation from one another. In this case, one might be inclined with Allan Bloom

[20] Eagleton (1990: 13), for one, locates the origin of aesthetics in the work of the 18th-cent. philosopher Alexander Baumgarten.

[21] D. Depew in Keyt and Miller (1991), 368; cf. Halliwell (1986), 190–8, 353–4.

[22] Halliwell (1986), 24–5.

[23] Lord (1982: 106) defends the integrity of *Pol.* 8. 7, observing that this chapter continues to address the question posed in chapter 6 as to whether music makes men banausic.

(though without implying any further agreement with the latter's reading of the works) to regard the *Poetics* as an appendix, a supplement, to the discussion of musical and literary education in the final books of the longer work.[24]

But coming to a decision about the significance of *Politics* $1341^{b}39$–40 is perhaps incidental to developing a reading of the *Poetics* both as a critical—that is, a discriminating—and as a political discourse. Overattention to the status of this passage threatens to divert attention from the potentially political dimensions of the *Poetic*—dimensions which are apart from the issue of catharsis and which might in turn assist understanding of this term. I want to defer discussion of catharsis until the end of the chapter in order to consider whether the *Poetics* recognizes alternative sites of politicization where tragedy is concerned. The one proper role for the Aristotelian citizen is leisure. In accordance with the discourse on the citizen and his pastimes articulated in the *Politics* and in the *Nicomachean Ethics* (e.g. $1177^{b}12$), leisure must be understood as for its own sake rather than as a respite from labour.[25] Literature is leisure, and thus is self-justifying. Intending to 'have my cake and eat it', I suggest that where the *Politics* deals with literary art in the context of education, the *Poetics* deals with the citizen's postpedagogic experience of literature, such that the experience of literature is to be seen as a form of leisure (now *diagōgē*). As Leon Golden argues, it thus concerns the activity of the mature, free, and educated citizen,[26] and so, against Plato, dramatic poetry is given a further political authorization in the *Poetics*.

IV

Aristotle foregrounds the issue of pleasure in the discussion of tragedy. In so doing, he directly addresses the very reason for which (as we shall see) other contemporary authors query the social utility of poetry against, say, oratory or history, and for which Plato seeks to exclude it from the ideal republic.[27] In chapter 4 of the *Poetics* he provides us with a general explanation for the origins of

[24] A. Bloom (1987), 72–3.
[25] In this I differ from Janko (1992: 343), who understands διαγωγή as 'educative entertainment'.
[26] Golden (1976), 354.
[27] Nussbaum (1986), 378.

imitation and so, implicitly, for the origins of dramatic art, which is
a form of imitation. He gives two different but related reasons for
imitation: first, human nature has a natural instinct for imitation
and secondly, individuals begin to learn through imitation.
Aristotle goes on to observe that *all* people delight in imitations,
even if they are painful ones, because they can delight in the detail
of the representative images. But representative detail is not the
whole explanation of tragic pleasure. The fact that men learn
through tragedy as a mode of imitation (*mimēsis*) produces delight,
since all men find learning pleasurable and not just philosophers,
who find learning the most pleasurable (*hēdiston*) ($1448^{b}11-12$ ff.).

Aristotle's discussion of tragedy in terms of pleasure is the site of
politicized and politically interested discourse in the *Poetics*. One
reader to identify and to elaborate it as such is the novelist and literary scholar Umberto Eco. In Eco's novel *The Name of the Rose*,
the blind librarian Borges attempts to regulate the reading of his
fellow monks; he keeps hidden the books or at least some of the
books which he deems to have a detrimental effect on the spirituality of his colleagues. The volume which Borges above all hides from
the eyes of readers in an attempt to constrain laughter, pleasure,
and passion in the monastery is the (otherwise actually lost) second
book of Aristotle's *Poetics*, on comedy. When several enterprising
monks individually discover the tome in one of the secret passages
of the library, their pleasure at discovering the book and their
enjoyment of the discourse on pleasure are cruelly cut short by
death. Borges has drugged the leaves of the book so that the readers are fatally poisoned when they lick their fingers to turn the
pages. Later he engages in the paramount act of censorship, the
burning of the library, to thwart the discovery by the hero of
the work, the investigative monk William de Baskerville, of his literary treasures and their secrets. The work concludes with images
of ironically self-consuming control—namely, the conflagration of
the monastery and the burning of three heretical brothers, who are
to be seen as promulgators of a discourse that lies outside canonical
doctrine.

While attesting to our exaggerated awe for the work (which a
number of scholars have shown to be at odds with its previous
insignificance[28]), Eco's fictional treatment of the *Poetics* associates

---

[28] The *Poetics* remained an obscure text until the end of the Middle Ages, circulating in the 12th cent. in Averroes' 'middle commentary' in Arabic, and then in the

it with an insidious attack on the freedom permitted to the written word precisely where pleasure and desire are concerned. The novel can be read as an attack on censorship, represented here as the institutional control of the Church: Borges's ruthless censorship of pleasure and its texts suggests that one aspect of Aristotle's discussion of dramatic poetry needs to be subject to a regulatory criticism.[29] *The Name of the Rose* is a fantasy that recovers a text kept from us by the accidents of textual preservation, only to lose it again as a result of anxieties about pleasure. But beyond this, it might be seen to stand as a powerful commentary on *our* existing *Poetics*, the first book on tragedy, in ways that are particularly germane for this study. I want to suggest that Aristotle's discussion of tragic literature is one which subjects the genre and its pleasures to rigorous discrimination against the background of, and in distinction from, a prior discourse which serves to exclude certain forms of literary pleasure from the community.

One of the first discussions of pleasure as a response to art is offered by the sophist and rhetorician Gorgias in his *Encomium of Helen*. In this work, which seeks to absolve Helen of any responsibility for adultery and implicitly for the Trojan War, the author argues that visual experience of events and objects, such as paintings or statues, can implant in their audiences emotions of fear or pleasure which are so overpowering that they lead them to act irrationally. Accordingly, Helen's pleasure at seeing Paris' body produced in her a desire for him that she could not resist.[30] In referring

Latin translations of this work by Hermannus Alemannus (1256) and William of Moerbeke (1278). The *Poetics* was the last of Aristotle's works to gain special prominence and authority, only gaining importance, in Italy, with Robertello's commentary of 1548 and only making its passage into France and England in the 17th cent. where, by a curious inversion of chronology, it began its life as a commentary on Horace's *Ars Poetica*. (As Cave (1988) shows, it attained the status of τέχνη, influencing the writing of drama in early modern Europe.) Yet even then the authority of Aristotle's treatise on drama was by no means guaranteed. It was challenged by 18th-cent. Romanticism, and required the work of the Chicago School of critics, Crane, McKeon, and Olson, to re-establish its place in formalist criticism of the 20th cent.—although Halliwell (1984c), 60, observes that the centrality of μίμησις in the treatise entails that it is impossible to see it as an exclusively formalistic doctrine of tragic poetry. Eco would have the reader of his novel think that the complete *Poetics* was part of the library of medieval monasteries. Almost certainly better known was the *On Poets*, which scholars now think to have had similarities to the *Poetics*. See Halliwell (1986), 291, 315, and Olson (1965).

[29] A. Patterson (1984), 21.

[30] Gorgias speaks of desire—τὸ ποθεῖν (18), ἔρωτα καὶ πόθον (18), and ἔρωτος τῇ ψυχῇ (19)—aroused by sight.

to the pathology of visual experience, non-artistic and artistic, as a 'disease' (*noson*), Gorgias proposes that pleasure might be something which individuals should be wary of and guard against, no less than rhetorical speech. Like the latter, pleasure introduces ignorance into the soul of the listener (18; cf. 8), and it resembles drugs (*pharmaka*), which have the capacity to induce sorrow, pleasure, or fear (cf. 14). The pharmaceutical metaphor suggests that a pleasurable response is not one that is in itself simply good or, conversely, simply bad, inasmuch as drugs can either heal or harm.

Other fifth- and fourth-century authors treat the issue of literary pleasure and taste as a marker of social identity (and so they readily invite the sort of cultural and political analysis of literature encouraged by modern thinkers, such as Raymond Williams and Pierre Bourdieu).[31] Aristophanes, for instance, ironically reinforces the view that comedy is a genre which appeals to the common rabble when he distances himself and his supposedly superior audience from the common people or mob (*dēmos*) in the parabaseis of several of his plays. In the *Knights* the chorus is careful to distance the comic poet's project from that of the Typhonic orator, Cleon, by observing that the production of a comedy is the most difficult task of all and one that pleases only a *few* people (516–17). The chorus implies a contrast between élite and mass tastes, allying Aristophanic comedy with the first and oratory with the latter. In the parabasis of the *Clouds*, the Cloud-chorus uses the fact that the poet's earlier play, the *Banqueters*, failed to please its original audience as evidence of the latter's integrity and of the refinement of his art (*Clouds* 524). The chorus states that it was forced to retreat 'by base men' (cf. *hup' andrōn phortikōn*, 524), who stand in contrast to the present audience, which it describes as wise (*sophoi*) and sophisticated (*dexioi*) (526–7, 535). Aristophanes suggests that the appropriate audience for his comedy is the intellectual élite rather than the mob, and the chorus forbids those who laugh at the forms of childish slapstick enumerated in 539 ff. to take delight in the poet's work (560). None the less, the poet typically disturbs his unproblematic identification with his ideal audience; the *Clouds* ends with

[31] R. Williams (1961: 43–4) has suggested that to be adequate a theory of 'culture' must be able to provide a mode of social definition, expressing a present way of life. Rejecting conventional philosophical and literary aesthetics, Bourdieu (1984: 485, 499–500) sees preference for certain aspects and types of culture as a reflection of social relationships and identity.

the shouting, the burning of buildings, and the general hubbub that the chorus had associated with a base audience.

Elsewhere Isocrates corroborates the Aristophanic dichotomies between base pleasure/the mob, and a less ready pleasure/the élite. For him, pleasure is a response that more unequivocally marks out comic drama as a popular and therefore unbeneficial form of discourse in the city. In *On the Peace* the speaker notes that demagoguery and comedy alone demonstrate licence of speech (*parrhēsia*) and that these earn the gratitude (*charis*) of their audience precisely because they reveal the shortcomings of Athens (14). *On the Peace* and the *Antidosis* insist that comedy has a populist and therefore base nature, and these two works also propose the need to prohibit various forms of buffoonery and abuse associated with comedy, especially where the young are concerned (cf. Arist. *Pol.* 1336ᵇ20 and 35). At *Antidosis* 284 the author objects to the widespread regard for buffoons and mockers as 'talented men' (*eupheis*).[32] According to Isocrates, the ideal pleasure does not come from base discourses like public oratory or comedy; rather, it is one which proceeds from discourses and deeds which demonstrate their civic utility (*Antid.* 132–3). This is a pleasure which can reconcile to his audience the prose writer who holds oligarchical leanings.

The socially discriminating discourse on literary pleasure is not confined to treatments of the nature of poetry. In Isocrates' *On the Peace*, the pacifist speaker offers a condemnation of public taste and of the orators who cater to it. He observes that the people tolerate only public speakers who satisfy their desires (3). Accordingly, contemporary orators do not practise or contemplate what is beneficial to the city-state; they utter only speeches which satisfy their mob audience (5). At section 10 the speaker draws a contrast between speakers who please and gratify their audience and those who have the integrity to speak what is beneficial in spite of and against popular wishes. The latter minority have integrity because they offer advice without regard for pleasure (*hēdonē*). Isocrates reinforces the perception that the popular, sycophantic public speakers are driven by their audiences' expectations. In the first prologue to the *Histories*, Thucydides states that, unlike professional speech-writers or logographers, he is not writing in order to

---

[32] J. Winkler in Griffith and Mastronarde (1990: 310) describes Isocrates as inscribing 'an apartheid between the high and low genres'.

give pleasure or to attract a listening audience (cf. *akroasei*) and thus prefers what is true to what is mythical (1. 21. 1). The historian rejects the spoken text and prefers the literary work because, as he says, his aim is to provide a lasting monument. But in this there is also an implicit rejection of popular taste. He observes that what is not mythical appears to be less pleasing to hear, suggesting that the written text which seeks fact and truth, like the *Histories*, does not satisfy popular demands and expectations (1. 22. 4). For Thucydides, popular taste becomes a political force requiring serious attention later in the work. He observes that the politicians who come into power after the death of Pericles cater to the pleasures of the people (cf. *kath' hēdonas tōi dēmōi*). It is this inclination to follow the mob which explains the disasters, most notably the Sicilian expedition, which plague Athens in the later years of the Peloponnesian War (cf. 2. 65. 10–11). The people, elsewhere figured as the mob (*homilos*), are by nature unreliable and fickle: they change their opinions frequently, as their response to Pericles' final speech in book 2 shows (2. 65. 4).

Plato's attitude towards pleasure is more complicated than might have been suggested by the *Republic*'s condemnation of all poetic pleasures on the grounds that they are obstacles to achieving the ideal state. In the *Laws* the Athenian Stranger states that it is necessary for music to be discriminated in terms of pleasure. He proposes that the finest poetry is that which delights citizens who are the best and sufficiently educated, and that if the citizens of better character have a better pleasure, it is the case that the opposite effect follows when music is undiscriminated (658e6–659a7). What the finest poetry might be is suggested when the Athenian Stranger speaks of the 'truest tragedy' as the polity which constitutes an imitation of the finest and most excellent life (817b3–5). This statement affirms the connection between social identity and literary genre when it proposes that tragedy does not simply signify the best constitution, but that it *is* the best constitution. This figuring of the state as a tragedy takes to its logical conclusion Plato's argument in the *Laws* that musical education, which of course includes literature, is responsible for the character of the citizen and the state (cf. 798c–d).

V

To understand how the *Poetics* situates itself in terms of the existing discourse of literary pleasure, it is important to consider what
tragic pleasure is. To this end, Halliwell undertakes a 'cognitive
analysis'—that is to say, one that is faithful to Aristotle's intention
to change the perception of tragedy as a sensual experience.[33] This
mode of enquiry focuses on the issue of how the audience perceives
tragedy, and, through perception, how it experiences pleasures. At
Poetics 1448^{b}15 ff. Aristotle explicitly locates pleasure in the
process of perception. Here the author observes that people can
derive pleasure from seeing an imitation on its own terms because
of its execution, its colour, or some other such thing and without
having seen its original referent. Later, in chapter 26, he observes
that tragedy has an advantage over epic in that its music and spectacle produce the most vivid pleasures (1462^{a}16–17). Aristotle
speaks of the particular pleasures that come from the aural and the
visual perception of music and spectacle, respectively.

The suggestion seems to be that pleasure is distinguished and
particularized not according to how the the individual's passions,
emotions, or moods particularize pleasure, but according to specific
perceptions and their actualizations. So if Aristotle had provided a
more exhaustive analysis of pleasure in the *Poetics*, he might have
detailed the manner in which the various elements of the drama—
its language, its spectacle, its music—produce their own proper
pleasure. But the reader can turn to the *Nicomachean Ethics* for
support for this view. In the final book of this work, Aristotle states
that in every act of perception there is pleasure, so that acts of seeing and acts of hearing are sweet (*hēdea*), and particularly so when
perception is strongest and most active (*EN* 1174^{b}26–9). What the
author emphasizes in this section of the work is the relationship of
pleasure to the activation (*energeia*) of perception, inasmuch as the
former brings the latter to its perfect state (1174^{b}32); without this
activation there can be no pleasure (1175^{a}5, 20–1). It is the case that
Aristotle distinguishes between the different pleasures which
inhere in different actions or operations (*energeia*). He elaborates
his point by stating that there is a pleasure proper to every *energeia*,
so that for a serious action (*tēi spoudaiai*) there is a proper, i.e.

[33] Halliwell (1986), 73.

reasonable, pleasure, and for a base one (*tēi phaulēi*), there is a proper, i.e. wicked, one (1175^{b}27–8). Pleasure, specifically a kind that is appropriate (*oikeia*), is what makes perception complete or perfect (1175^{a}30–1, 36). Aristotle explains what he means when he observes that for individuals to derive enjoyment (cf. *chairontes*) from someone playing the flute, it is not possible also to pay attention to the accompanying words: the pleasure (*hēdonē*) they derive from the flute would impair the perception of the words, and vice versa, one assumes (1175^{b}3–10). For the proper pleasure (*oikeia hēdonē*) to intensify the perception, it is important that those who experience pleasure 'distinguish' (cf. *krinousi*) and 'discriminate' (cf. *exakribousin*) between the activities which will involve them in perception (1175^{a}32–3). Otherwise, inappropriate pleasures (*hai alloitriai hēdonai*) have the same effect as appropriate pains; namely, they impair the perceptive activity (1175^{b}17, 22–3).

In keeping with one possible logic of a cognitive analysis, Halliwell reasonably pluralizes tragic pleasure. He establishes a taxonomy of pleasure *internal* to tragedy, discriminating between the varieties of pleasure in terms of how they are produced. He notes, in addition to a general pleasure which is particular to tragedy, an overall 'natural' pleasure which inheres in the audience's experience of learning from imitations, another pleasure derived from the execution of the work of art, another from the language, another from the spectacle, and another from the plot-structure. He proceeds, moreover, to impose a hierarchy within this taxonomy, ranking the pleasures of tragedy in order from lowest to highest according to their apparent importance as far as poetic skill is concerned. Thus the pleasure derived from spectacle is lowest because it is the least integral to the art of poetry (*Poet.* 1450^{b}16–18); the pleasures proceeding from language, rhythm, and music occupy the middle rank, inasmuch as diction is the fourth of Aristotle's elements of tragedy (cf. 1450^{b}12); while the pleasure which comes from tragedy as an intellectual process of understanding is the highest, in light of the connection between learning and pleasure drawn in *Poetics* chapter 4.[34]

---

[34] Halliwell (1986), 63 ff. Rorty (1992*b*: 16) follows Halliwell in insisting upon tragedy's multiple pleasures, 'Tragic drama involves and conjoins so many different kinds of pleasure that it is difficult to determine which is primary and which accidental'.

Yet in pursuing this interpretation, Halliwell unfortunately mis-reads the larger terms of the discourse on pleasure in the *Poetics*. While Plato had attempted to repress and manage (all but philo-sophical) desire as a part of a larger project to privilege the rational element of the soul over the irrational aspect, Aristotle admits lit-erary pleasure and desire into the community because it has been rigorously subjected to the critical process.[35] I suggest that as far as he is concerned, any attempt to distinguish and to rank *different pleasures within tragedy* dispenses with and denies the political aim of the *Poetics*. The author may conceive different sources of pleas-ure within tragedy; however, he does not for that reason propose that there are numerous pleasures belonging to tragedy, or for that matter to any other poetic genre, such as epic and comedy. The key to understanding the *Poetics* is to recognize that there is only a single, general, overall pleasure to be derived from the whole ex-perience of tragedy.

The *Poetics* most evidently asserts its critical status in the project of defining tragic pleasure and in distinguishing it from other avail-able literary pleasures. There is a propriety to be observed where tragedy and, for that matter, any other literary genre are concerned. When assessing the relative merits of tragedy and epic, Aristotle states that every art must aspire to create no random pleasure (cf. *ou tēn tuchousan hēdonēn*) but only that which has been mentioned, namely the pleasure *proper* to it (1462^b13–14). The discussion of tragic poetry does not admit *any* pleasure derived from imitative art. It discriminates between what is appropriate and therefore what is permitted for the different poetic genres, rather than between various, i.e. different, and plural forms of pleasure which adhere to tragedy, as Halliwell seems to suggest. Accordingly, tragic pleasure is the pleasure 'appropriate' or 'proper' to tragedy (cf. *oikeia hēdonē*).

Aristotle refers to tragedy's 'proper pleasure' at a number of places in the *Poetics*. At 1453^a30–6 he observes that a work which has opposite endings for good (*beltiosi*) and bad (*cheirosin*) charac-ters (he cites the *Odyssey* as an example of a work with such a reso-lution), such that justice seems to be done as an audience might wish, produces a pleasure which is more suited (cf. *mallon . . . oikeia*) to comedy than to tragedy. In the following chapter, he

---

[35] Cf. D. Depew in Keyt and Miller (1991), 379–80.

asserts that it is necessary to seek not every form of pleasure but only that which is proper (*oikeia*) to tragedy (1453ᵇ10–11), and for this reason the poet should seek to create fear and pity—elsewhere said to be the bases of the cathartic effect which produces pleasure—from the plot (*muthos*) rather than from spectacle. The idea that the plot is above all responsible for creating the pleasure peculiar to certain genres remanifests itself in the discussion of epic in chapter 23. Here the author states that a poetic narrative (*muthos*) should be composed as if it were a tragic plot, so that it has a whole and complete action and a beginning, middle, and end. As such, it will resemble a living creature—Aristotle invokes Plato's metaphor for literary unity from the *Phaedrus*—and generate 'the pleasure proper to it' (*oikeian hēdonēn*) (1459ᵃ17–21).

VI

Recent work on Athenian drama has concerned itself with the sociological and political aspects of Greek tragedy. This body of interpretation regards drama as reflecting the society in which it was written because it shapes, responds to, and engages with contemporary issues, and directs attention to the audience and the process of literary reception. Scholars have pointed to the way in which the Theatre of Dionysus arranged spectators so as to reflect and articulate social structures and groupings. According to them, the audience sat divided into the ten tribes, just as they would have sat in the Pnyx, where the full citizen Assembly met four times each month.[36] Jack Winkler has suggested that in addition to this tribal division all the members of the Council (*boulē*), fifty councillors from each tribe, sat together in a wedge, while non-citizens and perhaps citizen-wives occupied the outermost wedges of the theatre.[37] The theatre reflects in its physical layout the social structure and unity of the *polis* and in this sense stands as a sphere parallel to the law courts (*hēlaia*), to the Council (*boulē*), and to the Assembly (*ekklēsia*).[38] Josiah Ober proposes that the theatre is a 'political forum', where the mass audience of the *polis* might watch over competing élites, and would see them being humanized as they were brought before them.[39] The theatre is, in short, a mirror of

---

[36] See e.g. Winkler (1990), 40.

[37] Winkler (1990), 38–9 and notes.

[38] Euben (1986), 22.

[39] Ober (1989), 152–3.

Attic democracy, a microcosm of the civic community and its institutions, a place where civic identity is formed, negotiated, and reinforced.

While Ober and Strauss go on to suggest that seating in the theatre is 'egalitarian', they also have to concede that the Festival of
Dionysus presents a situation in which a text written and produced
by an élite is presented to the masses.[40] The theatre is thus also a
forum where superiorities are articulated. Winkler notes that
Dionysian dance was presented as a gift of the wealthy élite to the
many,[41] while the wealthy and aristocratic speakers of Attic oratory
often cast themselves as liturgists who have undertaken *chorēgiai*,
the funding and and training of choruses as a public service, from
their tremendous wealth. Moreover, the Great Dionysia was an
occasion on which Athenian power was made evident. During the
festival Athens' allies brought their tribute to the city and in this
acknowledged their indebtedness and dependence upon the
mother-*polis*.[42] Aristotle's account of how the audience experiences
tragic pleasure articulates a version of this élitist ideology.

The *Poetics* reflects this sociology, for the perception and experience of pleasure has its ontological and also its political contexts.
Different creatures and persons enjoy different things (cf. *EN*
1176ᵃ3). Tragic pleasure is contextualized both in terms of genre
and in terms of its audience. Aristotle attributes the experience of
tragedy as a proper pleasure to a subject, who is to be understood as
the proper recipient of this pleasure. This observation requires
careful qualification. Butcher has proposed that Aristotelian pleasure is individualistic and personalized and therefore flawed: pleasure depends largely on who you are. He writes, 'If the end of art is
to be found in a certain emotional effect, in a pleasure which is
purely subjective, the end becomes something arbitrary and accidental, and dependent on each individual's moods.'[43] Butcher goes
on to suggest that this stands uncomfortably with the author's
notion of art as a realization of an objective form, for his whole
philosophical system seems to require an externally determined
response to art.[44] But this is not the only way to understand how

---

[40] J. Ober and B. Strauss in Winkler and Zeitlin (1990), 239.
[41] Winkler (1990), 32.
[42] See S. Goldhill in Winkler and Zeitlin (1990), 101; also Isoc. *Peace* 82, and
scholium on Ar. *Ach*. 504.
[43] Butcher (1951), 208.   [44] Ibid. 209.

pleasure might be defined in terms of its receiving subject. For Aristotle, 'subjective' may entail that different people take delight in different things;[45] however, the adjective 'different' here is to be understood above all as marking distinctions in terms of different categories of social rank and class rather than according to the persons as individuals, however 'individual' is to be understood.

In Plato's and Aristotle's perspectives, literary art defines and forms political identity, although each writer advocates a somewhat different ideal of political identity. Stories, myths, and tragedies potentially provide the inhabitants of Plato's ideal society with models for who they might be—and are therefore to be carefully regulated—as they also provide models for the citizens of the communities implicitly envisaged in the *Politics*. As far as the *Poetics* is specifically concerned, poetry and the citizen-audience's responses to it reflect a class identity that is already in existence. Aristotle inscribes his account of the reception of tragedy within a literary class-consciousness wherein preference for a particular genre, whether tragedy or comedy, mirrors and also produces society's stratification. If at *Poetics* 1448^{b}13 ff. Aristotle comments on the pleasure that learning gives to philosophers amongst others, he elsewhere proposes that certain types of people—here the categories in question are philosophers and non-philosophers—experience different degrees of pleasure given what is on the face of it the same experience.[46] By analogy, where different people are concerned, there are different sources of pleasures: the same things give delight to and grieve different people, are painful and hateful to some and pleasurable and beloved to others (*EN* 1176^{a}11–12). Thus the class and individual described as morally superior and respectable (*spoudaios*) and the base man (*phaulos*) will find different things honourable (*timia*) and pleasurable (*hēdea*) (1176^{b}24–6). Likewise, in the final book of the *Politics*, Aristotle observes that

---

[45] Ibid. 211, for the argument that the subjectivity of pleasure is qualified by an 'objective validity' in the reception of tragedy, since Aristotle refers to higher, rather than lower and base, audience.

[46] In the *Nicomachean Ethics* the sweetest pleasure is one which proceeds from activity concerned with wisdom and the virtues. In chapter 7 of book 10 Aristotle states that the most pleasant (ἥδιστη) form of blessedness is one involving wisdom. Accordingly, philosophy, which he glosses as theoretical and so as opposed to the practical, has the most 'wonderful pleasures' (θαυμαστὰς ἡδονάς) (1177^{a}22–6). He continues by declaring that mental activity (cf. ἡ τοῦ νοῦ ἐνέργεια) has its own proper pleasure, which enhances mental activity and is a perfect blessedness, such that life is greater than human, indeed divine (1177^{b}19 ff.).

the different classes should be offered different types of music, so that their own natures produce what the reader is to assume to be the pleasure that is right for them (cf. *to kata phusin oikeion*, 1342ᵃ25 ff.). He states that there are two different classes of dramatic spectator, the one who is free (*eleutheros*) and educated (*pepaideumenos*) and another who is base (*phortikos*), because he works for his living, is a bondsman, or some other individual with an 'occupation' (1342ᵃ19–20).

In keeping with other classical Greek texts, the *Poetics* retraces the dichotomy between respectable/superior/élite and less respectable/inferior/popular pleasure in terms of the distinction between tragedy and non-tragic genres. Where it goes further is in providing a narrative of the development of the different literary genres which uses psychology to account for how they arose, and then why they appeal to certain types of individual and not others. Aristotle provides a history of genres which inscribes a dichotomy between high and low forms, ultimately and respectively tragedy and comedy. He characterizes comedy as base by merging its history with that of the *iambos*, a literary form that the *Politics* rigorously constrains. According to his narrative, more common individuals imitated the deeds of baser individuals, and produced satires, then *iamboi*, and, after Homer, comedy (*Poet.* 1449ᵃ2–6). *Iambos* is the specific forerunner of comedy. It was originally produced by writers who were less meticulous and discriminating and in turn represented citizens who were less than noble or fine: it is written about specific individuals (cf. 1451ᵇ14). It is clear from other parts of the Aristotelian corpus that the author's analysis of comedy would offer a psychological account of this genre as one which is to be associated with the less respectable citizen.

Elsewhere, the philosopher presents the comic, and particularly slapstick, as 'low culture'. In book 4 of the *Nicomachean Ethics* he speaks of the buffoon as being inferior to the comic (*geloios*) (1128ᵃ33–4). Buffoons exceed the limits of comedy. They seek only to create laughter rather than to speak what is seemly and to lament what causes the cautious individual grief. They are base, boorish, and rough (1128ᵃ5–9). The buffoons are aligned with those who are slavish in nature and uncultured, and are also defined by distinction from the free, the reasonable (*epieikēs*), and the cultured citizen (1128ᵃ18–22). Each of these groups of individuals have different criteria of discursive propriety, for the respectable individual both speaks and hears what is fitting for him to hear as a reasonable and free citizen (1128ᵃ17–18). In turn, he avoids what is inappropriate for him as a free citizen, seeking not what causes him grief but, rather, pleasure (1128ᵃ26–8). Such inappropriate forms of literature seem to include jests (cf. *skōmmata*), a sort of abuse which Aristotle identifies with and assimilates to legal slanders (*aporrhēta*) when he observes that legislators forbid certain forms of verbal behaviour (1128ᵃ30–1).

In the *Poetics* the philosopher observes that before Homer, who first showed his successors how to produce dramatic imitations, the earliest poets wrote either heroic or iambic verse, which gave rise to tragedy and comedy respectively (1448ᵇ33 ff.). Where comedy is a genre in which less discriminating individuals imitate the actions of the *phauloi* and which consequently represents individuals as being worse than in reality, tragedy is to be understood as a markedly élite genre as distinct from comedy. It is a genre in which more respectable individuals (*semnoteroi*) imitate the fine deeds of fine men (1448ᵃ16–17; cf. 1448ᵇ25–7, 1449ᵃ5–6, 1449ᵇ10, 1449ᵇ24–5, 1454ᵇ8–9). Tragedy is a superior art form in terms of its content, execution, and effect. But above all, the pleasure to be derived from tragedy is better (cf. *kreittōn*) than that produced by comedy and even by epic, due to tragedy's tighter structure (1462ᵇ10–15). Moreover, tragic drama is more discriminating about what it imitates, and accordingly appeals to a better audience; the author writes, 'if what is less base is better, such always appeals to a better audience (cf. *pros beltious theatas*), while it is clear that what imitates all things (*hē ⟨pros⟩ hapanta mimoumenē*) is base' (1461ᵇ27–9).

Homeric epic and tragedy, the genre which derives from epic, concern themselves with serious matters (*ta spoudaia*). *Ta spoudaia* requires attention, for in proposing this characterization of these literary forms, Aristotle significantly and emphatically invokes, only in order to reject, Plato's view that conventional tragedy in particular, but also epic, is not a *serious* form of imitation (cf. *ou spoudēn tēn mimēsin*) (*Rsp.* 602b8; cf. *Grg.* 502b and *Leg.* 816e–817a⁴⁷). To make this move successfully, Aristotle associates the adjective *spoudaios* with virtue. While Butcher takes *spoudaion* to mean 'poetically good',⁴⁸ George Grube insists that the phrase *ta*

---

⁴⁷ See also Zanker (1987), 137–8.
⁴⁸ Held (1984), 163 n. 24; Butcher (1951), 178–9.
⁴⁹ Grube (1958), pp. xxii–xxiii, n. 24.

spoudaia has moral and ethical implications.[49] Likewise, Leon Golden argues that *spoudaios* is to all intents and purposes the adjectival form of *arētē*, 'excellence' or 'virtue', following *Categories* 10ᵇ7–8—so 'excellent', 'good', 'noble'—and thus does not mean 'serious' in the way that a modern reader would normally understand this adjective.[50]

G. F. Held makes the point that the description 'serious' refers both to the nature of the tragic characters and to the action: the action of a tragic plot is 'serious' (*spoudaios*) because it is the product of characters who have 'serious', that is excellent or virtuous, characters. He goes on to suggest that there is a teleological implication of the adjective *spoudaios* and its related words. Pointing to book 10 of the *Nicomachean Ethics*, he observes that the *spoudaios*-adjective is used to describe contemplation, the self-sufficient activity by which individuals can gain their ideal end, namely happiness (*eudaimonia*) (cf. *EN* 1176ᵇ35–1177ᵃ6). It is no accident that in this passage Aristotle declares that serious matters (cf. *ta spoudaia*) are better than comic things (*tōn geloiōn*) and those which involve play, and that a 'serious' activity is characteristic of our better part and of a better man. Held extrapolates that, if tragedy is *spoudaia*, then it must be directed at happiness (*eudaimonia*), 'Tragedy exhibits to us characters who have, comedy characters who have not, the wherewithal to be happy and who demonstrate this by what they do in the play itself'.[51] He concedes that this happens despite the fact that tragic characters suffer misfortunes which are not consonant with happiness. Held's interpretation of the teleology of the *Poetics* requires qualification: it is not the action of the play itself which is directed at happiness, but rather the audience's response which leads to their happiness. From the response to the spectacle of theatre comes a 'serious' and appropriate pleasure for the audience which defines them as serious and respectable (*spoudaioi*) people, and thus as an exclusive group more likely to experience *eudaimonia* than any other segment of society.

As Depew observes, the philosopher criticizes Plato for including craftsmen and farmers in the *polis* such that they constitute a major-

---

[50] τῷ γὰρ ἀρετὴν ἔχειν σπουδαῖος λέγεται, ἀλλ' αὖ παρωνύμως ἀπὸ τῆς ἀρετῆς· (Arist. *Cat.* 10ᵇ7–9). See Golden (1965), 285–6; also Lucas (1968), 63–4, and Zanker (1987), 140–1.

[51] Held (1984), 170–4.

ity class who must then in turn be carefully constrained lest their desires affect the well-being of the state (*Pol.* 1264ᵃ25 ff.).[52] Aristotle here articulates the critical imperative where dramatic poetry is concerned. To all intents and purposes he excludes these individuals from his model of the city in book 1 of the *Poetics* because he concerns himself only with the discussion of tragic pleasure, one which is appropriate to a superior poetics and its audience. Discrimination ensures that poetry, in this case tragedy, as opposed to *iambos* or buffoonery, addresses itself to an élite audience, that is to the *spoudaioi*. This élite is quite literally an exclusive group that becomes by a radical metonymy the whole of the city and so reaffirms the character of a poetic discourse as one that is critical, that discriminates, and, in so doing, that produces a paradigm of civic identity.

VII

Asking how the audience experiences pleasure that is proper (*oikeia*) to tragedy and to itself as the proper audience eventually brings us to a notorious difficulty. The whole discussion of tragedy's superior and proper pleasure needs to be able to assimilate the discourse on pity and fear in the *Poetics* precisely because these affect states would appear to unsettle the notion that tragedy is a pleasurable experience. Aristotle declares that tragic pleasure is produced paradoxically, as it would appear at first, from pity and fear in response to dramatic imitation (1453ᵇ12). (The philosopher rejects the idea that tragic pity and fear proceed from an outcome in which justice is done in such a way that it satisfies a moral sense—in other words, so that it depicts villains receiving punishment and heroes receiving just rewards (1453ᵃ1 ff.).) Most scholars take up the discussion of precisely how pity and fear produce pleasure by turning to the notorious passage in which Aristotle states that a serious tragic imitation accomplishes through pity and fear a *katharsis* of these emotions (1449ᵇ27–8). They propose that *katharsis* denotes either a process that is analogous to or is the same as medical purgation (Bernays), a clarification of emotions, or else a 'getting clear' about obscure matters, as the consequence of 'clear-

---

[52] D. Depew in Keyt and Miller (1991), 376.
[53] Bernays in Barnes, Schofield, and Sorabji (1966), 154–65; Golden (1976); Nussbaum (1986), 388 ff.; (1992), 280–1; Nehemas (1992), 307.

ing up' cognitive issues (Nussbaum and Nehemas).[53]

Following Lear's analysis, I reject the views that *katharsis* involves either a purgation, because that assumes the need for a psychological cure in even virtuous and intellectually healthy individuals (*phronimoi*),[54] or an education of the emotions, precisely because the education is to be understood as already complete—in any case, Nussbaum's position involves something of a slippage in English idiom where 'clearing up' is seen to be synonymous with 'getting clear'.[55] The tragic spectacle is leisure for *its own sake*, and, as I earlier insisted, the *Poetics* is a discussion which chronologically extends the treatment of the literary arts in *Politics* books 5–8 when it treats the fully educated citizen's encounter with poetry. But this still leaves the reader somewhat perplexed, as Aristotle does not reveal a great deal about the roles of fear and pity in the reception of tragedy in the *Poetics* itself. The reader has to look elsewhere for enlightenment, and one important clue as to where she might find help is the philosopher's appeal to rhetorical ideas and terminology in chapter 24 of the work. Here the author invokes the argumentative principle of probability (*to eikos*) when he declares that the tragic poet must choose impossible plausibilities (*adunata eikota*) over implausible possibilities (*dunata apithana*) at 1460ᵃ26–7 (cf. 1454ᵃ36). The rhetorical strategy of appealing to common opinion (*doxa*), that is what the reasonable man believes to be the case, is invoked later at 1461ᵇ11–12. Aristotle defends the dramatic representation of what is impossible. According to him, it is sometimes necessary to plead the case of the impossible, due to the authority both of common opinion (*doxa*) and of the audience; thus in tragic discourse the persuasive impossibility is to be preferred to the unpersuasive possibility. Moreover, the defence of what is impossible in terms of common opinion is met by the comment that 'it is probable also for something to happen contrary to what is probable' (1461ᵇ14–15). This paradoxical form of probability only reinforces its importance, rather than undermines it, as the analysis of paradoxical probabilities at *Rhetoric* 1402ᵃ9 ff. reveals.

This explicitly rhetorical analysis of tragic plot evidently points to affinities between the treatment of tragedy in the *Poetics* and the *Rhetoric,* and with other scholars I look to the latter work for fur-

---

[54] Lear (1988), 299–301.   [55] Ibid. 304, 315.

ther guidance on the problem of *katharsis*. It has been noted that this text offers definitions of fear and pity which provide us with a cognitive analysis of the emotions involved in tragic *katharsis* and its pleasure that is quite distinct from the one offered by the *Nicomachean Ethics* and by Halliwell.[56] As Martha Nussbaum states, emotions for Aristotle are individuated 'not simply by the way they feel, but, more importantly, by the kinds of judgments or beliefs that are internal to each'.[57] That is to say, emotions involve a feeling of pleasure or pain and a certain belief about the way things are in the world. The *Rhetoric* makes this understanding of emotion explicit. At *Rhetoric* 1382^{a}21 ff. (cf. 1382^{b}29–31) Aristotle defines fear (*phobos*) as a pain (*lupē*) or distress caused by the belief that some destructive or painful evil is close at hand. At 1385^{b}13 ff. (cf. 1386^{a}29–30) he defines pity (*eleos*) as a pain (again *lupē*) at an apparent destructive or painful evil which comes upon someone who does deserve it and which an individual believes either he or someone connected with him may expect to suffer.[58] The belief that oneself or those connected with oneself can potentially also suffer the evil that afflicts someone else entails that one must be able to identify with the person one pities or because of whom one fears. It is the case that someone who despises the suffering individual cannot pity him because he regards him as inferior and therefore unlike him. Moreover, it is impossible to feel pity for someone who enjoys every good thing because it is impossible for this individual to suffer any evil (1385^{b}21–3).

The process of discovering what *katharsis* is leads to an analysis in which the social hierarchy implicit in the reception of tragedy is once more asserted. Although Aristotle states in the *Poetics* that tragedy involves an imitation of individuals who are better than the audience (e.g. 1454^{b}8–10), the understanding of *katharsis* as enlarged by the *Rhetoric* qualifies to what degree and in what way the tragic hero is better. It becomes clear that for pity to be possible, the tragic hero may not be so superior that the audience cannot identify with this character. This is why the philosopher stated at *Poetics* 1453^{a}5–6 that pity is for someone who does not deserve suffering and that fear is for someone like oneself. It is important to recognize that where rhetorical language is concerned, the *Rhetoric* for the most part concerns

---

[56] See the invocations of the *Rhetoric* by Halliwell (1992), 248–51, Nussbaum (1992), esp. 273 ff., and Nehemas (1992), esp. 300–2.

[57] Nussbaum (1986), 383; also Nussbaum (1992).   [58] Rorty (1992*b*), 14.

itself with the pathology of the well-educated, reasonable, and respectable citizen, namely the *epieikēs*. In this work Aristotle equates 'the respectable' (*to epieikes*) with not doing injustice ($1372^{b}18$), and so with justice as defined by written law (cf. $1374^{a}26-7$). At $1375^{a}31-2$ he proposes that *to epieikes* is stable, always remaining and never changing. The *Nicomachean Ethics* provides a more detailed discussion of what respectability and being a respectable person entails. In book 5 Aristotle offers an account of the relationship of *epieikeia* to justice (*dikaiosunē*), and of what is respectable (*epieikes*) to what is justice (*to dikaion*). According to him, what is respectable is a kind of just thing that is also better than what is just since it can offer a corrective supplement to legal justice, while both the respectable and the just are forms of what is serious/good/excellent (*spoudaion*) (*EN* $1137^{a}31-^{b}14$). From this analysis, it follows that the respectable person is someone who prefers what is just and acts upon this ($1137^{b}34-5$). Elsewhere in the work, the respectable individual is one who stands apart from the ordinary, undiscriminated citizen (cf. $1102^{b}10-11$), or else in contrast to the base man (*phaulos*) (cf. $1132^{a}2-3$). It becomes clear that Aristotle's respectable man is of the élite, a member of a ruling class in society. He observes that the reasonable and respectable man can produce a unity of mind (*homonoia*), aiming in common with others for what is just and beneficial, unlike the *phauloi* who are unable to agree, even though they are *philoi* ('dear', 'friends'), and aim instead for their own self-interests ($1167^{b}4-12$). At $1128^{a}17-18$ the philosopher affirms the relevance of this portrait of the respectable man to the portrait of the audience in Aristotle's discussions of literature. In this passage he posits the type of material uttered and heard by a respectable (cf. *tōi epieikei*) and a free (cf. *eleutheriōi*) individual as a normative ideal for literary discourse. As in the *Poetics,* what the élite audience—the serious, respectable and reasonable citizen—finds appealing is privileged over what the more common and less respectable audience finds pleasurable (cf. *NE* $1175^{b}24-8$ and, again, *Poet.* $1461^{b}28-9$).

Accordingly, the tragic hero of the *Poetics* will not be someone pre-eminent in virtue and justice nor will he be depraved and evil; rather, he must be someone between the two and prone to error (*hamartia*) ($1453^{a}7-10$). Nussbaum observes that it is this error which assures the tragic audience that the hero is not invulnerable

---

[59] Nussbaum (1986), 387.

and that it can therefore identify with the error.[59] The poet should produce a character with faults, e.g. irascibility, laziness, and so on, but none the less one who is still respectable (*epieikeis*), just as a painter might produce a portrait of reality which is both 'like' (*homoious*) and also 'more fine' (*kallious*) [than reality] (1454^b8-15). One final important qualification is necessary to the sociology of the tragic audience. The discussion of pity in the *Rhetoric* is insistent that those disposed to feel pity because they believe that someone else's evil can happen to them too are those who have already suffered and escaped it, namely the old (due to their wisdom and experience), the vulnerable, the excessively faint-hearted, and the educated (*hoi pepaideumenoi*) (*Rh.* 1385^b23-7). There is, however, a significant difference where the tragic audience is concerned. The *phronimos* ('sensible') viewer of tragedy is one who ideally realizes that the events on stage will not actually happen to him and thus is drawn to the theatre to experience its 'proper', that is 'specific', pleasure.[60] In the end, the tragic audience is a gathering of citizens who understand their distance from the terrible events occurring *in*, and only *in*, the tragedy and who are therefore able to feel fear, pity and then pleasure without any danger of complete identification with the staged emotions and actions, as Plato had feared.

VIII

In the *Politics* and the *Poetics* Aristole reinforces an image of a selective and stratified society in which the élite, namely the author himself and the citizen he depicts, dictate the acceptable forms of art and the appropriate responses to art. This is a society in which the author and his spectator regulate art to reinforce and to authorize their own identity as a select, exclusive class. The *Politics* offers overall an account of the process by which such a civic identity can come into being through a system of cultural and pedagogical socialization that scrupulously regulates and discriminates the experience of pleasure. Where the *Poetics* is concerned, the analysis of tragedy's psychology, of the pleasure, pity, and fear, is an analysis of the male élite citizen, variously termed the *kalos kagathos*, *spoudaios*, or *epieikēs*, and of his psychological response to

[60] Lear (1988), 323–6.

a particular form of leisure. The exclusive, élitist model of literary response in the *Poetics* effectively discriminates against other forms of pleasure, perhaps comedy and *iambos* discussed in book 2, and the groups who enjoy such forms. The philosopher authorizes a very specific form of literary leisure, and in so doing, he depicts the theatrical spectator as a metonymic figure for the *polis* as it ought to be and as it actually is in some small part. The community of the theatre, the audience which synechdochically stands for Athens, is one that Aristotle has subjected to rigorous discrimination such that it is far more exclusive than inclusive of the actual *dēmos*: the theatrical city makes no reference to the women, children, metics, and slaves who might have been members of the historical audience.

4

Cataloguing Texts:
Criticism in the Hellenistic Library

But is a period of transition, however momentous, by definition one of 'crisis'?

The problem lies partly in the interpreter's own outlook
and his choice of words. The word κρίσις is a highly specialized term in Greek medical literature, where it describes the
state of a patient whose life hangs in the balance. Applying this
term to the condition of an entire body of literature comes
close to falling into the Romantic trap of treating literature
and literary genres as if they were biological organisms that
pass through successive stages of birth, maturation, and death.
Thus understood, a crisis could lead to the unnatural or pre-
mature death of the literary patient, for example classical
literature.

Albert Henrichs in Bulloch et. al. (1993), 178

But, like sweaters, canons have an inherent tendency to
shrink: it is, after all an observed fact that social elites tend to
form smaller elites within themselves by the narcissism of
small differences, and the same impulse that canonizes Homer
within heroic epic is inevitably moved to ask the question
whether the *Iliad* or the *Odyssey* is the better poem; for once
we have been reminded of the shortness of our time and the
proximity of our death, no limit to urgency can be set.

Glenn Most (1992), 52

I

Twentieth-century scholars have characterized the Hellenistic
period as an 'age of criticism' (Sikes).[1] But this moment in the

---

[1] e.g. Pfeiffer (1968: 74) and Kennedy (in *CHLC* i. 200) on the importance of the
Museum and Library to Hellenistic literary scholarship. Cf. Sikes (1931: 159, 174),
who none the less denigrates the Alexandrian contribution to criticism.

history of literary reception is largely obscured to the modern gaze. We have the fragmentary poetry of Callimachus and, as Luciano Canfora makes clear, a body of subsequent works providing evidence of scholarly activities at Alexandria—the physical Library was consumed by fire in the Roman period.[2] The Library and its work, admittedly no less than the earlier criticisms examined in this book, now exist as a wholly textual construct, and so the discourse of Hellenistic criticism is, as far as the modern reader is concerned, in large part either sophisticated poetic discourse or a series of anecdotes, comments, and learned references collected in authors who are writing much later, in the Roman period.[3] From the material that exists, it might initially appear that criticism withdraws from the concerns of the world, being distinguished from other activities and behaviours to become a highly professionalized and rigorous occupation. Hellenistic scholarly activity together with the creative literary culture is marked by the abandonment of the 'great public genres', particularly epic with its Panhellenism but also tragedy with its civic ideology.[4] (The view, it would seem, proceeds from a perception of the written word and of a highly literate culture as introspective and interiorizing.[5]) Accordingly, even more than Aristotle's *Poetics*, the activities of the Hellenistic scholar-critics might at first sight contradict this book's main argument, that criticism is a political activity, that it seeks to produce a model of community by including and excluding particular languages and the political identities that these entail.

The present chapter calls into question this narrative at the point at which it disengages the critical process from the community.[6] I concern myself almost wholly with Alexandrian scholarship to interrogate the notion that 'professional' or 'institutional' activities are to be equated with 'apolitical' or 'disinterested'. My aim is to recover the political dimensions and environment of literary culture, and particularly literary scholarship, at Alexandria, and to explore the idea of *Greek* community as itself one in transi-

---

[2] Also Grube (1965), 124; the source is Aphthonius, *Progymnasmata* 12 (Walz p. 107).

[3] Canfora (1989).

[4] Kennedy in *CHLC* i. 201; also Russell (1981), 94, and Kennedy (1992), 225.

[5] See Ong (1982), 69; Toohey in Worthington (1994), 163.

[6] Gelzer (1993: 146) questions whether the Hellenistic scholarly culture is an 'ideology of refusal'. For a discussion of the way in which Hellenistic literary negotiates the community from within the 'archive', see Goldhill (1991), 223–83.

tion.[7] The retreat from the public sphere with which scholars characterize post-Aristotelian criticism, I suggest, constitutes rather a displacement and dislocation of its discriminated texts from their originative sites in order to appropriate their authority at a point when political and cultural authorities are being disseminated within the Mediterranean world. Criticism responds ultimately not with further dissemination but with an institutionalization of the work of earlier authors and of the individuals who read, judge, and discriminate literary texts as themselves the ideal political community.

II

Any analysis of Hellenistic criticism must involve an attempt to locate the activity in the recognition that this activity occurred in a variety of historical, physical spaces. Amongst these, Alexandria, founded in 331 BCE to become the refuge of what was to be deemed to be authoritatively Greek, is perhaps the most significant.[8] Here the connections between political authority and literary culture were to be firmly established and articulated. To manifest the North African city's status as an ideal monarchy, the first Ptolemy had the body of Alexander brought to the capital and established a cult around the tomb or *sēma*. Zenobius states that 'Ptolemy (Philopator) built in the middle of the city a *mnēma* [or 'memorial'], which is now called the Sema' (*Proverbia* 3. 94).[9] But Alexandria is, moreover, an ideal political text. Philo tells us that the Egyptian city was divided into five precincts, each named after a letter of the Greek alphabet—alpha (*A*), beta (*B*), gamma (*Γ*), delta (*Δ*), and epsilon (*Ξ*) (*In Flacc.* 973a). Callisthenes understood the lettered districts to be an aetiological acronym commemorating Alexandria's foundation: *A*lexandros *b*asileus *g*enos *d*ios *e*ktisen ('Alexander, the king, offspring of Zeus founded [this]').[10] Just as Hellenistic poetry presented its readers with *ktisis*- or foundation-myth poems, by its layout the very city declares its own *ktisis* to its inhabitants.

[7] Lewis (1986: 1), reminds us that the adjective 'Hellenistic', coined in the 18th cent., is a synonym for 'Greekish', which draws attention to a departure from what is properly and formerly Greek or which also recognizes an attempt to arrive at Greekness in an environment otherwise denied and recognized as other.

[8] Erskine (1995), 41.   [9] Jones (1932), 35 n. 4.

[10] See Goldhill (1994), 197.

In this textualized city, precinct Beta contained the tomb of
Alexander and the palace complex, within which was the fabled
Mouseion-Library. Geography thus makes explicit the intimate
connection between the gods (the tomb of the deified Alexander),
political authority (the palace), and literary culture (the Mouseion-
Library). The association between the divine, the political, and the
literary, for which Hesiod is the evident subtext, is elsewhere cele-
brated by Hellenistic poetry. The sense of the palace and scholarly
precinct as a surreal sphere comes from Herodas, *Mimiambus* 1,
where the brothel-keeper Gyllis visits her friend Meretriche,
whose husband or lover, Mandris, has been away for ten months in
Alexandria. To account for why Mandris has been absent for so
long, Gyllis offers a description of the cultural and political centre:
'There is the dwelling of the goddess. Everything, which is and
comes into being, is in Egypt: wealth, wrestling, power, prosperity,
reputation, shows, philosophers, gold, young men, the precinct of
the sibling gods, the best king, the Mouseion, wine, all the good
things which [one] wants, . . .' (ll. 26–31). Gyllis' list of what constitutes Alexandria draws attention to the activities that bespeak
élite Hellenic culture—wrestling, spectacles, philosophers, the
Mouseion, wine—and their association with the politically empowered and empowering—the gods and the king. In this passage of
Mimiambus 1 the contrast between Alexandrian society and the two
uneducated women, inhabitants of some inconspicuous town,
emphasizes the former's political, cultural, and material privilege.[11] Theocritus similarly plays with the contrast between high
and low in *Idyll* 15. The poem dramatizes the visit of the two bourgeois women, Gorgo and Praxinoa, to the royal palace and their
somewhat hesitant encounter with literary and visual culture there,
but it also sets these women against the thronging, multilingual
crowd of Alexandria.[12]

The Mouseion, literally glossed as the 'shrine to the Muses',[13]
itself foregrounds the political and religious dimensions of
Alexandrian literary culture, while the physical layout of the
Library also makes obvious the sense in which literary scholarship
at Alexandria takes place in the service of the gods and under their

---

[11] See Ussher (1980); Stern (1981).   [12] See Goldhill (1991), 275.
[13] See Ar. *Frogs* 93–4; Pl. *Phdr.* 278b; Arist. *Rh.* 1406ᵃ24–5; Diog. Laert. 4.1;
Philostr. *VS* 509; Eunap. *VS* 456. Also see Pfeiffer (1968: 98), who suggests that the
Library was located within the Mouseion, and Fraser (1972) i. 312–13.

authority. Diodorus Siculus stresses the physical proximity of books and divine statues in the Alexandrian courts. He observes that the sacred library (*hieran bibliothēkēn*), named the 'healing place of the soul', is to be found next to the statues of all the Egyptian gods, to each of whom the king is depicted as giving gifts (1. 49. 3).[14] Diodorus' account also tells the reader that adjacent to this library is a building which contains a dining-table with twenty couches on which recline images of Zeus, Hera, and the king, whose body is also buried there (1. 49. 4). Appropriately, the figure in charge of the scholarly community of the Mouseion is a priest-cum-head-librarian appointed by the kings—and in Strabo's time by Caesar. The priest-critic ministers to his books as if they were divine objects, and Panaetius, the Rhodian philosopher, extends the metaphor of priesthood to include interpretation. He describes the grammarian and critic Aristarchus as a prophet (*mantis*), who earns this description as a result of his exceptional ability to divine (cf. *katamanteuesthai*) the meaning of poems (Athenaeus 634c–d).

Like the king, the Alexandrian literary intellectual is a significant political figure. He is such by virtue of being linked to the political establishment through a structure of patronage.[15] In *Idyll* 17 the poet, Theocritus, announces that he takes his beginning from Zeus, and then proceeds to celebrate Ptolemy II (Philadelphus) as the noblest mortal (17. 1–7). In view of the Hellenistic king's claim to divine ancestry, the poet in effect declares the coincidence of divine and political patronage for his writing.[16] Through patronage, the Ptolemies establish and maintain the scholarly community, and they do so not by separating it from the larger world, but by incorporating the emblems of the political community into the scholarly one: the outside world is brought into the scholarly institution. Pindar had earlier rejected the professional and mercenary aspects of poetic culture in his day (cf. *Isthm.* 2. 1–15). By contrast, and offering a justification for patronage of the intellectual, Xenophanes lamented the fact that he received nothing for his contribution to the city, although his poetic wisdom and skill

[14] See Fraser (1972) i. 324. Canfora (1989: 77–8, 134) insists that we understand the word βιβλιοθήκη to denote 'shelves' or 'repository' rather than the building in which the books were placed, that is a library, by analogy with Isid. *Etym.* 6. 3. 3. Strabo (2. 1. 5) uses βιβλιοθήκη to refer to the Alexandrian Library to which Eratosthenes had access.

[15] Fraser (1972), i. 132; Thompson (1994), 67.

[16] See Lewis (1986), 4, and the excellent discussion by Koenen (1993), esp. 50 ff.

helped to set the city in good order, while for *his* achievement the athlete received a seat of honour and his meals at public expense.[17] Socrates later rehearsed this criticism of the state's tendency to undervalue the intellectual when he proposed that the Athenians should feed him in the *prytaneion* as if he were a victorious athlete (Pl. *Ap.* 36d–e). Theocritus picks up on the value of the poet in particular in *Idyll* 16, for this is the individual who sings of the deeds of the gods and of mortals (1–2). Poetic song ensures everlasting fame and it is for this reason that the rich man should not begrudge the man of letters patronage (58 ff.).[18]

The now privileged narrative generally attributes to Ptolemy I (Soter) the formalization of literary scholarship and study as a socially useful activity. The monarch professionalized literary study, and when he did so, he specifically committed himself and the Mouseion to a recognition of the scholar-poet's importance both as teacher and as cultural guardian. Plutarch writes as follows, 'Ptolemy the First brought together the Mouseion'[19] (*Mor.* 1095d). The participle 'brought together' (*sunagagōn*) has been the object of scholarly speculation. Pfeiffer argues that the participle is suitable in light of Strabo's description of the Mouseion as an 'assembly' (*sunodos*) [of scholars],[20] but *sunagagōn* is also appropriate for denoting the gathering of books and might appear to refer to establishment of the Library.[21] After all, Strabo uses the phrase 'bringing together (*sunagagōn*) books' (13. 1. 53) to denote book collecting, while Athenaeus speaks of 'the multitude of books . . . and the gathering in the Mouseion' (203e[22]).

In book 17 of his *Geography*, Strabo observes that in the Ptolemaic Mouseion at Alexandria, the scholars who work there, described as 'men who love words' (*philologoi andres*), have a common mess and share their goods in common (17. 1. 8). In his life of Dionysius of Milete, Philostratus suggests that, subsequently, meals given at public expense were synonymous with intellectual

---

[17] DK 21 B 2; cf. Bowra (1938). Kurke (1993: 154) notes that here Xenophanes prioritizes intellectual over athletic achievement in order to reject 'the symbolic economy that subtends athletic victory in favour of a material economy of civic acquisition'.

[18] See Gold (1987), 30–1. Griffiths (1979: 18–19) argues that by asking for a large fee, the poet ennobles his art.

[19] Πτολεμαῖος ὁ πρῶτος συναγαγὼν τὸ μουσεῖον. . . .

[20] Pfeiffer (1968), 96.   [21] Ibid. 97 n. 4.

[22] περὶ δὲ βιβλων πλήθους . . . καὶ τῆς εἰς τὸ Μουσεῖον συναγωγῆς.

prestige and honour. He refers to Hadrian enrolling Dionysius amongst the knights who received meals in a latter-day Mouseion, which he glosses as an 'Egyptian dining-table which summoned the most famous men in the earth' (*VS* 524). The common mess and property shared by the scholars affirms the recognition made by authors of the archaic and classical periods that literary culture has an important role and value in the community as a whole. The communal ownership of goods signifies the idealism of the community by enacting the proposal for public ownership of material goods in the ideal city of Plato's *Republic*. Furthermore, the mess was a feature of the Spartan state, and its establishment in the Mouseion suggests an implicit analogy between the poet and the soldier, one which corrects what Xenophanes had observed to be the traditional privileging of physical over intellectual prowess in the Greek city-state. It is perhaps not surprising that Jaroslav Pelikan ventures that the Library at Alexandria is a precedent for the modern university, which for him is a community that engages with social concerns.[23]

III

While the exact relationship of the Mouseion to the Library is uncertain, literary sources suggest that they are to be closely identified, or that the former contains the latter, or that they are identical.[24] In any case, the accounts of their foundation tend to be narratives of one or the other or of both together. If the setting up of the cult of Alexander symbolized the re-amalgamation of political authority that was otherwise fracturing out of control in the Mediterranean, then, through the founding of the Mouseion-Library, which collected and brought to their city largely Greek works, the Alexandrian leaders thus reassembled another significant constituent element of Greek culture and power.

Pliny notes that it is difficult to say whether it was the kings of Pergamum or of Alexandria who first created a library since they were engaged in a great struggle (*HN* 35. 2. 10). Following Varro, Pliny elsewhere remarks that competition between kings Ptolemy Epiphanes (205–185 BCE) and Eumenes caused Ptolemy to suppress

---

[23] Pelikan (1992), 110. [24] See e.g. Fraser (1972), i. 324.

the export of paper with the result that parchment was invented at Pergamum (*HN* 13. 21. 70). Competition, both hostile and friendly, is responsible for the foundation of book collections in another account. Vitruvius relates how jealousy and competitive greed stirred Ptolemy to copy the Attalid king in establishing his own library at Alexandria (7. pr. 4). He also established games in honour of the Muses and Apollo and awarded prizes so that authors had equal status with athletes. Vitruvius invokes the comparison between poet and athlete and between mental and physical virtue—which Plato and Xenophon had remarked upon as conventionally working to the disadvantage of the intellectual and his wisdom—to demonstrate how the status of intellectual activity has changed with the Hellenistic monarchs.

But I want to look beyond individual contributions for the reasons for the establishment of the Mouseion-Library. There were a number of precedents for such an institutionalized collection of texts. One of these is the founding of a public library (Ath. 3a) or else of a book collection by Pisistratus, the Athenian tyrant and the first Greek supposedly to have established such an institution (Gell. 7. 17).[25] In his discussion of libraries in the *Etymologies*, Isidore declares that in gathering texts into a library Ptolemy II (Philadephus) was emulating the Athenian tyrant Pisistratus (*Etym.* 6. 3. 3–5).[26] Isidore foregrounds the way in which the foundation of the Alexandrian Library is a conscious link to the Greek and Macedonian past. He proposes that the idea of the library, if not the library itself, is transferable across cultures, going on to observe that Xerxes later took Pisistratus' library to Persia while the Seleucid Nicanor subsequently returned it to Greece. After this, many other states sought to acquire texts and to translate them into Greek with the result that Alexander or his successors sought to collect all existing books into libraries. Another obvious precedent for the Alexandrian Library is the Athenian Metroon, the building which served to house the public archives and which contained the documents recording the official transactions of the city.

[25] Allen (1913), 51.

[26] 'Dehinc magnus Alexander vel successores eius instruendis omnium librorum bibliothecis animum intenderunt; maxime Ptolemaeius cognomento Philadephus omnis litteraturae sagacissimus, cum studio bibliothecarum Pisistratum aemularetur, non solum gentium scripturas, sed etiam et divinas litteras in bibliothecam suam contulit' (*Etym.* 6. 3. 5).

In an attempt to grant Hellenistic literary culture an Aristotelian genealogy, Strabo relates how Aristotle passed his collection of texts to his pupil Theophrastus, who in turn taught the Egyptian kings to gather and collect books. He continues his account, telling his reader that Theophrastus then bequeathed his own and Aristotle's libraries to his pupil, the philosopher Neleus, who took it to Scepsis, where his non-intellectual descendants (cf. *idiōtai anthrōpoi*) put the books away carelessly. The description of the books as lying neglected suggests the absence of order and arrange-ment in Aristotle's collection. A worse desecration is to befall the texts in Strabo's narrative. When Neleus' descendants hear that the books from their collection are being sought by the Attalid kings for the library at Pergamum, they bury them in a trench and so cause their decay. A bibliophile named Apellicon subsequently restores the texts, making new copies of them and incorrectly fill-ing the gaps. At Rome, the grammarian Tyrannion and certain booksellers acquire and then circulate poorly edited copies of these works (13. 1. 54). Strabo's narrative is in some sense a nightmare scenario of what happens when books fall into the ownership of individuals who do not understand their value.

Where the Metroon was by and large the memorial of political and legal activity in Athens, the Library-Mouseion had a more ambitious remit, serving as a cumulative record of Greek culture, redefining it as Alexandrian culture. Hellenistic scholarship had a totalizing tendency. This is in part articulated in the use of the adjective 'polymathic' (*polymathēs*) as a term of commendation. If earlier Athenian authors had criticized polymathia or multiple learning, equating it with superficial knowledge (cf. Heraclitus, DK 22 B 40; Pl. *Leg.* 811a–b; 819a; *Phdr.* 275a2–b1),[27] then the servant of the Muses, the Alexandrian scholar-poet, recovers the positive sense implicitly given to the term by Homer when he attributed omniscience to the Muses at *Iliad* 2. 485. The scholar-poet of the post-classical age needs to be knowledgeable in many things and in his pamphlet *Against Praxiphanes* (fr. 460 Pf.) Callimachus praised his contemporary Aratus for being 'learned (*polymathēs*) and the best poet'.[28] At *Aetia* 3. 75. 8–10 the poet observes that much knowledge (*poluidreiē*) is a bad thing when someone does not control their tongue, implying that it is otherwise

---

[27] Pfeiffer (1968), 138 n. 1.   [28] Ibid. 135–6.

a good thing. As someone who wrote works on many different top-ics, including geography, but mastered none in particular, Eratosthenes, the librarian (275–194 BCE), is perhaps an example of the Alexandrian polymath.[29]

What the Hellenistic scholar does is to map the totality of his and the community's knowledge on to Alexandria, or conversely to map Alexandria on to the totality of knowledge. It has been argued that the Ptolemies attempted to control *all* of Greek culture rather than just Athenian culture, and to establish their rule through this con-trol.[30] The Mouseion-Library is an institution which was intended to displace the hegemony of Attic textuality with one which was pronouncedly and literally Panhellenic, where the adjective '*pan-*' ambitiously denotes the sum of all Greek literature- and language-texts rather than simply what relates to the Greek states. Athenaeus informs his readers that the Ptolemies collected texts from the book trade conducted at Athens and Rhodes (Ath. 3b), while Galen says that Ptolemy copied all books which arrived at Alexandria by sea and had these copied texts inscribed with the phrase 'from the ships' (Gal. *Comm. in Hippoc. Epidem.* 17. 1. 606 Kühn).[31] It is worth noting that the phrase *kata tēn oikoumenēn* had been a con-ventional way of referring to the inhabited world since Herodotus (e.g. 1. 170. 3, 2. 32. 5, 4. 110. 2; also Soph. *Phil.* 221), and the use of it to define the provenance of the Library's books suggests that in appropriating and acquiring texts this institution defines the extent of Alexandrian political and cultural hegemony.

To record the contents of the Mouseion-Library, Callimachus produced the *Pinakes*, or Catalogues, of the holdings at Alexandria. The *Pinakes* ran to 120 volumes and purported to catalogue the entirety of Greek literature (*pasa paideia*) and the sum of knowl-edge.[32] According to Pfeiffer, Callimachus divided his Catalogues into several generic classes—e. g. rhetoric (cf. fr. 432 Pf.), laws (cf. fr. 433), treatises, epic, lyric, tragedy, comedy, philosophy, history, and medicine—and seems to have organized authors within each of these classes alphabetically with brief biographical notes.[33] (In his *Life of Homer*, Plutarch ascribes the division of the *Iliad* and the *Odyssey*, each into twenty-four books named after the letters of the

---

[29] Grube (1965), 127.   [30] See, most recently, Erskine (1995), 45.
[31] Davison (1962), 228–9; Fraser (1972), i. 325.
[32] Pfeiffer (1968), 128; also Hopkinson (1988), 83, and Blum (1991), 182 ff.
[33] Pfeiffer (1968), 128–9.

Ionic alphabet, to Aristarchus, or else to the scholar's disciples, although Stephanie West warns that this information may derive from conjecture.[34] Other evidence exists to suggest that the comedies of Aristophanes were also catalogued alphabetically.[35]) The parallelism between the organization of texts within the Mouseion-Library, of sections within large works like the Homeric epics, and of sections of the city-state strikingly reinforces the idea that the literary and the political spheres are in some sense analogous. The *Pinakes* seem to admit a diversity that against the background of critical history appears eccentric: diversity ought to produce a moral panic where the reception of literary discourse is concerned, and it will become apparent that the anxiety about multiplicity is managed somewhat differently. The totalizing aim of Hellenistic literary scholarship is attested by references to the 'table of various (or miscellaneous) things' (cf. *en tōi tōn pantodapōn pinaki*, fr. 434 = Ath. 244a) and to a 'table of various (or miscellaneous) compositions' (cf. *en tōi tōn pantodapōn suggrammatōn Pinaki*, fr. 435 = Ath. 643e). The titles of Callimachus' Catalogues acknowledge the 'manifold' (*pantodapa*) as a legitimate category, but there is a sense in which the *Pinakes* constitute a synopsis of Greek literature, like the *Epitomes* of Zenodotus, which stands for the totality of Greek mythology (Ath. 412a).

The *Pinakes* also attest to the inclination in Alexandrian scholarship to appropriate aspects of what might have previously and otherwise been regarded as 'other'. Strabo observes that Eratosthenes refrained from praising individuals who divide the world into the categories 'Greek' and 'barbarian' as well as from commending those who had advised Alexander to treat the Greeks as friends and the barbarians as enemies. In place of the conventional them/us distinction, Eratosthenes proposes a division of the world according to the moral categories of virtue and vice, where virtue is understood to involve the sort of lawful and civic behaviour to be associated with education and rhetoric, and where vice is the opposite of such behaviour (Strabo 1. 4. 9). In a similar vein, Callimachus' grammatical work *Barbarica nomima* (fr. 405), which some scholars regard as a supplement to Aristotle's ethnographical work by the same name (frs. 604–10 Rose), serves to reinforce the sense of Hellenistic culture and identity ostensibly by definition

---

[34] Eustathius 5. 29 and S. West (1965), 18–19.   [35] Pfeiffer (1968), 129.

against the barbarian 'other'; but less ostensibly they show that the 'other' is a crucial aspect of the discourse about Hellenistic identity.[36]

Josephus provides us with two separate accounts of how the Alexandrian Library expands the notion of Hellenistic culture by appropriation. In the *Jewish Antiquities* he notes that Ptolemy II was so taken with learning (*paideia*) and the collecting of books— the phrase 'collection of books' (*biblion sunagōgēn*) significantly recalls the creation of the Library—that he had the Jewish laws and constitution, namely the Hebrew scriptures, translated into Greek (1. 10 ff.). In the *Letter to Aristeas*, as cited in book 12 of the *Jewish Antiquities*, Ptolemy is reported as declaring his intention of having the Old Testament translated into Greek by seventy-two scholars, six from each of the twelve tribes, and deposited in his library (*bibliothēkēi*) (12. 47–9). Tertullian, at *Apologeticus* 18. 5, uses this same narrative to justify his description of the guardians of the Alexandrian libraries, the Ptolemies and Demetrius of Phalerum, as 'messengers' and 'prophets'. In recounting the translation of the Septuagint version of the Old Testament, the Christian author Isidore emphasizes the role of the Holy Spirit in ensuring the complete agreement of the translators. He observes that the Jewish scholars worked independently in separate rooms, but none the less concurred in their translations, so attesting to the authority of this version (*Etym.* 6. 4. 1–2).

IV

While Alexandrian literary culture may lay claim to all previously existing literature, it is none the less a selective and discriminating culture: the totality of Hellenic culture, articulated most obviously by Callimachus' *Pinakes* and of course by Alexandrian literary scholarship as a whole, is actually a metonymy.[37] The Hellenistic poet is simultaneously critic, judge, and discriminator of earlier works; he is the individual who decides which works will constitute

---

[36] See also Koenen (1993: 81 ff.) on Callimachus' Hellenization of Egyptian ideas and motifs in his poetry. Cf. Isid. *Etym.* 6. 3. 3; on the issue of self-definition against the 'other' in Greek thought, see Hall (1989).

[37] Compare Elsner (1995: 132), who argues that Pausanias' aim to depict πάντα τὰ ἑλλενικά (1. 26. 4) is 'a very selective kind of viewing'.

the institutionally validated culture. If readers have drawn attention to the way in which Hesiod is the subtext for Alexandrian poetics,[38] then I suggest that, as far as Callimachus is concerned, it is
this early poet who also justifies the critical imperative and the
identity of the Alexandrian intellectual as society's discriminator.
In *Iamb* 2 the scholar-poet presents his audience with an Aesopic
animal fable (cf. ll. 15–17). He speaks of a much earlier era when sea
creatures and animals where able to speak as 'Promethean clay',
that is as humans (ll. 1–3), until Zeus unjustly deprived these
beings of speech and gave it rather to mankind (ll. 6–10). The fable
is an aetiology of why particular individuals now speak as animals,
such that Eudemos has a dog's voice, Philton a donkey's, others
(von Arnim's supplement suggests 'orators'[39]) a parrot's, and tragic
poets those of sea creatures. It is in sum an explanation of why all
men speak too much (cf. *poulumuthoi*) and chatter (cf. *laloi*) (ll.
10–17).

Scholars have observed that it is puzzling for Zeus to give to
tragedians the voice of fish inasmuch as fish are silent creatures (cf.
Callim. fr. 533).[40] But Callimachus may not be referring to fish, to
which Babrius in any case could grant a voice (Babrius, pr. 1. 10).
In Hesiod's 'Typhonomachy', Zeus located the multivoiced
Typhon under the waves in order to render him inarticulate but not
silent inasmuch as he is transformed into the raging winds.
Callimachus may well be attributing the utterances of this polyphonous monster to tragedians, who, at least in Plato's depiction of
them, are indiscriminate imitators and cause others to produce
plural discourse (cf. *Resp.* 396b, 598d–e). After all, underlying
Iamb 2 are suggestions of a challenge to the gods. The reference to
Prometheus at line 3 evokes the Titan's trickery of Zeus, while the
Diegeseis-commentary on the poem notes that birds and animals
spoke as humans later would until 'the swan negotiated the destruction of old age with the gods and the fox dared to say that Zeus did
not rule justly'.[41] Speech passes to mankind the moment the fox, a

---

[38] See, for instance, Rosenmeyer (1973), esp. 21–2, 212–13; Reinsch-Werner
(1976); Halperin (1983), 245; Zanker (1987), 155.

[39] Trypanis (1958), 115.

[40] See Clayman (1980), 18; Bing (1981), 33; Courtney (1988), 276; but Platt
(1910) proposes that Callimachus has in mind seagulls.

[41] μέχρι | κατὰ λύσιν γήρως ἐπ[ρέ]σβευσεν ὁ κύ-| κνος πρὸς τοὺς καὶ
ἀλώπηξ τὸν | Δία ἐτόλμησεν μὴ δικαίως ἄρχειν φά-| ναι (*Dieg.* 6. 23–7). On the
difficulties posed to the reader by the commentary, see Barber (1939).

creature whom Archilochus had characterized as 'knowing many things' and had therefore associated with plurality, called Zeus' authority into question (*Dieg.* 6. 24–7; cf. Archilochus frs. 103, 201 West).

Callimachus' *Iamb* 2 is an oblique reworking of its Hesiodic source. As in the *Theogony*-episode, plural, animal-like discourses need to be constrained. Where Hesiod, as poet, works with Zeus to contain polyphony, the Alexandrian scholar now undertakes this task alone. He is engaged in correcting a divine shortcoming, for once upon a time Zeus directed the multiple animal utterances into humans, thereby proving that he was not yet just. Yet, it is important to recognize that not all polyphonies are the target of Alexandrian discrimination, for Frederick Griffiths observes that its poetics engages in plural ventriloquisms. Especially when they engage in praise of the ruler, Callimachus and Theocritus assume other voices: those of individuals who are clearly 'other'—Gorgo and Praxinoa (Theoc. *Id.* 15), the Spartan maidens (Theoc. *Id.* 18), the unborn Apollo (Callim. *Hymn to Delos*); those of otherwise inanimate objects—a nautilus shell (Callim. *Epigr.* 5), the lock of Berenice (Callim. *Lock of Berenice*, fr. 110).[42]

In *Iamb* 2 what Callimachus above all picks up from the Typhonomachy is a concern that identities might be mistaken, in particular that copies might be taken for the original. Alexandrian literary culture reflects this worry through the double impulses of continuity and discontinuity where the prior classical culture is concerned.[43] As far as the writing of poetry is concerned, Hellenistic authors may have acknowledged their indebtedness to archaic poetry, to the writings of Homer and Hesiod, by conscious use of the vocabulary, grammar, syntax, and themes of these poets. But they did so in such a way that their voices could never be mistaken for those of their antecedents.[44] Accordingly, Callimachus could say, 'I sing nothing unattested' (fr. 612), while in the prologue to the *Aetia* he recalls that Apollo has ordered him to take unworn paths, avoiding the common tracks and wide roads (1. 25–8). Certainly, Hellenistic poetry demonstrated its extreme self-consciousness about origins through the writing of foundation narratives (*ktiseis*) (where cities and festivals are concerned), and

---

[42] See Griffiths (1979), 82. [43] Gelzer (1993), 150; Goldhill (1991), 321–3.
[44] Griffiths (1979: 6) observes that Callimachus in particular rejected 'envy of Homer' (ζῆλος Ὁμηρικός), or the attempt to beat the epic poet at his own game.

aetiology (e.g. Callimachus' *Aetia*), which simultaneously referred the present to the Greek past and refounded the present as *differently* Greek.[45] Beyond this, as Kennedy observes, this body of writing made a point of treating topics which were not dealt with in classical poetry: in particular, 'scientific' or exceptionally technical matters such as the constellations, religion, and urban life. When these poets invoke myth, they select the localized, idiosyncratic traditions rather than the familiar, Panhellenic version. The topics of Hellenistic poetry might suggest, as they do to Kennedy, a concern with the imaginary or the intensely personal, rather than the here-and-now.[46]

Poetic textuality, moreover, is sacralized, and this sacralization entails rigorous discrimination, which results in a poetry marked by exclusivity and rarity. Callimachus ends the *Hymn to Apollo* with the observation that the Melissae—either bees, following the *Homeric Hymn to Hermes*, or the bee-priestesses, following Porphyry (*Cave of the Nymphs* 19)—carry to Deo (or Demeter) not water that comes from *every* fountain but only that which comes from a *little* stream, pure and unsullied on a peak. In contrast to this pure water is the 'Assyrian river', the Euphrates, with its *great* current that draws much sediment and filth along with it (ll. 108–12).[47] In that divine inspiration is also a strategy for defining poetry as a refined and erudite text which would appeal to a similarly refined and exclusive audience, it also proposes that originality is something rare in what is otherwise implied to be a world of fakes and copies. Hellenistic poetry becomes a dimension of the critical project in that its concern seems to be to show itself as a literary discourse that demonstrates both its archaic genealogies and its ability to establish an identity which is Greek but also distinct from Greek as articulated in the work of archaic poetry.

So as far as the reception of classical literature is concerned, scholarship seeks to authenticate and so to distinguish contemporary textuality from a past textuality. Ironically, however, it is precisely the project of reclaiming and preserving the past as the past which made this enterprise so necessary. The reconstruction

---

[45] For the simultaneously expanding and rupturing effect of aetiological narrative in Apollonius Rhodius' *Argonautica*, see Goldhill (1991), 321–3.

[46] Kennedy in *CHLC* i. (1989), 201–2.

[47] The Hellenistic poem marks itself as a discriminated text by being ideally small. Cf. e.g. Callim. *Aet.* 1. 1–12; *Epig.* 10; *Epig.* fr. 398; fr. 465 Pf. = Ath. 72a. See also Puelma (1954).

of earlier Hellenic culture under the Ptolemies was in large part to blame for the adulteration of this culture. Galen attests to the new phenomenon of forgeries. The libraries at Alexandria and Pergamum offered financial rewards to individuals who supplied them with volumes, and thus the falsification of works from an earlier age became a lucrative business (cf. *Comm. in Hippoc. De nat. homin.* 1. 44. 105[48]). The Alexandrian scholars thus had to ensure the correct identification of the voices of its literary texts and of their origins. Pfeiffer observes that Philetas of Cos is the first individual to be described as 'poet and critic' (*poiētēs hama kai kritikos*) (Strabo 14. 2. 19),[49] but it was the librarians Aristophanes and Aristarchus who were responsible for the establishment of what we might now call literary 'canons', where canonicity is constituted by entry of a title into the scholar's list or catalogue.[50]

Vitruvius' account of how Aristophanes became the first head librarian recognizes the dimension of Hellenistic librarianship concerned with authentication. Vitriuvius states that, after deciding to set up a library to rival Pergamum's, Ptolemy I established literary contests dedicated to the Muses and Apollo and sought educated judges (*iudices litterati*) to determine the victors of these contests. The king himself selected six individuals and had Aristophanes recommended to him by the governors of the Library as the seventh judge for the reason that he had diligently and carefully read all the books in the Library in order. When it came to the adjudication of the poetic competition, the first six judges agreed to give the prize to the poet who most pleased the crowd. Aristophanes alone, however, deemed that the prize should be awarded to the individual who had least gratified the audience with his composition (*De arch.* 7 pr. 5–6). To the angered king and audience Aristophanes justified his decision by showing that the individual he had selected as winner was the only one who had presented an original text, while the others had put forward plagiarized texts (cf. 'thefts', *furta*). He established that misappropriation had occurred by matching the stolen works to the texts from his bookcases. The king punished the offenders and made Aristophanes the head librarian.

---

[48] See text cited at Fraser (1972), ii. 481.   [49] Pfeiffer (1968), 89.

[50] The term 'canon', previously an ecclesiastical term to distinguish orthodox from heterodox writings (e.g. 'canon scripturarum', August. *On Christian Doctrine* 2. 8. 13; Isid. *Etym.* 6. 16. 1 ff.), was first used in this sense by David Ruhnken in his 1768 edition of Rutilius Lupus; see Pfeiffer (1968), 207.

The narrative justifies the latter's election to the post in terms of his ability to distinguish original work from fake.

Vitruvius' narrative perhaps recalls the *Contest of Hesiod and Homer* (see Ch. 1). After all, both texts depict a poetic competition in which the outcome is initially decided by popular vote only to be later overturned by an expert judge, and, more generally, they both rehearse the classical diatribe against popular taste. The *krisis* of poetic texts in these works is traced to and elided with legal judgement (*krisis*). Vitruvius casts the Ptolemaic king after the model of the Hesiodic king who figures the human ruler as just judge. The author also insists upon the overlap with the forensic scenario in his presentation of the offending poets as thieves who deserve to be punished for their misappropriations. Both in the *Contest* and in Vitruvius' text the authoritative judgement is that of the informed minority, suggesting that literary criticism is an exclusive activity. But Vitruvius' account of poetic judgement also differs from that depicted in the *Contest* at a number of significant moments. If King Paneides is the expert judge who invokes utility over pleasure in the *Contest*, it is the scholar Aristophanes who has to correct the king, Ptolemy, in the later work. Vitruvius' account of Hellenistic criticism suggests that critical and poetic authority is no longer straightforwardly coterminous with political authority but is to be distinguished from it by learning and study. It is precisely because Aristophanes has read all the books in order in the library, and because he can refer from memory to the texts held in his bookcases that he can overturn the decision of Ptolemy and the assembled crowd, justifying his appointment as the chief librarian. The critic selects as winner the poet who composes a new work, while exposing the individuals who plagiarize as mere reciters of the work of others (cf. 'ceteros aliena recitavisse'), and demoting them to the mere rank of rhapsode. Aristophanes' librarianship formalizes orderly and discriminating reading, which he literally enacts in his capacity as wise judge and by his careful maintenance of books. Vitruvius' account thus re-establishes poetic judgement as a process that involves the distinction of true text from false, original from illegitimate, rather than a distinction between pleasure and utility for the community.

As far as the account in *De architectura* is concerned, Aristophanes is the authenticator *par excellence*. But the standards set by Ptolemy's first librarian are not necessarily those of subsequent

scholars. Some of the criteria for inclusion in the Library catalogues might be regarded as quite arbitrary and without any literary basis. One consideration, for instance, was whether the
inclusion of an author would enable the librarians to structure their
canons into multiples of three or ten—so, nine lyric poets, three
Old comedians, six historians, ten orators.[51] Failure to recognize
the numerical grouping as an arbitrary structuring and discriminating principle of the canon has led some critics to query the
provenance of canon formation on some occasions. So Ian
Worthington queries whether the canon of the ten Attic orators can
be Alexandrian because it omits those who employ the emergent
Asiatic style (even though, in this instance, it is perhaps the exclusion of the Asiatic orators which attests to the Hellenic bias of the
canon and so to its likely Alexandrian origin[52]).

It is important to recognize that the librarian's authority can be
arbitrary and occasionally self-indulgent. In the opinion of later
authors, Callimachus is a librarian whose judgement is not always
to be trusted, even if he suggests that the man of culture must now
judge with his skill and learning to ensure that Typhonic babble is
contained (cf. Callim. *Aet.* 1. 17–18). Dionysius of Halicarnassus
corrects the Alexandrian librarian's attribution of *Against
Theocrines* to Demosthenes, placing it instead amongst the
speeches of Dinarchus (Dion. Hall. *Din.* 10 = Callim. fr. 444). He
also criticizes Callimachus and the Pergamene critics for not writing about Dinarchus in a careful manner (cf. *ouden akribes, Din.*
1 = Callim. fr. 447). Harpocration is the source for another disagreement between Dionysius and Callimachus when he notes that
the former declared spurious the *Against Critias*, which the latter
had identified as one of Demosthenes' speeches (Callim. fr. 445).
Photius says that the compiler of the *Pinakes* attributes to
Dinarchus a speech *Against Chairedemus* which others ascribe to
Demosthenes (cod. 265, p. 491^{b}31 = Callim. fr. 446).[53] Here
Photius describes Callimachus as 'not being sufficiently able to
judge'. Elsewhere, Athenaeus notes that Callimachus names a play
by Diphilus *Eunuch*, despite the fact that the dramatist has himself
called it the *Rampart Taker* (*Hairēsiteichēs*) (Ath. 496e–f). In the
face of misleading evidence given by the Hellenistic scholar,
Kenneth Dover concludes that Callimachus did not actually estab-

---

[51] Most (1990). 55.   [52] Worthington (1994), 249–50.
[53] Dover (1968), 23.

lish, so much as merely record, titles and attributions already given to the works.[54]

In his *Pinakes* Callimachus included both biographical and bibliographical information for each of the authors he listed, to the extent that Rudolf Blum attributes to him the invention of '*bio*bibliography'.[55] I suggest that, whatever this librarian's other failings, biography is perhaps where we must locate his concern to authenticate. The assumption that biographical detail might be a strategy for assisting the authorial designation of works has a much earlier basis. There was an established tradition of writing 'lives'. The research on Homer by the sixth-century Theagenes of Rhegium may be the first example of this, while there was also biographical writing of a kind in the classical period.[56] A body of classical biography grew up around the philosopher Socrates, seeking to establish him as an examplar of his own teaching and doctrine. Jaap Mansfeld observes that one of the axioms underlying this sort of scholarship was the understanding that a writer's life and his works and thoughts—his *logos*—were reflections of one another: the narrative of a 'life' becomes an ethopoeic text that corroborates the original sayings or writings and their intentionalities.[57]

The figure of the author, as constructed through the scholarly biographies of him, is thus a means of limiting the body of discourse that can be attributed to any one person, and a means of circumscribing interpretive possibilities. When Dionysius of Halicarnassus draws attention to the Hellenistic critics' failure to do adequate research on Dinarchus (Callim. fr. 447), he confirms biography as an important part of literary authentication: omission in this area is what explains the false attribution of speeches to the orator. The principle 'elucidate Homer from Homer', which makes its first appearance in Porphyry but has been thought to originate with Aristarchus, appears to espouse a purist, almost New Critical perspective on reading. But where twentieth-century New Criticism rejects biography, as being the basis for an interpretive fallacy, the ancient principle of 'Homer from Homer' may be an articulation of the understanding that the author and his biography are the authoritative basis for the authentication and exegesis of literary texts.[58]

---

[54] Ibid. 24–5   [55] Blum (1991), 1 and 244; also Mansfeld (1994), 60.
[56] See Momigliano (1971), 25–32.   [57] Mansfeld (1994), 180–91.
[58] ἀξιῶν δὲ ἐγὼ Ὅμηρον ἐξ Ὁμήρου σαφηνίζειν αὐτὸν ἐξηγούμενον ἑαυτὸν ὑπεδείκνυον, . . . The formula is first expressed by Porphyry, *Quaestiones Homericae ad Iliadem pertinentes*, p. 297. 16–17; see Mansfeld (1994), 204.

The redefinition and renegotiation of literary and political agents and authorities that are evident in the accounts of Alexandrian scholarship and in Alexandrian poetry must not be mistaken for the sort of political neutrality with which some modern scholars have attempted to characterize Hellenistic culture. Vitruvius' narrative emphatically reaccommodates critical skill within the political community and not only through the evocation of the legal *krisis*. The redefinition of criticism as a process which distinguishes original from fake is central to a realignment of literary culture and its reception *within* the political sphere. Against the background of critical history, I propose that the concern to preserve and to discern a genuine textual legacy be seen as a means of legitimating a culture which otherwise founds itself as a copy, a re-enactment, of the Greek city-state. Reappropriation of Athens' literature in its original forms perhaps becomes a strategy for denying that Hellenistic culture is an etiolated copy of Hellenic culture.

V

Hellenistic criticism's obsession with authenticity is most explicit where the reception of the Homeric corpus was concerned. From Diogenes Laertius (5. 80–1) we learn that Demetrius of Phaleron, for instance, whom Tertullian makes in part responsible for the Septuagint version of the Hebrew scriptures (Tert. *Apol.* 18. 5), wrote two books on the *Iliad*, four on the *Odyssey*, and a study *Concerning Homer*. The recovery of any classical Greek author, and especially Homer, constitutes an appropriation of cultural origins that curiously effaces alternative genealogies and that stands as an early example of what Edward Saïd terms 'Orientalism'. While Martin Bernal's *Black Athena* has notoriously, because less convincingly, argued that classical scholarship has concealed its Semitic and oriental influences, he is at least correct to observe that classical Greek texts do recognize the greater antiquity of Egyptian culture and its influence on certain aspects of Greek culture.[59] For example, Plato has Socrates and his interlocutors acknowledge the priority of Egyptian civilization in the *Timaeus* (21e ff.), but, as Dorothy Thompson observes, the Greeks ascribed the invention of

[59] Saïd (1978); Bernal (1987).

writing above all to the Egyptians (cf. the myth of Theuth at *Phaedrus* 274 ff.).[60] However one decides to interpret these references to Egypt—these texts also have literary contexts which may subvert or deny the importance of this culture—it is apparent that Egypt creates an anxiety about originality and influence. Criticism as practised at Alexandria has thus to serve as a strategy not just for establishing the authenticity of individual texts but also for asserting the priority and privilege of the Hellenic culture which produced them.

The concern to discriminate what was originally composed by Homer from the adulterations and additions produced by subsequent poets and performers of the epics is in large part the worry that imitations should be (mis)taken for the original voice, and that the voice of authority, Homer's, should be disseminated amongst pretenders. To guard against this the first librarian and editor of Homer, Zenodotus, engaged in what a modern scholar would recognize as textual criticism—although it is important to bear in mind that textual criticism is only one dimension of the critical project at Alexandria. His work on the *Iliad* reveals a tendency to omit altogether from the text suspected or spurious passages.[61] Apart from outright excision, Zenodotus identified specific bits of a text as being spurious or unacceptable by markings. He invented 'athetization' (*athetismos*), the marking process by which a passage of text is declared illegitimate. Significantly, *athetismos* derives from the verb *atheteō*, which later authors understand as meaning breaking faith with a treaty (cf. Polyb. 8. 36. 5) or as denoting deletion from public documentation.[62] This subsequent understanding of *atheteō* suggests that the scholarly marking of spurious lines might originally have been seen as a denial of the status of the passages in question as public, civic discourse.

Subsequent critics, such as Aristophanes and Aristarchus, were more tolerant of what they regarded as spurious passages. They more conservatively included them in their editions, but they still marked them as suspect. They described lines which were deemed to originate with rhapsodes and in localized editions of the text as

---

[60] Thompson (1994), 68.

[61] e.g. *Il.* 8. 284, 371–2, 385–7, 557–8, 9. 416, 694, 10. 240, 253, 497, 11. 13–14, 78–83, 179–80, 356, 12. 450, 14. 376–7.

[62] Cf. Dion. Hal. *Din.* 9 (δι᾽ ἣν ἕκαστον ἀθετοῦμεν αὐτῶν); Diog. Laert. 7. 34 (εἶτ᾽ ἀντιτεθῆναι αὐτά), cf. 3. 66; Cic *Att.* 6. 9. 3, where ἀθέτησις has the metaphorical sense of the rejection of an idea.

'illegitimate' (cf. *nothos*),[63] and expanded the system of notation to indicate a variety of critical opinions. A dotted *diplē* (*diplē periestigmenē*, $\dot{>}$) was Aristarchus' symbol to mark a disagreement between himself and Zenodotus.[64] Aristophanes of Byzantium used an obelos, a horizontal stroke in the left margin of the verse, to denote spurious lines, and a *diplē* (>) to draw attention to noteworthy points of language or content. Moreover, ancient scholia identify the critical interventions with phrases such as 'Aristarchus suspects' (*diastazei*) where *Odyssey* 7. 311–16 is concerned,[65] or else they declare passages such as *Odyssey* 4. 99 and 5. 105–11 'superfluous' (*perittos*). The scholium on *Odyssey* 5. 247–8 informs the reader that Aristophanes regarded these lines, which describe Odysseus' construction of his raft, as both saying the same thing (cf. *to auto . . . periechein*) and accordingly marked them with a *sigma* (C) and an *antisigma* (Ɔ) respectively (see Turner (1968), 112–18). As Van der Valk observes, the Alexandrians, not liking the repetition of lines, excised what they supposed to be superfluous passages.[66] This scholar also points to the athetization of *Odyssey* 18. 330–2 and 390–3, where the maid Melantho and the suitor Eurymachus use the same words to address the disguised Odysseus: a modern reader would understand the repetition as denoting the speakers' former sexual intimacy (cf. 18. 325). The Alexandrian scholars, furthermore, did not appear to tolerate what they regarded as unnecessary specificity or embellishment, such as the naming of the nymphs who mourn Patroclus (*Il.* 18. 39–49), or the description of the shield of Achilles (*Il.* 18. 483–608).

Textual criticism also concerned itself with the propriety of place in the epics. The scholars and their commentaries identify lines and passages which they consider to have originated elsewhere in the poem and to have been improperly transferred to their current place. So Aristophanes marks *Odyssey* 3. 72–4 with asterisks and obelisks to indicate that they have been dislocated from *Odyssey* 9. 253–5 where they are more appropriately (cf. *oikeioteron*) placed, and the scholium shows that the lines at *Odyssey* 13. 398–401 are marked with asterisks in the belief that they have been moved (cf.

---

[63] Cf. νόθαι δ' ἤνθησαν ἀοιδαί, 'illegitimate songs flourished', Callim. fr. 604.

[64] Grube (1965), 124–5; Reynolds and Wilson (1974), 9–11; Porter (1992), 72.

[65] e.g. *Od.* 11. 568–627, 13. 320–3, 15. 45, 16. 281–98, 17. 475–80, 501–4, 22. 31–3.

[66] Van der Valk (1949), 220.

metenēnegmenoi) from lines 430–3. The concern to remove later interpolations from the Homeric poems needs to be seen in the context of an understanding of the *Iliad* and the *Odyssey* as the very poems which from the fourth century onwards were to be regarded as the ultimate expression of Panhellenism. To possess the Panhellenic poems *par excellence* in their unadulterated form had always been to be able to lay claim to the discourse which historically defined Hellenism and its culture, one which extended beyond the confines of the city-state to comprehend all Greek-speaking peoples. The poems were performed and recited at Panhellenic festivals such as the Panathenaea, and there was an anxiety even then that they should be the texts of their original author. According to fifth-century sources, Pisistratus, as tyrant of Athens, gathered together at Athens the localized texts of the epics, the versions known as *kata poleis* (cf. ps.-Pl. *Hipparch.* 228b). There at Athens he had them edited to remove additions and variants introduced by rhapsodes and also by the various Greek states in an effort to further their local interests.[67] He produced an authorized edition and instituted the Panathenaic Rule, which stipulated that the poems were always to be performed in the same order and in the same way at the Panathenaic Festival, an occasion when the Greek states came together to celebrate Hellenic unity and identity through games and cultural contests.

Where Homer is concerned, the editorial aim of the Alexandrian scholars rehearses the Pisistratean imperative of re-establishing the original Homeric text and thus of delocalizing the poems. The poetry of Homer, possessed in its original form, becomes central to the establishment and definition of what it means to be Hellenic, and particularly Hellenistic, in a post-classical world that is geographically dislocated from the Greek world and whose ruling population is seeking to distinguish itself from the native Egyptian populace. The political, and specifically Panhellenic, motivation behind a number of critical interventions is evident despite George Grube's suggestion that the grounds for the exclusion of lines and passages were occasionally subjective.[68] The scholia remark that the phrase 'in Greece and the midst of Argos' (*kath' Hellada kai meson Argos*) at *Odyssey* 1. 344 is illegitimate (cf. *notha*). What this appears to suggest is an anxiety about distinguishing Argos from

[67] Davison (1962), 228.   [68] Grube (1965), 124.

the rest of Greece, and thus about a questioning of the poem's
Panhellenism. Similarly, Aristarchus athetizes *Iliad* 2. 529–30,
which describes Telamonian Ajax as surpassing the Panhellenes
and the Achaeans with his sword. Again, this passage, and particularly line 530, makes a distinction between the Greeks (cf.
Panhellēnas) as a nation and one particular group, the Achaiens (cf.
Achaious), who should be understood as also among the
Panhellenes. While How and Wells observe in their commentary
on Herodotus that the word '*Hellēnes*' originally and specifically
denoted the tribe of Achilles and only later denoted all Greeks in
contrast with the barbarians, both *Hellada* and *Panhellēnes* appear
to denote the Greeks as a whole. Later, in the Catalogue of the
Ships in book 2 of the *Iliad*, Aristarchus athetizes verse 558, which
mentions the 'phalanges of the Athenians'. What lies behind this is
a belief that either the tyrant Pisistratus or Solon had this line
inserted to advocate Athenian and therefore partisan interests.[69]
Preserving the Panhellenism of the Homeric poems in particular
was thus evidently one of the critical imperatives for the Hellenistic
scholars.

Cultural location is in part also a linguistic process. The
Alexandrians normalize spellings in their texts. They regularize
regional peculiarities with the Ionic alphabet, whereas until the end
of the fifth century, Athenians continued to employ an older alphabet in which long vowels and diphthongs remained undiscrimi-
nated, so that $\epsilon = \epsilon$, $\epsilon\iota$, and η, and $o = o$, ov, and ω.[70] Language is
what defines identity. Philology is a strategy of cultural definition.
Hence the subsequent *Treatise on Hellenism* (*Technē peri hellenis-
mou*), which various sources attest and which Jan Pinborg suggests
grows out of the work of Aristophanes of Byzantium and
Aristarchus, is perhaps to be regarded as more than a work about
linguistic matters: it is a work about Hellenic identity.[71] By nor-
malizing the dialectal forms of the Homeric epics the Alexandrian
scholar-critics also lay claim to the language which had been the
defining feature of autochthony, that is of Greek identity as a
birthright. In seeing language as the foremost criterion of national
identity, the Hellenistic editors follow classical authors.[72] At

---

[69] e. g. Diog. Laert. 1. 48; Plut. *Solon* 10; see N. J. Richardson in Lamberton and
Keaney (1992), 31.

[70] Reynolds and Wilson (1974), 8.   [71] Pinborg (1975), 108–9.

[72] Harris (1989), 116–17.

Histories I. 58 Herodotus insisted that the Greeks had always employed the same tongue, while the fact that the Pelasgians originally spoke a 'barbarian language' (*barbaron glōssan*) and changed their name provided evidence of their origins. At *Panegyricus* 50 Isocrates declared language, specifically Greek, the *sine qua non* of Hellenic identity. Later, in the *Rhetoric*, Aristotle used terms which indicate that his discussion of literary style is decidedly political. 'Speaking Greek' (*to hellēnizein*) is the 'beginning' or 'rule of style' (*archē tēs lexeōs*) (1407ᵃ19–20), and the discussion goes on to stress the importance of using what are literally 'authorized' (*ta kuria*) nouns and verbs (1404ᵇ5–6). Elsewhere, Aristotle identified misuse of language as a form of *barbarismos*, that is the sort of language that non-Greeks might employ (cf. *Soph. el.* 165ᵇ21; *Poet.* 1457ᵇ3–4).

VI

Hellenistic criticism is a mode of cultural dislocation and selection with the aim of assuming what was Hellenic. It is one which, in the description of this chapter, takes place through the physical situation of books in the Mouseion-Library and which treats texts as literal articulations of Hellenism. As part of this process of dissembled dislocation and appropriation, Hellenistic textual scholarship retains the moral, and implicitly political, project which is so central to the classical discriminations of public discourse. This is because following the third century the literature of fifth- and fourth-century Athens is again the school-text of the young citizen.[73] In making this point, I want to suggest that it is necessary to relinquish the idea of Hellenistic *paideia* as the glorious acme of ancient education and culture, as Henri Marrou most notably considers it to be, whether for its development of the curriculum of *engkuklios paideia*, for its technicalities, or for its inclusion of women in intellectual and artistic life.[74] None the less, Marrou concedes that this *paideia* is highly disciplinarian and far from respectful of the individual, even if it emphasized the fashioning of the citizen as an activity parallel to the plastic arts.[75] In early childhood, the *paedagogus* served as moral disciplinarian, while later on

[73] Thompson (1994), 76.   [74] Marrou (1956), 138, 243 ff., 302, and *passim*.
[75] Ibid. 141.

teachers resorted to physical brutality to ensure that their pupils learned their lessons. Teaching took the rather uninspired form of rote learning, repetition, and memorization. Not surprisingly, Hellenistic *paideia* ended up meaning in addition to 'culture' and 'education' also 'punishment' or 'chastisement'.[76]

The more advanced forms of literary culture at Alexandria no less reflect the disciplinarian aspect of Hellenistic *paideia*, especially as the poet and his writing continue to be the community's privileged teacher.[77] But the literary scholarship of the period takes very different forms. Outside Alexandria, others had been and were practising allegorical interpretation (cf. *huponoia* or *allēgoria*) as hermeneutic dislocation, to enable the appropriation of texts in such a manner that they became consonant with any variety of world pictures.[78] Allegory was a mode of reading which originated possibly in the sixth century and involved the cosmological exegesis of poetry; certainly, the Presocratic thinkers like Thales, Xenophanes, Anaxagoras, and Parmenides may be seen as the precursors of the Hellenistic allegorists in their use of poetry and poetic characters to articulate their philosophical ideas.[79] Theagenes of Rhegium, reputed to be the first person to write *about* Homer, is credited with the invention of allegory, while the names of Metrodorus of Lampsacus, Glaucon, and Stesimbrotus are also associated with this form of exegesis.[80] These individuals appear to have employed allegory in order to accommodate the recognition that poets can lie and, in particular, that they might misrepresent the gods.[81] It is in this sense that allegory is a mode of cultural reinscription, one which denies and then replaces the original cultural specificities of a text by disregarding authorial intention. Thus David Dawson proposes that 'Allegory is not so much about the meaning or lack of meaning in texts as it is a way of using texts and their meanings to situate oneself and one's community with respect to society and culture'.[82]

James Tate suggests that allegorism had reached its full develop-

---

[76] Marrou (1956), 220–1; also 201.   [77] Gelzer (1993), 140.

[78] Buffière (1956: 45) identifies ὑπονοία as the oldest word for allegory, cf. Pl. *Resp.* 378d and Xen. *Symp.* 3. 6.

[79] See Buffière (1956), 82–100.

[80] On Theagenes, see Buffière (1956), 103–5, and Pépin (1958), 95; on Metrodorus, see Pépin (1958), 99 and Pl. *Ion* 530c–d.

[81] Cf. Xenoph. DK 21 B 10 and 41; D. A. Russell (1981), 95.

[82] Dawson (1992), 236.

ment in the fifth century and that after this point the backlash began. Plato refers to the inadequacy of reading for the 'under-meanings' (*huponoiai*), so that stories of violence amongst the gods are made to mean other than they ostensibly appear to mean, because children cannot adequately judge between the literal and non-literal meanings (*Rsp.* 378d–e).[83] It would appear that the possibilities for cultural reinscription might be compatible with the Ptolemaic project of social appropriation of Hellenic culture, in particular in the appropriation of a Greek ideal of orderly community as far as the poetic ideal of propriety (*to prepon*) is concerned. The Roman rhetorician Quintilian defines 'allegory' as an extended use of metaphor (Greek '*metaphora*' or Latin '*translatio*') in a text (*Inst.* 8. 6. 14, 9. 2. 46–7), and this account of allegory helps to illuminate the potential social function of the trope. Aristotle speaks of metaphor as involving an 'attribution' (*epiphora*) where the attribution involves a shifting of language, either from genus (cf. *genos*) to species (cf. *eidos*), from species to genus, from species to species, or by analogy (cf. *Poet.* 1457^{b}7 ff.). Influenced by Aristotle, Roman writers treat 'metaphor' as a use of language which involves a *transference* from a natural linguistic usage to another that is less natural either because a proper word is lacking in the latter context or for the sake of literary effect.[84] Allegory, as a continuous use of metaphor, thus constitutes an extended displacement of language; and the spatialization of this process, as a shifting of words from one 'place'—Greek *topos* and Latin *locus*—to another 'place', foregrounds precisely the notion of displacement and transport. (As we shall see, the author of *On the Sublime* will develop this concept of linguistic transport in his treatise.)

As a strategy of reading, allegory enacts on a microcosmic level a displacement of culture. Modern readers tend to regard allegory as a mode of misappropriation and misreading. After all, allegory, as Dawson observes, involves 'using texts and their meanings to situate oneself to one's community with respect to society and culture', in other words to accommodate them.[85] It is beyond this, however, a way of making the other—the foreign, the morally reprehensible, and so on—acceptable to a community, and, consequently, it is a

---

[83] J. Tate (1929), 142.
[84] For *translatio* as *transferred* word, see e.g. *Rhet. Her.* 4. 34; Cic. *De or.* 3. 38. 155, 3. 39. 157; *Orat.* 27. 92; Quint. *Inst.* 8. 6. 6.
[85] Dawson (1992), 236.

mode of discipline. It is also the case that such reinscription has the capacity to efface the Hellenism of what is Hellenic, and this may explain the repudiation of allegorical reading by the Alexandrians, even if the Pergamene scholars and Crates of Mallus subscribe to this mode of reading.[86] From Eustasthius (3. 23[87]) we learn that Aristarchus regarded allegory as a lie. This scholar subscribed to a mode of reception rigorously based on philology, although it is the case that philology is not without its ideological assumptions and philosophical perspectives, as James Porter has suggested.[88] Indeed, by speaking to cultural purity and cultural hegemony, despite an obvious physical displacement of culture in the midst of a barbarian environment as constituted by the native Egyptian community, philological scholarship demonstrates its concern to articulate a view of the world. When in the *Geography* Strabo attests to the Alexandrian antipathy to allegory, he points out that everyone but Eratosthenes, appointed librarian in 246 BCE by Ptolemy III Euergetes, thought that Homeric poetry could be regarded as a philosophical inquiry (cf. *philosophēma*) (Strabo 1. 2. 17). Quite against the contemporary trend for allegorical reading, Eratosthenes directed his attention to the *Odyssey* and the hero's voyage as a geographical document (cf. Strabo 1. 2. 2–3).[89] Poetic appreciation is not the aim of this scholar's work.

The allegorical impulse in places of scholarly enterprise apart from Alexandria highlights the ways in which literary scholarship in the city of the Ptolemies was critical, that is discriminating, and, for the period, to some degree idiosyncratic for being such.

---

[86] Pépin (1958), 168. Porter (1992) argues that Crates' textual scholarship extended beyond the merely linguistic in that his linguistic doctrine presupposes a particular view of the world that would support the characterization of critic as 'architect'. Sextus Empiricus perhaps points to the political dimension of allegory when he attributes to Crates an important distinction between the grammarian and the critic: καὶ γάρ ἐκεῖνος ἔλεγε διαφέρειν τὸν κριτικὸν τοῦ γραμματικοῦ· καὶ τὸν μὲν κριτικὸν πάσης, φησί, δεῖ λογικῆς ἐπιστήμης ἔμπειρον εἶναι, τὸν δὲ γραμματικὸν ἁπλῶς ἐξηγητικὸν καὶ προσῳδίας ἀποδοτικὸν καὶ τῶν τούτοις παραπλησίων εἰδήμονα· παρὸ καὶ ἐοικέναι ἐκεῖνον μὲν ἀρχιτέκτονι τὸν δὲ γραμματικὸν ὑπηρέτῃ, 'He [Crates] said that the critic differs from the grammarian, for the critic must be experienced in the whole of linguistic knowledge, but the grammarian is simply an interpreter of dialects, and explainer of prosody and knowledgeable in things like this. Accordingly, the critic is like the architect and the grammarian, his subordinate (*Math.* 1. 79). According to Sextus Empiricus, the critic is to be something of a master planner, while the grammarian is confined to technicalities and is thus an inferior in literary and linguistic study.

[87] Roemer (1912), 153.   [88] Porter (1992), 73; also Pépin (1958), 170.
[89] Pépin (1958), 169.

Study of the literary text which is distinct from the more obviously biographical and textual constructions of literary authenticity displays the moralistic character of the scholarship of the Mouseion-Library, and also what we might perceive to be its failings. According to the critique that Strabo offers of Eratosthenes' Homeric scholarship in book 1 of his *Geography*, rejection of allegory does not entail a more enlightened or a more acceptable form of literary interpretation as far as we are concerned. It is a reading which uses knowledge as a criterion for judging the value and virtue of poetry, and thus continually accuses its author of ignorance (*agnōsis*) (cf. 1. 2. 25, 1. 2. 35, 1. 3. 3, 1. 3. 18, 1. 3. 22–3), where the more attuned Strabo sees poetic licence or fictionality for the sake of entertainment (cf. 1. 2. 8, 1. 2. 19). Strabo goes on to observe that if Eratosthenes privileges knowledge and facticity as poetic criteria, the latter places his faith in unreliable or insignificant authorities (1. 3. 1), and fails to accept the scientific findings of Archimedes despite being himself a mathematician (1. 3. 11). Above all, this Alexandrian critic—and he is not the only one, as Apollodorus and Demetrius of Scepsis are also found failing in this regard (1. 2. 35 and 1. 2. 38)—ironically demonstrates his own vast ignorance of poetry and its poetics as he faults Homer for his lack of knowledge. Yet Eratosthenes mistakes the specific for the universal in Homer (1. 2 .20), and he wants poetry to be an accurate mirror of a geographical reality.

What motivates and informs the over-literalistic treatment of earlier poetic texts or the rigorous marking of passages with the obelus is the recognition that literature, and particular poetry, may supply the reader with possible models of behaviour: texts are potential paradigms or templates for human life, as they are in the educational programme of Plato's *Republic*. If Strabo reports Eratosthenes as taking the view that poets seek to entertain, rather than to educate (1 .2. 3),[90] he observes that this critic inconsistently applies virtue (*aretē*) as a measure (cf. 1. 2. 12): the latter finds fault with the poets precisely because their texts do not assist the cultivation of virtue.

Eratosthenes' inclination to moralize is one that Alexandrian literary culture espouses in other, more evident ways. Theocritus' *Idylls* 16 and 17 make explicit the way in which Hellenistic poetry

---

[90] On this passage, see E. Asmis in Obbink (1995), 148.

might articulate a political programme as they declare poetry's aim to celebrate the glorious aspects of the divine and human worlds. Callimachus suggests how the post-classical poet might undertake this same project by rewriting his poetic inheritance. In the *Hymn to Zeus* he makes a point of correcting earlier poets for uttering lies about the gods when they speak of the three sons of Cronus each being assigned a different domain by lot: as far as the poet is concerned, Zeus has gained Olympus by virtue of his deeds and strength (59–66). Callimachus resumes the Hesiodic project of articulating the order of things as the order of Zeus, but he more openly concedes the manipulative character of such an enterprise when he declares that if he were to lie (cf. *pseudoimēn*), he would do so in such a way as to persuade his listener (64).

The fate of Sotades of Maronea, writer of a kind of obscene poetry known as *kinaidologos*, poignantly illustrates the role of poetry in speaking with the voice of the political establishment. Athenaeus reports that Sotades possessed an untimely outspokenness (*tēn akiaron parrhēsian*). He abused King Lysimachus when the latter was at Alexandria, and then, in Lysimachus' presence, he verbally assaulted Ptolemy Philadelphus and all the other princes of the cities. Athenaeus attributes to the poet the following abusive and tactless remark regarding Ptolemy's marriage to his sister Arsinoe, 'You are shoving a prick into an unholy eye of a needle'.[91] The story of Sotades tells how Ptolemy had his general Patroclus arrest the poet on the island of Caunus and drown him in a lead jar in the sea (see Ath. 620f–621a). The punishment highlights the risk involved in not conceding to poetry the function of praise, especially where the ruler is concerned, although the *ad hoc* nature of the punishment interestingly suggests that there was no formal structure or process for dealing with verbal transgressors such as Sotades.

If the Hellenistic poet is ideally the spokesman for the divine ruler and his human counterparts, the literary scholar is the moralist who ensures that reading contributes to the development of the reader as a virtuous citizen. He intervenes in the reception of Hellenic textual culture such that it only speaks to what is good and useful for the Greek world that this culture constructs in North Africa. In the *Deipnosophistae*, Athenaeus notes that Callimachus,

[91] εἰς οὐχ ὁσίην τρυμαλιὴν τὸ κέντρον ὠθεῖς (Ath. 14. 621a); some manuscripts have ὠθεῖ, 'he shoves'.

Aristophanes, and the librarians at Pergamum refused to enrol (cf. *anagrapsan*) Alexis' comedy *The Teacher of Profligacy* (*Asōtodidaskalos*) in their catalogues (336d–e). Where Athenaeus employs the verb *anagraphein* to denote the enrolment of works in the lists, others refer to the cataloguing of authors and their works by the verb 'to inscribe' (*engkrinein*) and its participle, 'having been inscribed' (*engkrinthentes*). The *Suda* refers to Dinarchus, one of the canonical Ten Attic Orators, as one of those who has been selected along with Demosthenes (*suda*, s.v. 'Dinarchus'), while Photius informs us that Phrynichus 'judged (*engkrinei*) Aeschines . . . to be amongst the best' (*Bibl.* 20ᵇ25).⁹² The use of *engkrinein* is significant: it acknowledges an indebtedness to Plato, who insisted that the leaders of the ideal state must select out (cf. *engkriteon*) fine stories and persuade nurses and mothers to tell only these discriminated stories (*engkrithentas*) to children (*Resp.* 377c).⁹³ *Engkrinein* points to the moralistic dimension of the Alexandrian canon.

Where the process denoted by *engkrinein* connotes only the moral dimension of librarianship, this aspect of literary scholarship is actually evidenced in editorial activity. The librarian-scholar athetizes lines not only because they appear 'illegitimate' but also on the basis that they cause offence by being indecent (*aprepēs*) or improper or vile (*eu.telēs*).⁹⁴ Plutarch is one of the most useful witnesses to this regulatory enterprise. In his treatise *How to Study Poetry* the Roman author provides important evidence for the moral aspect of Alexandrian criticism as he rehearses the anxiety about *aprepeia*. At 25e he observes that the contemporary young reader of poetry must be discerning and prepared to reject what he reads if it does not represent appropriate behaviour. He then proceeds to cite *Iliad* 16. 97–100, where Achilles prays that all the Trojans and Greeks may die and that he together with Patroclus may destroy Troy. Plutarch quotes four lines which Zenodotus and Aristarchus had athetized, perhaps on the basis of concerns about male homosexuality, as Grube proposes.⁹⁵ Later, at 26f–27a he makes apparent the precedents for his discriminations when he informs his reader that Aristarchus excised (*exeile*) from his edition

---

⁹² References from Pfeiffer (1968), 206 n. 2.

⁹³ To translate ἐγκρινεῖν and ἐγκρινθέντες Quintilian uses the phrases *in numerum redegerunt* and *in ordinem* [*redegerunt*]; see e.g. *Inst.* 1. 4. 3, 10. 1. 27, 10. 1. 54, 10. 1. 59.

⁹⁴ Roemer (1912), 316 ff.; Van der Valk (1949), 120; Dawson (1992), 67.

⁹⁵ Grube (1965), 125.

Iliad 9. 458–61, which present Phoenix's account of what anger is and the sort of deeds that men might do out of anger. Plutarch states that the reason for the excisions is not because they appeared to be later additions but due to Aristarchus' fear (*phobētheis*) regarding the effects of this passage. He observes that Homer then depicts Meleager as someone who is angry at the citizens of his community but subsequently soothes his anger and criticizes his own emotions (*ta pathē*). According to Plutarch, the poet praises this transformation of Meleager from anger to a peaceable state as good (*kalon*) and beneficial (*sumpheron*) (27a). What this reading of the Meleager-episode in book 9 of the *Iliad* does is articulate Aristarchus' anxiety about irrational emotions and passions that have the capacity to threaten order and harmony within the community. By highlighting Meleager's change of heart as 'good' and 'beneficial', Plutarch indicates that absence of anger is to be preferred in the community depicted in the poetic text, although he himself prefers the Homeric scene of instruction.

Following Alexandrian antecedents, Plutarch also expresses his own anxieties about *Odyssey* 6. 244–5, lines which depict Nausicaa telling her handmaidens that she hopes that Odysseus might stay among the Phaiacians so that she can marry him (27b). The Roman critic notes that Nausicaa demonstrates a boldness (*thrasus*) and lack of restraint (*akolasia*) which is blameworthy after seeing a stranger for such a short time. He articulates what he regards as the anxieties of Aristarchus, who first athetized both lines, although he was uncertain (cf. *diastazei*) about the first of them. Plutarch goes on to censure *Odyssey* 18. 282, which presents Odysseus perceiving Penelope to have persuaded the suitors to grant her numerous gifts and to have charmed their hearts. The critic censures the interpretation of this line which has the Homeric hero rejoice at the prospect of so much wealth, but he approves of an interpretation which draws an implicit contrast between the former's confidence and the suitors' false confidence (27c). Again, Plutarch here discusses a line which had caused the Alexandrian critics to worry. The scholia to Homer inform us that the line is 'vile/worthless' (*euteles*), using the term which is synonymous with impropriety (*aprepēs*), and that Aristophanes bracketed it with lightning rods (cf. *keraunion*).

Plutarch's importance is to draw retrospective attention to the concern of Alexandrian criticism to identify and excise what is improper (*aprepēs*) from the text of Homer. But even independently of the Roman scholar, it is evident that one concern of Alexandrian scholarship was to regulate sexuality through its representation. This is especially apparent in the athetization of the adultery of Ares and Aphrodite (*Od.* 8. 266 ff.). The scholia specifically inform us that a number of the 'transcriptions' (*en eniois antigraphois*), the scholarly editions which include those of the Alexandrians, omit *Odyssey* 8. 333–42. These lines depict Apollo and Hermes entertaining the possibility of the latter sleeping with the bound Aphrodite and for this reason they appear to be 'improper' (*aprepes*) (cf. 'through demonstrating impropriety' (*dia to aprepeian emphainein*)). It is in part the reason for the decision of Aristophanes and Aristarchus to place the end (*peras*) of the *Odyssey* at 23. 296, even if an anxiety to avoid repetition may also play a part in this decision as Odysseus rehearses the account of his adventures here. Nausicaa's dramatization of the hypothetical speech put into the mouth of a Phaeacian at *Odyssey* 6. 275–88 seems to reiterate the concern about modesty inasmuch as the passage shows the heroine entertaining thoughts of marriage to someone she has just met. Dawson notes that Aristarchus athetizes *Iliad* 24. 130–2, owing to his abhorrence at incest, here between mother and son, Thetis and Achilles.[96]

Beyond this, Nausicaa's imagined speech is an instance of the discourse of blame (*oneida*), which, as we saw in previous chapters, is regarded as being disruptive of order in the community and its identity. Notably, in the *Hymn to the Baths of Pallas* Callimachus depicts the goddess Athena commanding the mother of Tiresias to take back her angry words when her son is blinded for mistakenly seeing the deity and a nymph bathing. Athena declares that it is the laws of Cronus, rather than any action of hers, which have resulted in Tiresias' punishment, and thereby preserves her reputation as a bestower of good things (97–102). The imperative to avert blame, and so to protect name, is also apparent from other passages of commentary. Aristophanes and Aristarchus athetize *Iliad* 16. 261, where the Myrmidons are compared to boys who taunt (cf. *kertomeontes*) bees. Moreover, Aristophanes and those who follow him athetize *Odyssey* 11. 435–42/3, where Odysseus blames the plottings of women, namely Helen and Clytemnestra, for the death of many men. Zenodotus athetizes *Iliad* 2. 231–4, a section of

[96] Dawson (1992), 68.

Thersites' rebuke of Agamemnon, while Aristarchus athetizes Odysseus' response to Thersites, *Iliad* 2. 252–6, a passage which characterizes the latter's discourse as blame (cf. *oneidizōn*, 255; *kertomeōn*, 256).

The critical treatment of the Thersites episode also demonstrates a concern with the depiction of transgressions against authority, and this concern is elsewhere evident. The scholia inform us that *Odyssey* 11. 315–16 are athetized since, in saying that Otus and Ephialtes placed Pelion on Ossa, they depict an impossible event (cf. *adunatoi*). Of course, what they also represent is the consummate act of insubordination. This concern about the order of things may also be apparent in the decision to athetize *Odyssey* 4. 158–60—which have Pisistratus flatter Menelaus as someone who speaks with the 'mind of a god'—as *perittoi*, 'superfluous'. While Van der Valk quarrels with this athetization, warning of the need for critics, ancient and modern, to recognize that archaic culture expected deference and respect even between individuals of the same social status,[97] I suggest that it is precisely the comparison of a mortal to a god which causes the Hellenistic critics consternation. So, likewise, Zenodotus replaces *Iliad* 3. 423–6 with a single line— 'she sat opposite lord Paris'—since it is unfitting that the goddess Aphrodite should fetch a chair for the mortal Helen.[98]

From Athenaeus, the author who depicts the conversations of sophists at dinner, we learn that the Alexandrian critics wrote a number of commentaries on eating customs and food. There are references to a *Glossary of Cooking (Opsartutikai)* by Artemidorus, a pupil of Aristophanes (Ath. 387d). While it is tempting to characterize this concern with culinary and dietary matters as a dimension of the obsession with arcane and exotic learning, this may not wholly account for it. It is also the case that food and drink are traditionally associated with a discourse of order and virtue, in for instance the work of the archaic poet Xenophanes (cf. poem 1, DK 21 B 1) and in Xenophon's *Cyropaedia* (e.g. 1. 2. 8, 1. 2. 11–12, 1. 3. 4–5, 1. 5. 12, 4. 5. 4). This dimension of the concern with food and drink manifests itself in the literary analysis of individuals like Callimachus and Artemidorus. Athenaeus observes that the grammarian Aristarchus bracketed (*perigraphōn*) the lines, 'where have the boasts which you uttered in Lemnos gone when you were eat-

<hr />

[97] Van der Valk (1949), 199.   [98] See Dawson (1992), 67.

ing much meat and drinking mixing-bowls full of wine?' (= *Il.* 8. 229–31). The reasons behind the critic's excision are that the passage depicts the Greeks boasting after they have eaten meat and that boasting, along with ridicule and jesting, spring from an inclination towards falsehood (*pseudēs*) and away from common sense (*gnōmē*) (Ath. 39d–e). The moral concern of Alexandrian criticism may also be expressed in Zenodotus' insistence when commenting on *Iliad* 9.225 that Homer's description of a feast as 'equal' (*eisē*) indicates that it is 'good' (*agathē*) (Ath. 12d). Athenaeus proceeds to offer an etymology of the idea of the 'equal meal' as a 'good meal'. He surmises that because food was scarce for primitive men, they used to compete and fight for it: this led them into 'wickedness' (*atasthalia*), which Athenaeus traces to the word 'feast' (*thalia*) as the originating scene of such behaviour. Athenaeus' elaboration of Zenodotus presents the latter as being concerned to point out the orderliness of the society depicted in Homeric poetry—'equal' (*eisē*) suggests 'good' because without strife and fairly distributed—but it is also the case that the Hellenistic critic is not always sufficiently aware of the order of things. The author of the *Deipnosophistae* criticizes him for being unaware that the word 'feast' (*dais*) can only ever refer to a meal shared by human beings and not a meal consumed by animals or birds (12f).[99]

VII

In this chapter I have examined how the critical impetus to discriminate and to select certain discourses rather than a plenitude of others—despite claims to a totalizing Hellenism—results in dehistoricized traditions and their literary canons. Hellenistic criticism and literary scholarship are activities literally dislocated from their Hellenic origins; none the less, these activities constitute a series of appropriations, further dislocations, and reconstructions of genealogy in order to deny their atopicality and to refound selectively the culture of the classical Athenian city-state in North Africa. And

---

[99] Here the Hellenistic critics unusually engaged in allegorical interpretation, which, as Donald Russell suggests, helps to endow otherwise offensive or trivial material with important meaning. Athenaeus reports that Callimachus offered an allegorical interpretation of Aphrodite hiding Adonis in a lettuce-bed. The Alexandrian critic suggested that the constant eating of lettuce leads to impotence (Ath. 69c); cf. D. A. Russell (1981), 95.

they do so in such a way as to insist somewhat paradoxically that dislocation can confer originative status. The Alexandrian scholar-critics re-create a scenario in which texts are sacralized, and poet and king work in the service of the gods in the Mouseion-Library; and through this they establish the political and cultural identity of the Hellenistic world. Where the Hellenistic movement is involved, the post-Aristotelian discourse on literature is a language about reception that seeks to fashion alternative, idealized political worlds, that is to transform the Egyptian Alexandria into the textualized Greek city-state. There is a sense in which the discourse of reception is also and simultaneously about literary creation. The examination of the various scholarly activities which took place in the Alexandrian Mouseion-Library suggests the way in which identity and text become solipsisms. Biographical study confirms that the text is a reflection of the author's life, and vice versa, while editorial scholarship assumes that the audience will be formed by the text it reads. Taken to its logical conclusion, Hellenistic scholarship seems to suggest that there will eventually be an intersubjectivity between the now long-dead author and his contemporary reader, where the former through his writings informs and constructs the identity of the latter. It is above all in this sense that the Alexandrian intellectual enterprise is about the re-creation of an earlier Greece.

5

From Criticism to Self-Censorship, from Republic to Empire

> What is excluded as irrelevant by a discipline is designated as 'criminal'—*discernere* and *cerno* are the same at their roots. Discrimination normalizes not only by homogenizing and categorizing but also by eliminating and excluding those factors that wastefully 'unbalance' the 'delicate harmony' of the mind and 'society', as the case may be.
>
> Paul Bové (1986), 77

III

It is possible to write a narrative of literary criticism which stresses the continuities between the Greek critical enterprise and the Roman one. The texts I have examined up to this point show that critical activity in the sense of a process of literary *discrimination* and *judgement* is the norm rather than the exception where ancient communities are concerned. In the pre-Roman period, literary criticism is an activity that is imposed from outside upon the process of literary production by leaders, legislators, and their representatives and from within by the very authors who participate in the production of literary material. In the case of Plato and Aristotle, it is the writers of literary texts who themselves attempt to constrain the work of other authors, while the Alexandrian Mouseion-Library endeavours to formalize literary norms and ideals which the critic-poets also enact in their own work. Working from this background, this chapter seeks to demonstrate that this activity is not one confined to Hellenic culture. It examines the specificities of criticism in the Roman period in particular, to show how they articulate ideals of discursive order and constraint both around and against a rehistoricized Greek past and shifting contemporary political ideals.

I shall bring together a series of texts from the republican and imperial periods to (re)situate Rome within the history of criticism. In particular, I call into question the largely exaggerated portraits of the republic as a period of largely unbridled freedom of expression and of the empire as a period of unmitigated repression, and of repression as unmitigatingly negative. I show that, despite the nostalgic image of republican Rome produced by imperial writers and by modern scholars, this Rome observes various constraints on public discourse both in legal codes and in custom; and that where, according to modern scholarship, the absence of *libertas* at Rome has been taken as a sign of political dysfunction in the age of the emperors, a rather more qualified portrait of the constraints produced in this period is necessary. The material I examine in the later part of this chapter reveals that at imperial Rome the silences are not always imposed involuntarily and from without. Self-criticism becomes a necessity as authors and citizens regulate their own language as a strategy for survival in response to the external pressures that mark the change from republic to empire at Rome.

II

At Rome, reputation is first and foremost a verbal construction. This understanding is one that Cicero reflects in the preface to book 4 of the *Tusculan Disputations* when he cites Cato's *Origines* as the authority for believing that it was customary for Rome's ancestors to sing the praises and virtues of 'illustrious men' ('clari homines'). Song is perceived to have an important function: first, as a medium for providing a subtle form of instruction, and secondly, as a palliative for its audience (*Tusc.* 4. 2. 3). One of the grounds on which Cicero defends the claim of the poet Archias to Roman citizenship is the social value of his writing. Throughout the *Pro Archia* the author extols the benefit of poetry as a discourse that celebrates the fame and glory of the nation and its heroes. Poetry surpasses statues (12. 30), such that emperors cultivate their verse authors and the 'shrines of the Muses', no doubt a reference to the idea of the Mouseion (esp. 8. 18–9. 19, 11. 27, 12. 31).

The central importance of language, literary or otherwise, in the production of how society might think and speak about its members is, I suggest, what determines that republican *libertas* has to be a qualified 'freedom' or 'liberty'.[1] Certainly, according to Charles Wirzbuski,[2] *libertas* is defined in relation to an alternative political condition, connoting freedom from despotic mastery, while, according to Mason Hammond, it is a contingent condition, specifically a concomitant of orderly government.[3] On the basis of these understandings of *libertas*, republican Rome has to be viewed as a period of *relative* freedom of expression rather than of absolute freedom, and as a site in which public discourse was discriminated as being useful and/or permissible or, alternatively, as damaging and so impermissible as far as the stability and well-being of the overall community were concerned.

Criticism is founded in part in, and subsequently continues to inhabit, the legal arena, and at Rome this is particularly the case where defamation of the individual is concerned. According to later sources, the Twelve Tables, the oldest and most authoritative body of legislation at Rome, set prohibitions on language which was deemed to constitute libel or slander, and made death the punishment for such verbal misconduct (cf. Cic. *Rep.* 4. 12; August. *DCD* 2. 9)—the Twelve Tables (unlike twentieth-century legislation) did not distinguish the two categories of defamation from each other. The treatment of defamatory statements in the Twelve Tables occurs in Table VIII, a section of the legislation which concerns itself with injuries ('iniuriae') against the person, his reputation, and his property. Justinian's *Institutes* also prohibits oral and literary defamation under the category of injuries ('iniuriae'). Following the Twelve Tables (cf. VIII, 1 and 4, Crawford) and (as we shall see) the *Rhetorica ad Herennium*, book 4 of the *Institutes* legislates against injuries which include physical assault, e.g. punching, beating, theft of goods, and sexual threat as well as the composition and publication of any pamphlet ('libellum') and poetry ('carmen') which leads to the lessening of an individual's reputation by defamation (cf. 'ad infamiam alicuius') (*Inst. Iust.* 4. 4. 1). It becomes evident that the law on injuries is only for the benefit of citizens, their bodies, goods, and reputations, as a later section of the discussion reveals that *iniuria* cannot be committed against slaves (cf. 4. 4. 3). In classifying as injury the acts of following young men and women and of making threats to their

---

[1] On this point, see Masters in Elsner and Masters (1994), 170.
[2] Wirzbuski (1950), 1–14; Hammond (1963), 93.
[3] Hammond (1963), 94–5.

modesty (*pudicitia*) (e.g. *Inst.* Iust. 4. 4. 1), the law suggests that injury is also concerned with forms of behaviour which may cause the modesty and so the reputation of the victim to be called into question by others. Elsewhere in the *Institutes*, however, the concern to protect the reputation of citizens is expressed in the punishments set out against over-eager litigants in the section which discusses 'the penalty for those who litigate rashly' ('De poena temere litgantium', 4. 16). This law seeks to constrain malicious and excessive litigation, in an attempt to place a check on monetary penalties, and on oaths binding conscience, and also to stem the 'fear of notoriety' ('metus infamiae').

Justinian's *Codex*, another late imperial collection of legal pronouncements,[4] identifies a number of proscribed slurs—namely, calling a freedman a slave (9. 35. 9), falsely calling your grandmother a slave (9. 35. 10), and falsely calling a man an informer (9. 35. 3). These categories of prohibited language are clearly designed to safeguard the reputation of the citizen *qua* citizen—to call someone a slave is precisely to call that person's civic identity into question. They also insist on the idea that reputation is something to be protected: thus any perception that people are going around calumniating others or that it is all right to do so is dispelled by the action against informing. In the *Digest* of 533 CE, a legal compendium based on material that was at the time of publication more than 300 years old and ranged from Labeo (50 BCE–10 CE) to Ulpian (233 CE),[5] the law against libel comes under the heading of the Cornelian law on Injuries (*lex Cornelia de iniuriis*), which incidentally also contains prohibitions against the use of magic with a view to harm or kill.[6] It suggests what sort of offensive language the phrase 'by insult to the ears they violate' ('convicio aures . . . violent', i.e. *Rhet. Her.* 4. 25. 35) might constitute, for it identifies obscenity in particular as an injury ('iniuria', 47. 10. 15. 21).[7]

The broad range of behaviours covered by 'injury' in these legal texts proposes that language has potentially the same status as physical violence or theft, and this idea is corroborated by other Roman sources which elaborate the rather terse statements attributed to the Tables. The *Rhetorica Ad Herennium* provides us with

[4] Hammond (1963), 9.   [5] Birks and McLeod (1987), 16.
[6] See Butler and Owen (1914), 3–4.
[7] W. A. Hunter (1876), 3; see the *Digest* edition of Mommsen and Kreuger (1985).

the following text: 'Injuries are what violate the body by beating or what violate anyone's life by an insult to the ears or by some base allegation'.[8] Injury lies in damage not only to the body; it is also harm caused to the ear, and to an individual's reputation. This notion of injury confirms the perception that words, like sticks and stones, can also do harm and that verbal damage is either on a par with, or else is to be located on a spectrum of harms including bodily hurt. The phrase 'by insult to the ears' ('convicio auris') is noteworthy because, unlike the following prohibition on defamation, a form of language specifically directed at or against an individual, it implies that the offending discourse need not be deliberately intended to harm the named individual in order to offend. There is also evidence outside formal legal texts of a wariness of obscenity. Nonius (357. 12) attributes to Lucilius the following statement, ' "Obscenity" denotes also badly spoken . . . "Let the king of the gods turn away foul words" '.[9] In his commentary on Virgil, Servius observes that Ennius spoke 'equally obscene words' ('verba aeque obscena') to his detractors ('carinentes') when he provides a gloss on the verb 'to detract/carp' (*carinare*) (ad *Aen.* 8. 361).

Tenney Frank expresses disbelief that the Twelve Tables could have imposed the death penalty for libellous verses.[10] His response suggests an eagerness to uphold the view of republican *libertas* as ensuring individual freedom where the spoken and written word are concerned. It is possible to produce evidence for such a position. If Cicero argues for poetry's role in immortalizing great deeds in the *Pro Archia*, he might be cited as support for an idealized characterization of pre-imperial *libertas*. His references to legislation suggest that the republic is a community in which regulation speech is minimal. In the *Pro Sexto Roscio Amerino* 20. 55 he states that it benefits the state to have many accusers (*accusatores*) as a check on boldness (of speech) or *audacia* and to ensure that the guilty are brought to trial. He does concede, however, that there must be checks in turn on the accusers to contain their authority and influence, and he cites the Remmian law (*lex Remmia*), which

---

[8] 'iniuriae sunt quae aut pulsatione corpus aut convicio auris aut aliqua turpitudine vitam cuiuspiam violent' (*Rhet. Her.* 4. 25. 35).

[9] ' "obscenum" significat et male dictum . . . "Deum rex avertat verba obscena" ' (Lucil. 29. 858 Warmington).

[10] Frank (1927), 110.

penalized legal accusation of the innocent (i.e. *calumnia*). In the *Pro Cluentio* 110, the author recalls that Sulla curtailed the tribune's voice with the result that the people became unaccustomed to the 'old custom' ('vetera consuetudo') of public speech. The surrender of this traditional outspokenness had a bad effect, for when oratory made its return, Quinctus was for a time able to deceive the people, who had meanwhile become unused to oratory.

But Cicero is anything but a supporter of gratuitous slander. He elsewhere demonstrates awareness that Roman law prohibits language which is slanderous. In book 4 of the *Tusculan Disputations* he cites the sanction in the Twelve Tables against defamatory song, 'None the less, they sanction by law that it [i.e. defamatory song] should not occur to the injury of another person'.[11] In *On the Republic* 4. 12 (cf. August. *DCD* 2. 9), Cicero writes that the Twelve Tables counted amongst capital crimes the singing or composition of a song ('carmen') which caused defamation or insult to another individual. Cornutus, in his comment on Persius, *Satire* 1. 123, provides further confirmation that slander is regarded as a serious crime when he notes the warning that 'whoever uttered a slander in public would be beaten [to death] with clubs'.[12] Scholars have suggested that the *carmen* mentioned in the law must refer to a magical spell, preferring to identify defamation as articulated in the Twelve Tables as sorcery. They note, for instance, that Pliny refers to the prohibition against casting spells on crops and fruit (*HN* 28. 4. 17–18; cf. also Hor. *Sat.* 2. 1. 82). They observe that the verb *occentare* ('enchant'), which appears in Pliny, has the same sense as the verbs *incantare* and *excantare*, which both denote magical incantation.[13] Hendrickson, however, notes that Festus thinks that *occentare* has the sense of 'to do a verbal injury' (*convicium facere*),[14] while Momigliano rejects the idea that the verb has a magical sense when it occurs in appeals in Plautus (e.g. *Curc.* 145; *Merc.* 408; *Persa* 569).[15]

---

[11] 'quamquam id . . . ne liceret fieri ad alterius iniuriam, lege sanxerunt' (*Tusc.* 4. 2. 4).

[12] 'cautum est ut fustibus feriretur qui publice invehebatur' (Cornutus on Pers. *Satire* 1. 123 Jahn, p. 276).

[13] Cf. Van Gigch (1852).

[14] ' "Occentassit" antiqui dicebant quod nunc *convicium* fecerit dicimus' (Festus, p. 190. 32–4 Lindsay); cf. Hendrickson (1925), 289.

[15] Momigliano (1942), 121.

Thus, in contrast to Frank, other scholars draw attention to the severity of the punishment set out in the texts of Cicero and Cornutus, and they thereby qualify republican *libertas* by drawing attention to the significance of this severity. Arnaldo Momigliano emphasizes the disparity between the punishments for libel and slander in Athens and Rome and explains this in terms of the élitist and exclusivist nature of Roman law. If the penalty in Athens is only five drachmas, this was because the law did not distinguish between citizens according to social rank, while the death penalty in early Roman law suggests the greater importance placed upon the reputation and standing of the citizen who is to be understood as someone of rank.[16] There is a sense in which the imperative to protect reputation might be seen as largely due to the fact that the individual's name bore a relationship to his standing and authority in society. The idea of censorship, literally 'the counting' (*census* from *censeo*), at Rome offers support for this understanding of the Twelve Tables. The office of the censor, established in 443 or 437 BCE, oversaw the division of citizens into property classes according to their wealth, and, in addition to this, also had the authority to degrade people for actions deemed to constitute bad citizenship, for instance, cowardice in battle, misuse of public money, and cruelty. In his punitive function, the censor pronounced the offender infamous (*infamis*) and so held to be disgraced as if he had been sentenced in a lawcourt.[17] As discourses which would potentially impugn a citizen's reputation and perhaps his status, defamation and slander thus presume to function in what is literally a censorious role and without official sanction.

Less inclined than even Momigliano to play down the legislation against defamation is E. H. Warmington. This scholar regards the penalty as indicating the gravity with which defamation was regarded. Calling into question the good name of a citizen is a serious crime precisely because it constituted a 'breach of public peace' rather than a private wrong.[18] Warmington's interpretation implies that the disparagement of the identity of a particular citizen has a synechdochic implication: a threat or harm to the identity of the individual figures a threat or harm to the identity of the Roman citizen in general, and so to the whole citizen body. Support for this interpretation comes from Paulus who states that the reputation of

[16] Ibid. 122.   [17] Cary (1954), 115–16.   [18] Warmington (1938), 474 n.

each individual must be protected from base songs ('turpia carmina') in the interests of public discipline.[19] According to Momigliano and Warmington, the law on injurious song (*carmen*) is concerned with the interests of those with reputations to protect because their interests are not distinct from those of the state.

Whereas the 'literary' is a category which might provide what would otherwise be verbal 'harm' with a defence (as we shall see in Chapter 8), in Roman law the literary nature or context of verbal injury was not a mitigating factor. The author of the *Rhetorica ad Herennium* produces as a hypothetical example of an 'absolute issue' ('absoluta [constitutio]') Accius' suit against a mime who abused him by name on stage (*Rhet. Her.* 1. 14. 24). Accius lodges his suit for injury; the mime actor defends himself on the right to use the name of someone (cf. 'nominari eum') who has given his name to a dramatic composition. Later, in book 2 of the work the reader learns that Publius Mucius Scaevola condemned the mime, but also learns that Gaius Caelius let off the man who had slandered by name the poet Lucilius (cf. 'C. Caelius iudex absolvit iniuriarum eum qui Lucilium poeta in scaena nominatim laeserat', 2. 13. 19). The author of *Rhetorica ad Herennium* notably figures the poet as defamed, rather than as defamer, and discredits slander by associating it with a mime actor, a figure who signifies loose morals and therefore un-Roman behaviour. Aulus Gellius tells that the poet Naevius wrote two plays, the *Hariolus* and the *Leontes*, when he was imprisoned on account of his continual tirade of insults ('ob assiduam maledicentiam') and shameful invective ('probra') against the leaders of the state in the manner of Greek poets ('de Graecorum poetarum') (Gell. *NA* 3. 3. 15). *Maledicentia*, literally 'what is badly said', is insult, abuse, bad-mouthing, and so to the detriment of its subjects; it stands in opposition to praise, which is to the credit of its subjects. It is worth noting that at *NA* 7. 8. 5 Aulus Gellius reports a tradition that Naevius wrote a verse against Scipio Africanus portraying him as being dragged away from a girlfriend by his own father. According to Gellius, Naevius charged one of the republic's heroes with sexual misconduct. In the earlier text (*NA* 3. 3. 15, above), this author compares Naevius' outspokenness to that of the Greek poets, implicitly invoking iambists like Archilochus and Hipponax.

---

[19] 'interest enim publicae disciplinae opinionem uniuscuiusque a turpis carminis infamia vindicare' (Paulus, *Sent.* 5. 4. 15); cited in Hendrickson (1925), 289.

Attempting to preserve the pre-imperial Rome as the *locus* of unhindered expression, Frank has suggested that the punishment of Naevius was unusual and there is a sense in which its frequent citation and the manner of its citation by scholars would seem to indicate as much.[20] But the weight of the evidence argues against this idealizing view. However, if, as H. D. Jocelyn has persuasively argued, it is unlikely that the migrant Naevius would actually have dared to criticize the powerful élite, the literary anecdotes, none the less, provide a valuable representation of the anxieties surrounding verbal licence.[21] We see that literary slander is portrayed as inexcusable, while Greek literature comes to stand for lack of restraint and moderation, perhaps *licentia*, as it does also in Cicero, *Pro Flacco*. 7. 16 and later (as we shall see) at Augustine, *City of God* 2. 9. The Greek past is set against the republican present to characterize slander as an un-Roman, and thus barbarian, discourse.

III

Evidence of constraints against defamatory discourse in the republic establishes an important subtext for the verbal constraints and silences of the empire, for this legal framework calls into question the starkness of the contrast between these two Romes as far as verbal freedoms are concerned. It is against this background that I want to reject the stereotypical portrait of imperial repression and to offer instead a redescription of verbal regulation in the empire as a supplementing and tightening of pre-existing constraints on public language. Beyond this, I intend to demonstrate that imperial repression has complicated agencies. It is not the case that the state and its agents alone silence political comment, for authors to some extent reinforce the critical imperative even as they engage in opposition to the state. What authorial response to the state control of language produces, as we shall see, is a self-censorship in the form of either subtle or else explicit discrimination of its own voices— either by assimilation or by opposition—from that of the state's official one.

Horace is one of the first poets to identify himself, and to be identified, with the Augustan era, and it is with him that literary

---

[20] Cf. Momigliano (1942), 120.   [21] Jocelyn (1969), esp. 34.

discrimination seeks not only to regulate the discourse of others but also takes the form of self-criticism. Horace's carefully fashioned departure for the history of literary criticism is produced against a background of earlier critical authorities. Historians of Roman literature have often pointed to the poet's appropriation of Hellenistic postures—for instance, the persona of the poet-priest—but they have not so far drawn attention to the broader implications for Horatian criticism of a Hellenistic culture where literary production occurs in the service of the state and its leader, the king, and where it is an expression of the authority of the state, fashioned after the classical Greek state. The poet's *vates-persona* is one which marks him as the individual who has assumed the authority to determine which texts may or may not circulate in the public domain with the approval of the community's political figurehead. At *Satire* 1. 10. 74 ff. Horace puts on display the privilege and authority granted by imperial patronage. He declares his preference for an élite audience, namely the few readers ('paucis lectoribus'), rather than the masses of the vulgar games (cf. 'vilibus in ludis') (74–5). The poet's ideal audience is the select and knowledgeable Augustan circle, which counts amongst its members the *princeps*, who is named as 'Octavius', his deputy Maecenas, and their learned cultural spokesmen, Virgil, Pollio, Bassus, Macer, and of course, Horace himself (cf. 'doctos' and 'amicos', 87). This is the society which has no place for the sycophantic and chatty boor, who attempts to insinuate himself by latching on to the poet in *Satire* 1. 9.

In keeping with the tradition in which Greek writers, such as Plato and Isocrates, for instance, employ epistolary literature to dispense didactic material and advice to leaders,[22] Horace uses *Epistles* book 2 to fashion his critical identity and its authority. In *Epistle* 2. 1 to Augustus he presents criticism as a mode of literary discrimination for the benefit of the state and its leaders. He makes explicit the link between the ruler and himself, as a writer, with the opening address to Augustus in lines 1–10.[23] In the sycophantic rhetoric of *captatio benevolentiae* the poet acknowledges that poetry is a hindrance to matters of state and a further burden to a busy ruler such as the addressee. But it is the case that, amongst other things, *Epistle* 2. 1 sets out a defence of poetry as a tool of state

---

[22] Atkins (1934), ii. 61.
[23] For a discussion of Hor. *Epist.* 2. 1. 1–4, see Ahl (1984*b*), 58.

authority. The emperor Augustus is a figure parallel to the poet, who observes that the *princeps* embellishes the state with morality (cf. 'moribus ornes') and emends it with laws (cf. 'legibus emendes') (ll. 2–3). The state is akin to a poetic text that a poet might adorn and correct. *Epistle* 2. 1 later reinforces the idea that art has a political dimension, as Horace implies that the appropriation of other cultures to one's own is a form of political domination. He alludes to Rome's acquisition of all that is best in Greek literature at lines 27–30, while his comment that 'captive Greece . . . took captive [Rome]' at line 156 indicates that the domination is not one-sided but mutual.

Rome's élite, the *equites*, and no doubt the emperor watch over the poet's activity as authorized judges and critics (cf. *Sat.* 1. 10. 76; also *Epist.* 2. 1. 19, 84–5). But in turn the literary artist is the community's overseer and teacher. The citizen is ideally an individual who will be useful to the city (cf. 'utilis urbi', *Epist.* 2. 1. 124), and the poet will help him to be such by educating him and regulating his behaviour. The poet regulates the discourse of Roman youth, discriminating in the service of morality and taste in his community. He turns his audience's ear away from obscene speech ('*obscenus . . . sermo*'), a form of prohibited discourse (126–7), and he is the adjudicator of envy and anger ('irae', 129).[24] If this is a curious statement, given Horace's identity as a satirist and given the association of satire and diatribe, the poet none the less presents himself as the judge and guardian of public discourse. He is a moralist (128–30); he teaches by example, both his own and that set by others (128–31); he supplies advice regarding the institutions of marriage and religion (132–5); and he provides the prayers which assist the state (136–44).

Horace underscores the sense in which his role is constructed by and constructs political authority with his closing allusion to Alexandrian, and especially Callimachean, poetic doctrine as he praises the 'poem which is woven with a fine thread ('tenui deducta poemata filo', *Epist.* 2. 1. 225; cf. 179–86). Moreover, he gives the poet's activities a historical perspective which serves to align them with the state's government. He recalls the Fescinnine licence ('Fescennina . . . licentia', 145), which permitted playful insults to be uttered on festival occasions until the jokes turned savage and

---

[24] Rudd (1989), 98–9.

began to threaten the reputation of honest families. In response, the community brought in legislation which punished anyone who made another the subject of a wicked song ('malum . . . carmen'), and so poetry returned to its function of praising ('ad bene dicendum') and delighting its readers ('delectandumque') (145–55; cf. on 'mala carmina', *Sat.* 2. 1. 82–4). Horace suggests that the republican era is one of excessive licence rather than *libertas*, but slightly later, his historicization rejects classical Greek literature as inferior to its later Roman counterpart. The question of whether the Greek tragedians produced any benefit (cf. 'utile') proposes the superiority of Roman poetics as a public, political language and reinforces the standard historicization of Greek literary culture as a discourse which is too free, too unconstrained, and so ungoverned (*Ep.* 2. 1. 163).

Scholars have regarded *Epistle* 2. 3 to the Pisones, now commonly known as the *Ars poetica* (following Quintilian, *Inst.* 8. 3. 60 and *Ep. ad Tryph.* 2), as the author's most important critical text and as one of the central works of ancient literary criticism.[25] I prefer to locate this text within the history of criticism in the context of a broader discussion about the construction of the ideal poem, its history, and the poet's role in society. My wish is to recharacterize it as a work which reflects a number of the social and legal constraints upon public literary language in the early empire. In the historical portion of the letter Horace addresses the issue of propriety in drama. He instructs his audience, most immediately the sons of Calpurnius Piso, to avoid stage representation of things that are 'unworthy' ('indigna') but rather to have them enacted behind the scenes (sc. 'intus digna geri') or else narrated. He cites as examples of 'unworthy things' the revolting violence involved in Medea killing her sons, Atreus cooking human flesh, Procne turning into a bird, and the grotesque metamorphosis of Cadmus into a snake (179–88).

From his subsequent treatment of satyr-plays, it becomes clear that Horace is engaging in a historicization of literary regulation which again implies the superiority of Roman critical standards, and particularly those belonging to the social and political élite. The poet introduces this genre at line 220 by characterizing it as a contest for the sake of a 'vile goat' ('vilem . . . ob hircum') with a

---

[25] e.g. Russell and Winterbottom (1972), 279–91, and of course, the magisterial study of the *Ars poetica* in three volumes by Brink (1963–82).

view to providing an etymology for tragedy as a 'goat song' (*tragos + oidos*).[26] He continues by pointing to the nudity of the rustic ('agrestes') satyrs and then observes that the audience watches, transfixed by the newness of the entertainment and the festive occasion which renders the event free of all laws (sc. 'exlex') (223–4). Horace concludes his analysis of the satyr-play by cautioning against the emergence of 'filthy and ignominious language' ('immunda . . . ignominiosaque dicta', 247). The poet's allegiance to an élite class-identity becomes apparent from his association of such diction with crossroads and market-places (245) and with his suggestion that such work would offend those who are knights or fathers, or who have substantial wealth (248). The impression that historical Greece is a *locus* of discursive licence is reinforced yet again (as in *Sat.* 1. 4) by the following reference to Old Comedy, whose freedom (*libertas*) became harmful and powerful to the extent that it had to be controlled by laws. According to Horace, the chorus fell silent once comic licence lost its capacity to do harm and was subject to regulation (282–5).

Kenneth Quinn remarks that Horace mounts a literary opposition to the more traditional critical establishment as a champion of the new literature and as a newly-made man.[27] This is perhaps a somewhat misleading picture. If Augustan patronage establishes the poet as a member of a literary and political élite, it simultaneously imposes a series of obligations upon its recipient.[28] The critical and political validation of the poet implied by the Alexandrian pose now also requires the stringent regulation of the poetic voice, and it emerges furthermore as a voice which masks the tensions between literary production and political authority by assimilating itself to the latter in a way that is not so evident in the work of other authors. The poet is required to regulate his own discourse out of deference, and Horace undertakes this by a poetic self-definition which positions itself against prior literary figures. He begins *Satire* 2. 1 by revealing that some people think him too harsh and regard him as going beyond the law ('ultra legem'), although others think him not sufficiently daring (1–3). Later he suggests that Lucilius is his model inasmuch as his predecessor first dared to compose verses which show people for what they really are:

---

[26] Cf. Rudd (1989), 187. [27] Quinn (1982), 172.
[28] On Horace's insecurity, see the discussion by Gold (1987), 111–18.

> When Lucilius first dared
> to compose poems in this manner,
> to draw away the outer skin where each person would show himself
> smart and shiny, but [be] base within . . .[29]

Horace represents Lucilian invective as a truthful depiction of its victim (rather than as a dirtying of reputation) in order to seek approval for Lucilius' work and his own, which, in this respect, he declares inferior to his predecessor's (cf. 'infra Lucili censum ingeniumque', 75). But in *Satire* 1. 10 Horace disowns Lucilius, so as to make apparent the importance of discursive self-regulation in the imperial circle. Here the author's predecessor is presented as a poet who sacrificed refinement and revision for quantity. This satirist's poetry is characterized in terms of an uncomposed foot ('incompositus pes') and it is compared to a gushing, muddy river (1. 10. 1–4, 35–64). Above all, Lucilius falls short in failing to revise his work: as *Satire* 1. 10. 65–74 makes clear, the process of revision is a necessary element of Horatian/Augustan poetics. Good poetry is the product not just of writing but also of reconsiderations, constant erasures, and rewritings. The image of the muddy river accuses Lucilius of lack of discrimination: mud is the residue and debris, the licence, which clouds the Hellenistic image of the poetic river.

The critique of Lucilius deliberately recapitulates an earlier attack on the satirist in *Satire* 1. 4. This earlier poem provides a significant context, for it reveals Horatian discrimination as one that occurs in large part through the discourse of literary history. Here the earlier satirist's outpourings are associated and identified with the licence (*licentia*) of the Athenian Old Comic poets, Cratinus and Aristophanes, who regularly flout the constraints against slander and libel in their communities. Horace sharply calls into question Aristophanes' own critical agency when he depicts the comic poet as a figure of discursive impropriety here. He engages in a radical revision of the rushing river, originally the image that Aristophanes used to dismiss Cratinus, the exemplar of comic slander against a named individual (*onomasti kōmōdein*) (cf. *Knights* 526–8).[30] As far as Horace's literary historicization is concerned,

---

[29] 'quid, cum est Lucilius ausus | primus in hunc operis componere carmina morem, | detrahere et pellem, nitidus qua quisque per ora | cederet, introrsum turpis . . .?' (*Sat.* 2. 1. 62–5).

[30] See R. M. Rosen (1988), 38, and his ch. 3 for discussion of Cratinus.

the past is an undifferentiated era of discursive anarchy and crudeness. Lucilius is elided with his Greek authorial ancestors, and the differences between Aristophanes and Cratinus are to be effaced. The last two become the authors to justify for classical Greece its description as a site of 'great liberty' (cf. 'multa cum libertate', I. 4. 5).

The boor of *Satire* I. 9 is excluded from Rome's cultural élite because he does not regulate his own language, but self-criticism is not by itself a sufficient condition for acceptance within this circle. The poet is also the judge of the community's discourse. Horace implicitly equates the poet's self-criticism and self-censorship with the state's mechanisms for discursive regulation in a way that restores literary *iudicium* to the critical figures privileged by Hesiod, namely the individuals who represent poetic and political authority in the community. Hence Horace is at pains to reject any scenarios of literary production and performance where *iudicium* might involve individuals other than the literary and political élite, for to do otherwise would enable the dissemination of critical authority. The mass audience, comprised of the *plebs*, requires the poet to curry its favour and that of the *grammatici*. It compels participation in an unsavoury mode of literary politics as Quinn observes,[31] and it demands that the writer take 'trivial compositions' or 'trifles' ('nugae') seriously (cf. *Epist.* I. 19. 35–49). Accordingly, the poet declares that he does not permit the recitation of his works in verse contests or competitions nor in theatres (cf. *Sat.* I. 10. 37–9). If poetic contests are to take place in temples (cf. *Sat.* I. 10. 38),[32] then Horace presides as *vates* over his own rather more exclusive temple in, for instance, the *Odes* (e.g. 3. 1. 1–4). As far as the poet is concerned, criticism ideally takes place away from the public sphere so that the possibility of input from a broader community is denied.

IV

The poetry of Ovid supports the understanding of the Augustan literary project as an extension of the emperor's power and authority but in quite a different way. Where Horace appropriates himself

---

[31] Quinn (1982), 150.   [32] Ibid. 146–7.

to this politico-literary enterprise, Ovid disassociates himself from
it. Unlike Horace, Ovid is a member of the nobility by birth (cf. *Tr.*
4. 10. 7–8) and confidently lays claim to a literary authority, to a
poetic genealogy which includes members of the Augustan coterie,
which is none the less distinct from the emperor's (cf. *Tr.* 4. 10.
45–51 and 55). Ovid's poetry demonstrates a critical difference,
namely over who may determine what sorts of discourse may be
circulated or not circulated in the community and then what sorts
of discourse are to be privileged at the expense of others. The
author's career, ending as it did in exile on the Black Sea at Tomi,
reveals the consequence of attempting to establish literary authori-
tiy apart from the emperor at Rome.

Leo Curran has suggested that even more than the *Ars amatoria*,
with its ostensibly sexual theme, the *Metamorphoses* should have
been an offensive and threatening work to Augustus given that it is
a more obviously political poem.[33] In support of Curran's thesis, I
venture that what the epic demonstrates are the possible injustices
of a critical scenario in which the authority for literary judgement
is exclusively political in its basis. Book 6 of the poem presents us
with two artistic contests in which gods compete with non-deities.
This book opens with the extended narrative of the weaving competition ('certamen') between Minerva and Arachne. While the
goddess represents a highly disciplined portrait of the gods in all
their authority and power (70–102), the doomed girl produces a
more impressionistic tapestry which depicts a series of rapes of
young females by the gods (103–28). At the conclusion of the contest, the poet remarks that neither Minerva herself nor Envy could
fault the work of Arachne (129–30), and scholars understand the
deity to judge the tapestries to be of equal accomplishment.[34] None
the less, the goddess, angered by the subject of Arachne's weaving,
transforms the doomed girl into a spider (131–8). Divine judgement is thus anything but disinterested; rather, it here seeks to
maintain the reputation of the gods (cf. also 'yield to the goddess'
('cede deae'), 6. 32). The outcome of the contest between Minerva
and Arachne indicates that any *agōn* between gods and lower beings
is a foregone conclusion: the gods authorize their own victories.

---

[33] Curran (1972), 90; see also Holleman (1971) on the political background to the
epic.
[34] See Anderson (1968), 103, and Curran (1972), 84.

This notion is reinforced by the subsequent narrative of the defeat and gruesome flaying of the satyr Marsyas following a musical contest with Apollo. To make it clear that the conclusion of any competition with the gods is one that is predetermined, the narrative dwells not on the actual competition itself but rather on the details of the punishment and the horrified response of the community (see *Met*. 6. 382–400). Together, the Marsyas and Arachne episodes show up the unpleasant side of literary judgement as a political strategy of authorization for the Augustan age: the fates of these two artists demonstrate that those without authority cannot win and are mercilessly silenced if they challenge the discourses of those in power. Ovid's critique of divine judgement goes deeper, for the gods are hardly reliable or blameless judges. As Holleman and Curran argue, the *Metamorphoses* devalues divinity by showing the Olympian gods Jupiter and Apollo to be less than dignified soon after their initial appearances and by placing the deification of Rome's historical and recent leaders, Aeneas, Romulus, Julius Caesar, and Augustus, on a par with the less than ideal transformations of other figures, e.g. Daphne, Lycaon, and Glaucon.[35]

Ovid's exile poetry further develops the view that imperial literary criticism is arbitrary, and even undermining of its own authority.[36] *Tristia* 2 offers a defence of the author's *carmina*, the poetry which has caused him to be exiled. 'Poem and transgression ('carmen et error') are the two crimes which led to his downfall. He declares that he will remain silent about the transgression ('error'), for it is the 'base poem' ('turpe carmen') which has caused him to be known as the 'doctor of obscene adultery' ('obsceni doctor adulterii') (207–12). This description of poetry (*carmen*) as *crimen* ('crime') reflects the literary constraints in Augustan Rome and, before them, the historical prohibition on injurious *carmina* in the Twelve Tables. But this is an account that Ovid denies as far as his own work is concerned. There is no *crimen* in his poetry, not even in the erotic *Ars amatoria* (240), even if he deems it unworthy reading material for Caesar (241–2) and for Roman gentlewomen (252–8), intended as it was for prostitutes alone (cf. 'solis meretricibus', 303). To establish that his poetry (*carmen*) is without *crimen*, he claims at 249–50 to write only of what is legitimate and of what

---

[35] Holleman (1971), 460; Curran (1972), 83.
[36] Wiedemann (1975: 264), rejects the view that Ovid's exile poetry is merely sycophantic.

are permitted trysts (cf. 'legitimum concessaque furta'; cf. also 'non facinus causam, sed suus error habet', *Tr.* 3. 1. 52). He rejects the accusation that he named individuals, or as he puts it, used actual, literally 'naked', names (cf. 'nomina nuda') in his 'liber' (408): 'nuda' suggests an equation between licence and the immoral (cf. Apuleius, *Apol.* 10–11).

Ovid vindicates his own verse by drawing a contrast between it and other forms of entertainment more likely to contribute to immorality at Rome, for instance, the gladiatorial games, theatrical displays, and the Circus (*Tr.* 2. 275–83). He observes that other authors also write works describing time-wasting games (471–96), while the state provides some support for even obscene mimes (cf. 'mimos obscena iocantes'), since senators attend them (497–502).[37] As with Horace, literary history is an important strategy of literary self-authorization. Ovid invokes the alignment of past/licence and present/literary restraint to his advantage, drawing a contrast between himself and his poetic ancestors.[38] At 361 ff. he notes in defence of the *Ars amatoria* that there is a whole prior tradition of writing about erotic matters with impunity. He cites the attention given to love by Greek epic and lyric poets, whom he catalogues at ll. 364–80, by Greek tragedians (381–409), and then by Roman poets, who are also mentioned by name (421–70). It is amongst this third group that Ovid explicitly locates himself as the sucessor to Tibullus and Propertius (467–8). He justifies this earlier, normative licence by arguing that the effect of a poem depends on the reader's mindset and perceptions: if one reads his poetry with the right mind ('recta si mente legatur') it is evident that it cannot harm anyone (275–6). Without this liberal attitude, all books will have 'crimen' (265); even the circus, where men and women sit squashed together, will no longer be safe (cf. 'non tuta licentia Circi est', 283). This defence is one that is picked up later by the epigrammatist Martial, who prefaces book 1 of his poems with the observation that earlier authors ('antiqui auctores')—he names Catullus, Marsus, Pedo, Gaeticulus, and 'anyone else who is now read'—

---

[37] Wiedemann (1975: 270–1), observes that Augustus supported mimes, and pornography.

[38] Compare Juvenalian satire, which presents itself as attempting to reclaim licence, dealing, for instance, with fear, anger, desire, pleasures (Juv. *Sat.* 1. 85–6; cf. 170–1), using names (153), employing insults which the victims may not forgive (154). This outspokenness Juvenal valorizes as the simplicity of his predecessors (cf. 'priorum | scribendi . . . simplicitas', 1. 151–2).

enjoyed the opportunity to abuse and revile true and great names. He glosses this frankness, now recovered in his epigrams, as a 'licentious truth of words' ('*lasciviam verborum veritatem*', 1. pr.). In the preface to book 2, he states that unlike comedy and tragedy, which cannot speak for themselves, perhaps because the author is represented by actors, epigrams do not require a 'curio' ('herald', 'crier') and are satisfied with their own 'lingua' ('speech'), which he describes as being wicked ('mala'). 'mala lingua' glosses verbal licence in the form of verbal abuse ('maledictio'). Interestingly, like Ovid, Martial suggests that any constraints on poetic language come above all from the disapproval of the audience itself. It is the wicked interpreter ('malus interpres') who takes offence and complains about frank speech.

Ovid protests that exile in a barbaric land silences him by causing his Latin to fail (*Tr.* 3. 14. 45–52). But the silencing effect of exile is above all achieved through removal from the privileged cultural and political centre, Rome. If Horace had demonstrated the political privilege of proximity to the *princeps* in poems such as *Satire* 1. 10 and *Epistle* 2. 1, then *Tristia* 3. 1 articulates the author's banishment from Rome as a separation from the privilege that the favour of the imperial ruler-judge can grant and this separation in turn as a mode of censorship. The author sends this poem to Rome, instructing it to seek an audience for itself and in this way to remedy the fact that it has been denied a resting-place in the Augustan libraries in the temple of Apollo (*Tr.* 3. 1. 63–4), in the Octavian portico near the theatre of Marcellus (67–9), and in the library founded in the temple of Liberty by Asinius Pollio (71–2).[39] Irony is of course intended by the reference to the fact that Ovid's work is barred from the shrine of Libertas.

A. J. Marshall writes that imperial libraries were an oblique means of enacting censorship: inclusion in them would ensure a work's status as a 'classic' as in the case of Virgil and Livy (cf. Suet. *Calig.* 34. 2), while exclusion determined the work's demise.[40] The scholarly community in its turn reinforced the critical function of the imperial book collection and its canonizations, for Augustus prompted commentaries on the works of the Greek poets whose

---

[39] Marshall (1976: 262), suggests that the *Ars amatoria* was banished from all three libraries during Ovid's lifetime.

[40] Marshall (1976), 262–3.

busts he placed in his library (cf. Suet. *Tib.* 70).[41] The work of
Quintilian, Rome's latter-day librarian and judge under the
patronage of the emperor Vespasian, emphatically underscores
the relationship between literary and political judgement.[42] The
rhetorician enunciates the coincidence of literary language and
power in terms of authorial discrimination. He rehearses his critical
authority in terms of roles established by the Alexandrians, this
time of the scholar-critic rather than of the poet.[43] Like his North
African predecessors, the imperial librarian is a priest of the Muses.
In the *Institutio oratoria*, his long treatise on the training of the
ideal orator, he observes that, if Aratus invoked Zeus (in the
Phaenomena) as a starting-point, then he will invoke Homer as he
embarks upon his catalogue of texts which are to be canonical
specifically for the future orator at 10. 1. 46. His self-fashioning as
literary priest is reinforced in his comparison of Ennius to a sacred
grove ('sacros . . . lucos') and by his attribution of 'religio' to his
poetry at 10. 1. 88, and also in his description of himself as someone who cherishes 'sacred scriptures' ('sacra litterarum', 10. 1. 92).
To the urbane prose-writer Calvus, significantly an author who
engages in rigorous self-criticism (cf. 'nimia contra se calumnia'
and 'castigata'), he attributes 'holy speech' ('sancta . . . oratio') (10.
1. 115). Through Calvus Quintilian extends the idea of the scholar-
priest to the professional teacher of rhetoric (cf. Apuleius, *Flor.* 1).

Quintilian produces a rhetoric of literary institution that not only
dispenses with the actual physical site of literary activity more
emphatically than Horace does with his textual temple but is also
an important anticipation of [Longinus] (see Chapter 6). He establishes his own *Pinakes*, the catalogue of Greek and Roman authors,
in book 10. As his Hellenistic predecessors, he identifies excellence
as the chief criterion for inclusion in the catalogue. He states that
no author, except an excellent ('optimus') one, should be read by
the student of oratory at the beginning (10. 1. 20); later, when the
student is tired of excellence, he may read selections from baser
authors (10. 1. 57). What establishes and authorizes excellence is
judgement ('iudicium'), which is in turn given a genealogy that
locates the origins of this mode of judgement in the Hellenistic age.
Significantly, Quintilian's arrangement of his own catalogue of

---

[41] Marshall (1976), 263.   [42] See Woodside (1942).
[43] Kennedy has suggested that book 10 of the *Institutio oratoria* offers a means of
understanding the project of Hellenistic criticism; see Kennedy (1992), 225.

authors and texts evokes to an extent the Callimachean catalogues. But where his predecessor employed a generic and alphabetical classification, the Roman rhetorician offers a generic and then a chronological classification, beginning with Greek authors and then moving on to Roman authors.[44]

Quintilian exercises *iudicium* in establishing the authors that the future orator should study and read, and in so doing he offers his audience a paradigm of the critical process. The 'most exacting judgement' ('exactissimo iudicio') is to be exercised in determining which authors to imitate (10. 2. 14) and in ensuring that the future orator avoids the faults of style which now afflict popular rhetoric (10. 2. 15; cf. 10. 1. 18–19). Quintilian affirms the social function of the critical process, depicting it as an activity which anticipates the public judgement of the lawcourt. At 11. 1. 43 he affirms that it matters not only who and for whom one speaks but also in whose presence one speaks ('apud quem dicas'), for this person's position will make a difference ('discrimen'). Indeed, the final sections of book 10 conflate literary judgement with the whole issue of legal judgement. One becomes a judge ('iudex') of the canonical authors and of one's own work in order to anticipate the 'bystanding judges' ('circumstantes iudices') of the public lawcourt and assembly, characterized as a noisy mob at 10. 3. 30. The orator has to take into account the mental disposition of the legal judge (cf. 'qui iudicis animus') (10. 3. 15), and to reconcile the jury's position with his own, even if it is hostile (11. 1. 8–9; cf. 11. 1. 75 ff.).

If Ovid recognizes the power of the library, his recognition takes the form of an attempt to interrogate the institution's authority. I suggest that even despite his banishment from Rome, the poet sets himself up as an alternative critical presence. He challenges the Augustan library-system as a critical institution, and with it, the position of the emperor as divinely ordained ruler and literary judge. The poet manages to give his poetry a voice and to resist the silence of exile to some degree. If he himself has been physically banished from Rome, it is the case that he maintains his other

[44] So at Quint. *Inst.* 10. 1. 46 the Greek catalogue commences with a list of epic poets; it moves to archaic and Hellenistic poetry at 10. 1. 56; to Old Comedy at 10. 1. 65; to tragedy at 10. 1. 66; to history at 10. 1. 73; to oratory as represented by the Attic canon of ten orators at 10. 1. 76; and to philosophy at 10. 1. 81. At 10. 1. 85 he observes that the same order ('ordo') is to be retained for Latin authors, first epic poets, then elegiac authors (10. 1. 93), tragedians (10. 1. 97), historians (10. 1. 101), orators (10. 1. 105), and, finally, philosophers (10. 1. 123).

privileges and rights as a citizen (*Tr.* 4. 9. 12). Despite his physical exclusion, he has the means to construct a virtual presence for himself in the imperial capital through the continued circulation of his writings, both the poetry written before his exile and his subsequent *Tristia* and *Epistulae ex Ponto*. Elizabeth Block has observed that in *Epistulae ex Ponto* the poet intrudes himself into the poem less as a poet and more as a critic.[45] In making this remark, Block points perceptively to Ovid's strategy for self-authorization in the exile poetry. The poet fears that his reputation and name will not survive in his absence (cf. *Tr.* 3. 10. 1–2); however, he has the means to grant his writing a presence at Rome. At *Tristia* 3. 3. 77–80 he makes it plain that his books are his memorial. Accordingly, at 3. 14. 8–10, he tells an unnamed friend to retain his body ('corpus') of books in the city since his own exile does not also require the exile of his works. Furthermore and finally, it is the case that the physical distance from Rome and its emperor-critic ironically entail a greater freedom for the poet. While Ovid is careful not to incriminate his intimates by mentioning their names in his poetry (cf. esp. *Tr.* 3. 6 and 3. 14), he is able to mention Augustus frequently in his poetry, and his subject is powerless to prevent this (*Tr.* 4. 4. 14–16).

IV

In the *Catiline* Sallust observes that political authority ('regium imperium') initially sought to preserve *libertas* and to increase the republic, yet later turned to arrogance and domination of its subjects (6. 7). In the final section of this chapter I examine first what Tacitus and then what Lucan have to say as a strategy for dislodging this otherwise absolutist rhetoric. Tacitus I suggest needs to be acknowledged as the author who offers the most noteworthy and also the most complex account of authorial self-silencing and discursive repression by the state. Frederick Ahl has observed that scholars have placed too much faith in the Tacitean portrait of a silenced intellectual and political community, arguing that as a consequence little attention has been paid to the various strategies for expression available to authors even under repressive regimes.[46]

[45] Block (1982), 22.
[46] On the figure of the silenced intellectual, see Y. L. Too in Elsner and Masters (1994).

Ahl's objection on the first point is correct and justified: for, as we shall see, Tacitean Rome is something of a caricature. Yet the historian's response to the discourse of the earlier imperial age, however, requires further thought because it disregards the issue of self-censorship which, as will be seen, Tacitus both specifically and explicitly advocates and implicitly supports.[47] As the foremost historian of imperial Rome, the author makes the destruction of literary expression and freedom a topos of his representation of the city in that era.

At the beginning of the *Agricola* the historian observes that his ancestors were able to commemorate the deeds and characters of famous men ('clari viri'), while at present such a literary account of the deeds and virtues of one's ancestors is exceptional. Literary commemorations and memorials to past accomplishments exist *despite* public vice, ignorance of what is right, and envy (1. 1). Tacitus states that he lives in an era hostile to virtue (1. 4) and that the reader is for this reason to be all the more impressed with his biography of Julius Agricola. The historian goes on to produce a portrait of the imperial city which substantiates his portrait of it as a repressive state. He recounts how Domitian put to death Arulenus Rusticus and Herennius Senecio for praising Thrasea Paetus and Helvidius Priscus in their books (2. 1). Dio elaborates the story of martyrdom, informing his reader that Arulenus' crime was to call Thrasea a saint (67. 13). For this, he was supposedly accused by Regulus for being the 'ape of the Stoics' (Pliny, *Ep.* 1. 5. 2). With him Herennius was tried by Mettius Carus (Tac. *Agr.* 45. 1; Dio Cass. 67. 13). According to Tacitus, the *laudandi* of the offending works were imperial dissenters. The Stoic Thrasea committed suicide, an act of defiance, under Nero (*Ann.* 16. 21, 16. 35), while Suetonius records Helvidius as failing to show proper respect to Vespasian (*Vesp.* 8. 15).

In the Tacitean narrative, censorship takes place not in the interests of society but for the purpose of silencing opposition to the emperor, as Tacitus makes explicit. The writings of the offending intellectuals are burned in public as the historian reports in the *Agricola*: 'By that fire they deem the voice of the Roman people, the liberty of the senate, and the conscience of humankind to have been consumed. In addition the advocates of wisdom were driven out as

---

[47] Ahl (1984*b*), 101–2.

was every good art exiled, lest any honest deed ever occurred.'[48] The fire which consumes the works of Arulenus and Herennius is presented as destroying 'the voice of the Roman people, the liberty (*libertas*) of the senate, and the conscience of the human race'. According to Tacitus' narrative, criticism at Rome has departed from its original function of protecting the voice of the people and has now assimilated itself to the authoritarian voice of the state.

Tacitus invokes book-burning, which Seneca the Elder would have his reader believe is a familiar topic for declamation in the Roman rhetorical schools. In *Suasoria* 7 he presents a hypothetical situation. Antony offers to spare Cicero's life on the condition that he burns his own books, and Cicero has to decide what to do in the face of arguments by Quintus Haterius, Cestius Pius, Publius Asprenas, Pompeius Silo, Triarius, Argentarius, and Arellius Fuscus the Elder that he preserve his books at any cost. This rhetorical show-piece rehearses again and again the idea that the man of letters, who is to be perceived as the advocate of free speech, must not compromise his voice—to the extent that Seneca points out that everyone worries more about Cicero's books than about Cicero himself (*Suas.* 7. 10–11). In the course of the various arguments, it becomes clear that not all freedoms are equal: freedom of expression and freedom to criticize are privileged beyond all others. Pompeius Silo, deemed the best advocate of *libertas* by Seneca, is presented as suggesting that life cannot be worth living if it is owed to Antony and even less so now that the state has exchanged 'liberty' ('libertas') for 'licence' ('licentia') (7. 5).

In the *Annals*, as in the *Agricola*, *libertas* is the feature that distinguishes the republic from a contemporary Rome inhospitable to writers and free speech. The work opens with the statement that Brutus established 'freedoms and the consulship' ('libertates et consulatum') (1. 1; cf. 1. 33. 4; Livy 2. 1. 7, 3. 38. 2, etc.). Tacitus locates the cause for the demise of freedom of expression in the imperial period to the reign of Augustus. The historian notes how Augustus was the first to handle a case concerning defamatory pamphlets ('famosi libelli') as a case of treason ('maiestas'). The emperor punished Cassius Severus for sullying the reputations of illustrious ('inlustris') men and women with his writings (*Ann.* 1.

---

[48] 'scilicet illo igne vocem populi Romani et libertatem senatus et conscientiam generis humani aboleri arbitrantur, expulsis insuper sapientiae professoribus atque omni bona arte in exilium acta, ne quid usquam honestum occurreret' (*Ag.* 2. 2).

72; cf. 4. 21). Significantly, libel actions under Augustus reassert the non-populist character of the law.[49] The description of Severus' texts as cheeky writings ('procacia scripta'), and the reference to his sexual appetite, equates defamation with sexual immorality, which Augustus' moral programme sought to combat.

Following Augustus, the freedom supposedly ushered in by the reign of Tiberius is revealed by Tacitus to be nothing more than a mere illusion (*Ann.* 1. 82). In *Annals* 4 he recounts the fate of the poet Cremutius Cordus, described by F. H. Cramer as the most famous case of silencing in the early principate.[50] Cordus is charged with what the author describes as 'a new and until then unheard of crime' ('novo ac tunc primo audito crimine', 4. 34), namely treasonous injury. Cordus had praised the republican hero Brutus and named C. Cassius 'the last of the Romans' in his annals. Against the accusation of Satrius Secundus and Pinarius Natta, Sejanus' clients, he defends his words ('verba'), asserting that by praising Brutus and Cassius, he has not committed treason (cf. *lex maiestatis*) against Tiberius or his stepfather Augustus. He cites a list of venerable predecessors, Livy, Asinus Pollio, Messala Corvinus, Cicero, Antonius, Bibaculus, and Catullus, in order to make his point that other authors have praised republican heroes without any repercussions. He cautiously alludes to the *libertas* enjoyed by the Greeks for further justification (4. 35). Despite his defence, Cordus' books, like those of Arulenus and Herennius in the *Agricola*, are burned, although, as Tacitus notes, hidden copies continue to be circulated. The picture Tacitus gives in the *Annals* is of a Rome which ironically constrains the praise that would otherwise contribute to the good name of its citizens and set the community an ideal. Rather, Rome nurtures slander, the discourse which detracts from the reputation of its good citizens.

At the beginning of the *Histories* Tacitus reinforces the narrative of decline from republic, from freedom of speech (*libertas*), and from truth, to empire, dissimulation, and falsehood. The first chapter of the work begins with an account of an original Rome in which writers and citizens could recall political affairs and accomplishments with both eloquence and freedom ('pari eloquentia ac libertate', 1. 1). The next sentence in the chapter takes the reader post-Actium, to the originative moment of the empire, and also to

[49] Smith (1951), 179.   [50] Cramer (1945), 191.

the point at which literary genius ceased to be, truth became distorted, and lack of knowledge is the condition of citizens who know
their state not as their own but as a foreign one.[51] Tacitus' analysis
produces as the reasons for this state of affairs sycophancy, the
desire of writers to win approval, and partiality in the form of
hatred for Rome's ruler. The author goes on to characterize the
craft of authorship in the imperial period as one in which writers
manifested their ambition through spite and envy, while audiences
received such outpourings with eager ears. It is this perversion of
the historian's craft which reinforces the evils of imperial literary
culture by concealing the facts that flattery is merely another form
of servitude, and hostility towards the leader only a false form of
liberty. Tacitus offers a critique of authorial practice in the empire
as one which is a form of compromise and as one which does not
constitute a legitimate mode of self-criticism. The displays of sycophancy or, alternatively, of open hostility are aspects of political
accommodation or non-accommodation which do nothing to further actual literary protest.[52] Sycophancy explicitly approves of the
empire and is liable to be read at face value, while hostility leaves its
author vulnerable and offers a false sense of accomplishment
through verbal protest.

   This faulting of polemical discourse may offer a reading of
Tacitus' dramatized discussion on oratory, the *Dialogus*.[53] The
work opens with the characters in disagreement over whether to
privilege freedom of expression, here instanced as political critique
expressed through the medium of literary texts, over personal
safety in a repressive regime. Secundus and Aper visit the poet
Maternus to caution him against reciting his *Cato*, a play which has
as its main character the anti-imperial icon and representative *par
excellence* of republican ancestral customs ('mos maiorum'). The
visitors inform the playwright that he is seen to have offended the
political authorities (2. 1) and with his well-being in mind they
attempt to persuade him to omit material which is liable to be con-

[51] 'magna illa ingenia cessere; simul veritas pluribus modis infracta, primum
inscita rei publicae ut alienae, mox libidine adsentandi aut rursus odio adversus
dominantis' (*Hist.* 1. 1).

[52] 'adulationi foedum crimen servitutis, malignitati falsa species libertatis inest'
(*Hist.* 1. 3).

[53] Scholars variously locate the date of the dialogue. Murgia (1980) believes the
Dialogus to be Tacitus' earliest work and dates it to 97 CE, while Syme (1958: 670–3)
and Woodman (1975: 294–5) date the work to 102 CE or even later.

strued as criticism of the state and its ruler. Aper advocates a revised *Cato*, or, as he puts it, 'although not a better *Cato*, a safer (*securiorem*) one' (3. 2). Maternus, however, declares his intention to recite in the near future his *Thyestes*, a drama which he insists will be even more critical of the current regime and thereby make up for what he perceives to be the deficiencies of the *Cato*.

In the intervening discussion, the characters highlight the potential social functions of public speech. They go on to make their cases for the various merits and advantages of writing and performing two of the community's privileged languages, poetry and rhetoric—the latter both in its older, Ciceronian, form and in its newer forms. It is only at the very end of the *Dialogus* that Tacitus takes up the issue of the tension between *libertas* and verbal self-censorship. Here he appears to make explicitly the point that *libertas* cannot be accommodated under a despotic leader and that there is accordingly no space for the rhetorical arts in a repressive state. In chapter 40, when Maternus speaks again, he responds to the claims that Aper and Messalla make for oratory. He observes that great eloquence is the 'offspring of licence' ('alumna licentiae'), which stupid people misname and mistake for *libertas*. According to Maternus, rhetorical eloquence accompanies seditions, inciting the people to frenzy, and for this reason does not manifest itself in well-governed states such as the historical Sparta and Crete (40. 2–3). According to Maternus, the eloquence of the Gracchi and Cicero is not worth the instability and trouble it produces (40. 4) and he concludes by declaring that the dearth of great eloquence, indeed one lamented at the beginning of the *Dialogus* (1. 1), is due to the fact that great speeches and orators are not called for in the present state (41. 5). Tacitus links oratory with discord, a judgement that serves, as Shadi Bartsch notes, to reject the frequent association that Cicero makes between rhetoric and peace in his writings.[54]

The conclusion of the *Dialogus* has left scholars in fierce debate as to what Tacitus' actual intentions might be: does the historian reject rhetoric as a mode of public language because of its destabilizing effect in a presently peaceful state? or does he rather present Maternus' rejection of oratory as a veiled critique of a repressive

---

[54] See e.g. Cic. *Brut.* 12. 45 and *Arch.* 3.5 ('et hic Romae propter tranquillitatem rei publicae [studia] non neglegebantur'); on *otium*, see Wirzbuski (1950), 92–3, and Bartsch (1994), 110.

state, as characterized by the anxieties about the reception of the *Cato*?[55] My intention is not to advocate one or the other of these stark alternatives. After all, Roman rhetoric shows up the impracticality and foreignness of an all-or-nothing stance, where outspokenness and reticence are concerned. In his treatise *On Style*, Demetrius declares that figured language must be employed if somebody wishes to address and to criticize either a tyrant or a powerful individual, and he advocates this as a middle course between flattery, which is base, and direct criticism, which is dangerous (289 and 294). Ahl notes, in an essay entitled 'The Art of Safe Criticism', that Quintilian, Vespasian's imperial rhetorician, subsequently elaborates Demetrius' account of the political use of figured language at *Institutio oratoria* 9. 2. 66.[56] Quintilian sets out three different occasions on which figured language, which he defines as language that is changed from its most obvious and uncomplicated usage by poetic or oratorical usage (9. 1. 13), may be employed. The first of these concerns when it is dangerous to speak openly; the second concerns propriety—where the Latin 'it is not fitting/suitable' ('non decet') perhaps renders the Greek 'improper' (*aprepes*); while the third advocates the use of figured language where the novelty of such structures may produce delight and pleasure.[57] Of these three occasions, the first is the most obviously political, and what Quintilian proposes is a need for the author in question to tread warily around authority, particularly as author and political leader may be at odds. The following section of the work suggests that the rhetorician has in mind the empire, figured as tyranny: he cites the use of rhetorical figures in school exercises which require pupils to produce speeches to instigate rebellion against despots without speaking too plainly to tyrants (9. 2. 67).

Rhetorical culture is not the only factor which prompts a more qualified interpretation of the *Dialogus*. I want to suggest that the ideal of *libertas* is itself a regulated freedom of expression, and where Tacitus' work is specifically concerned, Bartsch subscribes

---

[55] e.g. G. Williams (1978: 41 with n. 81), sees Maternus' praise for the docility of Rome's subjects as being ironic (41. 3)

[56] W. Rhys Roberts, *Demetrius On Style*, in W. H. Fyfe, *Aristotle, The Poetics; 'Longinus', On the Sublime; Demetrius on Style* (Cambridge, Mass. 1960). See Ahl (1984a).

[57] 'eius [schematos] triplex usus est: unus, si dicere palam parum tutum est, alter, si non decet, tertius, qui venustatis modo gratia adhibetur et ipsa novitate ac varietate magis, quam si relatio sit recta, delectat' (*Inst.* 9. 2. 66).

to the view of Tacitean complexity as a mode of self-censorship. She proposes that Maternus' final speech as different readings for different audiences, and so shifts the emphasis away from authorial intention and towards the instability of readerly reception. For her, Maternus' language demonstrates the absence of freedom of speech because it engages in a sycophantic approval of the current state, even despite the evidently republican sentiments displayed by his plays.[58] As Tacitus shows in the *Annals*, particularly with the case of Cremutius Cordus, and in the *Histories*, patent criticism in the form of hostile polemic is ineffective. Wirzbuski notes elsewhere that Tacitus condemns intransigence, as in the case of Helvidius at *Agricola* 42. 4 f.[59] Thus the options left to the pragmatist are withdrawal from political activity, or the masking of politico-literary criticism, and it is this latter option which describes Tacitus' approach. As Inez Ryberg pointed out in a study of the *Annals* in 1942, it is characteristic of Tacitus to refuse to commit himself openly to accusation of the emperor Tiberius. The historian rather resorts to indirection, to hearsay, innuendo, and opinion.[60] Where Ryberg goes on to suggest that the force of tradition and public opinion enable the historian to declare his prejudice against the emperor Nero in the second half of the *Annals*, I prefer to argue that the later demonstration of directness here serves rather as an antidote specifically to the dissimulations of the emperor-actor.[61]

If Bartsch makes the departure from an over-simplistic view of the *Dialogus* as a work that *either* rejects oratory *or else* offers a criticism of the state, and that qualifies the authoritativeness of a face-value reading of Maternus' statements, she still perhaps does not adequately address the awkward discrepancy between Maternus' own dramatic discourse, which advocates thinly disguised critique of the state, and his statements in the dialogue, which reject the no more obvious critique of rhetorical discourse. Doubt about the possibility of even this level of (dis)closure is raised by the suggestion of Messalla that he would refute Maternus if there were more time (42. 1). I suggest that the comment is poignant precisely because Messalla's speech in the middle of the *Dialogus* indicates

[58] Bartsch (1994), 115, 125.   [59] Wirzbuski (1950), 147.
[60] Ryberg (1942).
[61] On Nero as emperor-actor, see e.g. C. Edwards in Elsner and Masters (1994), 83–97, and Bartsch (1994), 6–17.

that there might be considerations and constraints upon discourse other than those set out by Secundus and Aper—namely fear of retribution—and even by Maternus—namely the need for civic harmony. T. J. Luce proposes that the speech of Messalla offers an account of a supposedly traditional education which conforms to the *ideal* that Cicero set out in the *Brutus* and the *De oratore* rather than to any genuine historical actuality.[62] I would argue instead that Tacitus' speaker is providing his readers less with an instance of Ciceronian revisionism than with an echo of Plato's *Republic*, the paradigmatic text about the ideal society and the structures and discourses which produce it. The orator observes that in contemporary Rome Greek nursemaids tell stories ('fabulae') which nurture neither honesty ('probitas') nor modesty ('modestia') in the youth: no one takes any thought for what they should say and do in front of infants. As a result children become used to lewdness ('lasciviae') and sarcasm ('dicacitas') (29. 1–2). Messalla works on the assumption that youthful minds are impressionable and vulnerable, formed by what they experience early on. He suggests that it is precisely the fables told by Greek nurses which account for the city's current vices—that is to say, its obsession with the theatre and gladiatorial shows (29. 3). Where Plato advocates state schooling, the conservative Messalla laments the demise of the family as the site of Roman education,[63] and it is with this ideal of familial schooling in mind that he also attacks the subsequent education of youths. Instead of concerning themselves with the works of well-known authors who present the deeds and figures of antiquity, which Plato's *Protagoras* reveals to have been the traditional curriculum of classical Greece, Roman youths go to the rhetorical schools where they receive anything but a broad and liberal education (30. 1–5). It is for this reason that I suggest seeing the speeches of Messalla and Maternus, who are ostensibly characterized as antagonists in the *Dialogus*, as together offering an explanation of why oratorical virtue has been constrained. If Maternus asserts that it is because the state does not require it, then Messala shows why the state cannot accommodate it—the citizens have been corrupted into cheering for the theatre and the gladiators—and proposes a return to an alternative critical framework. Beyond this, what Messalla's speech also does is to rehearse the critical programme of

---

[62] Luce (1993), 20; also Gwynn (1926), 243.   [63] Gwynn (1926), 243.

an ideal state, advocating a realignment of criticism and the state as a means of revising the latter.

Thus, in articulating his complaints against the repressiveness of the post-Augustan principate, Tacitus does not simply or without qualification idealize freedom of expression. If the constraints on expression, literary and political, are to be criticized as being at odds with the requirements for good government, then there is also a sense in which *libertas* is to be tolerated only to the extent that it is for the good of the community. Here Mark Morford's analysis of what *libertas* means for Tacitus is extremely helpful. Morford observes that in the historian's first work, the *Agricola*, freedom of expression is closely tied into a notion of virtue (*virtus*) and guarantees 'a universal standard of moral values'. He argues, moreover, that this conceptualization is programmatic for the rest of his works. Accordingly, the peoples conquered by the Romans, namely the Britons and the Germans, can manifest 'liberty' because their behaviour is founded on virtue (cf. *Agr.* 30–2 and *Germ.* 7. 1).[64] This moral aspect of *libertas* is crucial because it highlights Tacitus' adherence to the fundamental principal of criticism, namely that discrimination of circulated discourse must occur for the sake of establishing a well-ordered community. Hence, as Morford points out, *libertas* is to be granted to one, relatively limited group of individuals in the empire, the senatorial class, and not to the whole community lest arbitrariness and confusion plague government.[65] Tacitus proposes that freedom of speech is only ideal in rather more restricted conditions than Cicero did when he simply cast it as the companion of peace and order at *Brutus* 12. 45. Speaking through Maternus at the end of the *Dialogus*, the historian sees *libertas* as being possible only when the republic is under a good leader ('princeps'), which is clearly not the situation in the Rome that Tacitus depicts (cf. *Dial.* 41. 4).[66] Precisely in offering a critique of the excesses of silence in the empire, Tacitus' works as a whole affirm that the critical process, ideally one which is enacted by the individuals who themselves produce the discourse in circulation, is a necessary and normative requirement of a well-governed and orderly community. Yet it is also the case that the historian insists that his readers assume a critical stance. By invoking innuendo in the *Annals* and by writing the *Dialogus* in a dialogue form

---

[64] Morford (1991), 3424–5.   [65] Ibid. 3423–4.   [66] Ibid. 3426.

(following most obviously Cicero but also Plato), the author insists that the text's audience discriminate between the various, possible, and available interpretations in the face of authorial and intentional self-effacement enacted by these literary forms.

Even as he depicts a Rome in which state repression is an indicator of civic dysfunction, Tacitus none the less implies that criticism, particularly self-imposed criticism, is a necessary aspect of political conduct. The historian is not alone in this position, for Lucan, I suggest, explicitly argues for criticism as the basic ordering principle of the political community in the *Bellum civile*. Jamie Masters has recently argued that the epic may be read as a litmus test for freedom of speech in the Neronian age—if the author survived despite writing an apparently anti-Caesarian polemic, then the emperor's support of *libertas* is vindicated; if he perished, as indeed Lucan did (for whatever reason), then the poem and the poet's fate become a testimony to what was in actuality a repressive regime.[67] I want to venture here that apart from any position it may take on Nero's Rome—and Masters has persuaded us to view the *Bellum civile* as a parody of what anti-imperial propaganda might look like[68]—the epic demonstrates that political structure is crucially predicated on a critical imperative inasmuch as undiscriminated language is both symptomatic of and responsible for a confused and chaotic world at the political and cosmic levels. The immediate subject of the poem, civil war, is characterized as the abandonment of distinct boundaries. This situation is emblematized by the verb *miscere*, 'to mix', and if 'mixing' can suggest harmony or unity and also the mixing that is 'the bringing-together-into-conflict', it is also the case that when a state turns on itself the joining in harmony and aggression cannot always be distinguished.[69] Boundaries are transgressed in such a way that one's brother becomes not one's ally but one's enemy, as Caesar's men realize when they survey the 'enemy' at the battle of Ilerda in book 4 (cf. *BC* 4. 170 ff.). The transgression entailed in civil war is reinforced as Caesar wilfully crosses the natural boundary of the river Sicoris, in an evocation of the Rubicon and Xerxes' Hellespont.[70] As scholars have observed, there is a sense in which civil war resembles the Stoic ecpyrosis or conflagration where the order of the universe collapses on to itself such that the stars plunge into the

---

[67] Masters in Elsner and Masters (1994), 169–70.   [68] Ibid. 168.

[69] Masters (1992), 111.   [70] Ibid. 66–70.

sea, and land and waters become mingled (1. 70–83; cf. 642–71).[71] But even in the chaos and indiscrimination of a civil war, where blood ties are confused by factional alliances, criticism is not entirely absent. War between the Caesarian and Pompeian factions at Rome is not simply dissolution of the state, but a series of *discrimina*, of moments of definition and crisis that will result in the imperial state.[72]

At one level, the *Bellum civile* tolerates the dichotomy between republicanism/speech and Caesarianism/repression. Caesar is the figure who commands silence. The general and his actions render mobs and whole peoples silent with grief and fear where they would otherwise speak or at least murmur (e.g. 1. 247, 1. 259, 1. 298, 3. 81, 4. 171–2). The meaning of Caesar as a symbol of imperial repression is far from unclear. Yet to read the *Bellum civile* as a work that simplistically instates the division between republic and empire as one between free expression and silence is to misread the epic. The poet calls into question the simplistic identification of imperialism with silence and republicanism with *libertas*, itself a discrimination between political ideologies that his portrait of civil war renders void. The world of the *Bellum civile* is not a world able to tolerate unrestrained speech. Dennis Feeney has argued that the republican hero Pompey is merely the shadow of *libertas* that Cato vows to follow (cf. 2. 303).[73] Pompey is markedly unvocal in the poem, and at the moment of his death, he notably prevents himself from speaking, thus giving a display of Stoic self-control and restraint ('talis custodia Magno/mentis erat', 'such was the custody of Magnus' mind', 8. 635–6). In place of speech, the poet articulates the leader's thoughts on resignation to fate (8. 615–36). In fact, the epic is a text which makes the point that Rome can only tolerate freedom of speech up to a point. Lucan declares that the Romans could not bear 'liberty' (1. 171–2), that 'Freedom' rouses wrath (3. 112–14).

On other occasions, speech is identified with death. In book 1 Curio employs his 'mercenary tongue' to incite Caesar to civil war, offering it to the general to win over allies (1. 272–95). And the

---

[71] Morford (1967), 47; also Masters (1992: 64–5), who observes that the natural cataclysm is preferable to civil war inasmuch as the latter event produces a violent and destructive disruption of definitions, of laws, of boundaries, whereas ecpyrosis results in the formlessness out of which new order may emerge.

[72] Masters (1992), 64 n. 50, 113.   [73] Feeney (1986), 242.

associations of speech with death are above all and most conspicuously presented in the case of prophetic utterance. In book 1 the
Etruscan priestess refuses to divulge the turmoils planned by the
gods for Rome, concealing the prefigurations in ambiguity (1.
631–7). The poet tells his reader that kings silenced the Delphic
oracle out of fear of the future (5. 113–14; cf. 9. 573–4), that is until
Appius forces the priestess Phemonoe to consult the tripod. The
description of prophetic inspiration is significantly described as a
volcanic explosion, like Typhonic Etna (5. 99–101), and then as the
convergence of all time (5. 177–82). Delphic prophecy is a discourse which defies discriminations even as it portends crisis (cf.
'tanti discrimini', 5. 194), and that explains why Apollo has to cur-
tail it, allowing Phemonoe only to assure Appius of his own lack of
role in the war (cf. 5. 194–6). Yet there is one occasion when
prophetic speech is notably disassociated from death. In book 10
Caesar consults the Egyptian priest Acoreus about the future,
promising to abandon civil war if he is assured of reaching the Nile
(10. 191–2). Acoreus accordingly obliges him with a prophecy,
declaring that it is permitted to disclose such secrets regarding the
order of the heavens (194 ff.).

What unfettered prophecy would entail is perhaps dramatized by
the witch Erichtho, as her confused and undiscriminated voices
invoke and then speak of death and destruction (6. 684–93):

> Tum vox Lethaeos cunctis pollentior herbis
> Excantare deos confudit murmura primum
> Dissona et humanae multum discordia linguae.
> Latratus habet illa canum gemitusque luporum,
> Quod trepidus bubo, quod strix nocturna queruntur,
> Quod stridunt ululantque ferae, quod sibilat anguis;
> Exprimit et planctus inlisae cautibus undae
> Silvarumque sonum fractae quae tonitura nubis.
> Tot rerum vox una fuit.

> Last comes her voice, bewitching the gods of Lethe
> more potently than any drug, first composed of jumbled noises,
> jarring, utterly discordant with human speech:
> the bark of dogs and howl of wolves,
> the owl's cry of alarm, the screech-owl's night-time moan,
> the wild beasts' shriek and wail, the serpent's hiss;
> it utters too the beating of the cliff-smashed wave,
> the sound of forests, and the thundering of the fissured cloud;
> of so many noises was one voice the source.

Erichtho produces the utterances of dogs, wolves, owls, serpents, the sound of waves, forests, and thunder-clouds. With Erichtho, the plural voices of the Hesiodic Typhon return yet again, this time to the Roman world, as a destructive and indiscriminate cacophony (cf. *'confudit'* (685), 'dissona' and 'discordia' (686)). The deity intones the utterances of various unpleasant creatures, and she produces the sounds of the natural upheavals of which the Hesiodic Titan is the cause after he has been metamorphosed by Zeus. It is in this way that the goddess vocally re-enacts the indiscrimination of civil war. That such is the import of Erichtho's speech is made evident at 6. 750 ff., as the witch subsequently resurrects a corpse to describe the carnage of war—that is, to declare the reality that oracles only obliquely signal (6. 770–2). Erichtho may thus be read as the figure who symbolizes the consequences for a world that has abandoned the critical imperative.

V

In this chapter I have examined the different ways in which Rome historicizes itself as a place of discursive control in the republican and imperial periods. What emerges from the texts examined is a historicization in which the past, whether of classical Greece or the Roman Republic, is cast as a period of greater discursive liberty, either excessive in the case of Greece or ideal in the case of the republic. Roman criticism is thus a rhetoric of negotiation which has its complex intertextualities with prior and contemporary criticisms. If in the early imperial period Horace engages in self-criticism as a manifestation of political constraints on the circulation of language, literary and otherwise, Tacitus and Lucan later recognize the need for both external constraints and self-imposed ones, which become apparent as a negotiation of the former as repression intensifies. If these later authors call into question both silence and polemical discourse as strategies for coping with discursive restraints, then they, and particularly Tacitus, also suggest the various forms of indirection that authorial self-criticism may take. Ovid is perhaps the figure who more than any other stands apart from this complicated system of implicit negotiations. But this is not the whole story of Roman criticism, for what the following chapter will show is how the more formal discourse on the production of a rhetorical text in the Roman period offers the individual author a means of negotiating an external critical structure through displacement.

6

Dislocating States and the Sublimity
of Criticism

At that time Longinus was a breathing library and walking
museum, and he was entrusted with the task of judging
ancient [authors] just as many others before him.

Eunapius, *Lives of the Sophists* 456[1]

I

Where the previous chapter considered the way in which ancient
authors and contemporary scholarship characterize the Roman
empire as a space of repression that needs to be negotiated either
through silence or through self-selecting discourses, my present
concern is to see how another aspect of criticism in the Roman
period continues to negotiate the post-Aristotelian project of cultural discrimination and appropriation. The critical scenario I now
consider is the privileged public discourse of rhetoric. The work of
Ahl, Bartsch, and others has drawn attention to the ways in which
discourse and authority are in conflict in imperial Rome in poetic
and historical texts, and also to the ways in which rhetoric highlights this predicament. My particular concern in this chapter is to
consider how one of the most tantalizing, if also one of the most
puzzling and apparently idiosyncratic, texts about literature enacts
criticism in the rhetorical domain. The author of *On the Sublime*,
whom I shall refer to as [Longinus] in keeping with scholarly custom,[2] proposes an extremely rigorous discrimination of literary

---

[1] Λογγῖνος δὲ κατὰ τὸν χρόνον ἐκεῖνον βιβλιοθήκη τις ἦν ἔμψυχος καὶ
περιπατοῦν μουσεῖον, καὶ κρίνειν γε τοὺς παλαιοὺς ἐπετέτραπτο, καθάπερ πρὸ
ἐκείνου πολλοί τινες ἕτεροι.

[2] The ascriptions in a number of the manuscripts associate a Longinus with the
treatise. The Codex Parisinus (2036) offers 'Dionsyius Longinus' as the author of
the work; another, 'Dionysius or Longinus'; while the Laurentinus simply presents

texts as the basis of the sublime, and the sublime in turn becomes
the means of achieving the radical cultural dislocation of the reading subject.

II

Allen Tate points out that subsequent writings on the 'sublime'
make its ancient author responsible for much that he did not originally intend.[3] One of the chief products of mistaken intentions is the
use of the ancient sublime by later writers and authors seeking an
apolitical and wholly aestheticizing basis for later theories of art,
whether their own or those of other subsequent writers and
authors. Because *On the Sublime* often appears to be a work which
is without social and historical context, it has made itself available
for appropriation to Romanticism as a disinterested and disembodied aesthetic. Charles Segal, accordingly, describes the sublime as
being timeless and as aiming at the eternal,[4] while Ernst Curtius
sees the creative spirit of the sublime as transcending political and
economic concerns.[5]

Almost entirely dislodged from the political and public spheres,
the sublime thus seems at first glance to mark a departure in particular from rhetoric, the shared language of a community inasmuch as it constructs itself in terms of common opinion (*doxa*) and
probability (*to eikos*)—that is, what the majority of people in the
community believe likely to be the case or likely to be true. After
all, the wondrousness (*to thaumasion*) which characterizes the sublime strikes out or drives away what is persuasive and what is pleasurable, effectively subordinating the latter to itself (*Subl.* 1. 4).
Such an interpretation of the sublime might suggest that this ecstatic literary quality furthermore rejects social and literary conventions of all kinds, the metaphorical or textual 'places' (*topoi*) to
which authors return again and again and which readers recognize
as the common shared language of literature. Yet, following Frank
Lentricchia, who correctly insists that it is a mistake to view

us with 'Longinus'. See Lamb (1993), for a discussion of the biographical traditions
which explicitly politicize the sublime as a discourse of resistance to authority,
including its own.

  [3] A. Tate (1953), 131–51.   [4] C. P. Segal (1959), 124.
  [5] Curtius (1953), 398; cf. Lentricchia (1983), 128.

[Longinus] as cutting the ties between literature and rhetoric, I seek to recover the interestedness of the sublime precisely where the latter discourse is concerned.[6]

To make this important move, I have to dispel the common assumption that rhetoric is a discourse which above all seeks to *persuade* its audience.[7] Rhetoric is not synonymous with persuasion, even if the latter is its goal. The Greek word for 'persuasion' is *peithō*, while 'rhetoric' derives from *eirō*, which supplies some of the parts of the verb *legein*, 'to speak'. It is on this basis that Pierre Chantraine goes on to define a 'rhetorician' simply as 'celui qui parle en public' or 'orateur à l'assemblée, homme politique', so that 'rhetoric' is to be understood properly as the shared language of an author's contemporary community.[8] The author of *On the Sublime* thus rhetorically situates his work when he identifies the public sphere as the realm of his address. The author's immediate addressee, Postumius Terentianus, who is to be regarded as an intimate friend (cf. the epithets *philtate*, 1. 1, 12. 4, 29. 2, 44. 1, and *hēdiste*, 1. 4, 4. 3), helps to mediate the text to a more general audience. As a confidant and a partisan to [Longinus'] views of rhetoric (1. 1, 1. 3, 44. 1 ff.), Terentianus represents the sympathetic respondent to his engagement with Caecilius' published work on the sublime, and beyond this he is emblematic of the 'politicians' (*andres politikoi*, 1. 2) for whom the treatise is intended. That the politicians are to be regarded as orators, as the very individuals who speak in the public domain, becomes clear from [Longinus'] frequent invocations of the figure of the orator (*rhētor*), both as the recipient of his work and as exemplar (cf. 1. 4, 8. 3, 9. 3, 11. 2, 12. 3, 15. 10, 17. 1, 30. 1, 32. 3, 32. 8).

It is above all the characterization of the sublime (*to hupsos*) in *On the Sublime* as literary movement which articulates its rhetoricity. As the author insists, sublime language is mobile and in this respect emphatically distinct from plastic art. At 36. 3 he observes that where statues are concerned, likeness (*to homoion*) to the original is the virtue sought by the artistic; on the other hand, where language is concerned, the desideratum is transcending (*to huperairon*), and

---

[6] Lentricchia (1983), 128.

[7] Note Kennedy (1963: 7), 'Wherever persuasion is the end, rhetoric is present'; also Guthrie (1971), 50; Vickers (1988), 1. Also, Dodds (1959: 4), 'Rhetoric was the Art of Success'.

[8] Chantraine (1968), i. 326, s.v. εἴρω 2; also Benveniste (1948), 52–4.

therefore going beyond, what is human. He elaborates a conventional contrast between verbal representation as mobile and responsive, perhaps as a gloss on the idea of the 'winged word', and plastic art as static and unmoving. The sophist Alcidamas had favoured spontaneous orations over bronze and wooden statues and paintings (*On the Sophists* 27), while Isocrates justified his encomium of the Cyprian leader Evagoras, declaring that a written speech is more able to represent the virtues of his subject than any plastic or painted similitude (*Evagoras* 75). In the *Apology* Apuleius rehearses the same objection to statues and other non-verbal representations, observing that they freeze their subject and render him or her immobile, unlike language (14).

More radically, the sublime displaces its audience and lifts it up. According to the treatise *On the Sublime*, the sublime (*to hupsos*) is a quality which proceeds from what is supernatural (*ta huperphua*) and wondrous (*to thaumasion*).[9] It leads its audience to a state of ecstasy (*ekstasis*), to a coming out of oneself and particularly out of a (resting-)place (*stasis*). Elsewhere, the author depicts it as a quality and effect of literature that elevates its recipient, that constitutes a lifting up (*to huperairon*) of what is otherwise merely human (36. 3; cf. also *sunairesis*, 7. 2, 10. 3). The Longinian sublime is a discourse that moves and is moved precisely because it is a rhetorical language. One of the most important passages for understanding the dislocating effect of the sublime upon the reading subject is 7. 2, where [Longinus] observes, 'our souls are lifted up (*epairetai*) naturally by the true sublime. They are filled with joy and self-congratulations as if they have themselves produced the text they have heard.'[10] The verb 'lifted up' (*epairetai*) foregrounds the idea of *ekstasis*, of shifting from one place to another, while the use of the passive voice denotes the surrendering of the listener's agency to the sublime in order that this individual might paradoxically re-identify him- or herself as the agent of the sublime. By lifting him or her up, the sublime transforms the reader, as recipient of the work, into its surrogate author, perhaps its re-creator, and it refig-

---

[9] Newman (1987: 152–5) suggests that ὀνόματα κύρια and μεγαλοπρεπή give the treatise a religious dimension; in particular the phrase ὀνόματα κύρια suggests to him 'inspired' language. On this basis this scholar wants to attribute to *On the Sublime* as late a date as possible.

[10] φύσει γάρ πως ὑπὸ τἀληθοῦς ὕψους ἐπαίρεταί τε ἡμῶν ἡ ψυχὴ καὶ γαῦρόν τι †ἀνάθημα λαμβάνουσα πληροῦται χαρᾶς καὶ μεγαλαυχίας, ὡς αὐτὴ γεννήσασα ὅπερ ἤκουσεν (*Subl.* 7. 2).

ures the audience as someone who will not only receive but also produce texts. When Suzanne Guerlac examines the way in which *On the Sublime* challenges the stability and unity of the writing and reading subjects, she proposes that the sublime creates the fiction of the audience as being identical with the speaker. Guerlac identifies what we shall see presently to be the intersubjectivity of the sublime.

III

The background for understanding the Longinian sublime as a rhetorical discourse is the body of Roman rhetorical writing which conceives of this language as structuring itself in terms of space and place. Varro supposes that the verb 'to speak' (*loqui*) derives from the noun 'place' (*locus*) in *De lingua Latina* 6. 56. Whatever authority we grant to this etymology, Quintilian certainly makes apparent the identity of public language as one which both assumes and articulates itself as a language of artificed placement, of orientation, and of movement. In the first book of the *Institutio oratoria*, Quintilian declares that it is important to avoid barbarism and solecism. He gives as examples of the former linguistic fault the addition of either a letter or syllable to a word, or alternatively its subtraction, so that the letter or syllable takes the place of another one or else is misplaced: 'each person can imagine for himself that he could add a letter or syllable to which word he wishes, or subtract it, either putting one in place of another or the same one in a place other than that which is correct' (1. 5. 11). This characterization of barbarism suggests that if bad rhetorical language does not know its proper place ('locus'), good rhetorical language does, because it is fixed in it. In book 8, the author states that clarity requires that the orator uses language which resides in propriety ('proprietas'), in a condition where words by nature correspond to things and do not wander (cf. 'errare') (e.g. 8. 2. 1–3). In book 9 of the *Institutio*, Quintilian declares that rhetorical composition requires the orator to know which word sits best in which place (cf. 'quoque loco') (9. 4. 60). This idea of propriety extends to larger structures of language. In the discussion of the parts of a legal speech in book 4 of the *Institutio*, Quintilian declares that there is a place ('locus'), for different elements of the speech, such as the

narrative of events (4. 2. 5, also 33) or the proofs (cf. 'loco proba-
tionis', 4. 2. 49), and he then proceeds to establish where these
ought to be (also 4. 2. 62, 4. 2. 66 ff.). Among these is the treatment
of actual, literal places ('loca'), which together with the proper
establishment of times and other such elements of setting, help to
make an oration's narrative convincing (4. 2. 53–5).

It is the case, however, that an orator would not always want or
be able to employ language in its natural situation.[11] In book 3
Quintilian states that the orator aims to teach ('docere'), move
('movere'), and please ('delectare') his audience, who is above all
the legal judge (3. 5. 2). The idea that the orator *moves* (cf.
'movere') his listener indicates that public speech and the persuasion produced through public speech operate in part by shifting the
latter individual from one position to another. To effect this,
rhetoric operates as a discourse that is liable to be transferred and
to be moved within limits. After all, as a whole, Roman rhetoric is
a language transferred from Greek culture. As Quintilian observes,
the Romans have translated, literally 'transferred' ('transferentes'),
the Greek term *rhētorikēn* into the Latin 'oratoriam' or 'oratricem'
and they make use of much that is Greek (2. 14. 1–4).

Transference manifests itself in a variety of other ways. In the
discussion of legal argumentation in book 3, the author speaks of
'translatio', literally 'transference'—the very word which also
denotes 'metaphor' (see below)—as an important aspect of forensic
oratory. In his articulation of stasis theory, Quintilian suggests that
various considerations might be brought into, that is transferred
('translatio', 'transfertur') into, a defence to mitigate blame (cf. 3.
6. 69–84 *passim*). So, for instance, treatment of persons, times, and
actions amongst other things may be introduced ('transferuntur')
to help explain the cause of a particular action, such as a homicide
(3. 6. 70). The discussion of rhetorical figures and tropes highlights
the ways in which transference and dislocation contribute to the
discourse of persuasion. Figures and tropes are the rhetorical
strategies which permit the orator to shape his discourse and to
allow it to depart from strict propriety. The word 'figures' (*figurae*;
Greek *schēmata*) identifies this language as shaped and configured

---

[11] Dio Chrysostom demonstrates the literal truth of this when he makes an
encomium of rustic poverty palatable by juxtaposing it against moral criticism of
urban prosperity in the *Euboicus* (*Or.* 7); see Trapp (1995: esp. 164–5) for a discussion of the importance of place in the work of Dio Chrysostom.

(cf. 9. 1. 1; 'conformatio' 9. 1. 4), while tropes 'turn speech' ('ver-tant orationem', 9. 1. 2) and also involve the transference of speech from its natural and principal meaning to another one for the sake of embellishment (cf. 9. 1. 4). Quintilian emphasizes the spatialized conceptualization of a trope, remarking that the majority of grammarians define it as an utterance transferred ('translata') from the place ('loco') in which it is proper to that in which it is not proper.[12] So, among the figures discussed in book 8 of the *Institutio*, metonymy (*metonymia*) is the positioning of one word in place of another (8. 6. 23); catachresis (*katachresis* or *abusio*) involves a transference—the word 'translatio' is again used—when a proper term already exists and is thus to be distinguished from metaphor (8. 6. 35–6); hypberbaton (*hyperbaton*) is a transgression, a conceit in which a word is cast ('traicitur') far away from its proper position for the sake of beauty, and particularly when it involves an inversion (cf. *reversio* and *anastrophē*) (8. 6. 65). Hyperbaton can also be harsh and uneven if words have to be thrust back into some sort of order to avoid chaos (8 .6. 62).

Metaphor is the figure which most obviously insists upon the spatialization and dislocation of language. The writer of the *Rhetorica ad Herennium*, an anonymous rhetorical treatise composed in the early first century CE, speaks of *translatio* as follows, 'a word is transferred from one thing to another thing because it will seem right that it can be transferred on account of their similarity' (4. 34. 45). This author regards metaphor as a verbal transference justified or motivated by an apparent similarity between the objects. In Cicero's *De oratore* 3. 38. 155 Crassus views metaphor as a transference of a word from one object to another either for stylistic embellishment or else to make up for the absence of a word to denote an object.[13] Quintilian invokes these prior definitions of metaphor when he contrasts 'proper words' ('propria verba'), those which signify what they have always signified, and 'transferred words' ('translata'), those which are understood in one way by nature and in another by their placement.[14] Later, in book 8, he speaks of metaphor, literally a 'transference ('translatio'), as involving the dislocation of a word from its proper place to another place

---

[12] 'ut plerique grammatici finiunt, dictio ab eo loco, in quo propria est, translata in eum, in quo propria non est' (*Inst*. 9. 1. 4).

[13] Also Cic. *De or*. 3. 39. 157; *Orat*. 27. 92; and Quint. *Inst*. 8. 6. 6.

[14] 'cum alium natura intellectum, alium loco praebent' (*Inst*. 1. 5. 71).

('locus') for a better or for a more seemly effect (8. 6. 4). In particular, a *translatio* can help a speaker to escape base language or to appropriate words where no proper ones are available (8. 6. 5), so that, ironically, linguistic transference, as a form of language that does not itself constitute propriety, allows the speaker to avoid a moral or stylistic impropriety. The author also states that context, specifically the location of the metaphor within the speech, is necessary to valorize metaphor, for without this, it can have no virtue in itself (8. 3. 38).

The orator has to disrupt the natural linguistic structures and their collocations—that is, he has to resort to figures and tropes, to avoid obscenities and to find words where none otherwise exist, but the comment at 8. 3. 38 reveals an anxiety that metaphor might threaten to take dislocation to such an extreme that these structures are no longer rhetorically acceptable. Indeed, elsewhere, in book 4, the rhetorician warns the orator to avoid insolent language, overdaring borrowings, obsolete archaism, or poetic licence if he wishes to maintain the favour of his audience at the beginning of the oration (4. 1 .58). In his treatise *On Style*, Demetrius insists upon the need to guard against overuse of metaphor in particular (78) and observes that one can mitigate the effect of this figure by converting it to a simile (80), or else by adding epithets (85).

IV

To see the sublime as a quality of a spatialized and moved language is to entail coming to terms with the sublime as a figured language, and to begin to recognize the relationship of *On the Sublime* to the public sphere. It is also to recognize that the rhetoric of the sublime in particular can hardly risk being gratuitous because it is always on the verge of collapsing as a result of its extreme rhetoricity. At 35. 5 the author observes that what is paradoxical or 'contrary to expectation'—to give 'paradox' (from Greek: *para* and *doxan*, 'against expectation/opinion') its etymological gloss—evokes wonder, as the sublime is expected to do. In offering this account, [Longinus] in turn poses to his reader a curious and idiosyncratic paradox, namely an implicit repudiation of the linguistic 'space' which makes the sublime possible. The Longinian treatise on the sublime may discuss many of the figures and tropes of the more conventional rhetorical treatise but it also undertakes a far more daring project of rhetorical displacement. What might help to explain this impetus to ecstasy and to transcendence (cf. *to huperairon*) is the recognition that rhetorical propriety and impropriety are contingent on external circumstances. Figurality and tropicality deliberately and consciously shape and shift discourse in such a way that they make *space* for otherwise politically sensitive comment. But where [Longinus] is concerned, the sublime seeks furthermore to move the reading subject, both in the sense of persuading him or her but also in the sense of transporting this individual to an entirely different 'place', as literally and metaphorically understood. As we shall see, the sublime assumes a parallel between linguistic dislocation and cultural dislocation and reinstitution.

On the Sublime is a taxonomy of linguistic dislocations which in turn shifts the reading subject, enabling a series of alternative identifications of the reader.[15] It is a rhetorical treatise which to a considerable extent dramatizes its own 'theory', demonstrating and enacting the power and effect of the figures and tropes of public discourse that it describes and analyses. One of the ways in which it seeks to disorient its reader is by refusing to conform to any straightforward or conventional models of literary unity. In Plato's *Phaedrus*, Socrates offers what has become an authoritative discussion of literary unity when he suggests that a speech (*logos*) should be like a living-creature, having a head, body, and feet each in their proper arrangement (264c2–5). [Longinus] explicitly recalls Plato's comparison when in chapter 10 he observes that since the parts of every topic have places assigned 'by nature' (*phusei*), it is necessary to select (*eklegein*) what is most timely and opportune (*ta kairiōtata*) and to arrange them with respect to one another so as to create a single body (*hen ti sōma*). He goes on to state that the audience 'is led' (*prosagetai*)—the verb perhaps reflects Plato's use of the noun *psychagōgia* at *Phaedrus* 271c10—both by the choice of passages and by their density (10. 1).

If Lucan emphasizes the need for language to observe distinctions and boundaries lest the world collapse into an apocalyptic confusion from which it might never recover (see Chapter 5), the author of the treatise *On the Sublime* takes quite a different approach. He proposes that the structure of the sublime text is an

[15] Walsh (1988: 262–4) sees the sublime as a departure from natural language through tecnhnicality.

artificial order, consisting in a contrived rearrangement of only
certain aspects of natural literary structure. Yet [Longinus'] own
prose calls into question conventional textual unities, and it enacts
precisely the sort of dislocations which he discusses as being characteristic and required of the sublime. For Neil Hertz, this occurs
most evidently in the way in which the author cites exemplary texts
in his treatise. He observes that [Longinus] does not follow a linear
structure. Instead, he 'thickens' the texture of his work, on the
grounds that density of citations creates the sublime (10. 1). He
piles citations and images on top of each other in rapid succes-
sion.[16] Passages, linked by shared images and often only by a single
shared word, are jarringly juxtaposed to produce interesting meanings.[17]

The treatment of Sappho's poem (fr. 31 L–P) at chapter 10. 2 ff.
illustrates precisely this quality of [Longinus'] language.[18] Hertz
points to the layering effect of the text, here venturing that the reference to death (cf. *tethnakēn*) in the final stanza of Sappho's poem
provides an obvious link to, and a pretext for citing, a passage from
Homer, a description of a storm bringing sailors near death at 10. 5
(cf. *Il.* 15. 625–8). Apart from the common motif of death, Hertz
notes further complex transitions between the citations from
Sappho and Homer which associate them. He notes that the effect
of passion, namely shivering, on Sappho's body (cf. fr. 31. 13–14)
is paralleled by the sailors shuddering when their ship is tossed and
beaten by the waves (cf. *tromeousi*, *Il.* 15. 627). The stress that
Sappho experiences in her body is, moreover, like the stress to
which Homer subjects the language of his works: the epic poet tor-
tures, forces, and batters his words together (10. 6).[19] In
[Longinus'] analysis, it is as if Sappho's own personal suffering
informs the chronologically earlier Homeric textuality, highlighting the way in which author and reader (who is here also an author)
may merge through the power of the sublime. To make emphatically the point that the sublime does not require linear continuity
or chronology, [Longinus] intersperses a passage from the
Arimaspea between the citations of Sappho's poem and the lines

---

[16] Hertz (1985), 8.   [17] Ibid. 2–3.
[18] Guerlac (1985: 282) reads Sappho's text as an example of a sublime structure
because it scatters and also draws together a whole series of different bodily perceptions, so that the body is presented both as the literal, physical body of the speaking
voice and as the metaphorical, textual 'body'.
[19] Hertz (1985), 6–7.

from Homer at 10. 4 and then a line from Aratus at 10. 6. Because the artificial continuity produced through the intertextuality of *On the Sublime* does not lie in a natural consecutive order, neither the *Arimaspeia* nor the verse from Aratus, despite being ineffective texts, diminishes the effect of the sublime.

Chapter 10 clearly marks the dramatization of sublime structure through the citation of texts from Sappho, Homer, and Aratus. But it is not the only passage in the treatise to grant a privileged status to artificial order. In chapter 9, the author ostensibly discusses the way in which what is lofty (*megalophues*) is one of the crucial factors for producing the sublime. He offers a further citation from Homer, presenting what appears to be a continuous description of a theomachy, or battle of the gods, from the *Iliad* (9. 6). Closer inspection of the lines reveals that they are actually an amalgamation of two separate passages which are undisturbed in the manuscript tradition, *Iliad* 21. 388 and *Iliad* 20. 61–5. The author conflates separate elements of Homer's poem in order to dramatize cosmic disorder. The commentary he provides at 9. 6–7 makes apparent his intention to re-create in his own text the chaos described by Homer when he declares that 'everything together, heaven, hell, mortals, immortals' (*panth' hama ouranos hadēs, ta thnēta ta athanata*), is in conflict. The author's own asyndeton constitutes at the linguistic level a rejection of linearity by closely juxtaposing words which here denote contrary spaces and domains. At the level of cosmology, asyndeton illustrates the point offered at 9. 7, that the poet makes men appear to be as gods in terms of their power, and he renders gods as men in the *Iliad*. Later in the same chapter, at 9. 8, [Longinus] again shows that the structure of the sublime can be constituted out of a deliberate dislocation of texts. Taking liberties with the text of the *Iliad*, he offers a sublime description of Poseidon which combines lines from different parts of the epic, namely 13. 18, 20. 60, and 13. 27–9.

On the Sublime also works at displacing its reading subject through more specific literary structures—that is, through rhetorical figures (*schēmata*). In chapter 16 [Longinus] explains how apostrophe (*apostrophē*), whose very name denotes a turning away or a dissociation, can create the state of ecstasy. Jonathan Culler suggests that apostrophe deflects a message; it disrupts what this critic calls 'the circuit of communication', because it gestures to an addressee, namely a fictional and absent one, other than the text's immediate readers or hearers.[20] Already in antiquity, [Longinus] recognizes what apostrophe can do. He cites a passage from Demosthenes' *On the Crown* which shows how this figure can make those who are addressed through it perceive themselves to be elsewhere than they actually are. He comments that when the orator invokes the ancestors of his contemporary Athenians, he dissociates his actual audience from their present circumstances and transports them back into their own past. In particular, he returns them to the jubilant celebration of the victory over the Persians at Marathon (16. 2).[21] The logic of apostrophe holds that by citing this passage, the author of *On the Sublime* in his turn transports his own contemporaries to the great Athenian democratic past and lifts them out of their current circumstances.

Also among the tropes which break up the more conventional continuities of the text, and so produce an ecstatic effect, is hyperbaton, literally an order of expression or thought that has been moved (cf. *kekinēmenē taxis*, 22. 1). Hyperbaton signifies agitated emotion—as we have seen, Quintilian defines it as a mode of linguistic 'transgression'. [Longinus] cites from the text of Herodotus part of Dionysius of Phocaea's speech which serves to warn the Ionians about the pressing Persian threat:

Just as the Phocaean Dionysius says in Herodotus, 'Our affairs are on a razor's edge, O Ionian men, as to whether we are free or slaves, and as for the latter, runaway slaves. Thus if you now wish to undertake labour, toil is at hand and you will be able to surpass the enemy. (22. 1–2; cf. Hdt. 6.1)

[Longinus] goes on to analyse the passage, commenting that Herodotus has dislocated the natural orders of syntax and chronology. He observes that the historian has delayed the vocative 'O Ionian men'. He has transposed (*huperebibase*) it in order to draw attention to the imminent danger from the enemy; he has pushed ahead (*proeisebalen*) his addressees to address fear; and he has thus overturned (*apestrepse*) the order of ideas (22. 2). By delaying the address to the Ionians, the speaker Dionysius stresses the urgency of the immediate danger. The hyperbaton in turn transports the audience into a state of fear, in effect dragging along (*sunepispōmenos*) its audience into the action of the text (22. 3). Other historians use the figure of hyperbaton to draw their audi-

---

[20] Culler (1981), 135.   [21] Guerlac (1985), 280.

ences into events depicted in their texts. [Longinus] observes that
Thucydides is especially skilled at leading by hyperbata what is
unified and cannot be divided from elsewhere, reinforcing the idea
that the author of *On the Sublime* is engaged in a radical revision of
literary unity. He notes, furthermore, that Demosthenes, although
not as daring as Thucydides, still throws (*embalōn*) his audience off
balance and into fear. Through hyperbata, this fear makes the
audience able to sympathize with the danger, literally, 'to share
the danger' (*sunapokinduneuein*), experienced by the text's speaker
(22. 4).

Change of person is another figure that resituates and displaces
the reading subject, locating him or her in another time and place.
A shift of speaking voice and identity, say from the third to the second person, can make the audience think it is in the midst of the
dangers being represented in the text, as in the case of the examples
that [Longinus] cites from Homer (*Il.* 15. 697), Aratus (*Phaen.*
287), and Herodotus (2. 29) at 26. 1–2. The author of *On the
Sublime* observes how, of these three authors, Herodotus conveys
the hearer's soul through the geographical locations he mentions in
the work, Elephantine and Meroe, to create the impression that his
hearer can see, and then how he sets him in the midst of the action
(*tōn energoumenōn*, 26. 2). [Longinus]' own commentary scripts the
displacing effect of the figure for the reader of his work. He asks his
addressee, 'Do you see?' (*oras*) in what way the soul is led through
the geographical sites and made, as it were, to visualize what it has
heard (*tēn akoēn opsin poiōn*).

The analysis of the Herodotean text imposes upon the reading
audience a mode of intersubjectivity which [Longinus] earlier
ascribes to *phantasia*, the method of verbal image-making.[22] At
15. 1 ff., the author glosses *phantasia* as a thought which is 'productive of speech', and he goes on to declare that the term conventionally describes a situation 'when under the influence of
inspiration and emotion *you* seem to see what you say, and *you* place
it before the eyes of the listeners/audience'. What one remarks
about this description of *phantasia* is the way in which it becomes
impossible to distinguish between the author and the audience.
The second person singular, 'you', denotes both individuals, so
that 'you' both produces and views the description. The audience

[22] See also the discussion of Hellenistic ekphrasis in Zanker (1987), 39–41;
Goldhill (1994), 208–13, esp. 213; Elsner (1995), 26–8.

is not just the passive viewer, but is cast as someone who creates, forms, and fashions the viewed world through what is implicitly his cultural expertise.[23] But there is perhaps a paradox involved in this intersubjectivity, for *phantasia* makes visible what even the artist himself has not seen. In the *Life of Apollonius of Tyana*, Philostratus distinguishes *phantasia* from imitation when he speaks of the former as being able by mental analogy with reality to produce an image of what the artist has not viewed, and in this way as being able to do justice to depictions of the gods.[24]

But the literary sublime engages in the dislocation of the audience as far more than viewer. Furthermore, in chapter 26 [Longinus] uses the word 'places' (*topoi*) to denote the different places through which the reader's soul is guided and at which he is set down (26. 2). His language is significantly the vocabulary of metaphor, the trope which, as we have seen, operates by the transfer (*translatio*) of words from one metaphorical 'place' to another 'place' (see e.g. *Rhet. Her.* 4. 34. 45; Cic. *De or.* 3. 39. 157; Quint. *Inst.* 8. 6. 5). The reader is drawn into the treatise—note the apostrophe to Terentianus as 'friend' (*hetaire*) at 26. 2—then he is transported from literal and metaphorical place to place, and then finally into the locations identified in Herodotus' work as cited in the treatise.[25] Through this textual journey, his or her senses are augmented; hearing is given sight and in this way the sublime is achieved. Elsewhere, Quintilian observes that sublimity ('sublimitas') can be produced by daring transference ('translatio'), particularly when it attributes sense to otherwise inanimate objects: 'a wondrous sublime arises especially from these things which create danger by daring and by transference (*translatione*) when we attribute actions and consciousness to things which [otherwise] lack sensation.[26]'

---

[23] See the recent excellent discussion by Goldhill (1994), 208–10; also Kennedy in *CHLC* i. 211.

[24] Cf. μίμησις μὲν γὰρ δημιουργήσει, ὃ εἶδεν, φαντασία δὲ καὶ ὃ μὴ εἶδεν, ὑποθήσεται γὰρ αὐτὸ πρὸς τὴν ἀναφορὰν τοῦ ὄντος, . . . (Philostr. *VA* 6. 19). See also Trimpi (1983: 103 n. 6), who sees Philostratus as criticizing the (Aristotelian) notion of μίμησις as verisimilar reproduction.

[25] On ἐνάργεια as vividness in rhetorical and poetic texts, see Zanker (1981), (1987), 39 ff. and Goldhill (1994), 208.

[26] 'praecipueque ex his oritur mira sublimitas, quae audaci et proxime periculum translatione tolluntur, cum rebus sensu carentibus actus quendam et animos damus' (*Inst.* 8. 6. 11).

Plato proscribes the dramatic voice as pluralizing identity. [Longinus], however, regards it as a means of constituting the sublime. A figure related to change of person assists the destabilization of the identity of the subject in the service of the sublime. An author can suddenly shift (cf. *antimethistatai*) into his character's person and dramatize his emotional state (27. 1). [Longinus] cites *Iliad* 15. 346–9, where Homer first narrates Hector's summons to the Trojans and then has Hector himself instruct his men to rush at the ships. [Longinus] proceeds to describe this change from third-person narration into dramatic discourse as a change from person into person, which effaces any distinction between the author's own real identity and the identity of his fictional character (27. 2). The exchange of voice and person need not always be so explicitly figured as [Longinus] himself shows in his commentary on a passage from Euripides' *Phaethon*. Following a citation of a description of Phaethon mounting the chariot of the sun, the author observes that the tragedian's soul has itself virtually mounted the chariot and shared the risk of flying with Phaethon's father's horses (15. 4). The verbs, literally rendered as 'mount together' (*sunepibainei*) and 'fly with' (*sunepterōtai*), and the participle, 'being in danger together' (*sungkiduneuousa*), emphasize the sympathy and identification of Euripides with his fictional character. Similarly, question and answer is another aspect of the rhetoric of the sublime, displacing its audience through the impression that the listener or reader is actually face to face with the interlocutor (18. 1). A confluence of figures is also effective in moving (*kinein*) the recipient of a literary text (20. 1).

Other sections of *On the Sublime* are more specifically concerned with how the rhetoric of the sublime can transform the conditions which the reading subject finds or thinks him- or herself in. Chapter 25 shows how temporal location may be shifted through language. Here the author demonstrates that use of the present tense in narrating past events can create the impression that the past is now happening and present (cf. *hōs ginomea kai paronta*). He cites from Xenophon's *Cyropaedia* a description of a man 'falling' under Cyrus' horse, 'striking' (*paiei*) the horse's underbelly with his sword, and shaking the ruler off his horse (*Cyr.* 7. 1. 37). The citation of the *Cyropaedia* again enacts the temporal dislocation which he attributes to Xenophon's text as it re-presents the incident for his own audience, while the citation is significantly introduced with a vivid present, 'Xenophon says' (*phēsin ho Xenophōn*), which projects the narrative act into the more contemporary *On the Sublime*. [Longinus] states that the use of present tenses in speaking of the past is a narrative technique also commonly used by Thucydides.

The destabilizing power of the sublime and its figures is again evident in the various figures which produce change at the linguistic level. Polyptoton (*poluptōton*) is a term which covers a variety of devices such as accumulation (*athrōismos*), variation (*metabolē*), and climax, all involving the transformation of grammatical case and number (23. 1). [Longinus] illustrates polyptoton by citing a passage from Sophocles' *Oedipus Tyrannus*. He observes that by referring to Oedipus and Jocasta's marriage as numerous, indeterminate 'marriages' (*gamoi*) in the drama, the dramatist multiplies and increases their misfortunes (23. 3; cf. *OT* 1403 ff.). By corollary, the designation of numerous individuals or things by a singular, denoting them as a class, amalgamates them as a unity. It is thus that language demonstrates its capacity to transform reality, and the author of the treatise notes that this trope of number produces a 'startling change of facts into their opposite state' (24. 2).

V

On the Sublime effectively enables its audience to identify with the author, both past and present (as [Longinus] acknowledges at 7. 2), with literary characters and figures, and with fictive worlds. Assimilated to rhetoric and particularly to an understanding of rhetoric as a discourse which displaces, disrupts, and elevates, the sublime poses two large questions. The first of these is how it might be understood as a critical discourse in the sense explored by this book. The second is where the sublime leaves both itself and its reading subject at the end. I suggest that the attempt to answer the first of these questions makes apparent the way in which the sublime is a discriminating and exclusive discourse with a distinct social and political teleology.

Writers in the eighteenth century addressed the second question by seeing the 'sublime' as a signifier of potential limitlessness and of an aesthetics of limitlessness. They suggested that the sublime could lead to the disintegration and dissipation of the text and its reading subject. Since it was a language that could, in the case of a literary or artistic object, allow the reading and viewing subject to be endlessly transported, Pete de Bolla (1989) observes that in aesthetic discourse the sublime constituted a discourse of excess and licence that needed to be rigorously curtailed and constrained through careful legislation. Even in economic and social discourses, the sublime became identified with hyperinflation and again showed the necessity of strict regulation. De Bolla's analysis provides a context in which the idea of the sublime must be strictly controlled in order to ensure that it does not get out of hand, and it furthermore reveals one of its significant political dimensions in subsequent appropriations of it. This reading of the sublime therefore calls into question what we began by seeing to be the Romantic characterization of the sublime as an entirely apolitical transport into a realm of hypostasized beauty.

I want to offer yet another rehistoricization of the sublime, namely one which locates it directly within critical history. If some later authors who took up and developed the theory of the sublime regarded this literary and cultural quality as one that requires regulation to be imposed from without, they none the less failed to recognize that [Longinus] had already established a series of boundaries and safeguards against infinite dislocation. The author of *On the Sublime*, as a rhetorical theorist, demonstrates his conventionality, rather than his eccentricity, where anxiety about excessive movement of language is concerned. The sublime does involve textual dislocation; however, it is the case that to be feasible such dislocation has to be *discriminating*. Certainly, when [Longinus] considers the relationship between the sublime and figurality at chapter 17, he expresses an anxiety about lack of restraint. He observes that rhetorical figures have an effect which is contrary to and fights against (*summachei*) the sublime, since an ostentatious use of figures arouses suspicion and creates the sense of insincerity. He asserts that the best figure is one which conceals its own figurality.[27] [Longinus] implies that a successful figure hides its own figurality exactly by enacting its figurality, by engaging in a set of moves, which perhaps shows how one might also disguise the schematic quality of discourse by explicitly forswearing that quality. Thus Guerlac locates a paradox of the sublime here, noting that

---

[27] διόπερ καὶ τότε ἄριστον δοκεῖ τὸ σχῆμα, ὅταν αὐτὸ τοῦτο διαλανθάνῃ, ὅτι σχῆμά ἐστι (*Subl.* 17. 1).

the author prescribes more effective dissimulation to cure the appearance of dissimulation: this effective duplicity engenders ecstasy no less than actual sincerity does.[28] But where Guerlac implicitly equates figurality with the sublime, [Longinus] maintains that they are distinct and proposes that the antidote (*alexēma*) to figurality is the avoidance not of figures but of the sublime and emotion, whose brilliant light blinds the audience to the artifice (*technē*) of figures (17. 2; also 32. 4).

Dissimulation is not where the critical imperative most obviously manifests itself where the sublime is concerned. The need to be discriminating presents itself rather and above all where [Longinus] patently foregrounds the importance of selecting certain works over others in the discussion and production of the sublime. It is no accident that he begins the treatise by observing that his rival Caecilius, whom Donald Russell has identified as Caecilius of Caleacte, the first-century BCE author on figures,[29] has attempted to illustrate to his readers through a myriad ways (*dia muriōn hosōn . . . deiknunai*) just what sort of thing the sublime is and thus treated his audience as ignorant of his topic (1. 1). The point is that Caecilius has been indiscriminate, so that his work as a whole appears to be rather feeble (*tapeinoteron*) (1. 1). That the sublime must in turn be the product of the criticism, that is of the discrimination, as far as the material available to an author is concerned, becomes explicit from chapter 43. 2–3 of [Longinus'] treatise. Here the author cites an account of the Persian expedition into Egypt from the work of the historian Theopompus, the reputed pupil of Isocrates and possibly thus one of the Isocrateans who is faulted in chapter 21 for overusing connectives. [Longinus] observes that the narrative passes from the lofty to the base because the historian was unable to leave out any detail (cf. *ta hola diebale*, 43. 2). He was indiscriminate in his account of the *katabasis*. In this way the historian significantly enacted the *katabasis*, literally a 'descent', on a linguistic level by producing a bathetic plunge which is a counterpoint to the sublime, conceptualized as a lifting up. [Longinus] goes on to echo the discourse of legal criticism when he remarks that ideally one would imitate the human artistic nature which does

---

[28] Guerlac (1985), 281, 285; see also Walsh (1988: 266–7), who notes that the sublime overcomes its audience through violence rather than through deceit.

[29] D. A. Russell (1964), 58.

not set in view the 'unsayables' (*aporrhēta*) or the accoutrements of tumidity (43. 5).

It is important to recognize that part of the author's definition of the sublime (*to hupsos*) involves a differentiation of this literary quality from excess. In his discussion of the literary sublime in a letter addressed to a Lupercus, Pliny the Younger speaks of the need to distinguish between the tumid ('tumida') and the sublime ('sublimia'), the improper ('improba') and the daring ('audentia'), the excessive ('nimia') and the full ('plena') (*Ep.* 9. 26. 5).[30] It is thus that he asserts the need for a rhetorical rule and limit, such as the language of Demosthenes is; cf. 'sed Demosthenes ipse, ille norma oratoris et regula, num se cohibet et comprimit, . . .' (*Ep.* 9. 26. 8). As Pliny, [Longinus] vociferously asserts that the discourse which constitutes the sublime has its constraints. This assertion calls into question the conventional characterization of this literary trait in terms of extremity and excess. In chapter 12, he makes a distinction between the sublime and mere rhetorical amplification (*auxēsis*), which resides in multitude (*en plēthei*, 12. 1). In addition, if frigidity (*psuchron*) stands in opposition to the sublime, then tumidity (*ongkos*), literally 'swelling', is the sublime transgressed. To illustrate this fault, the author cites at chapter 3 a passage from Aeschylus' now lost *Oreithyia* to declare the lines which Boreas speaks paratragedy rather than what is tragic: the tragedian's image of the heavens vomiting, and his characterization of the wind Boreas as a flute-player are declared to have departed from the properly tragic. Describing this example of literary excess as swollenness (*ongkos*) and tumidity or bombast (*stomphos*) (3. 1)—or to take Hamilton-Fyfe's (1927) translation, 'high-falutin' (*meteōra*)—[Longinus] insists that it is anything but sublime (*hupsēla*) (3. 2). Tumidity results in part from trying to outdo the sublime (4). Because Cicero has recourse to tumidity (*en ongkōi*), he falls short in a comparison with Demosthenes, who is later in the treatise presented as a 'limit' or 'boundary' (*horos*) where the use of certain figures is concerned (12. 4; for Demosthenes, see 32. 1).

Unlike Caecilius, [Longinus] demands that his audience be discriminating and discerning in its attempts to encounter and to experience the sublime. In turn, his account of the sublime will be selective. Rather than teach his audiences as if they were complete

[30] See Armisen-Marchetti (1990), 90.

novices, he will only remind them of this quality, declaring that his analysis (*theōria*) of it will be neither excessive nor useless (2. 3). In response to those who might question the validity of his own technical rhetoric, he later insists that he is not detailing everything (*to panta diakriboun*) which produces the sublime; rather, he presents only a few (*oliga*) of the figures responsible for this literary quality (16. 1). In an evocation of legal discrimination, the author invites his named addressee, Postumius Terentianus, to give his *judgement* (*sunepikrineis*) on his project (1. 2). Legal judgement, one of the paradigmatic critical scenarios, is precisely the ability required for the recognition of the sublime. Later in the treatise, [Longinus] invites his addressee to make a sound judgement—'you may judge (*epikrinoite*) these things better'—by concurring with him that the writing of Demosthenes is superior to that of Cicero, given the economy of Demosthenes (12. 5). Elsewhere, in chapter 6, the author informs Terentianus that it is important to acquire knowledge of and the ability to discern (*epikrisis*) the true sublime. He adds that the judgement (*krisis*) of speeches is the final product of much experience, and in the following chapter, he suggests that this is not a skill demonstrated by a small group of readers (7. 4). An incontrovertible proof of the sublime is presented when individuals of differing backgrounds, dispositions, ages, and so on agree in their judgement (*krisis*) of what is sublime (7. 4). But judgement needs to be properly applied so that the reader does not 'deem'— again the verb *krinein* is used—the shortcomings of truly great and daring authors, such as Homer, Archilochus, Pindar, Sophocles, and Demosthenes, to discredit them completely, with the result that one ends up preferring writers who are technically more perfect. The latter group, individuals such as Apollonius, Theocritus, Eratosthenes, Bacchylides, and Hyperides, are perfect only in a limited sense, for their literary aspirations and goals are lower (33. 5–34. 1; cf. 36. 4).

The sublime, according to [Longinus'] account, is a quality of discourse that itself discriminates. It is 'an excellence' (*akrotēs*) and 'an outstanding quality' (*exochē*) of speech proceeding from the greatest poets and prose writers in their excellence (1. 3). [Longinus] suggests that a personified human nature has selected mankind for this quality inasmuch as it has 'judged' (*ekrine*) him a creature neither base nor ignoble (35. 2). To learn how to produce the sublime entails that one must learn not from any random author but from skill (*technē*, 2. 3). Judgement and discrimination are in turn also required in the production of the sublime, although [Longinus] observes that the current social environment produces only corrupt judges who seek personal profit and gain, and are in part responsible for the decline of literature in the community (44. 9)—the author implicitly casts his society as a re-enactment of the cruel and unjust Fifth Age of Hesiod's *Works and Days*. As we have seen, he contends that this literary quality may proceed from the selection (*eklegein*) of the most timely elements (*ta kairiōtata*) and from their arrangement into a coherent structure (10. 1). In the discussion of diction, the author asserts that the selection (*eklogē*) of appropriate and grand words persuades and charms an audience (30. 1).[31] In chapter 14, he imagines earlier sublime authors such as Homer and Demosthenes to be the heroic judges (*kritais*) and witnesses, that is the audience, of the work that is currently being produced, in order to stress the rigour of the literary standards demanded of and by the sublime (14. 2).

VI

It is with regard to such circumscription that I suggest the sublime cannot indeterminately dislocate its reading subject—indeed one does not simply get lost in the sublime. Here an awareness of a prior literary culture becomes of paramount importance in the construction of a limit for the dislocation of subject language and of its recipient. Fifth- and fourth-century Athenian authors had established the dichotomy between the old and the new in literature together with its moral characterization, associating tradition (*ta archaia*) with preservation not only of traditional literature but also with respect for the customs and laws of one's ancestors. In contrast, novel things (*ta kaina*) were depicted as a rejection of the teachings and customs of one's fathers that conventionally manifested itself in the Oedipal scenario of the son beating the father, as

---

[31] The selection or choice (ἐκλογή) of words seems to have been a conventional topic of rhetorical treatises; see Arist. *Rh.* 3. 2. 1, 5. 1; Phld. *Rh.* 1. 162s; *Rhet. Her.* 4. 12. 17; Cic. *Brut.* 72. 252–3. In *On Literary Composition* 1, 2, and 3, Dionysius of Halicarnassus insists, however, that selection of words (ἐκλογή τῶν ὀνομάτων) takes second place to arrangement (συνθέσις); see also Usher (1985), 19 n. and 22–3 n.

in the comedies of Aristophanes.[32] The critique of what is novel
and contemporary makes evident the retrospective yearning of *On
the Sublime*. [Longinus] disapprovingly observes that current writers presume to reject tradition and what is ancestral (*ta archaia*).
They are now completely taken by desire for novelty (*kain-
ospoudaion*). This infatuation with what is new constitutes a lack of
continuity between past and present, between father and son—
which Hesiod articulates as the nightmarish situation of his own
age, in which fathers do not resemble their offspring (*WD* 182)—
between origins and descent. It constitutes a rejection of the past
and its authors, such as Homer, Plato and Demosthenes, whom
[Longinus] regards as the pinnacle of literary achievement and who
offer to the present a means of recovering the sublime.

Eagerness for what is novel explains why contemporary literature is so uninspired and insipid. Not accidently is the response to
Caecilius in *On the Sublime* precisely a critique of the love of novelty.[33] Caecilius and his writing support the view that there is a
dearth of sublime natures at the present (44. 1). This critic's work
fails to demonstrate sublimity. It appears enervated as a whole and
does not succeed in meeting opportune moments (*kairoi*), which is
a necessary requirement of a sublime text (cf. 1. 4). Caecilius shows
his hate for Plato and his preference for Lysias (32. 8), and accordingly his concern with accuracy over ambition to achieve the sublime (*ta hupsa*) (cf. 36. 3). He emblematizes the literary
inadequacies of the current age, no less than the unnamed philosopher of the work's final chapter who, rather, blames the decline of
literature on repressive government (44. 1).[34]

Ewen Bowie has argued that the intellectual movement we now
call the Second Sophistic had an archaizing tendency, particularly
where linguistic and literary matters of culture were concerned,
which served to offer the past as an alternative to a defective present; while Jas Elsner views the Greek past as simultaneously pos-

---

[32] For the dichotomy between τὰ ἀρχαῖα and τὰ καινά, see Too (1995), 54 ff.

[33] D. A. Russell (1979: 128) notes that ps.-Dionysius, author of the treatise
Mistakes, rejected archaism and an apparently irrational aesthetics such as the
Longinian sublime.

[34] Arieti and Crossett (1985: 224) have suggested that the latter individual may
be a figure representative of a particular group, philosophers, in that he serves as an
amalgam of all the contemporary philosophical sects, Stoics, Epicureans,
Peripatetics, and Cynics.

sessed and as recognized as awesomely alien.[35] The preferred and
ideal past was that of Athens, the privileged language was Attic
Greek, and the latter-day sophist's canon was the literature of classical Athens, all of which ostensibly aimed to produce a cultural
resurgence in what was regarded as a defective Roman present. *On
the Sublime* may well be contemporary with this subsequent
sophistic movement, and it is the case that the sublime, despite or
perhaps because of its disruptive nature, is a deeply conservative
force. Hertz has suggested quite specifically that the overall
impression created by the work is a desire to depart from imperial
Rome through nostalgia, a wistful yearning for the past, for the
golden age of fifth- and fourth-century Athens, which supplies
most of the author's literary examples and models. (He offers, as an
analogous figure for [Longinus], Walter Benjamin who recalls a
Europe which existed in a more ideal age before the disintegrating
Europe of the 1930s.[36])

Of course, the invocation of classical Greek, and especially Attic,
literary culture itself has a precedent in the critical project of
Hellenistic Alexandria. With respect to this, the epigraph at the
head of this chapter becomes extremely interesting. Eunapius characterizes the philosopher Porphyry's teacher, Longinus—who,
notably, is not identified as the author of *On the Sublime*—as a
latter-day Hellenistic critic. This Longinus is compared to a
'breathing library' and a 'walking museum', the institutions which
were active in the wholesale appropriation of Homer, archaic
poetry, classical Greek literature and, in the case of the Septuagint,
the Hebrew Bible by an élite Alexandrian culture and its representative agents. Eunapius' biographical sketch of the historical
Longinus and his work puts the ideas of both judgement and dislocation in the foreground through its evocation of the idea of the
Mouseion, which it also personalizes. Where the original
Mouseion-Library was constituted by a complex of buildings, the
body of professional literati who worked there, and their books, the
historical individual Longinus now personifies the critical institution as a 'breathing library and walking museum'. He adjudicates
the work of earlier writers and, as in the case of his predecessors,
great learning and authorship validate his position as judge. The
biographer goes on to declare that his literary judgement (*krisis*)

[35] Bowie (1970), esp. 36 and 41; Elsner (1996), 249.   [36] Hertz (1985), 14.

was required to legitimate the critical positions of his contemporaries. Eunapius may not be speaking of our [Longinus]; however, it is the case that *On the Sublime* engages in a visibly Hellenistic technique of appropriation of a prior, alien culture, although its archaizing inclination constitutes a rejection of Hellenistic literature. Just as Ptolemy II had the Old Testament translated out of Hebrew into Greek, so the treatise likewise brings the story of the Creation from the Book of Genesis to its Greek-reading audience through translation, one that is conspicuously erroneous (cf. 9. 9).[37]

[Longinus] also envisages a much more fundamental recovery of the past and a more radical transport of the reading subject from his or her present situation. The Longinian sublime presents imitation (*mimēsis*) as a strategy—the metaphor he employs is that of a 'road'—for the reclamation of past authors and the literary tradition that make the sublime possible. In chapter 13 the author discusses imitation and zealousness (*zēlosis*), for the great prose and poetic authors of an earlier age breathe into the soul of the latter-day writer the great natures (cf. *apo tēs tōn archaiōn megalophuias*) of their predecessors, just as a divine breath from the earth inspires the Pythia (13. 2). This statement is extraordinary because, as Russell has observed, imitation itself and the desire to emulate or imitate are distinct for Dionysius of Halicarnassus' (*On Imitation*, p. 200 Usener–Radermacher). For the author of the present work, they are, however, indistinguishable and so speak to the power of the sublime text to move and rouse the soul to admiration.[38] Imitation is not a mechanical or technical process of modelling oneself after a paradigm, and could not be so on the understanding of the sublime as a literary quality that can 'other' the self; it is an inspirational experience, thus attesting to the sublime as a creative and re-creative quality.[39] [Longinus] elaborates his account of imitation by explaining that it is not a theft but a remodelling (*apotupōsis*) on the basis of fine and beautiful characters and artworks. By his juxtaposition of 'characters', 'creations', and 'artworks', he proposes that the artist cannot ultimately be distinguished from his art (13. 4). He sheds light on the way in which the sublime can be understood to lift up the soul of an audi-

---

[37] See D. A. Russell (1979), 113–14.
[38] D. A. Russell in West and Woodman (1979), 9–10.
[39] See D. A. Russell in West and Woodman (1979), 11, 16.

ence so that it believes itself to have produced what it has heard (*hōs autē gennēsasa hoper ēkousen*), and thus the sublime effectively transfers the recipient into the position of author (cf. 7. 2). Remodelling (*apotupōsis*) redeems plastic art by ascribing to it a mode of mobility that is characteristic precisely of language and in particular of rhetorical language, and insists again upon the inter-subjectivity of author and audience. It is in this way that the dis-course of imitation is explicitly transcended by, and now appropriated to, the sort of imaginative process denoted by the term *phantasia*.

If [Longinus] rejects contemporary literary predilections, he, nevertheless, presents a qualified critique of the present. With Segal, I suggest that he repudiates the position of the nameless philosopher who is reported as supposing that the dire state of lit-erature is due to the social environment. The unnamed intellectual blames current cultural conditions on the absence of true democ-racy and freedom (which is the 'nursemaid' of lofty discourse at 44. 1–5), and he thus takes refuge in a rhetorical commonplace con-cerning the decline of oratory, found for instance in Tacitus' *Dialogus* (in one reading of the dialogue), in Velleius Paterculus (1. 16–18), and in Quintilian (*Inst.* 8. 6. 76).[40] Where the philo-sopher insists that no rhetorician can be a slave (44. 4), [Longinus] rejects as an explanation for the state of literature and the writer's soul the rather simplistic argument that oppression cannot nurture eloquence. Instead he proceeds to observe that it is the human con-dition to find fault with present circumstances, when in fact they are not responsible for greatness in nature and literature (44. 6). Segal, who inclines towards a depoliticizing and Romanticizing interpretation of the sublime, understands this refutation to imply that for the author of the treatise there is no correlation between the state and literary art.[41] This scholar maintains that for the latter to see man as bound by his material circumstances seems to contradict his ideal of the sublime as a quality which transcends such circum-stances.[42]

If [Longinus] dismisses the idea that society wholly determines the condition of literature in society, he is not, on the other hand, saying that there is no correlation between the state and art. In fact,

[40] See Luce (1993: 13) for a fuller list of passages in which this commonplace can be found.

[41] D. A. Russell (1964), 185 ff.   [42] C. P. Segal (1959), 139–40.

the condition of the political community is intimately connected
with literary culture and its condition. For the author, sublime
literature proceeds from sublime souls and natures, which are the
constituent elements of the polity. The psychological dimension of
the Longinian sublime becomes evident from M. Armisen-
Marchetti's observation that this is not a necessary aspect of the literary sublime. This reader notes that unlike [Longinus] and
Seneca, Pliny does not associate the literary quality with the
grandeur of soul, but sees it only as a superior eloquence for which
the orator will take risks.[43]

I want to suggest, in addition, that the psychological quality of
the sublime is one with an important political genealogy. The link
between the state of literature and the community is an obvious
precedent in the soul–state analogy in Plato's *Republic*. [Longinus]
deliberately refers the reader back to a Platonic theory of constitutional identity which regards as its microcosm the individual's
soul-type—whether democratic, oligarchic, aristocratic, or tyrannical—in order to personalize the idea of constitution. At chapter
13. 1 he cites with approval *Republic* 586a, which characterizes men
without intelligence and virtue as failing to gaze up above, where
true pleasure lies, but as looking downwards and feeding themselves at tables as if cattle. In the larger context of *On the Sublime*,
the Platonic citation serves as an explanation of the genesis of various historical states, although the sublime state is, more clearly
than the Platonic republic, only a textual and psychological entity.
For [Longinus], the corrupt condition of the human soul in his
time specifically explains both the unfortunate condition of the
state and the scarcity of the sublime in literature. Wealth, honour,
reputation, and tyrannies, like the mere appearance of grandeur, do
not constitute the sublime (7. 1). It is the case that now love of
money and love of pleasure enslave (*doulagōgousi*) men, while
wealth produces offspring, namely pride, lawlessness, and shame-
lessness, which become masters (*despotas*) of their souls (44. 7).
Men accordingly become enslaved less by any ruler of the contemporary state, and more by their own moral condition.

When the account of literary decline in *On the Sublime* invokes
the tyranny as a metaphor for a psychological condition, it reinforces the idea that the sphere of the political has shifted from the

---

[43] Armisen-Marchetti (1990), 97.

external state to the individual and his inner state. In fact, the treatise simultaneously and somewhat paradoxically destabilizes and reconstructs a public sphere for literary and rhetorical discourse. The use of political metaphor in chapter 44 constitutes a dislocation of the state from the external, physical sphere to one which is internal and psychological, and which in turn provides the author's account with its social context. What the metaphor does is both to confirm and to highlight the assumption that language—and especially an intersubjective rhetorical language which merges reader with the original author and his text, as the discourse of the sublime is and does—creates social reality, and in particular the social identity of the citizen.

The sublime operates *within* the contemporary public sphere in order to depart from it, and the transport (i.e. *ekstasis*) of the audience which the sublime produces is one which thus reconstitutes civic identity elsewhere. In her study of sophistic culture at imperial Rome, Maud Gleason notes that an individual had to manifest and embody society's *paideia*, a term that is synonymous with 'culture', in the absence of formal degrees and educational qualifications.[44] How the individual did this was above all through language. Thus in this context, the rhetoric of the sublime resituates language, and through language it relocates the reading subject for the good of the community, namely for the preservation of freedom against a slavery of the soul. By doing this, it offers the writer and his reader an escape from otherwise constraining social and political circumstances. The destination identified for its audience is most obviously the sublime text, the circumstances, and the individuals which the sublime text portrays. (Perhaps, as in the case of the philosophical state of Plato's *Republic*, the ideal under discussion exists nowhere else but in the text itself.)

Where *On the Sublime* itself is specifically concerned, the implication is that the reader finds him- or herself transported into the author's own rhetoric of the sublime as constituted in the treatise. But as this sublime is constituted by a series of historical texts and by the author's own citation of them, the displacement this rhetoric entails is above all a movement towards and an appropriation of this literary past as constituted. Illustrated and constituted by the work of earlier authors, this Longinian rhetoric leads the reader to

[44] See Gleason (1995), pp. xxi–xxiv.

identify with these exemplary texts and with the original audiences envisioned by Homer, Demosthenes, or Plato. So just as through the figure of apostrophe in chapter 16, Demosthenes' own contemporary audience is made to identify with the Athenians who fought the battle of Marathon, [Longinus'] own audience is made to identify with the immediate Demosthenian audience and in turn with the latter's ancestors through the treatise's rehearsal of apostrophe. With good reason the author proclaims that the capacity to be read again and again (*anatheōrēsai*) is one of the qualities of a truly sublime text (cf. 7. 3).

The sublime is pronouncedly discriminating in the past that it chooses to recover, and imitation is a critical strategy inasmuch as it disrupts and denies conventional chronologies and continuities. It enables literary history to be foreshortened by bringing into contact with each other the members of the élite literary community who are otherwise separated by time. Homer's imitators, Herodotus, Stesichorus, Archilochus, and above all Plato, bring themselves under the inspiration of the epic poet, and they in turn share the Homeric sublime with their respective communities (13. 3). That the influence of Homer is apparent in each of these successive authors affirms [Longinus'] belief that the sublime should transcend its current temporal context. It furthermore explains why the writer who aspires to achieve the sublime should imagine a future age (*pas . . . aiōn*) and not only his paradigms Homer and Demosthenes as his audience, who are now figured as 'judges' and 'witnesses' in the lawcourt and theatre (14. 2–3). [Longinus]' description of Homer and Demosthenes presents the critical process with its aetiology, and it also poignantly stresses the atemporality of the sublime's address, for the classical lawcourt and theatre are patently anachronistic contexts in which to locate Homer.

[Longinus'] vocabulary indicates that the 'judges' of the sublime text are witnesses to a literary contest or struggle (*agōn*). At 13. 4 he speaks of *mimēsis* as involving a fine struggle for fame (cf. *eukleias agōn*) between a young contestant (*antagōnistēs neos*) and a more established and esteemed contestant.[45] So Eurylochus' lines from the *Odyssey* are said to suggest a contest (*agōnia*, 19); hyperbaton creates the impression of an 'agonistic suffering' (cf. *enagōniou pathous*, 22. 1); while the figure of polyptoton is very agonistic

---

[45] For the idea that a work must enter into a contest (*agōn*) with tradition to become part of the literary canon, see H. Bloom (1994), 6.

(*agōnistika*, 23). As a whole the sublime makes its spectators (*theatas*) the most honourable contestants (*agōnistas*, 35. 2). The contest is one in which freedom and particularly freedom of the soul is at stake. At 21. 2 the author observes that the connectives hinder passion and emotion in a text, impeding freedom of movement (*tēn . . . eleutherian . . . tou dromou*). Following this logic, asyndeton, literally an 'unjoining', is conducive to syntactical and emotive freedom. In chapter 39 he discusses melody as a wondrous instrument of freedom and emotion, suggesting that it may have an effect analogous to word order (39. 1).[46]

Linguistic 'freedom' is, furthermore, closely paralleled with political freedom. The apostrophe cited from Demosthenes in chapter 16 is presented as an encouragement to the Athenians to resist the onslaught of Philip of Macedon just as their ancestors defeated the Persians. Both Demosthenes' present predicament and his historical exemplar concern a struggle (*agōna*) over the freedom of the Greeks (16. 2). [Longinus] suggests that the apostrophe resembles divine inspiration (*empneustheis . . . hupo theou*), implying an analogy between the effect of this figure and literary imitation (*mimēsis*), which likewise inspires a subsequent generation. The larger implication is that the apostrophe might affect subsequent audiences of the figure, including those of *On the Sublime*. [Longinus] cites Demosthenes again in chapter 32, when he uses the latter as a standard for the degree to which an author may use figurality. He quotes *On the Crown* 296, a text in which the orator criticizes individuals who have surrendered the freedom of the Greeks to Philip and Alexander, and who thereby have given up the limits (*horoi*) and the requirements (*kanones*) of Greek identity, namely freedom and the rejection of despotic masters (32. 2). The introduction of Demosthenes as the limit (*horos*) for the use of metaphors and other figures insists that text and polity are coterminous, or at least analogous (32. 1). Bathetic literary discourse, as represented by the passage from Theopompus cited at 43. 2, is to be associated with lack of freedom: thus the historian writes in an unelevated manner about the Persian invasion (*katabasis*) of Egypt.

The contest (*agōn*) is of course the site which evokes literary discrimination in the form of the legal judgements by the Hesiodic kings, by Lysias' speaker in *Oration* 10, and by Aristophanes of

[46] Toll, however, replaces μετ' ἐλευθερίας with μεγαληγορίας (see A. O. Prickard (ed.), *Libellus de Sublimitate Dionysio Longino* (Oxford, 1947), app. crit. ad loc.).

Byzantium. It is a site which patently acknowledges the social and political significance of criticism as a process which seeks the benefit for the community as a whole by judging in favour of certain discourses and against others. Yet if this struggle seeks to wrench the individual, namely the reading subject, from his or her material circumstances into a series of prior worlds represented through its text, and in this way to reconstruct the polity as a more ideal community, the sublime also involves a bizarre paradox. In order to bring the citizen into a community characterized by linguistic and so political freedom, the sublime has to compel the reader into submission. The sublime produces an extraordinarily powerful effect, which [Longinus] leads us to perceive as being analogous to an exertion of political and military authority. He observes that it exerts a mastery (*dunasteia*) and invincible power (*bia amachos*) which subdues its audience, and he speaks of the sublime text's *oikonomia*, using a term that most immediately denotes the control of the household but often serves as a metaphor for the organization of the political state (1. 4). At 9. 6 he comments that a passage he has cited from the *Iliad*—as we have seen, actually a conflation of 21. 388 and 20. 61–5—produces sublimity in its description of heaven, underworld, mortals, and immortals, all fighting and taking risks of battle together (*sumpolemei kai sugkinduneuei machēi*). Here the limits between sign and signified break down, as the representation of war denotes and rehearses the capacity of the sublime to subdue and conquer its audience. At 17. 1 the author speaks of literary figures 'fighting together' (*summachei*) with the sublime and 'profiting from this alliance' (*antisummacheitai*). If figures alone rouse the suspicion of tyrants, kings, and rulers, in tandem with the sublime and emotion they manage to disguise figurality, and thus assert their authority over actual political authorities (17. 2). [Longinus] shifts the political sphere from the state to the individual through the figure of metaphor, which the author presents as one of the writer's instruments for achieving the sublime in chapter 32. This, perhaps, is the ultimate paradox of the sublime, that it is a literary quality which enslaves the individual in order to free the state.

VII

The sublime creates its own political community and, in this respect, [Longinus]' rhetorical project is consonant with the largely prescriptive, pedagogical aims of Plato and Aristotle *vis-à-vis* the production of an ideal civic identity through the control of poetic texts. The sublime's rhetoric of dislocation supplies its author with a strategy for repositioning critical agency in the Roman state. It transforms the physical transport, criticism, and translation of literature undertaken in the Alexandrian Mouseion-Library into a metaphorical and psychological process in which the *individual reader* becomes both the agent and the object of cultural dislocation through the force of the sublime (*to hupsos*). The text's ideal of the sublime involves a removal of author, reader, and text from the social and temporal contexts that constitute the material public sphere in order to remake the political state and its citizen in a realm of textual and psychological freedom. But such freedom is produced as the result of constraints, as the result of a rejection of a series of discourses and textualities which the author-critic regards as bathetic and low (*tapeina*), and, in fact, as the result of the discrimination of and against all that is contemporary Roman culture. The critical process as enacted in *On the Sublime* is in effect rigorous to the point that all it maintains as being acceptable and useful for the political community are a very few excellent, that is sublime, texts produced by a mere handful of authors: Homer, Plato, Demosthenes, and the treatise's own author. The acceptability and usefulness of these texts lies precisely in their capacity to detach the recipient from the larger body of contemporary texts through ecstatic response.

7

Augustine on Reinventing the Discourse of Community

> For Augustine, however, all language is a metaphorical detour
> in the road to God because no sequence of words, even
> 'proper' words, can adequately represent an atemporal and
> holistic significance.
>
> Margaret Ferguson (1992), 70–1

I

In earlier chapters I have considered both how critical activities
became and might have become institutionalized and how the
statements produced about literature in various institutional contexts serve to authorize a cultural tradition for a set of different
communities, both textual and, less frequently, historical. In
Chapters 4 and 6 in particular, I suggested that criticism involves
more than the exclusion of texts which challenge the hegemonic
discourse but may also require the scrupulously discriminated displacement of one set of hegemonic discourses by another one. The
present chapter now examines the way in which the apparently
contradictory institutionalizing and dislocating aspects of criticism
come together at the end of the classical era. I return to the literary
culture of North Africa to consider the contribution made by
Augustine in the re-establishment of criticism as a political discourse which specifically transforms the ideal of the Graeco-
Roman city into a Christian ideal of community. While Augustine
treats issues of literary production and reception, especially as
regards scriptural interpretation, in many works of his vast corpus,
I shall concentrate on the *Confessions*[1] and *The City of God* (also

---

[1] I have cited throughout this chapter Henry Chadwick's translation of the
Confessions (Chadwick (1991)).

DCD) as texts which accessibly discuss literary texts, even though they are not usually read for this reason. My concern in these two texts is with the author's engagement with classical material and its models of criticism through which he develops strategies for their regulation in the service of the Word of God. My explicit aim is to argue that where criticism is concerned, Christian late antiquity marks less a rupture and point of departure in literary history than a recuperation and revalorization of the principles established by much earlier authors and their communities.

II

The majority of readers of the *Confessions* take the work as it comes. Reading the work involves reading from book 1 onwards to the 'end', either book 10, where Augustine's account of how he became Christian reaches its climax and most readers stop reading, and less frequently, the work's actual end, book 13, which contains an analysis and commentary on the Book of Genesis. This structure of reception accentuates the dichotomy between the text's pagan narrative, which has broad interest and accessibility as an account of the author's 'conversion', and its Christian one, which is by and large the concern of the theologian and philosopher. But this approach also entails an uncomfortable disjunction between books 1 to 9 and the subsequent hermeneutic and philosophical books.[2] Thus Georg Misch influentially justified the juxtaposition of the explicitly personal and of the more theoretical elements of the work by placing 'autobiography' within a tradition of Christian self-examination and introspection.[3] Inscribing the *Confessions* within two distinct histories of autobiography in his account of the genre, Misch presented it as the culmination of a discourse of the self whose actual beginnings he traces to earlier Near and Middle Eastern civilizations, and, in a subsequent orientalistic recharacterization, as the incipit of a Western tradition of autobiographical discourse, represented and developed by such authors as Petrarch, St Theresa of Avila, and Rousseau.[4]

[2] Cranz (1954: 288) proposes that the *Confessions* be seen as falling into two main sections, books 1–9 and books 11–13, with book 10 standing apart.
[3] Misch (1950), i. 17; also Brown (1967), 169, and Vance (1973*a*), 5–6.
[4] Misch (1950), i. 18, ii. 669.

My approach to the 'problem' of unity in the *Confessions* abandons 'autobiography' as an anachronistic description of the text. (As Pierre Lejeune, amongst others, has shown, 'autobiography' is after all an eighteenth-century coinage.[5]) In place of generic description, I offer a preliminary narratological analysis which involves a distinction between 'story', the actual order of events, and 'discourse', the narrative of events in order to situate the work within a critical context.[6] In *Time and Narrative*, Paul Ricoeur worked with the rift between actual and narrative times to suggest that the discussion of time in book 11 chronologizes eternity by making past, present, and future appear as 'modalities of the present'.[7] My reading is concerned with another disruption of chronology in the work. It seeks to draw attention to another anachronism, this time the work's rhetoric of the preposterous, of *hysteron proteron*, which has the author dislocate the historical beginning, the discussion of the Creation, to the work's final books. I suggest that it is not insignificant that a commentary on the Book of Genesis should be the culmination of the *Confessions*. On at least four other occasions, the author shows interest in the initial book of the Old Testament, most notably in *De Genesi contra Manichaeos* (388/9 CE), *De Genesi ad litteram inperfectus liber* (*c*.393), *De Genesi ad litteram* (404–15), and *City of God* 11 (417/18).

But I also note that by itself this observation fails to locate adequately the deferral of Beginning in terms of the narrative structure of the *Confessions*. To address this issue I venture that book 13 retrospectively contextualizes the concern of the overall work to highlight the role of a particular type of textuality, the Word of God, in the establishment of community, specifically a Christian community. Augustine's concluding commentary on Genesis in the *Confessions* explicates a narrative in which the Word ('Verbum') of God creates the world, and in this way it makes evident the power of this language to establish both the community that humans and other living beings occupy and the identity of the living beings themselves (13. 2. 2–3; cf. Gen. 1: 1–2: 2). In Hebrew, the term *dabar* is one which denotes both 'word' and 'thing', granting to

---

[5] Lejeune (1973), 137. Vance (1973*a*: 1) suggests that 'autobiography' is a 19th-cent. neologism. Clark (1993: 34 ff.) proposes that the *Confessions* might not be an autobiography in any conventional contemporary sense and identifies the work as a narrative of the individual with reference to God. By this move, conversion, understood as the production of Christian identity, is surrendered.

[6] Culler (1981), 169–70.   [7] Ricoeur (1984), 8, 30.

language a material reality which cuts across the conventional rhetorical dichotomy between speech and action/reality. Augustine introduces into book 13 citations from the Old Testament which declare the physicality of language. At 13. 15. 16 he cites both Isaiah 34: 4, which speaks of the heavens 'folded together like a book', and Psalm 103: 2, which describes the heavens as a skin or parchment, to suggest the synonymity between scriptural world and physical world.[8] At 13. 18. 23 he recalls this earlier chapter and its scriptural subtexts when he describes the heavens as 'the firmament of the book' ('firmamenti scripturae tuae'; cf. 'in libro tuo, firmamento tuo') under which the angels fly. These passages simultaneously textualize the physical world and reify language.

The poetics of Genesis is more than a materialist one; it is an *ex nihilo* poetics. But Creation is far more than an actualization of language through language. Book 13 of the *Confessions* also characterizes the establishment of the world as a process of criticism in its etymological sense as 'distinction', 'separation', and 'judgement'. The narrative of Creation entails above all an account of the separation and the distinction of good from bad. At 13. 20. 26 Augustine speaks of the 'mouth of God' 'separating the precious from the vile'.[9] The commentary of book 13 continues by declaring that the earth is separated from the sea to produce a living soul (13. 21. 29; cf. Gen. 1: 24), spiritual are distinguished from carnal men through the ability of spiritual persons to judge thus (13. 23. 33), and good from bad people (13. 34. 49).[10] Not all distinctions are so absolute, for God will also make more precise differentiations amongst good things—for instance, fruit, which is to be understood as the good and right will of a giver, and a gift, which is to be understood as a human benefaction (13. 26. 41[11]). Moreover, God inscribes and presides over the social-political order of which he is divine critic and of which the Christian is the human administrator. God judges between what is right and wrong, while the Christian believer blesses and prays for the will of God, and interprets, explains, and disputes on this issue, supplementing and

---

[8] Vance (1973*b*), 169.

[9] Cf. 'separantes enim pretiosum a vili facti estis os dei' (*Conf.* 13. 20. 26).

[10] 'cum iam distincta sit terra fidelis ab aquis maris infidelitate a maris' (ibid. 13. 21. 29); 'neque de illa distinctione iudicat spiritalium videlicet atque carnalium hominum' (ibid. 13. 23. 33); 'et iustificasti impios et distinxisti eos ab iniquis' (ibid. 13. 34. 49).

[11] 'didici at te, deus meus, inter datum et fructum discernere' (ibid. 13. 26. 41).

imitating divine discourse (13. 23. 23–4). In this way, Augustine rehearses what is to be regarded as the paradigmatic Hesiodic narrative which legitimates judgement (*krisis*) as a process authorizing the public circulation of certain discourses at the expense of others.

The commentary on Genesis retrospectively informs interpretation of the whole preceding narrative of the *Confessions* as an account of how criticism might provide a paradigm for Christian identity and so for the (re-)creation of the individual as a believer. The author provides several invitations to such a literally retrospective reading. Book 13 begins with an invocation to the God 'who made me [Augustine]' (13. 1. 1), locating Augustine's conversation within the scriptural narrative of Creation. Subsequently, the author offers a comparison of the Creation of the world to a 'conversion':

> It [the world] would have been dissimilar to you unless by your Word it had been *converted* to the same Word by whom it was made, so that, illuminated by him, it became light and, though not in an equal measure, became conformed to a form equal to you (tr. Chadwick (1991); my italics)[12]

As a textualized reality, Creation involves a turning of matter to the Word to resemble the Word. As Margaret Ferguson has argued, it is similitude and likeness to God and his language which denote closeness to and communion with God, while unlikeness constitutes spiritual exile.[13] It is is precisely this understanding of Creation which indicates an analogy between this event and the conversion of an individual, such as Augustine: the commentary on Genesis, as a commentary on the archetypal conversion, is then a logical supplement to the foregoing transformation of Augustine from pagan to Christian. The analogy between Creation and divine discourse assumes several things. It suggests more than just the role of the Word in fashioning the identity of the believing individual. The assumption is, as for earlier classical authors, that identity is produced by means of imitation, most frequently, of traditional pagan literary models, such as Aeneas. Or else, for the Christian, it is produced by imitation of Christ, so that the individual comes to be like Christ. But the analogy also assumes the role of the critical

---

[12] 'per idem verbum converteretur ad idem, a quo facta est, atque ab eo inluminata lux fieret, quamvis non aequaliter et tamen conformis formae aequali tibi' (*Conf.* 13. 2. 3); cf. 13. 20. 27 and 13. 14. 15 for the Word as 'lamp'.

[13] Ferguson (1992).

process in privileging the Word above other secular and more conventional discourses. As with the earlier Greek and Roman tradition of literary criticism, the relationship between word and deed is for Augustine undeniable. Criticism must be an attempt to control the number of textual models available to the community and, in so doing, to privilege the 'good' discursive model, presented variously as 'just', 'true', 'philosophical', 'Christian', over those which are 'bad', 'unchristian', 'deceptive', and so on. If the discussion of literary reception and production that takes place in the work is not essentially different from what we find in the classical tradition of 'literary criticism' as represented by Hesiod's *Theogony*, Plato's *Republic*, Aristotle's *Poetics*, or *On the Sublime*, what *is* particular to Augustine is the prioritization of a specific Christian textuality. This reading requires that we reject the naïve view that the *Confessions* is a narrative of the author's *own* life and self.[14]

III

The first book of the *Confessions* makes it apparent why the Christian's rejection of the secular world must be a process of literary discrimination. In book 1, Augustine presents his infancy, quite literally the preverbal state of his life (cf. *infans* = 'unspeaking'), as a stage which confirms that human beings are by their very nature bound up in sin and that conventional secular language reinforces their sinful condition. At 1. 6. 7–8 the author recalls that he produced inarticulate noises and cries which signified his passions and his desires for food. In addition, these sounds express his further wish to have the adults around him 'obey' him and satisfy his wants:

When I did not get my way, either because I was not understood or lest it be harmful to me, I used to be indignant with my seniors for their disobedience, and with free people who were not slaves to my interests; and I would revenge myself upon them by weeping. (1. 6. 8)

According to this passage, infantile discourse is an indication of man's fallen nature. The baby's calls for food and for attention are

---

[14] Cf. Vance (1973b: 163–4), 'L'acte autobiographique ne se définira ni en termes d'un sujet qui se "couche" sur papier ou sur parchemin avec sincérité, ni en termes d'un *persona* qui appartient au domaine du langage, mais doit plutôt apparaître comme une dialectique entre les deux.'

acts of disobedience where the adults and God are concerned. And as such, they recall and rehearse the narrative of Original Sin, the disobedience of Adam and Eve in eating the fruit forbidden to them (cf. Gen. ch. 3). Augustine alludes to the theological teaching that humans have inherited sin even at birth and therefore need redemption, which he defended against the Pelagians in various works.[15] Slightly later, at 1. 7. 11, he reinforces the allusion, interpreting his infantile crying as signifying an appetite for food which is implicitly sexualized. The infant opens his mouth wide to grasp at the breasts of either his nurse or his mother in an attempt to be satisfied by her and in a fit of jealousy at the brother who might share this milk (1. 7. 11).[16] For Augustine, the infant's noises are not part of a pre-socialized discourse: rather they are part of the vocabulary of an unconverted and unreconstructed community of what we shall see to be the other city of the *City of God*.

Augustine moves on to expose the iniquity of the discourse by which the young boy is conventionally brought up and in which he is instructed. If the traditional literary and rhetorical education is important for providing the individual with his subsequent social identity and role, it also necessarily reinforces his entanglement in the language of the world, in the sinful desires that this language articulates, and in the enforcement of these desires upon others. At book 1, chapter 9, the author recalls his primary education. He recounts how he is coerced into learning society's language and its structures through a system of rewards, namely the wealth and honour promised by rhetorical skill. Secular pedagogy commodifies grammar and rhetoric, presenting these disciplines as the means of achieving material gain. But the rewards offered to schoolchildren are qualified, since they are offset by the punishments and so increase the sorrows and hardships suffered by the 'sons of Adam' (1. 9. 14; cf. Gen. 3: 16). The pupils pray for deliverance from the schoolmaster's beatings, just as the Israelites sought deliverance from their slavery in Egypt. Augustine figures the intricacies of rhetorical language as bonds (cf. 'the bonds of our tongues') to emphasize the analogy between secular education and the bondage of the Israelites in Egypt. Notably, in keeping with the doctrine of Original Sin, the abused schoolchildren are not entirely

---

[15] Rist (1994), 17–18.

[16] Of course, Adam and Eve's taking of the forbidden fruit is most explicitly recalled in the story of the pears at 2 .4. 9.

guiltless, as the author draws attention to their laziness when it comes to learning (1. 9. 15). New Testament allegoresis reinforces the critique of conventional rhetorical pedagogy offered by the allusion to the Pentateuch. The identification of the children as 'sons of Adam' is a biblical reference to the first man who was destined to perish, as against the second, redemptory Adam, Christ (cf. 1 Cor. 15: 22; also v. 45).

At 1. 13 Augustine continues his narrative by focusing in particular on his literary education. He begins by declaring his aversion to the Greek language and its literature, a statement that need not be taken at face value and that may be read in the light of a rejection of the immorality of this literary culture, which begins with Homer's depiction of the gods (1. 13. 20; cf. also 1. 14. 23 and 1. 16. 25). What he admits to is a predilection for Latin, and especially for Virgil's *Aeneid* (cf. 1. 14. 23). But his narrative also proposes the idea that pagan literature, which he terms 'fables' ('fabulae'), is to be superseded. He compares this body of literature—tradition, as far as the Roman world was concerned—to the 'veils of the temple'. The scriptural allusion is here to the curtain in the Temple in Jerusalem which distinguishes the high priest from the Jewish believer (e.g. Matt. 27: 51), and which is to be interpreted here as a symbol of the imperfect knowledge presented by pagan literature. The analysis of the impact made upon the author by the *Aeneid* and by its characters involves the Platonic critique of literary myth, not so much as a discourse that can lead to the multiplication of roles, but rather as one which may engage its audience in an empathy and enactment of its language to the detriment of the recipient's soul. Augustine recalls how, in reading the *Aeneid* he wept at the account of Dido's death rather than at his own lack of love for God, and also how he mourned, in reading of the love of Dido and Aeneas. The point is that he identified with these characters to such a degree that the act of reading became synonymous with the fornication about which he reads (1. 13. 21). The challenge to discover a critical strategy is there precisely because language has the potential to become an aspect of the reader's psycho-sexual being.

Augustine further develops the idea that the reception, the reading, and the reciting of literature is in itself a form of social activity. According to his analysis, literature involves the reader in a re-enactment of its narrative and emotions. Reception of a text so reifies language that reading about sexual immorality is itself a form of sexual immorality, and such that the association between pagan discourse and passion or desire is affirmed. Augustine's narrative of reading acknowledges that traditional, pagan education emphatically enacts the Hebraic understanding of 'word' as synonymous with 'thing', although in such a way that 'thing' is far from ideal. It also reveals as an additional problem the failure of the secular teachers of rhetoric to recognize the relationship between the sign and what the sign signifies. Pupils are forced to imitate the anger and sorrow of the goddess Juno in school declamations without any regard for the truth (1. 17. 27), and they are exposed to myths about the gods raping mortal women without any recognition of the possible consequences and effects, namely that the depicted acts may themselves be enacted. This lack of consciousness is highlighted at 1. 18 where Augustine describes how pedagogues get upset if one of their students commits a grammatical fault, such as a barbarism or solecism, while taking delight in explaining their *own* immoralities: they follow the law of the letter but they neglect the more important law of the spirit or deed (1. 18. 28–9). The comparison of these narratives to a form of 'drunkenness' suggests that the effect of mythical discourse is to diminish responsibility (1. 16. 26).

Augustine's subsequent narrative makes more explicit the way in which literature determines the sort of person its recipient becomes through inevitable enactment of it. The author reinforces the Platonic view that language can be a stimulus to negative desires (e.g. *Republic* 2 and 3, *Phaedrus, Ion*) as he characterizes his subsequent rhetorical career. Book 2 establishes the literal and metaphorical erotics of rhetorical language. At 2. 2. 2 the author declares that as an adolescent he had a 'single desire . . . to love and to be loved', with the result that he was unable to distinguish between true love and lust. The phrase 'to love and to be loved' ('amare et amari') has as its most obvious reference the young Augustine's discovery of his sexuality and his acquisition of a mistress when he was 16, but it also connotes his own desire to be a good teacher of rhetoric, a desire which, as book 1 (and, as we shall see, book 4) suggests, strengthens the bondage of younger students in the very web of language and desire in which he himself had been caught (cf. 2. 2. 4).

The following book of Augustine's narrative exhibits the specific way in which literary texts can offer a negative paradigm for an individual's actions and character. The beginning of book 3 finds

Augustine arriving at Carthage ('Cartago'), where a cauldron ('sartago') of 'illicit loves' seethes (3. 1. 1). The similarity of the Latin words *Cartago* and *sartago* reminds the reader of the *Confessions*—and many readers have remarked on the pun—that in this poetics of verbal construction, language is instantiated either for good or for bad outcomes. Accordingly, Augustine now presents his own desire for love, and the emotions that this desire entails, as the chains and rods which constitute this linguistic bondage: 'I was glad to be in bondage, tied with troublesome chains, with the result that I was flogged with the red-hot iron rods of jealousy, suspicion, fear, anger, and contention' (3. 1. 1). His sojourn at Carthage and the development of his rhetorical skills and his sexuality are actualizations of the *Aeneid*, especially of the voyage of Aeneas to Carthage and of his ill-fated affair with Dido. Augustine's journey to Carthage makes patent the consonance of linguistic and sexual desire. The author moreover recounts how he found himself infected (cf. 'turpi scabie foedarer') by the theatre and the emotions it produced. He points to the pleasure that its enactments of pain produced, observing that he loved to mourn ('dolere amabam', 3. 2. 4). In this, Augustine clearly rejects Aristotle's ideal of tragic pleasure as a superior one, in order to elaborate the earlier Platonic critique of drama as a spectacle that now satisfies the perverse, fallen desires which do an individual harm rather than good.

Augustine's reference to the origin of his relationship with a girl while at a church service (3. 3. 5) again contextualizes desire for the literary arts against a background of sexual desire and lust. In book 4 Augustine emphasizes the connection between erotics and rhetoric as he depicts himself, *qua* teacher of rhetoric, as an individual whose life consisted 'of being seduced and seducing, being deceived and deceiving', both literally and metaphorically, by language and by women, and thus as someone who enacts his desire 'to love and to be loved' (cf. 2. 2. 3). The teacher of public language sells language, fulfilling the role of sophist, who is antiquity's linguistic mercenary—although in this case he gives the lie to the appellation of rhetoric as a 'liberal art' (4. 1. 1), inasmuch as its aim is to 'overcome' and so to dominate the speaker's opponent (4. 2. 2). The author's first book, *On the Beautiful and the Fitting* (*De pulchro et apto*), a study of lower, physical things, as he himself recalls, appropriately articulates the connection between his rhetorical concerns and his involvement with 'beautiful things of a lower order' (4. 13. 20). Even more poignantly, at this moment in his life Augustine acquires a mistress (4. 2. 2), making literal his linguistic seductions. The corporeality of conventional rhetoric will entail that the author must resign his professorship of rhetoric before being baptized (9. 5. 13).

If the early books of the *Confessions* suggest the intimate relationship between word as sign and paradigm, and deed as the signified enactment of the verbal paradigm, they also reveal the tenuousness of this relationship. If the recipients of the texts in question dramatize what they read, it is also the case that the signs are without a prior presence: it is only through imitation that the texts acquire any reality. Pagan texts are lies ('fabulae'), or phantoms: so the author speaks of the 'vain spectacle of the wooden horse' or the 'very ghost of Creusa' from the *Aeneid* (1. 13. 22); the non-existent words ascribed to Juno in rhetorical declamation (1. 17. 27); and the *lies* of forensic rhetoric taught by the teacher (4. 2. 2). But the fragility of the word-deed/thing relationship of pagan discourse becomes most apparent in Manichaean teaching with which Augustine becomes involved when the Manichee bishop, Faustus, arrives at Carthage (5. 3. 3). Manichaean language is sign without reference: its authors produce words which are dreamlike 'fantasies' ('phantasmata', 3. 6. 10). In book 5 we learn that Faustus is an accomplished rhetorical master, and his eloquence renders him 'a great trap of the devil' ('magnus laqueus diaboli', 5. 3. 3; cf. 1 Tim. 3: 7; also *Conf.* 5. 6. 10) or 'a snare of death' ('laqueus mortis', 5. 7. 13; cf. Ps. 17: 6), which deceives many, while his teaching, compared to food to be consumed by the disciple, is allusively compared to the forbidden fruit (5. 3. 3; also 5. 6. 10). Faustus is renowned and admired for his skill in the 'liberal art' ('artes liberales') of the traditional rhetorical and literary education; however, the discrepancy between the description of his abilities as 'liberal' and their enslaving effect emblematizes the emptiness of Manichee doctrine, its departure from facts, things, and actions. Even Augustine's initial assessment of Faustus' teachings leads him to conclude their 'lengthy fables' are less convincing than the doctrines of philosophers (5. 3. 3 and 5. 7. 12; cf. 'fabulous matters', 5. 10. 19). Later he comes to a realization that Faustus' eloquence is a distraction, a mere veneer—'the fitting language which flowed with facility to clothe his ideas'—which conceals the absence of truth and the fact that this knowledge is limited only to grammar and to the canonical literary and philosophical texts (5. 6. 11). The bishop refuses, on the grounds of apparent modesty, to engage in dialogue with his disciples on the matters of astrology discussed in Manichee books (5. 7. 12). In this he shows himself a failure at employing the mode of discourse which, according to *De magistro*, facilitates learning (cf. *De magistro* 12. 40).

The insubstantiality of Manichee doctrine is further articulated in the fact that the sect's theology lacks, what is by Christian standards, a spiritual dimension, for its teaching on the divine is one which concerns itself only with matter. The author depicts the Manichees as displacing true spirituality, namely love of God, with physicality in the veneration of the sun and moon as deities (3. 6. 10), and also in complicated dietary rules which do not permit a Manichee holy man to pick fruit lest it weeps (3. 10. 18). The physicality of the sect's theology is above all manifested in its dualism which holds that the world is divided into two minds which in turn entail two contrasting types of matter, one good and the other evil (8. 10. 22–3; 5. 10. 20). Where the critical imperative enters into Christianity in a rejection of what is evil, Manichaeism enacts criticism in a way which is defective because incomplete. Its theology is one which refuses to cancel out or to reject completely what is evil. So difficulties in making decisions, e.g. whether to go to church or to go to the theatre, are understood as conflicts of two opposed and irreconcilable wills, one good, the other bad (8. 10. 24). Evil remains an essential component of the Manichee universe. Hence the sect propounds a mistaken creation theology, denying that the act of creation lies precisely in an act of criticism, of separation of what is good/holy/spiritual from what is bad/unholy/ unspiritual, by ascribing the intrusion of evil to a competing being (13. 30. 45). The absence of truth and doctrinal substance in Manichaeism has the overall effect of turning Augustine away from the ideas of Mani and his teachers (5. 7. 13), inverting the Platonic view that an individual has desire (*erōs*) for what s/he knows s/he does not have (cf. Pl. *Symp.* 202a ff.).

IV

Augustine's portrayal of pagan literature, of rhetorical education, and the Word's deceptive other, Manichaean doctrine, in the *Confessions* disinherits these discourses for the new Christian culture and its discourse. Yet if the pre-conversion Augustine is a figure who becomes what he reads, it is important to recognize that the author's conversion no less involves the reading of both Christian and non-Christian texts. For the author, pagan literature is antecedent to the Christian Word, which he attempts to institute as the discourse of a new community, just as the Old Testament and its teaching are prior to and anticipate the New Testament and its doctrine. So, following the analogy of prefiguration, the traditional classical canon is not something to be entirely dispensed with; rather it is to become a body of texts to be transcended and superseded. That creation takes place through the agency of the Word suggests that it is a process in which certain discourses, those which are divine, are authorized partly in order to regulate other discourses.

John Rist notes that while Tertullian uncompromisingly repudiated non-Christian society and culture, other late antique authors suggested that Christianity might 'despoil the Egyptians', appropriating pagan culture in the service of a Christian culture.[17] Accordingly, in the *Confessions*, pagan literature comes to serve as a propaedeutic to Christian teaching, a point which the author suggests in this text and which he more explicitly champions in other works.[18] It is in this ancillary mode that the importance of aspects of pagan textuality become obvious. In book 3 the author tells his reader that in his study of rhetoric he came across Cicero's (now lost) philosophical treatise *Hortensius* (3. 4. 7). As Augustine recalls it, his encounter with this work marks an important moment on the path to his conversion, for it establishes for the first time in him the desire for something other than bodily pleasure and satisfaction. He observes that the *Hortensius* transformed his passions in that, as its reader, he was affected not by its language and style, but by its content. The Ciceronian work, which includes 'an exhortation to

[17] Rist (1994), 207 and n. 8.

[18] In book 2 of *De ordine*, Augustine admits poetic literature and its myths in the service of helping the pupil distinguish between truth and falsehood; cf. *De ord.* 2. 12. 37–42.

study philosophy', appropriately stirred in its reader a desire to seek God through philosophy ('philosophia'), which he glosses as 'love of wisdom': God is retrospectively understood as the source of wisdom (3. 4. 8).

The next stage in Augustine's textual conversion leads him in book 5 to Rome where he discovers, as Aeneas before him, a whole new idea of community and a new textuality to go with it (5. 8. 14). It brings him into contact with the Manichaean bishop's Christian counterpart and opposite number, Ambrose, and through his association with Ambrose, with a very different kind of erotics. Augustine's acquaintance with the Christian bishop of Milan marks what is a notable and literal departure from the Virgilian subtext for identity, for he leaves the Virgilian city, Rome, and arrives at Milan to take up his new post as teacher of rhetoric (5. 13. 23). Furthermore, if rhetoric is conventionally characterized as a discourse which is erotically heterosexual because it has its counterpart in fornication, the relationship between the Christian bishop and the author is now presented as a homosocial one which is careful to exclude any hint of physical sexuality. Augustine characterizes Ambrose as a surrogate father in such a way as to prefigure the loving relationship of the author, *qua* male believer, to Christ. He recalls how the bishop welcomed him to Milan with fatherly kindness, and he observes that he began to 'love' ('amare') him and then to be enthralled by the eloquence of his preaching even though he continued to despise Christianity.

Furthermore, Ambrose reveals to Augustine a relationship between text and thing or action which is distinct from anything he has previously encountered. At the end of book 5 he admits to a predilection for the bishop's words, one which subsequently leads him to a knowledge of Christian doctrine. Where pagan myths and Manichee doctrines signify only falsehoods, Ambrose's words make meaning and truth present in such a way that the word–thing dichotomy is denied, '. . . together with the words which I was enjoying ('diligebam'), the subject-matter, in which I was unconcerned, came to make an entry into my mind. I could not separate them'. Ambrose's language cannot be distinguished from its message for another reason. The bishop expounds the Old Testament 'figuratively', that is allegorically, such that the literal text is given a spiritual meaning and such that the words are liberated from an otherwise constraining physicality (5. 14. 24). As an exegetical

methodology, Christian allegorical reading allows for pagan literature to be reinterpreted and reread so that it has its uses. Thus, the
temple-veil presented by Virgil's *Aeneid* at *Confessions* 1. 9 can be
drawn back in such a way that Aeneas' travels anticipate or fore-
shadow the metaphorical wanderings of Augustine on his path to
conversion.

The critique of Manichaeism suggests that the Christian reifica-
tion of language must entail more than a physical instantiation. So
Ambrose's textuality signifies both its reality and its spirituality by
being notably disembodied. In book 6 the author draws attention to
Ambrose's peculiar habit of reading silently to himself, and of
using only his eyes and heart to receive the words. While scholars
have used this passage as evidence for the thesis that reading was
voiced in antiquity, I suggest that Augustine's comment should not
be taken *only* literally.[19] The author speculates that silent reading
prevents students and onlookers from interrupting the bishop's
perusals and helps to save the bishop's frail voice for preaching,
but he also concludes the chapter by admitting his uncertainty for
the latter's actual motives (6. 3. 3). A further implicit reading
beyond this gloss is available, and perhaps invited in light of the
passage's narrative of non-literal reading. The overall context of
the narrative offers silent reading as a mode of textuality which
appropriates itself to a prior text—here the scriptures—and then
represents Christian discourse as one which is non-physical
despite, or since, producing desire for God. It figures the separation of Christian language from the body and from the conventional rhetorical situation in which eloquence serves as a mode of
seduction.

The unvoiced text is the spiritual one which enables the reader to
listen to the 'inner teacher', God.[20] The account of how learning
occurs in *De magistro* offers a reading of the silent 'voice'. In this
dialogue the interlocutors, Augustine and his son Adeodatus,
establish that language is a medium by which teaching and learning
occur, in that it serves to signify reality (e.g. *De mag.* 1. 1 and 9. 26).
As the teacher figure, Augustine goes on to propose that receiving
the words themselves does not constitute the act of learning, since
the realities that spoken or written words signify may not be understood. The example he gives is of hearing foreign words or names,

[19] Knox (1968), 422; also see the fascinating discussion by Ferguson (1992), 85.
[20] Mazzeo (1962), 190–2.

such as those of the three youths, Ananias, Azarius, and Misael, who are thrust into the Babylonian furnace, and of failing to understand what they might mean (cf. 11. 36). Understanding, and so learning, thus take place not through the externalities of language, that is speaking and hearing language, but through an interior truth which 'presides over the mind itself from within' (11. 38; tr. R. P. Russell).[21] Learning is an interior process which takes place above all through the agency of God, the divine Teacher, so that the role of human teacher is to ask the sort of questions which make it possible for the student to 'hear' the Teacher who instructs from within (12. 40). It follows thus that prayer and silent reading or meditation will be the forms of discourse which most approximate the language by which we properly learn.

The vision at Ostia, in the *Confessions*, which is narrated just before the death of Augustine's mother, Monica, also helps us to understand more fully the importance of Ambrose's silent reading. Mother and son discourse about the eternal life of the saints and experience the greatest fleshly pleasure, and Augustine recalls that they proceeded beyond and transcended aural language by interior thought and language, that is by another unvoiced and spiritual discourse (9. 10. 24). Later in this chapter, Augustine recalls his and his mother's recognition that it is only through this transcendent silence that humans become aware of God as creator and are able to hear his words (9. 10. 25). The silent 'voice' is one that speaks to the angels and to the spiritual, interior ear which Augustine attributes to himself in book 13. At 13. 15. 18 Augustine declares that the angels do not need to read as humans do in order to know God's Word; rather, they have a scroll which is always open before them, namely the presence of God, figured as his face, which they peruse without syllables. These passages figure a being's relationship with God as the reading of a text. Thus, comprehension of a text is imperfect when it marks a relationship that is imperfect or is in the process of coming into being. Augustine cites 1 Corinthians 14: 22 in observing that spiritual tongues, which cannot be comprehended as they constitute a spiritual language, are intended to be a sign to unbelievers (13. 21. 29).

Full comprehension takes place when a perfect relationship, like that which the Christian or the angels enjoy with God, exists. The

---

[21] Cited from R. P. Russell (1968).

process of reading which culminates in enlightenment is metaphorical and the text which is read is read figuratively. Augustine establishes his spiritual identity when he notes that nothing prevents him from understanding figurative statements in the scriptures (13. 24. 36–7). This characterization of God's Word as something quite distinct from normal, human speech is elsewhere and later rehearsed in book 11 of the *City of God*:

Thus God does not speak with man through any bodily creation, uttering to corporeal ears so that the air reverberates between the one who speaks and the one who hears. Nor [does he speak] in such a spiritual manner which is figured as corporeal likenesses [cf. *De Genesi ad litteram* 12. 4–8], just as in dreams or in any such sort of manner—for thus he speaks as to bodily ears since he speaks as if through the body and as if with the intervention of corporeal spaces. It is the case that such things are seen to be similar for the most part to bodily things. [God] speaks by truth itself if any is suitable to hear by the mind and not by the body.[22]

God's speech is incorporeal. It does not need to travel through the air or to take any bodily form; rather, it speaks with truth to the audience's mind. At 16. 6 of this same work Augustine declares that when human beings receive God's Word, an ineffable and eternal discourse, through their 'inward ears' ('interioribus auribus'), they become like the angels.

V

If Ambrose's discourse reveals that the Christian text converts its audience away from the pleasures of the body and towards a desire for God, book 8 of the *Confessions* presents Augustine's conversion as one which occurs through text and through example based on text. At 8. 2. 3 the author relates how he went to Simplicianus, the individual who had sponsored Ambrose in the latter's own conversion and served as the latter's spiritual 'father'. To Simplicianus, he

---

[22] 'Sic enim Deus cum homine non per aliquam creaturam loquitur corporalem, corporalibus instrepens auribus, ut inter sonantem et audientem aeria spatia verberentur, neque per eius modi spiritualem quae corporum similitudinibus figuratur, sicut in somnis vel quo alio tali modo; nam et sic velut corporis auribus loquitur, quia velut per corpus loquitur et velut interposito corporalium locorum intervallo; multum enim similia sunt talia visa corporibus: sed loquitur ipsa veritate si quis sit idoneus ad audiendum mente, non corpore' (*DCD* 11. 2; cf. also *De Genesi ad Manicheos* 1. 9. 15).

explains his 'wanderings', both the literal ones which led him from Madaura to Carthage, Rome, and Milan, and his implied textual ones through Platonic texts in the Latin translation of Victorinus. Victorinus, the African professor, who 'was extremely learned and most expert in all the liberal disciplines' and who practised rhetoric at Rome, is a significant figure in the narrative. Victorinus provides Augustine and consequently the reader of the *Confessions* with a paradigm of an individual who gives up the discourse of the world for Christianity and its language and who makes his conversion at Rome public (8. 2. 5). Victorinus' open profession of faith is one which displaces the conventional rhetorical occasion, redefining the performative occasion as one in which the orator now speaks God's words rather than his own. Where Augustine is concerned, Simplicianus' protreptic intention succeeds, for the author confirms that this story produces a burning desire in him to follow ('exarsi ad imitandum') the rhetorician's example, although he is prevented from immediately doing so by the 'chain' of his will, which now replaces the bondage of rhetoric and the liberal arts (8. 5. 10).

Victorinus' is only the first of several inset narratives which attest to the capacity for Christian discourse to be reified. The visit of the court-official Ponticianus to Augustine's house becomes the next stage in the latter's textual conversion (8. 6. 14). Sitting down to converse with his host, Ponticianus notices a book on a table and discovers it to be by the apostle Paul. Already a Christian, he proceeds to relate a series of stories which emphasize the power of the Christian Word ('Verbum'). His first story concerns the Egyptian monk Antony and the story's indirect role in a series of subsequent conversions. The speaker tells Augustine how two of his friends had entered a Christian household and found a *Life of Antony*, which one of them began to read (8. 6. 15).[23] The biography produces in one of the readers a 'holy love' and a sense of shame, with the result that he resolves to give up his current political career and the dangers that attend such a career to become a Christian. This reader becomes an example to his companion, who is also convinced to join him. The friends' experience in turn serves as a paradigm for the conversions of Ponticianus and his friend, which in their turn prompt the conversions of their fiancées, who decide to

---

[23] Chadwick (1991: 143 n. 11) identifies the *Life* as that by Athanasius of Alexandria in its Latin translation by Evagrius of Antioch.

dedicate their virginity to God. It is thus that the *Life of Antony* renounces the sexuality of language.

These stories serve as preludes to Augustine's own (literary) conversion in the following chapters of the *Confessions*, for the immediate effect of Ponticianus' narrative on Augustine is to involve him in an act of self-recognition, figured as the author being set before himself (cf. 'you set me before myself again', 'et tu me rursus opponebas mihi', 8. 7. 16). Augustine comes to see the person he is really is, and this is a significant moment, for the author's self is made apparent to the reader only in this brief but pivotal moment in the narrative of the *Confessions*. But a paradox is also involved, since recognition of the self simultaneously involves the privileging of otherness, namely Christian identity. Augustine's phraseology, 'you set me before myself', evokes the notion of presence as expressed in the New Testament by the phrase 'face to face' (cf. 2 John 12; 3 John 14). Conversion (cf. *converto* = 'to turn') begins quite literally in Augustine turning back to himself and to a full examination of himself, but, as an instantiation of the Creation, which also consists in a 'turning' of Word to Word, it also consists in the author's turning towards God's word. At 8. 7. 17 Augustine significantly recalls his earlier encounter with Cicero's *Hortensius* and the impact that it had in instilling a desire for wisdom in him, again reinforcing the idea that texts have the power to influence action.

Ponticianus' narratives do not in themselves turn the reader to God's Word; this is left appropriately to the Scriptures. Experiencing an internal conflict of wills, Augustine withdraws from his friend Alypius, the male companion whose friendship had earlier prevented the author from marrying and who clearly represents the homoerotic dimension of traditional philosophy, to sit in his garden under a fig-tree (8. 12. 28; cf. 6. 12. 21). Here, he hears a voice from a neighbouring house repeatedly commanding its listener to 'take up and read' ('tolle, lege'), and he interprets this as a command from God to open his scriptural text and to read the first verse he comes across. The voice which urges the author to read the scriptural text is described as being that of a child of indeterminate sex, 'it might be a boy or a girl (I do not know which)' (8. 12. 29). In being childlike and ungendered, the voice is asexual. Its rhetoric is for this reason distinct from that of the conventional practitioner of public discourse, who is presented as seducing his audience and in turn as prostituting himself.

The random selection of a text recalls the *sortes Vergilianae*, the practice which employs the text of Virgil as an instrument of divination; however, the author is careful to efface this subtext and to cite instead the model of Antony randomly opening a text of the gospel in search of instruction. Augustine opens the Bible at Romans 13: 13–14, which forbids its reader to engage in the pleasures of the flesh—riots, drunken parties, eroticism—and to 'put on the Lord Jesus Christ'. The passage which Augustine picks out explicitly denies the role of the body and its passions in its discourses, leading him in turn to leave aside thoughts of marriage and worldly ambition, namely honour achieved through rhetoric, which is to be understood as the discourse which has its own corrupt erotics (8. 12. 30). Silent reading of Romans 13 brings to a climax the ongoing redefinition of the erotics of the text in the *Confessions* as a whole and particularly in book 8.[24] It constitutes not just Augustine's transformation into a Christian but also the transformation of reading in the context of Christianity. Urging the reader to 'put on the Lord Jesus Christ', the scriptural verses displace Virgil's *Aeneid* as the text which individuals allow to control their behaviour through a random consultation of its verses for inspiration; they replace the mimetic model offered by Aeneas and pagan literature with the idea of *imitatio Christi*. This instance of *sortes Christianae* re-enacts the creation of the individual and of his community as a discrimination through the Word of God. If criticism is the act of divine creation, most obviously as the separation of light from dark and firmament from water as presented in the narrative of Genesis and rehearsed in the commentary of book 13, it also here involves the discrimination of texts, philosophical and scriptural, from those which are pagan, poetic, and erotic, to provide the reader with a paradigm of identity in this world.

VI

The *City of God* extends the critical project of the *Confessions*, relocating the distinction between and separation of discourses in the more explicitly political framework of the 'city'. Augustinian criticism articulates the civic ideology and identity of the divine city,

[24] Mazzeo (1962), 190–2.

distinguishing it as a spiritual, eternal community with a very particular discourse that is quite different from the earthly, pagan, and corrupt community, and its languages. If public discourse was regulated and discriminated in the archaic and classical Greek and Roman communities, or more accurately in the communities as depicted in texts of the relevant periods, the divine city envisaged by Augustine no less imposes a series of constraints upon what might be said, written, and circulated.The material from the archaic poets down to the authors of imperial Rome offers a language of ideal statehood inasmuch as it reflects what is for the good and bad of the community, and Augustine no less carefully discriminates and regulates language to produce the textual construction of the 'city of God'. The work opens by stating the author's aim to mount a quasi-legal defence of the divine city against paganism and its discourse (cf. 'hoc opere . . . debito defendere', *DCD* 1. pr.; 'defendenda est Dei civitas', 1.1). Augustine's intention is to negate all other discourses which challenge or threaten the former—namely false theologies, demonologies, pagan doctrines, and poetic fictions about the gods—and which in turn are the basis of the non-divine and demonic city. The *City of God* as a whole enacts this defence through a legitimation of the discourse which participates in the writing of the divine city, namely the Word of God as constituted by the scriptures and their theology.

In the *Confessions*, Virgil's *Aeneid* was the text which provided the paradigm for the secular world, and Augustine briefly recognizes this at *City of God* 1. 3, when he observes that Rome's great poet is drunk up ('ebibitus') by young minds. But the literary character of paganism in this later work needs to be qualified. There is now a new premiss: if God is ultimately to be regarded as the 'author' of the world and in particular of the divine community, then demons or evil spirits and their human agents are responsible for drama as the privileged literary texts of the historical city and in this way for the moral identity of the historical city at particular moments. Peter Brown observes that in the *City of God* the bishop of Hippo (as Augustine then was) appears to mount an attack on a paganism that exists only in libraries as he neglects to address the contemporary mystery cults, oriental religions, and Mithraism.[25] Cities and theatres are the human works which stand contrary to

[25] Brown (1967), 305.

the world as God's work—the word for 'work' ('opus'), denotes both physical labour and artistic undertaking (6. 6. 1).[26] The critical emphasis in the text shifts to drama, which Plato (in the *Republic*) and Aristotle (in the *Poetics*) had previously analysed as a discourse which offered an image of the classical Greek city-state, and the origins of which Augustine ascribes to demons. At 1. 32 he refers to the origins of drama at Rome as the beginning of 'spectacles of base acts' ('spectacula turpitudinum') and licence ('licentia') to vanity. He offers a genealogy of drama which traces the genre not to the vices of mortal men but to the gods. He relates how the latter beings commanded that dramas be performed in their honour in order to put an end to a disease in the state.[27] The result of this is an obsession with stage plays which displaces a former obsession with circus games. In consequence spectators become mad with desire for actors, and this desire becomes an even more serious plague which infects the morality of the Roman people.

In subsequent books the author affirms the role of these malevolent gods in establishing the forms of dramatic literature in the classical Roman city. Against the prevalent view that the immoral acts depicted in art and literature are the product of poetic fictions, he reiterates the point already made at 1. 32, that plays ('ludi scaenici') are a product of demonic imperative. This literary form was established during a plague at the command ('imperando') of the gods as received by priests (2. 8)—what the gerund *imperando* implies is that the gods are in charge of the historical Rome. Augustine, moreover, establishes a moral hierarchy for the dramatic genres. According to him, while comedies and tragedies contain much that is base, they are not like those which contain obscene language, and they are therefore included in the curriculum of so-called 'liberal education' presented to young boys. The origins of dramatic art are discussed yet again in book 4, where the author rebukes Cicero for the failings of his literary criticism. While the philosopher reviles mythology for its anthropomorphizing treatment of the gods, he omits to fault stage plays, which display the crimes of the divinities ('poetica numinum crimina') (4. 26; cf. Cic. *Tusc.* 1. 26. 65; *Nat. D.* 1. 42; also Xenophanes, DK 21 B 11, 15). Augustine provides a

---

[26] 'cum mundus opus sit divinum, urbes vero et theatra opera sint hominum' (*DCD* 6. 6).

[27] Cf. 'deorum vestrorum iussis Romae instituti sunt. . . . dii propter sedandam corporum pestilentiam ludos sibi scaenicos exhiberi iubebant (ibid. 1. 32).

rationale for this mistaken position. He proceeds to rehearse a tradition which declares the divine institution of drama and the dire
consequences to mortals for failing to perform stage plays.[28]
According to this tradition, a farmer named Titus Latinius has a
dream in which the gods instruct him that the Ludi Romani must
be repeated, since their pleasure in the performance was spoiled by
the execution of a criminal on the first day of the games. When the
farmer suffers from a lack of nerve and fails to inform the senate as
ordered, he loses his son. On the following evening he has another
dream in which he is warned of harsher consequences. Failing once
more to act, he is warned a third time of dire punishment and then
falls ill. Finally, he tells a magistrate what has happened and the
plays are repeated. Where Hesiod and Plato (disapprovingly) indicate that one of the functions of the poet is to uphold and pronounce justice in the community, the author of the *City of God*
seeks to discredit the idea that the gods would punish humans for
their literary shortcomings. He argues that because the gods provide models of violent or shameful behaviour, they cannot be
regarded as arbiters of justice. The gods do not have the capacity to
be offended by the poetic account of Paris' adultery, a wrongful
action, and thus could not have been responsible for destroying
Troy. The gods are 'authors and teachers of sins' ('auctores . . .
doctoresque peccatorum') rather than the avengers of wrongdoing
(3. 3).

Augustine characterizes the pagan gods as the ultimate authors of
the sin and wrongdoing of the city's inhabitants: they are depicted
as the authority ('auctoritas') for violent behaviour (2. 25. 1). He
notes that the fact of the gods fighting with one another on a plain
in Campania provides humans with a paradigm for actions that he
describes as execrable ('execranda'): it is the case that on the very
same spot two Roman armies later clashed in civil war, engaging in
conflict that threatened the stability of the civic community. The
pagan gods, however, deny their role in instigating the conflict for
they perceive 'no crime' ('nullum nefas') in civil war. But it is above
all by being responsible for the establishment of dramatic art at
Rome that these divinities supply the human community with bad
examples. When these gods inaugurated dramas and musical performances in which immoralities are committed, they necessarily

---

[28] The narrative is previously related by Cicero (*Div.* 1. 26. 55), Livy (2. 36. 1 ff.),
and Valerius Maximus (1. 7. 31).

corrupted the morals of Rome's citizens: the spectators of these spectacles were and are deceived into thinking that they can imitate what they see on stage with impunity ('securus imitaretur'). The conviction that life will imitate art is repeated slightly later at 2. 27 where Augustine declares that myths ('fabulae') portraying gods doing shameful and criminal actions instruct the whole state in such deeds. The idea of the city 'learning' immoral deeds from literary texts and spectacles deliberately recalls the author's account of his rhetorical education in the *Confessions*, while the status of these texts as paradigms for identity and behaviour is emphasized by his observation that actors were regarded as base ('turpes') and notorious ('infames'). The point is that by performing dramatic texts, actors enact the sinful behaviour depicted in them (cf. 2. 13). Later in the *City of God*, at 18. 12, Augustine closes down the rift between reception and action when he declares that to enjoy the crimes of gods as depicted in plays, even if they are false, constitutes an actual crime ('crimen . . . verum') precisely because these stage plays are produced to win the favour of these false divinities.

In books 8 and 9 Augustine reassigns roles and identities to the authorial gods. He reidentifies them as 'demons ('daemones'). He appropriates the terminology of Neoplatonism, which he declares in this chapter to have affinities with the Christianity he espouses, in order to reserve the term 'god' for the Judaeo-Christian God. Citing support from Apuleius, he later declares that the attribution of the title 'gods' to demons, and thereby to imply that they are gods, constitutes a fiction created by poets ('fictio poetarum', 9. 7). These demons are confined to creating only what is external and physical, namely the body and its passions. Furthermore, he presents the 'gods', who are the authors of literary culture and of the immorality that it produces, as readers of their own art. Also, at 8. 5 he observes that mythical theology is a discourse in which the 'gods' operate as dramatic producers, putting on display their own crimes and passions to excite their spectators. These 'gods' are as well the audience, for they become spectators of the immoral forms of behaviour that humans exhibit when the latter enact what they have previously viewed on stage. Because the demons are spectators to the dramas which they instigate, and if these dramas are about their actions, it follows that these beings view themselves and their own actions. The reception of conventional dramatic art might serve as a mode of self-recognition, as when Augustine sees himself 'face to face' as in a mirror at the moment of his conversion in the *Confessions*. Where demons are concerned, such self-viewing is a form of narcissism, of self-love, which renders impossible the *imitatio Christi* that Christ enables through his incarnation and that forms the basis of identity in the divine community (9. 21; cf. 14. 28).[29] Augustine describes the demons as 'loving' stage plays, requiring that they be performed in their honour, and he concludes that they must be evil for so doing (8. 13). What justifies this moral judgement is that these divine viewers take delight in things hated by good and prudent men, namely the violent fictions created by poets (9. 1).[30] Beyond this, however, is the recognition that narcissism or self-love is only another aspect of that love of personal gain and power which is so characteristic of the secular city and which determines that this community must be flawed.[31]

VII

The heretical Donatists regarded the (that is, their) Church as an alternative to secular society, characterizing themselves as a pure and persecuted minority.[32] By contrast, the Catholicism of Augustine adopted a far less defensive position. The Christian Church was growing and expanding, and the bishop of Hippo rejected a simplistic dichotomy between secular and pagan.[33] The Church was an institution that could through discipline and opportunity hope to be coterminous with society, although secular institutions and politics are to be understood as distinct from the divine community.[34] The Church would assimilate the world; it would tolerate the 'chaff' until the final harvest,[35] but this meant that it could not in turn entertain, and thus it undertook to persecute, the more discriminating Donatist heresy after 405 CE.

This complex and at times apparently ambivalent relation between Augustine's Church and the world shows itself in the crit-

---

[29] Cf. *DCD* 14. 28, and Markus (1970), 60.

[30] 'daemones, qui talibus gaudent qualia boni et prudentes homines aversantur et damnant, id est sacrilega flagitiosa facinerosa non de quolibet homine, sed de ipsis diis figmenta poetarum et magicarum artium sceleratam puniendamque violentiam . . .' (*DCD* 9. 1).

[31] Rist (1994), 217–18.   [32] Brown (1967), 203, 214, 224.

[33] Markus (1970), 60, 70–1.   [34] Brown (1964), 112; (1967), 224.

[35] Markus (1970), 108.

ical dimensions of the *City of God*. As a creation of the divine
Word, the 'city of God' marks a discontinuity with the historical
city, as represented by Athens and above all by Rome. None the
less, it does not reject certain aspects of government and authority,
which Augustine declares to be partly human and partly divine in
De ordine (2. 9. 27). If the discourses of the divine and secular states
are quite distinct, the author demonstrates that each of these
different cities establishes its structure by authorizing its own particular discourse and by excluding others as dangerous or undesirable. He legitimizes the discrimination of literary discourse within
the theological state that privileges the Word in the larger framework of a history of criticism in which the Roman city serves as an
imperfect model for the divine city, indeed its opposite. So part of
what the *City of God* does in the process of 'despoiling the
Egyptians' is to historicize a secular authority for the critical
impulse in Christian society which is being established. Augustine
draws a series of contrasts in attitudes towards censorship. He sets
in opposition attitudes to the regulation of public discourse in classical Greece (especially in historical Athens), and classical Rome,
and then a larger one between attitudes in the classical state and the
divine state. Above all, the contrasts serve to repudiate the example
set by the Greeks. Following Roman authors such as Horace, he
characterizes Hellenic culture as one which harbours and tolerates
dangerous licence. He admits that the ancient Greeks were consistent in allowing individuals to be criticized and to be named in Old
Comedy, referring to the convention of slandering by name, i.e.
onomasti kōmōidein (cf. 'nominatim', 2. 9); however, poetic licence,
which is entirely consistent with the democratic culture of litigation and rhetoric, is such that it makes possible not only the defaming of bad leaders, such as the demagogues Cleon, Cleophon, and
Hyperbolus, whom Augustine names and who themselves take
democratic outspokenness (*parrhēsia*) to an extreme, but also the
defaming of good leaders, such as Pericles. Later in the same chapter Augustine observes that the Greeks permitted defamatory
charges ('opprobium') against both men and gods at the prompting
of the gods themselves.

Augustine acknowledges republican Rome as one of the precedents for his own censure of poetic licence. He notes that in
contradistinction to the Greeks, the Romans placed restrictions
on public literary language. The author refers to the laws on the

proscription of libel and defamation in the Twelve Tables, the originative, hallowed text of Roman law, and the earliest evidence for prohibitions on certain types of language at Rome. He cites the relevant text as it is mediated by Cicero's *Republic* (4. 12), a work which he quotes again at 2. 9 as proof that the Romans did not want any living citizen to be praised or blamed on stage: '. . . our Twelve Tables ordained the death penalty for very few crimes, but among those punished in this way they included the crime of singing or composing a song which brought ill repute or disgrace on another person'.[36] This law regulates against, and sets out the punishment for, defamatory or harmful verses, and by citing it the author of the *City of God* implicitly presents us with the origin of subsequent laws regarding regulation of language at ancient Rome. This reference to the Twelve Tables provides the *City of God* with a set of precedents for his own critical infrastructure. It may be understood as an acknowledgement that the construction of an ideal society— whether Plato's *Republic*, Cicero's own republic in *On the Republic*, or Augustine's city of God, no less than the historical community— involves the discrimination of discourses as beneficial or acceptable, or not, by its legislator or lawgiver.

The constraints of the 'city of God' surpass in rigour the regulations on discourse of these prior ideal and historical communities. If Augustine invokes the history of discursive regulation at pre-imperial Rome, he also proceeds to attack it on grounds of inconsistency and illogicality. He notes that, while making the defamation of citizens a capital crime, the state allowed its poets to slander its gods. In a reference to the accounts of Aulus Gellius and the author of the *Rhetorica ad Herennium* regarding enforcement of the legal restrictions on defamation in public literary language, he reminds his audience that the dramatists Plautus and Naevius were prohibited from defaming the politicians Publius or Gnaeus Scripio. He observes that there is, however, an inconsistency, as the comic poet Terence was able to depict Jupiter as lascivious, with the result that he aroused youthful passions (*DCD* 2. 12). In 2. 13 Augustine calls further attention to the inadequacy of restraints placed on the representation of gods and men. Theatrical plays could show the gods whom the Romans worship in an unfavourable

---

[36] 'nostrae . . . contra duodecim tabulae cum perpaucas res capite sanxissent, in his hanc quoque sanciendam putaverunt, si quis occentavisset sive carmen condidisset, quod infamiam faceret flagitiumve alteri' (*DCD* 2. 9).

light, even if the civil rights and privileges of actors who participated in these plays were restricted. He goes on to suggest that in
honouring their actors, the Greeks were more fair because they
worked on the premiss that both gods and the humans who played
them deserved recognition. Augustine makes these observations
for a *reductio ad absurdum*: the Christian can only conclude that the
pagan gods are not to be honoured. In the following chapter, at
2. 14, Augustine exposes a further problem with the Roman attitude to stage plays. Apart from the inconsistency of protecting the
reputation of citizens but not that of its gods, Rome regarded only
actors, and not poets, whom the Twelve Tables regulate, as disrep-
utable. Once more, ancient Greece serves as a point for comparison, although with quite a different purpose in mind. The author
praises Plato for banishing from the ideal state poets who would
otherwise deceive the citizens, and he expresses the view that for
banning the production of immoral performances the Athenian
philosopher is worthy of civic honours. Taking his lead from
Labeo, he proposes that the philosopher should be honoured above
the heroes and pagan gods as a 'semi-god' ('semideus'). Plato's
Republic becomes an explicit model for the divine state and its
regulation of literature.

VIII

In the first half of the *City of God*, Augustine presents his reader
with a critique of the inconsistent attitudes that the Roman republic displayed with regard to the regulation of literary, and particularly dramatic, discourse. He contrasts pre-imperial Rome with the
Greek city-state, which, while it sustained licence, at least was less
arbitrary in supporting the overall establishment of dramatic literature. What the initial part of the work involves is an attempt to
repress through logical argument the discourse which authorizes
the secular state and its religion, and at the same time legitimates
these structures. Augustine rewrites the history of literary criticism
for Rome, seeking to exclude or to dismantle secular discourses and
presenting licence ('licentia') as the basis of immorality. Where
imperial authors contextualize freedom of expression as a condition
of a better past, and regulation of discourse as being in opposition
to the interests of society, the Christian author seeks the silencing

of pagan discourses as the strategy for an ideal divine community. This in turn suggests that the 'city of God' is a state whose authority lies in the presence of the Word of God to the exclusion of all other words. Where pagan theology has authorship disseminated amongst demons and its human spokespersons, the poets, Christianity limits authorship. Hence Augustine takes pains to deny the angels a role in creation (13. 25. 12), and he instates God as the sole *author* of the divine state and of its texts, and so as their sole *authority* (12. 25; cf. 13. 24). To this extent the *City of God* rehearses the Hesiodic anxiety over multiple and plural voices as productive of discourses which may deceive their audiences into regarding them as authoritative, that is as a legitimate theology.

Accordingly, the *City of God* presents diversity of languages, and the misunderstanding which ensues, as the product of human sin. At 16. 4 Augustine provides an explication of the narrative of the Tower of Babel (Gen. 11: 1–9), recasting it as an account of the founding of Babylon, the earthly city of indiscrimination (cf. 'civitas impiorum confusionis nomen accipit', 16. 11). For the author, the event explains the existence of different languages and of the ensuing confusion ('confusio') as God's disempowering punishment for presumptuous transgression. The multiplication of languages undermines the power of a ruler, namely his tongue (cf. 'dominatio imperantis in lingua'). So, when the ruler Nebuchadnezzar refused to obey God by building the Tower of Babel, his sphere of dominance was reduced through the confounding of language.[37] Later, in book 19, Augustine explains that the diversity of languages in the world poses a bar to social unity, serving as the cause of misunderstanding and war between communities. According to him, it is easier for dumb animals to associate than for two individuals who speak different languages and who are compelled to stay together. The author invokes a number of commonplaces, only to reject them. The first of these is the view that speech distinguishes animals from human beings, and the second is the characterization of *logos* as the element which unites and creates the political community.[38] Augustine affirms

---

[37] 'quoniam dominatio imperantis in lingua est, ibi est damnata superbia, ut non intellegeretur iubens homini qui noluit intellegere ut oboediret Deo iubenti' (*DCD* 16. 4).

[38] Cf. Isoc. *Nicocles* 6–9; *Antid.* 253–7; *Paneg.* 48 ff.; for discussion of this commonplace, see Too (1995), 3 n. 7.

the importance of speech, and particularly shared speech, as the basis of political community and power. He notes that imperial Rome imposed her language, Latin, upon all of her conquered peoples to ensure peace by means of interpreters or translators, although it achieved this first through slaughter and bloodshed (19. 7).

If the city of God as envisaged by Augustine is a community which comes into being through the separation of good languages from bad ones, it is also one where the multiplicity of languages cannot be permitted to confound or to de-authorize divine discourse. Divine textuality may appear in its original and authoritative manifestation as the Hebrew language, which Augustine presents as being once spoken by the whole human race and so as uniting it (16. 11. 1–2). Subsequently, it becomes the language of the chosen people in particular, first the historical people of Israel and then of the communities which continue to enjoy God's favour. Moses appointed individuals called 'leaders in letters' (*grammatoeisagōgoi*) to instruct young children in the language, so that Hebrew culture surpasses all other pagan cultures in antiquity (18. 39). What the author presents is a doctrine of cultural hegemony as articulated by the pre-eminence of a particular language. For Augustine, Hebrew, the original language of God's people, continues to be the discourse of the saints (cf. 16. 3. 2). But in a historically post-Babel world, the Christian community has to find means of resisting the actual plurality of languages in the world. Translation becomes an important and necessary means of recovering the Word of God, as Augustine's retelling of the Babel episode shows. He provides his reader with a rendering of Genesis 11: 1–9 in such a way as to undo the linguistic and literal diaspora following the construction of Babel. As a way of marking his treatment of the text as one which involves translation, he conspicuously corrects the mistranslation of the phrase 'hunter *against* the Lord' ('venator contra Dominum'), which describes Nebuchadnezzar as an opponent of God and thus as a potentially bad example of a mortal ruler. He notes that others have misinterpreted the ambiguous Greek *enantion* to mean 'before' rather than 'against' the Lord. His translation resists discrimination in another respect, as he deliberately confuses the ancient city of Babel with Babylon, the city, beyond its association with confusion, which is synonymous with sin in the Book of Revelation.

Elsewhere, Augustine takes pains to authorize the faithfulness of translation to original authorial intention. In book 18 he uses the agreement of the Septuagint translation to make this point. Recalling the aetiological narrative of the Alexandrian Library, he relates how Ptolemy II (Philadelphus) asked for six scholars from each of the twelve Jewish tribes to translate the Hebrew Bible into Greek. When the Egyptian ruler inspected their work, he found a remarkable consensus in choice of words and in syntax, so that it appeared that one translator had been at work. Augustine himself attributes this miraculous unity to the work of the Holy Spirit, which had authorized the text in the first place (18. 42), and perhaps thereby offers a commentary on the narrative of Pentecost as an occasion on which different individuals each heard the others praying in his own language (cf. Acts 2: 1–13). At 18. 43 Augustine affirms the authority of the Septuagint over other Greek translations, those by Aquila, Symmachus, Theodotion, and the anonymous 'fifth' scholar, stating that the Septuagint serves as the basis for subsequent Latin translations of the Old Testament and as the standard by which to measure other renderings. Again, the legitimacy of translation rests on the consensus of the scholars who mediate the Word of God through his Spirit and thus speak with the same inspiration as the prophets.[39] Earlier, in book 15, the author says that because the seventy received a prophetic spirit, they none the less produced the words of God ('divinitus dictum') even when they departed from the original text.[40] The idea of the Septuagint as a standard or basis for determining the value of other translations offers a gloss on the idea of 'canon', literally a 'rule' or 'measure'. But given Augustine's characterization of the production of this Greek version of the Scripture as authorship rather than mere translation, canonicity resides not in the Septuagint *qua* translation but in the text's status as a manifestation of the Word of God. The author applies the term 'canonical' to denote the

---

[39] 'Spiritus enim qui in prophetis erat quando illa dixerunt, idem ipse erat etiam in septuaginta viris quando illa interpretati sunt, qui profecto auctoritate divina et aliud dicere potuit, tamquam propheta ille utrumque dixisset, quia utrumque idem Spiritus diceret, . . .' (*DCD* 18. 43).

[40] 'merito enim creduntur septuaginta interpretes accepisse propheticum spiritum, ut, si quid eius auctoritate mutarent atque aliter quam erat quod interpretabantur dicerent, neque hoc divinitus dictum esse dubitaretur . . .' (ibid. 15. 23).

Scriptures as a divinely authorized discourse.[41] But it is important to recognize that for Augustine, originality is not the sole criterion that qualifies a text for inclusion in the canon. He states that some works, like the prophecies of Enoch, referred to at Jude 14, are deemed too ancient to be received into the privileged canon of God's Word (18. 38), while others that have authorships falsely attributed to them may be excluded from the canon despite having an authority ('auctoritas') approved by God. The latter works may be included in the Apocrypha.

At 18. 43 Augustine emphasizes that the unity of a text involves consensus of meaning rather than of verbal form, since the Holy Spirit can articulate the same thing in different ways. Thus it does not matter that the Septuagint refers to angels both as 'sons of God' and as 'sons of gods' (15. 23). Likewise, in *On Christian Doctrine*, Augustine objects to the idea that a grammatical solecism in itself should alter or affect the meaning of a text (2. 13. 19), although punctuation, which structures language, can introduce ambiguities (3. 2. 2 f.). This emphasis on meaning, rather than on the words themselves, marks another radical departure from classical rhetorical culture, which stresses the impact of verbal form, that is style, upon an audience. What this emphasis on meaning ultimately leads to is a concern with modes of non-literal interpretation, above all to allegory, an interpretive method which he had already introduced through the figure of Ambrose in the *Confessions*. At *City of God* 20. 28 Augustine proposes that God will distinguish ('tam magnum futurum . . . discrimen') between those who disobey the law and those who understand the law in its spiritual sense ('spiritaliter'). Spiritual understanding is necessary if sin is to be avoided. In this same chapter, he cites Malachi 3: 14–15 to make the point that those who take the Scriptures in a carnal sense ('carnaliter'), that is literally, will have rejected service to God as being vain: literal understanding leads to complaints against God.

Again, in *On Christian Doctrine*, the author warns against taking literally figurative or metaphorical expressions (cf. 'figuratam locutionem, id est, translatam') and, vice versa, against taking what should be understood literally in a figurative or metaphorical

---

[41] e. g. 'scripturam condidit quae canonica nominatur, eminentissimae auctoritatis' (*DCD* 11. 3); 'in scripturis sanctis quae appellantur canonicae' (ibid. 18. 36); 'in auctoritatis canone' (ibid. 18. 37), where the phrase denotes the status of the writings of Moses as the first canonical texts of Scripture.

manner (3. 10. 14). (The use of the phrase 'locutio translata' indicates that figurative discourse is a 'transferred' or 'translated' discourse, perhaps no less than the Septuagint is a translated version of the Hebrew Old Testament.) Augustine goes on to cite and then to redefine what we have seen to be the Hellenistic criterion of 'propriety' as the standard for determining which model of translation should be employed: if the literal text does not correspond to virtuous behaviour or to the true faith, namely love of God and of one's neighbour, then the text must be understood figuratively. Several chapters later, he suggests that almost all of the deeds depicted in the Old Testament are to be read both figuratively and literally, lest they appear inappropriate to the morality and teaching of the New Testament. If the reader understands them literally, he is, however, to be careful not to see them as providing a model for his own 'mores' (3. 22. 32). Augustine recovers allegory as a way of maintaining the authority of scriptural texts which would otherwise be categorized as 'immoral', 'unjust', or 'unhelpful'; allegory in turn recovers and reappropriates a discourse that is otherwise historically out of touch. More generally, the discussion of allegory in *On Christian Doctrine* elaborates the means by which Christian culture might appropriate and subordinate pagan literary culture. On the one hand, Augustine rejects pagan myth regarding the Muses as the daughters of Zeus and Memory, citing evidence from Varro that these goddesses are actually only statues (2. 17. 27)—he takes the position previously articulated by Xenophanes and by Plato, for instance, that Hesiod is a poet who fabricates lies about the gods. Yet, on the other hand, he concedes that even pagan learning can communicate some element of (Christian) truth, although one is not to seek this 'truth' from the theatre (2. 18. 28). One can learn history even outside the confines of the Church—the *City of God* attempts to produce a history from within—and the benefits of secular history become apparent when the author notes that chronology can establish the indebtedness of Plato and Pythagoras to the Old Testament prophets, rather than the latter's debt to pagan philosophy (2. 28. 42–3).

I suggest that the discussion of allegory in the *City of God* and *On Christian Doctrine* provides literary criticism with its teleology . At *City of God* 20. 28 Augustine declares that it is necessary to read the law of Moses spiritually ('spiritaliter') and to find in it Christ, who judges between the good and the bad. He associates the allegorical recuperation of the Old Testament with the Last Judgement through reference to Christ, the judge. Reading thus anticipates the Last Judgement, figured implicitly and explicitly as the reading of a book, an occasion which quite literally involves an act of reading and discernment of the text. (It is important to insist that reading can only be a rehearsal of the Last Judgement, for Augustine resisted the Donatist view that the Church was an already judged and discriminated community, which held only a few pure elect.[42]) Earlier in the same book, he translates Revelation 20: 12, where John writes of a vision in which books are opened, as is another book of each individual's life, according to which his or her deeds are judged: 'And he said, "I saw the dead, great and small, and the books were opened. And another book was opened, which is of the life of each person, and the dead were judged according to what was written in the book about their deeds." '[43] Augustine interprets the plural books mentioned first in this passage as being the Old and New Testaments in which God revealed his commandments, and the singular book mentioned secondly as the text which records whether each individual obeyed or disobeyed these commandments. This latter book is one which cannot be measured in physical or material terms (cf. 'carnaliter'), nor can its reading be measured in normal temporal terms. Rather the text is called to mind swiftly and is understood by mental intuition ('mentis intuitu'), by which God's Word is revealed to the angels and his people. What this chapter of book 20 of the *City of God* confirms is that the discrimination of texts which occurs in the city of God rehearses the reading which constitutes divine judgement and discrimination between those who are good and those who are bad or wicked, as portrayed in this work and in the Book of Revelation.

IX

Augustine is often thought to mark the end of the classical world and its culture. Yet, if this characterization is at all valid, it must be conceded that the bishop of Hippo nevertheless perpetuates one

[42] Rist (1994), 229.
[43] 'et vidi, inquit, mortuos magnos et pusillos, et aperti sunt libri; et alius liber apertus est, qui est vitae uniuscuiusque; et iudicati sunt mortui ex ipsis scripturis librorum secundum facta sua' (*DCD* 20. 14).

aspect of the pagan world—the critical imperative, which holds that communities must discriminate between the discourses available to them if they are to ensure their existence. My reading of *Confessions* and *City of God* shows that Augustine, characterized by contemporary scholars as 'le patriarche des persécuteurs', can be perceived as putting into practice a principle inherited from pagan Greek and Roman antiquity.[44] The Christian author's accounts of the divine community point to the continued need to discriminate between discourses as good/divine or bad/demonic, in the community authorized by God rather than by the gods. At stake now is the salvation of the individual, who needs to renounce the discourses of the world in order to become a citizen of the Christian community and who is required to become a critical agent lest he incur the terrible judgement of God.

[44] Brown (1964: 116) qualifies the characterization of Augustine as 'le patriarche des persécuteurs'.

8

Criticism in the Present Time?

We forget in fact that freedom of speech . . . is always freedom
from the speech of others, or rather control of their silence . . .

Pierre Bourdieu (1988), 192

I

This study began by proposing that histories of literary criticism
have by and large decontextualized, by insufficiently contextualiz-
ing, the writings that they perceive to constitute ancient literary
criticism. It argues that they cite them out of context and hyposta-
size individual terms, such as *mimēsis* and the sublime, and so in
turn deny the opportunity to consider in what ways critical discourses in antiquity respond to a concern that texts can do something good or bad to the individual and society. The Greek and
Roman texts from antiquity examined in this study reveal again
and again a recognition that literature is potentially more than just
a text to be received by the audience's ears and eyes: literary texts
can have an effect on the individual, which may in turn have implications for the larger community. It is for this reason that authors
seek either to authorize and privilege them (assuming that the texts
in question have a desired effect), or else to exclude them from their
communities (assuming that the texts in question have an undesirable effect).

Michel Foucault may have argued that continuity is by no means
the only or even a desirable feature of history, whether this be a history of criticism or of some other body of discourse.[1] If the task of
this study has been to relocate 'ancient literary criticism' by opening to scrutiny in particular the term 'criticism' and to a lesser
degree the term 'literary' (see Conclusion below), then it has done

---

[1] Foucault (1989), 21; Lentricchia (1980), 205.

so by introducing a historical discontinuity between a more conventional literary history and the discourse that this history has
been attempting to appropriate for itself as an alternative history of
criticism. It has, moreover, emphasized the discontinuity between
ancient criticism and aesthetic or evaluative criticism, which is concerned with the work in itself—perhaps best exemplified by New
Criticism—and with standards of beauty instrinsic to the work.

But it is not always possible to follow the pull towards discontinuity, and, if anything, I depart from the more conventional historicization which insists upon the rupture between pre-modern
and modern criticism. Indeed, my intention is to resist the introduction of precisely such an irreconcilable break between ancient/
classical/ élite/hegemonic and modern/bourgeois/protest, which the
literary histories produced by the left require for their own self-
authorizations. To conclude my analysis at late antiquity, however,
leaves literary history incomplete and renders ancient critical discourse without any contemporary descendants or analogies (not that
these are necessary requirements for this study to be valid). For this
reason, in this final chapter I shall propose that it is possible to re-
establish the historical continuity of literary criticism. I shall
attempt to find modern analogies for ancient criticism which may be
located elsewhere than in the realm of what is often termed contemporary criticism. In particular, whereas earlier chapters of this book
have succeeded in showing that ancient criticism is both an evaluative and a regulative practice with a social teleology, that it is a mode
of what we might nowadays term 'censorship' (see the Introduction),
this final chapter considers whether, after antiquity, what we conventionally regard as censorship is in any way analogous to ancient
criticism. The sites of discourse to which I direct attention are the
contentious ones of obscenity, pornography, and the higher education curriculum, which late twentieth-century American scholarship
has been most vociferous in recognizing as crucially, because politically, significant. Because the academy is today a cosmopolitan one,
significant debates and arenas of contention in one part of world have
implications for those in other parts, and it is for this reason that the
particularly American preoccupations with freedom of speech and
censorship deserve attention.[2]

---

[2] Robbins (1993), 185. S. Hall in Dunant (1994: 164–83) observes that, because
the American issue of 'PC' has travelled into British culture, it is important to pay
attention to what happens on the other side of the Atlantic.

II

I want to reaffirm—albeit now retrospectively—the political nature of ancient criticism by drawing attention to the analogies offered by contemporary forms of literary discrimination and judgement. My aim is to recover these analogies in the realization that the literary historian can reclaim these discourses for other than élite quarters and aims, and place them in a broader public sphere. If literary historians of modernity or of the left have refrained from including in the critical canon texts produced about literature by particular élites in antiquity on the basis that these works serve to articulate the tastes and interests of the élite against the mass and in order to resist their ostensible politics, they have ironically restricted the historicity of the narrative of criticism in a manner that is not unlike the traditional histories that propound the idea of 'ancient literary criticism'. I intend to demonstrate that the sort of critical discriminations and selections which characterize ancient or pre-modern criticism also persist in a post-Enlightenment literary culture, not simply despite the greater democratization of the book trade but precisely because of it. Censorship manifests itself for the good and for the preservation of the community not simply in twentieth-century autocratic or totalitarian regimes—for instance, Nazi Germany or the former Communist states—but also in democratic Western countries. For the reason that this study does not see censorship as a necessary concomitant of despotic repression, I suggest that it is especially important to be sensitive to the forms of discursive exclusion in democratic cultures of whatever form.

Whereas literary and cultural theorists like Raymond Williams, Peter Hohendahl, and Terry Eagleton characterize criticism as a creation of the eighteenth century and its bourgeoisie, I suggest rather that criticism *continues* in and after the eighteenth century. Instead of looking for a discourse of political and cultural protest, as these thinkers do, I begin by drawing attention to literary discrimination as it takes the form of prohibition against obscene material—significantly, a prosecutable offence in modern Europe beginning in the eighteenth century.[3] In Britain, a body of

---

[3] Rolph (1969), 55. The first book to be found obscene in an English common law court, *Venus in the Cloister, or the Nun in Her Smock* published in 1724 by Edward Curll, was so declared in 1727. As punishment, Curll was placed in the pillory for corrupting 'the morals of the King's subjects'. Saunders (1990: 438) observes that

legislation which came into force in the 1950s, a period not insignif-
icantly often invoked in late twentieth-century nostalgia as the
locus of family values and moral standards,[4] manifests assumptions
which are certainly familiar from Plato's *Republic* and Augustine's
Confessions amongst the other ancient texts considered in this book.
(It is significantly in recognition of these precedents that C. H.
Rolph offers the *Republic* as the originative text for contemporary
censorship laws.[5]) Characteristic of literary criticism, this cluster of
contemporary legislation and legal decision regarding obscene
material concerns itself with issues of public good or harm. In
1959, the British Government passed the Obscene Publications Act
in order to penalize any individual who *publishes an obscene article*,
whether for gain or not. It defines the 'obscene' in the following
terms:

An article is obscene 'if its effect or (where the article comprises two or
more distinct items) the effect of any one of its items is, if taken as a whole,
such as tends to deprave and corrupt persons who are likely, having regard
to all relevant circumstances, to read, see or hear the matter contained or
embodied in it'.   (Section 1 of the Obscene Publications Act 1959)[6]

The Act assumes a prophylactic position in an attempt to avoid a
situation where word or picture might lead to antisocial action or
behaviour—that is, 'deprave and corrupt'. The 1959 Act makes an
important qualification to the above definition of 'obscene':

(2) It is hereby declared that the opinion of experts as to the literary, artistic, scientific or other merits of an article may be admitted in any proceed-
ings under this Act either to establish or to negative the said ground (i.e.,
the ground that publication is 'justified' in the interests of science, literature, etc.).   (1959 Act, Section 4, Sub-section 2)[7]

in the 19th cent. British obscenity law sought for the most part to control otherwise
diversified social spaces—for instance, street corners or other places in which pornographic material might be circulated.

   [4] The Children and Young Persons (Harmful Publications) Act 1955 sought to
regulate the influence of juvenile reading material, penalizing: 'any book, magazine
or other like work which is of a kind likely to fall into the hands of children or young
persons and consists wholly or mainly of stories told in pictures (with or without the
addition of written matter), being stories portraying (*a*) the commission of crimes,
or (*b*) acts of violence or cruelty, or (*c*) incidents of a repulsive or horrible nature, in
such a way that the work as a whole would tend to corrupt a child or young person
into whose hands it might fall.' As Rolph (1969: 107–8) observes, the intent was to
control the explosion of American 'horror comics' and their potential effect on children.
   [5] Ibid. 28–9.   [6] Cited from Rolph (1969), 14–15.   [7] Ibid. 26.

The law permits the mitigation of obscenity. What the Act recognizes is that benefit or utility, figured here as 'the interests of science, literature' and so on, that is knowledge or culture, or its furtherance, can redeem material that might otherwise constitute the 'obscene'. The definition in Section 1 and the qualification of Section 4, Subsection 2 together frame the law as one of greater good for the larger community: these sections of the 1959 Act distinguish between what is harmful, that is what actually or potentially leads to a detriment, and what is beneficial for the audiences of the material in question. In a subsequent amendment to the Act, the distribution, i.e. the multiplication, of obscene material is highlighted as an issue. The Obscene Publications Act of 1964 seeks to penalize the wholesaler and in this way to cut off access to the offending material for the bookseller and the public.[8]

Christie Davies comments that in the progression of legislation against the obscene there is a significant shift away from a moralistic position that, like the Children and Young Persons (Harmful Publications) Act 1955, saw material as being intrinsically bad. She observes a move towards a causalistic argument that, like the Obscene Publications Act 1959, attempts to establish the detrimental effect of proscribed material.[9] The progression from the moral to the causal marks a shift of responsibility from the author to the audience. Where moralists might regard the *author's* intention as important in deciding whether to ban material, causalists consider it unimportant and, as Rajeev Dhavan notes, they argue that people can decide for themselves what to receive.[10] But beyond the shift from a concern with what the obscene might do to the whole person to an anxiety about specific actions, the 1959 Act in particular insists upon the unfixity, and therefore the arbitrariness, of what constitutes the obscene. To 'deprave and corrupt' potentially leaves a broad remit for the 'obscene', rendering liable to proscription gay and lesbian material, and texts regarding women's fertility.[11] The law invokes the 'average person', in effect the lay counterpart of the 'reasonable man', to serve as judge in determining merit or harm.

No less does the escape clause in the 1959 Act, which excuses obscene material on the basis of 'literary merit', demonstrate the

---

[8] Ibid. 47.
[10] Dhavan (1978), 58–9.

[9] Davies in Dhavan and Davies (1978), 2.
[11] Itzin (1992), 402, 408.

instability of the 'obscene'.[12] Hunter, Saunders, and Williamson observe that post-1959, literary critics or 'experts' are brought in to pronounce on the artistic merit of a work in question to establish its legality, or else on its lack of merit, and so to define its illegal status.[13] Hence Penguin Books Ltd. successfully defended its decision to publish D. H. Lawrence's *Lady Chatterly's Lover* on the basis of its 'literary merits' in 1960.[14] The assumption is that the literary is opposed to the functional and therefore obviates the possibility of a work being able to harm, and, certainly, the expert witnesses claimed that Lawrence's novel was 'for the public good'. By way of comparison, in the United States, the legal definition of obscenity, phrased in 1973, raises the same problems of determining the illegality of the material in question when it conceives as obscene such material as 'appeals to the prurient interest; . . . depicts and describes in a patently offensive way' and 'taken as a whole, lacks serious literary, artistic, political or scientific value'.[15]

III

The legislation on obscenity also assists in extending the critical paradigm to other issues, such as pornography, where prohibitive legislation is for the most part absent and where for this reason debate is all the more important and vociferous. Against the background of ancient criticism, those who stand in opposition to pornography, and have accordingly demanded prohibitive legislation, more evidently propose the continuity of ancient and modern criticism. Historically, these individuals have insisted on pornography's damaging effect, denying the separation of word/image and action where pornography is concerned, no less than, say, Plato in the *Republic* or Augustine in the *Confessions*, where literature is in question. They have rallied, and occasionally still rally, around the cry 'pornography is the theory, rape is the practice'.[16] Numerous studies exist that seek to establish—frequently, uncompromisingly—the link between pornography and actual harm, sexual

---

[12] Saunders (1990), 440.
[13] Hunter, Saunders, and Williamson (1993), 15, 147.
[14] Rolph (1969), 108.   [15] MacKinnon (1992), 464 and n.
[16] See Kappeler (1986: 35), who calls for more sophisticated language to address the issue.

exploitation, abuse, violence, and even murder.[17] In her now classic *Pornography: Men Possessing Women*, Andrea Dworkin insists upon the actuality of harm entailed in pornographic images. Dworkin begins her study by evoking the idea of obscenity, and she then proceeds to dismiss it as a category of material that 'requires a judgment of value' to be considered harmful. For her, pornography is *in ipso facto* an actualized harm in that it consists in 'the graphic depiction of whores', that is the graphic depiction of women as whores.[18] In order to emphasize the harm for women in the pornographic image, Dworkin draws analogies between the pen or camera which depict the woman and the sabre that penetrates the vagina,[19] and presents the actions of the Marquis de Sade as paradigmatic of the pornographer-rapist.[20]

Perhaps, the most eloquent and powerful claims of the harms of pornography come from the lawyer and sometime ally of Dworkin, Catherine MacKinnon. Agreeing in principle with Dworkin, MacKinnon has proposed that 'Pornography is more act-like and thought-like',[21] and in her most recent book, ironically entitled *Only Words*, she insists on an unmitigated and unmitigating statement of the link between text and action as an argument for the need for laws against sexually explicit material. In direct response to the literary defence, she beings by stating that pornography is 'not the basis of literature' because it concerns the unspeakable, namely abuse, terror, and traumas.[22] Words *are* an actual cause of harm in such instances as libel, blackmail, bribery, conspiracy, sexual harassment, and—adds Catherine Itzin, for that matter—racial harassment.[23] MacKinnon makes an argument for the damaging effect of pornographic images which deftly sets aside as irrelevant issues of intentionality. She sets out to argue that words are indeed not 'only words', nor for that matter are pictures only pictures. Where law might protect pornography as a 'viewpoint' on women and on the basis of freedom of speech, she maintains that pornography is an instance of expression which is not distinct from

[17] For the suggestion that child pornography is a record of child sexual abuse, see Kelly (1992), 121. See D. E. Russell (1992: 313) for discussion of work which suggests that depictions of rape may increase the likelihood of rape.

[18] Dworkin (1981), 9, 200.   [19] Ibid. 25.   [20] Ibid. 70 ff.

[21] MacKinnon (1992), 484.   [22] MacKinnon (1993), 3.

[23] C. MacKinnon, 'Not a Moral Issue', *Yale Law and Policy Review* 2. 2 (1984), 337, and Itzin (1992), 412–13.

what it expresses, namely violence, abuse, and sex.[24] Throughout *Only Words* MacKinnon argues that words actually *do* things, to all intents and purposes offering an unsubtle version of J. L. Austin's concept of the speech-act (see J. L. Austin, *How To Do Things With Words* (Oxford, 1962)). She suggests a variety of analogies to illustrate her point that text can actually produce real damage and harm to those involved in its production and in its reception: saying 'kill' to a trained dog in the presence of another person can be translated to mean, 'I want you [i.e. the other person] dead', and is to all intents and purposes an act of destruction; burning a cross in the United States is an act of racism; uttering unwelcome sexual words or statements is to all intents and purposes sex, as in the Anita Hill–Clarence Thomas case.[25] Later, MacKinnon goes on to show that sexual language is quite literally unspeakable, citing Anita Hill's difficulty in repeating the actual words that were allegedly used against her.[26] Shame in recounting sexual violence is now the defining criterion for MacKinnon's definition of the 'unspeakable'.[27]

MacKinnon makes a case for seeing pornography as harmful for the individuals willingly and unwillingly involved in its production. She maintains the need to censor such material precisely because it harms the individuals represented in its images—women and children may be raped, maimed, or even killed in the production of pornography, as in so-called 'snuff' films. It is from this position that she moves on to make the more controversial argument that pornography may also lead to sexually violent behaviour among those who receive its images.[28]

Bald arguments in terms of harm or, if not benefit, non-harm are not, however, by any means representative of the sum of critical discourse. Kappeler draws attention to the fallacious pressure to defend pornography and freedom of speech as a liberal or sexual radical, and to distance oneself from 'prigs and prudes' and repressive censors.[29] The construction of this alliance effaces significant differences between the various interested parties. It assumes that all acts of censorship in the late twentieth century are identical and are to be set simplistically and unproblematically in opposition to the right to free speech, invoked in the United States as the First Amendment or in the United Kingdom as 'liberty'. When such

[24] MacKinnon (1993), 11–17.   [25] Ibid. 12, 33, 65.   [26] Ibid. 65.
[27] Ibid. 66.   [28] Ibid. 17.   [29] Kappeler (1992), 88.

black-and-white contrasts are drawn between freedom and repression, where freedom is identified with the left and repression with the right, a whole crucial level of contextual argument which helps to justify discrimination in the sense of censorship is lacking.

Contextualization is precisely one of the strategies which responds to the calls for liberalness and fair-mindedness from conservatives who seek to undermine feminist argument. Indeed, Stanley Fish argues for seeing the importance of social context in calling into question the liberal assumptions of conservatives. In *There's No Such Thing as Free Speech and It's a Good Thing, Too*, a book which calls into question a series of liberal assumptions about discourse and scholarship, Fish observes that he has been characterized as being on the 'right' by critics for teaching the texts of the traditional canon and for his theoretical positions.[30] In his turn, he cites the legal theorist Frederick Schauer who argues that free-speech arguments are not neutral but rather have 'all the earmarks of an ideology', that is a series of presuppositions about what is good and bad for society.[31] Those like the legal theorist Ronald Dworkin, who support free speech in the form of the First Amendment to the US Constitution, will appeal to the greater good that free expression will have for society, on the basis that it constitutes one of the democratic foundations of Western society. For Fish, 'free speech' is undeniably a loaded, partisan term, like 'merit' and 'fairness', which crop up as privileged and ideal terms in the writing of right-wing thinkers like Allan Bloom and Dinesh D' Souza.[32] The problem with these words and phrases is that they assume that everyone operates by nature or historically on a level playing-ground, with equal access to speech, advancement, or protection from exploitation.

Against D' Souza, who cites the apparent excesses of political correctness and codes on racial and sexual harassment in universities, Fish defends such constraints for the reason that they are necessary to preserve the rights of certain groups, such as racial minorities or women, who have been and continue to be socially and historically disadvantaged.[33] He argues that freedom of speech is not a satisfactory point of reference where anti-Semitic

---

[30] Fish (1994), 53.

[31] Ibid. 13, and Frederick Schauer, 'The First Amendment as Ideology', *William and Mary Law Review*, 33 (1992), 856.

[32] Fish (1994), 16.   [33] Ibid. 102–19.

propaganda surfaces, whether this is in a school, as in the Jim Keegstra case in Alberta, Canada, or under the umbrella of academic discussion. The holocaust has shown what the effects of such material might be. Thus for Fish, history—here that of the Afro-American communities in the United States—obviates the charge of 'reverse racism' where affirmative action is concerned, although he concedes that this position does raise the important question as to whether the injustices and discriminations of the past can ever be righted by legislative action or policy.[34] In the end, he dismisses a gradualist system of exclusion for a 'safe rather than sorry' policy, stating that he would rather run the risk of censoring 'art' and 'literature' than tolerate the risks, the hate, and violence, that they might incite.[35]

The rejection of absolutist arguments in favour of or against freedom of speech is a necessary move if practicalities are to be considered. Social context is necessary for an intellectually rigorous defence of the discrimination of pornographic material: it is important to consider what pornographic material implies both for men and for women in contemporary society. Moreover, to invoke social and cultural context in arguing against the circulation of pornography is in turn to distinguish one's position from that of the conservatives and to dislodge this embarrassing collusion. Contextualization interrogates the simple-minded account of causality. Certainly, when we go beyond the characterization of individuals as simply 'pro-' or 'anti-' pornography, we do find more than literalistic and absolutist statements that this or that image is detrimental. After all, the anti-porn position is a vulnerable one inasmuch as it is always difficult to establish the role of pornographic material in causing a particular rape or act of violence. Deborah Cameron and Liz Frazer observe that porn-blaming needs to be recognized as something of a cultural cliché, an explanation that feminism or those who simplistically invoke it can have recourse to. Accordingly, when the night before his execution mass-murderer Ted Bundy 'confessed' that he enacted scenarios derived from the pornographic material with which he was obsessed, his admission was less an acknowledgement of pornography's damaging influence than an invocation of a particular feminist conviction by a man who no longer had anything to protect.[36]

[34] Fish (1994), 60–9.   [35] Ibid. 114–15.
[36] Cameron and Frazer (1992), 361–6.

Kappeler may cite the slogan, 'Pornography is the theory, rape is the practice', but she does so in order to call for a more sophisticated language to deal with the problem. Where the Williams Report criticizes feminists for failing to trouble themselves with an overall critique of culture, Kappeler argues that a critique of culture is precisely what feminist theorists are engaged in. In fact, the refuge that the Report takes in the 'literary' and the 'aesthetic' is itself a case of decontextualization which ignores the processes of literary and pornographic production and their economics to which Kappeler draws attention. She shows that because literary judgements and values are largely produced by men, it is the case that sexualized material will be an expression of a patriarchal society.[37] Kappeler deliberately invokes, as a call to reconsider, Dworkin's analysis of the photograph 'Beaver Hunters' in which a woman is tied to the hood of a black jeep carrying two white male hunters. She begins by framing her analysis of pornography with the case of Thomas Kasire, the black worker who was tied up, beaten, photographed, and finally murdered at the hands of a white farmer in Namibia.[38] While the account of Kasire might be regarded as a case for the analogy between violence and pornographic depiction, or else for the mis-analogy between racism and sexism, Kappler is not making a point about the literalism of violence in the production of pornographic images.[39] What she draws out of the scenario is the sense in which understanding social dynamics—a Namibia in which the white man assumes it his right to torture blacks and in which the white courts do not sufficiently penalize such behaviour— is crucial for comprehending the larger systematic violence and degradation to Kasire. Kappeler sets up an argument that presents pornography as sexism, which is to be understood as somehow analogous to the institutionalized racism which Kasire suffered.

James Boyd White suggests that where American culture is concerned it would be extremely difficult to find some other structure or discourse to displace law '. . . for power, for decency, for correspondence with the facts, for willingness to modify itself, and so on'.[40] Advocating the analogies between law and literary language, White proposes legal discourse as a 'constitutive rhetoric', as a

[37] Kappeler (1986), 110–22.
[38] See Dworkin (1981: 25 ff.), who used the 'Beaver Hunters' photograph to make the point that society conventionally regards women as the property of men.
[39] Kappeler (1986), 14–15, and (1992), 84.   [40] J. B. White (1985), 241–2.

shared language which individuals employ and negotiate to produce a community, ostensibly with justice as its aim.[41] This characterization of legal language helps us to understand how with
MacKinnon, as perhaps its most significant protagonist, criticism
goes beyond the level of protest and campaign and returns to the
original forum of the legal contest (*agōn*). The absolutist rhetoric
that the reader encounters in *Only Words* must not be allowed to
mask the social analysis which serves as her subtext. In her 1979
book *Sexual Harassment of Working Women*, MacKinnon argued
that sexual harassment of women constituted sex discrimination on
the grounds that it served to close off opportunities to an already
structurally disadvantaged group in society.[42] What she argued was
that particular, individual cases were not just that, and so not just
private, personal issues, but were, rather, symptomatic of the way
that society treated women at work and at home, and therefore a
legitimate issue for the law. MacKinnon has attempted to bring
this larger social context into the campaign against pornography
and to establish that it too is a form of sex discrimination to be proscribed by legislation. On this basis she was responsible with
Andrea Dworkin for introducing and wording legislation against
pornography in the Human Rights Ordinance of the City of
Minneapolis 1983.[43] Rejecting the idea entrenched in the First
Amendment that equality lies in freedom of expression, she presented the view that pornography constitutes discrimination
against women, because it subordinates them and renders them
second-class citizens, if even that.[44]

MacKinnon's criticism attempted to discriminate against a discourse which poses a detriment to a segment of society: damage to
society now entails what prevents particular segments from enjoying respect and equality of opportunity. But the critical process
locates itself in a larger social principle of discrimination. In a later
account of her legislation, MacKinnon took pains to distinguish the
Minneapolis legislation from the cause–effect model of earlier discussions of pornography, and to locate it in the discourse *against
discrimination* as 'discrimination' is commonly understood. She
emphasizes the ordinance's concern to prohibit sexualized depictions *that subordinate* rather than to direct the ban against sexual-

[41] J. B. White (1985), 28.   [42] MacKinnon (1979).
[43] Dworkin (1992).   [44] MacKinnon (1993), 11.

ized depictions *of subordination* of women.[45] The difference between 'that' and 'of' in the wording is significant because it recognizes that subordination is not simply restricted to the depictions themselves, but that the depictions are an element of a larger system of disadvantage to women in society. The Minneapolis Ordinance, in particular, demonstrates the political efficacy of contextual argument. The recognition that pornography must be viewed against the situation of women in contemporary society provides this form of discriminatory material with a rigorous and persuasive intellectual case. Furthermore, it also serves to establish that the exclusion of sexually explicit or exploitative material would provide society with a greater good than the preservation of freedom of speech at all costs, for it makes the point that the disadvantaging of women would be a greater social harm.

A more sophisticated critical stance, which to a considerable degree rejects MacKinnon's position, comes from Drucilla Cornell. Where pornography is concerned, Cornell proposes to shift the critical imperative away from the legal sphere to the domain of the 'imaginary', where the sense of individual personhood is formed against and despite different social forces which attack and fracture the self.[46] Her aim is to return to women in particular the possibilities for taking responsibility for their own individual personhood, and she argues that heterosexual pornography is precisely one of the obstacles to the achievement of this goal. Heterosexual pornography is an imposition of male fantasy structures upon others in such a way as to deny and degrade selfhood, especially where women are concerned.[47] (Unlike MacKinnon, Cornell refuses to assimilate gay and lesbian pornography to more conventional porn, arguing that the former may be seeking to articulate a sense of sexual self from within the gay community.) For Cornell, pornography must be recognized as a necessarily complex fantasy structure so that it becomes difficult to think of it in terms of the coercive speech act, as indeed MacKinnon does—although I would not want to exclude this possibility altogether. It is for this reason that Cornell regards the feminist programme as ideally being to control the distribution of pornographic images in such a way as to prevent them from dominating the public sphere and

---

[45] MacKinnon (1992), 466.   [46] Cornell (1995), 18 ff.
[47] Ibid. 141.

threatening the imaginary.[48] For her, this does not necessarily have to entail the prohibition or the criminalizing of pornographic images and their production.

If liberalism claims to be universally and eternally valid, then sensitive and responsible argument is relativistic, addressing a social scenario at a particular moment. What this means is that the view that sexual or, for that matter, racial material is discriminatory may in turn have its legitimacy called into question. Intellectual arguments can be put forward for changing the categories of what is to be proscribed as society is transformed or reconstructed. In some sense, where pornography or racially discriminatory material is concerned, censorship and regulation are working precisely towards this aim: namely, the structural establishment of greater opportunities for women and other presently culturally disadvantaged groups, so that these groups begin from the proverbial 'level playing-field'. This alternative writing of the history of literary criticism demonstrates precisely that the categories of what are deemed to be good, just, or advantageous, and, conversely, bad, unjust, or detrimental change because they reflect the ideals of the community and of the individual who inhabits the community.

IV

To follow the call for cultural precision and context in making my case for the necessity of the critical process, I now want to reject the notion that *all* contemporary forms of discursive exclusion are for the good or benefit of society, if only because we recognize that texts have different ways of meaning. In particular, I interrogate the validity of the critical imperative, where criticism is for the sake of discriminating against *multiple kinds* of discourse rather than *multiple copies* of a particular kind. Where criticism, under the name of 'literary criticism' or more commonly, of 'liberalism', seeks to regulate and limit the discourses available for the academic community and its pedagogies, then the role of discrimination becomes questionable.

In the United States, in particular, education is regarded as a form of socialization. Henry Louis Gates critically observes that

[48] Cornell (1995), 141.

'few American theorists of American education . . . have separated pedagogy from the needs of citizenship'. The academy is often seen to be an important marker of issues in the political sphere and is sometimes indistinct from it, so that undergraduate study is to be viewed as a template for civic identity and behaviour where civic identity is above all identified with the white male.[49] Accordingly, individuals on the right, and especially the extreme right, have blamed the intellectual community for the fragmentation of common or shared identity, and, as Bruce Robbins observes, they have accused literary departments of substituting *multiculturalism* for 'Culture'. None the less, the opposition to multiculturalism is an absurd one because it constitutes a repudiation of American culture itself. As Robert Hughes observes, it is precisely 'This polyphony of voices, this constant eddying of claims to identity, . . . that makes America America.'[50] The dominant anxieties are detached from cultural contexts, and are addressed to the destabilization of Truth, to the eclipsing of the Universal by particularities, and to the supposedly heightened profile given to work and issues concerning race, gender, class, and ideologies such as Marxism or feminism.[51] These issues, one might note, are significantly those which call into question the identity of the academic as a white, male citizen and in some sense rehearse legislation of the nineteenth century and the earlier part of the twentieth century to regulate and control immigration in the United States.[52] What we find is an often ironic identification of valid academic issues set against or in contrast to (amongst other things) feminism and post-structuralist theory as less valid academic discourses which are seen as threatening to displace the traditional languages of scholarship, and which moreover erode the foundations of Western society as based on justice, fairness, and freedom of speech and expression.

[49] Gates (1992), 106; also Lentricchia (1983), 2; Giroux (1992), 119–44; Brant and Too (1994), 15.

[50] Robbins (1993), 180; Hughes (1994), 83.

[51] Bromwich (1992: 26) writes about the 'faculty loyalty oath', which requires faculty at certain American universities and colleges to 'incorporate such "nontraditional" perspectives as gender, race and class' in their teaching. Bromwich charges policies of this kind with engendering a restrictive group identity and mentality in contemporary higher education.

[52] Mann (1979: 88 ff., 116, 126), notes that American immigration policy and practice demonstrated a definite bias in favour of Northerners, that is those who were of Anglo-Saxon origin.

The envisaged relationship between education and citizenship is more than theoretical.[53] In the United States, one of the mainstays of an education which seeks to socialize has been the 'Great Books' curriculum and its prior incarnations, particularly 'Western Civilization'.[54] Originally conceived as a historical component of the curriculum in 1919, Great Books ensured that all students would read a fixed set of works—e.g. Plato, Aristotle, Shakespeare, Milton—seen to be important to Western consciousness and crucial to the initiation of the student into the ranks of Western culture. Scholars have pointed out that the establishment of the Western civilization course at Columbia, which scholars trace as the origins of 'great books', actually grew out of 'War Issues' courses held at the beginning of World War I at various universities to familiarize US soldiers with the European culture and heritage that they were to defend.[55] More to the point, they offered a recuperation of the Arnoldian programme of classical and European literature as a civilizing force. W. B. Carnochan offers an alternative, but complementary explanation—that the historical programmes of study were in part originally established in response to a sense of the need to integrate and homogenize a growing immigrant population.[56] It is worth noting that, against the background of this justification for 'great books' teaching, this now conservative curriculum did not always have an assured position in the liberal arts curriculum. As Gerald Graff notes, when English first began to be institutionalized as a subject of study in American colleges and universities at the beginning of the twentieth century, teachers concerned with 'ideas' rather than with philology, with its claims to scientific objectivity, were accused of *belletrism*.[57]

'Great books' pedagogy is also an aetiological discourse. Lee Patterson poignantly observes that in the later nineteenth and early twentieth centuries, literary studies had become so concerned with historical context that literary works were no longer read as literary texts. He remarks that it became important to 'reformulate the atemporality of [the 'champions of literary culture's] classics in

---

[53] See McDonald (1992: 46 ff.), who traces the idea that education constructs society to the French Revolution.

[54] Keeping alive Charles William Eliot's (one of the founders) ideal of a pluralistic and competitive university, Harvard did not institute such a requirement, despite its 'core curriculum'. Carnochan (1993), 79, 119.

[55] See M. L. Pratt (1992), 13–31; Hughes (1994), 55–7.

[56] Carnochan (1993), 69.   [57] Graff (1992*b*), 134.

terms that would resist the acid of historicism; or to deploy the methods of historicism itself in such a way that they could not dissolve the values they were employed to discover'.[58] But ironically, the 'great books' tradition is one that for the most part effaces the historical context with which it initially aimed to provide students, operating as both a historicism and transcendentalism. In its effort to communicate a series of humanist values, its curriculum presumed the transferability of its texts, downplaying differences and contextual specificities.[59]

Defenders of the 'great books' curriculum seek to limit the extent of repudiating the plural and diverse discourse that would threaten the curriculum's privilged position. (I note that the voices of male classicists have been especially prominent among them.[60]) For Allan Bloom, the supposedly inordinate attention granted to the literary and cultural achievements of non-European and non-male authors potentially undermines the superiority of Western intellectual culture. By making space within undergraduate study for women and for 'minority' authors, current pedagogical practice invites a cultural relativism, with the result that students are no longer able to distinguish the greatness of a culture based on the classical canon.[61] One must of course wonder at the logic of such a position, inasmuch as it unwittingly points to the fragility of a hegemonic 'Western culture'. This rather crude paternalism finds expression elsewhere with Roger Kimball, who begins by lamenting the crisis in higher education in the United States.[62] He takes to task academics, and in particular literary critics such as Stanley Fish, Margaret Ferguson, and Jonathan Culler, for breaking up the cultural consensus of the American undergraduate curriculum with their methodologies and instatement of feminist and ethnic canons. He proposes that the politics of minority interests has 'corrupted' higher education in the United States, and he cites in particular the displacement of Western culture by feminism, black studies, deconstructionism, and so on, pointing, like D' Souza, to the existence and outcome of harassment cases as an example of where this corruption has occurred.[63]

---

[58] See Patterson (1987), 101–2.

[59] See also Lentricchia (1983), 125–6, and the Introduction above, pp. 2–5.

[60] See Brenkman (1993: 90), who identifies amongst others Donald Kagan, author of several substantial studies on Greek history.

[61] A. Bloom (1987), 39.   [62] Kimball (1990).

[63] Ibid. pp. xvi–xvii, 28.

In his recent book, suggestively titled *The Oldest Dead White European Males* in an attempt to reclaim the term 'DWEM' ('dead white European males') for classics, Bernard Knox takes issue with nameless and indiscriminate multiculturalists and feminists for rejecting ancient Greek authors in an attempt to redraw the literary canon. Knox advocates the view that we should continue to read Greek authors because they demonstrate a high value and that newer works should compete with these for inclusion in the canon.[64] What Knox reveals here is an anxiety about the expansion of the literary canon to include more texts and the potentially numerous, alternative voices that these texts may present. In identifying his opponents as 'multiculturalists' and 'feminists', he suggests that these newer works express the points of view to be identified with these individuals. Harold Bloom offers an argument that is not dissimilar to Knox's when he proposes that to become part of the canon a work must enter into and survive a contest—his word is *agōn*—with tradition.[65] The literary quality important in this version of Oedipal struggle is originality 'that either cannot be assimilated, or that so assimilates us that we cease to see it as strange'.[66] To engage in canon revision without *agōn* results, as far as Bloom is concerned, in the inclusion of women, black, and other 'minority' writers who are not the 'best' but who embody resentment of what is the 'best'.[67] For this critic, the contest returns as a limiting, critical strategy.

What lends emotive force to pronouncements such as these is the explicit recognition (not unchallenged, as Harold Bloom's own idiosyncratic defence of the canon reveals[68]) that 'great books' embodies the values and paradigms for contemporary democratic society.[69] Allan Bloom has made explicit the political assumptions behind controlling and limiting the curriculum. As his argument for the reinstatement of 'great books' in *The Closing of the American Mind* shows, this curriculum furthers what is a patently self-interested and nationalistic project while ironically proclaiming

---

[64] Knox (1993), 21, 26.   [65] H. Bloom (1994), 6.   [66] Ibid. 4.

[67] Ibid. 7. Fox-Genovese (1986: 141–2) observes that those who seek to expand the canon find few women or minority authors to draw upon, not because such authors are inferior but because the historically white- and male-dominated 'republic of letters' has historically excluded them.

[68] H. Bloom (1994: 30) insists that reading the canon should not be about citizenship.

[69] See Derrida (1992), 25; McDonald (1992), 47.

itself a universalizing and timeless discourse. He has argued that the traditional liberal arts programme makes the undergraduate properly socialized in democratic ideology and tradition: thus by failing to read Plato's *Republic*, the undergraduate student will have no basis for understanding justice and virtue. If 'great books' upholds democratic values, Frank Lentricchia points out that it does so by being 'politically tranquilizing', by refusing to allow its students an opportunity to do anything other than 'just read'.[70]

Elsewhere, the idea that a Western curriculum, above all one derived from democratic Athens, enshrines Western, that is democratic, values becomes a doctrinaire refrain. D' Souza observes that while the democratization of campuses has brought new curricula involving texts by women and non-white authors, this educational revolution does not actually produce greater liberality or fairness. D' Souza sets out to prove that the scourge of 'political correctness' which has afflicted North American campuses has resulted in forms of discrimination that now disregard or penalize academic merit. He points to quota systems based on race which result in well-qualified Asian-American students being barred from Berkeley.[71] Characterizing himself as a champion of academic 'merit', he attributes the failings of affirmative action to the fact that this new form of institutionalized 'racism' has its basis in non-Western cultures which have no developed tradition of racial equality.[72] Yet D' Souza threatens to 'throw out the baby with the bath water', for his criticisms are far from constructive, unlike those of Robert Hughes, who, while disagreeing with the rigging of university admissions on the basis of race alone, insists that affirmative action should none the less help the 'intelligent disadvantaged.[73] D' Souza proceeds to accuse anti-discrimination provisions of challenging the American First Amendment—which enshrines freedom of expression—through the emphasis on a non-white canon, and this in turn necessitates a departure from the traditional curriculum together with the constraints imposed by policies on racial and sexual harassment.[74] The polemical position of *Illiberal Education* is that changes in higher education, which D' Souza exaggerates by focusing on the few remarkable instances as indicative of the whole academic culture, attack the basis of democracy in the United States.

[70] Lentricchia (1983), 126; A. Patterson (1993), 29.
[71] D' Souza (1992), 24.　　　　　　[72] Ibid. 79, 240–1.
[73] Hughes (1994), 57.　　　　　　[74] D' Souza (1992), 142–4.

Knox unwittingly discloses the problem with this line of argumentation. He implies that harm is to be incurred from accepting politics initiated from the 'left' within current society, observing that prior to the nineteenth century the humanities—above all as constituted by ancient Greek literature—were regarded as an education for democracy.[75] There is none the less a curious contradiction in Knox's argument as he attempts to justify the value of Greek authors by identifying them with innovation and change, and Herodotus in particular with multiculturalism.[76] It would appear that multicultural discourse is to be permitted to have its say only when it is produced from within the canon. Larger contradictions are involved in current defences of 'great books', which admittedly have great persuasive power for a less considering audience. For Bloom and his supporters, the great books and authors are the texts which every educated person needs to read because they articulate the concerns that educated people necessarily and always think about and engage with. It is this universalizing character of the texts subsumed within this canon which grants them an unassailable authority. The importance of cultural and historical specificities, the significance of detail, and the possibility of multiple and alternative interpretations are sacrificed, so that history itself is virtually rendered irrelevant.

Impetus for these positionings doubtless derived from the fact that in the 1980s, two of the most influential voices in the US supporting the preservation of the hegemonic white canon and its curriculum were individuals who were appointed by the government. It is the Zeus-like prerogative of the President to appoint the chairman of the National Endowment for the Humanities, the chief body for distributing academic funding and determining educational policy. Accordingly, as President, Ronald Reagan set a conservative direction for higher education policy when he appointed as chairpersons William Bennett, and then Lynne Cheney. As Secretary of Education Bennett published in November 1984 his report *To Reclaim a Legacy: A Report on the Humanities in Higher Education* (Washington, DC), in which he defended his enduring vision of Western culture, the important 'legacy' to be passed down from generation to generation. The title of his report implies an ideally patrilineal descent of the cultural 'legacy', which traces

[75] Knox (1993), 103.   [76] Ibid. 18–20.

itself back to classical antiquity—though Gerald Graff has shown that this programme owes its origins to the unenlightened pre-democratic college curriculum, which focused on the study of the Greek and Latin classics, and which often produced mediocre results rather than the nostalgically idealized high standards.[77] Bennett suggests that instead of enjoying a respectful reception, the inheritance of this glorious past suffers in the late twentieth century from an Arnoldian *decline* in culture that may precipitate anarchy.[78] He regards this politicization of the curriculum, and of current literary scholarship in particular, as a symptom of the loss of nerve and faith in certainties which has afflicted American culture since the 1960s.[79] Cheney followed up her predecessor's critique of the left with a report entitled *Humanities in America: A Report to the President, the Congress, and the American People* (Washington, DC, 1988).[80] Cheney's subtitle suggests that the state of the academy is an important concern for society as a political community, and in an interview with the *Chronicle of Higher Education*, she is cited as standing in opposition to the 'radical anti-Americanism' of her targets.[81] Subsequently, Peter Brooks has cited Cheney as saying, 'Viewing humanities texts as though they were primarily political documents is the most noticeable trend in academic study of the humanities today. Truth and beauty and excellence are regarded as irrelevant: questions of intellectual and aesthetic quality, dismissed.'[82] Cheney's complaint is one of those made in response to contemporary debates regarding curriculum and canon in higher education in the United States which seek to stem the debate by discrediting the interest in politics as a fashionable trend and therefore as a passing interest.

The reports of Bennett and Cheney were directed against the apparent multiplicity of voices and discourses produced by professionalized critical activity within modern academia. The power of the National Endowment for the Humanities (NEH) and its directors to control and regulate academic discourse becomes especially apparent when one considers the way in which it distributes financial support. As Catherine Stimpson notes, NEH funds for projects

[77] Graff (1987), 20 ff.; (1992*b*), 88, 128.   [78] Graff (1987), 4–5.
[79] Graff (1993), 126.   [80] Kimball (1990), 4, 35.
[81] Graff (1992*b*), 165.
[82] Peter Brooks, 'Western Civ at Bay', *Times Literary Supplement* (25 January 1991), 5.

and scholarship involving women and minorities dropped drastically in the early 1980s, from seven-figure sums to six-figure
ones.[83] It is not surprising, then, that Bennett and Cheney in turn
helped to consolidate the neo-conservative right and produced a
now familiar warning that the introduction of other voices into the
literary canon undermines the authority and identity of the state.

V

Fortunately, there is still anything but a monopoly on the discourse
about the state of higher education, so that the (perhaps, Typhonic)
voices which present arguments against the attempt to regulate
language and textuality for higher education and more generally,
society, are still heard. Accordingly, we are presented with a situation analogous to an *agōn* or a contest, rather than the prejudged or
already discriminated outcome we find in ancient critical texts.
What these positions suggest is that criticism as a form of silencing
and canonization as practised by the individuals considered above
may now be superseded or indefensible on the terms currently
invoked by the right. The academic right has argued for its views
on the basis of the relationship between literature and cultural context, particularly citizenship; however, it is not only the right which
claims this assumption as its privileged preserve. (It is of course the
basis of this study that criticism assumes that there is a close link
between texts and the effect that they might have on society.)
Academics on the left, particularly multiculturalists and feminists,
also use the social importance of what we read as one of the foundations of their arguments, and John Brenkman is careful to distinguish the critique produced by multiculturalism from political
correctness and naïve rejections of Western culture.[84]

Henry Gates articulates his view that education has important
implications for American society and culture. He goes on from
this position to distinguish himself from the right by suggesting
that it is crucial for education to comprehend what he terms the
'diversity of human culture'.[85] Gates's ideal pupils are to be 'citizens of a world culture', taught in African, Asian, and Middle
Eastern literatures rather than just in the limited canons espoused

[83] Stimpson (1990), 76–7.   [84] Robbins (1993), 180; Brenkman (1993), 91.
[85] Gates (1992) pp. xii, xv.

by Bennett and Allan Bloom.[86] But this does not entail that individuals will be alienated or taught to be *other*, precisely because
these traditions, and particularly the African-American one, cannot be separated from American tradition.[87] What Gates suggests
is a broader remit for what education can offer by way of preparation for citizenship. More radically, in his study of the academic
profession, Bruce Robbins shows how citizenship can be called up
as a justification in the service of multiculturalism. He suggests that
to be an intellectual today means being cosmopolitan, that is a
figure who transcends various cultures and communities, whether
ethnically, sexually, or ideologically defined, and where being cosmopolitan does not entail a new way of being Western.[88] Where
Raymond Williams might have lamented the distancing of the
intellectual from society, where Terry Eagleton might complain
that critical activity no longer has a cultural or political brief, and
where a volume such as the collection of essays co-edited by
Lennard Davis and Bella Mirabella can in part look back and reflect
on the greater political engagement and activism of higher education in the 1960s,[89] Robbins's work optimistically proposes that
these do not have to be entirely detrimental developments.[90] The
contemporary intellectual is a figure without any fixed or rooted
territory or domain: she is a figure who, in a comparison which
invokes J. S. Mill, can be transferred like capital.[91] Thus interdisciplinarity may be seen as what should follow logically from this
displacement of the intellectual. Not incidentally does Stanley Fish
note that interdisciplinarity—which is often and perhaps somewhat
wearily associated with feminism, Marxism, and deconstruction—
is generally seen to challenge the authorities both of social structure
and of academic discipline, although he cautions that disciplinary
boundaries themselves will continue to exist, if only because they
are appropriated across subjects and disciplines.[92]

The work of the 'multiculturalists' and 'feminists' that the right
blames for the erosion of a common Western culture and its tradition puts forward multiple voices produced not just from different
constituencies, namely women and non-white authors, but also
from the possibilities of reading texts in different and plural ways:
the academic left stresses the importance of reading, of rereading,

[86] Ibid. 42.   [87] Ibid. 150–1.   [88] Robbins (1993), 182, 195.
[89] Davis and Mirabella (1990).   [90] Robbins (1993), 58, 76.
[91] Ibid. 182.   [92] Fish (1994), 231, 239–40.

and of multiple readings. Certainly, crucial to this is the recognition, made most explicit to us by reader-reception theory, that there is more than one way to read and receive texts precisely because individuals read texts in different ways.[93] After all, theoretical arguments against pornography in particular and developments in the canon debate by academics on the left have radically called into question the role of literary texts in determining social identity, and, with that, the sense that criticism needs to operate as a regulative and constraining discourse. Here, it is perhaps that the transferability of criticism as a methodological approach from antiquity into the twentieth century must be called into question, so that the assumption that literary theory offers a paradigm for reading is thrown into question. Where ancient writers were concerned primarily with *what* society might read rather than *how* it would read, perhaps with the exception of the allegorists, one of the concerns of modern academia has been with making it apparent that texts cannot just be read in themselves but that the process of reading itself needs careful attention as to what it might entail. The emphasis has shifted from *what* we read to *how* we read, or at least has grown to include the latter option. Moreover, it has taken on board the recognition that texts can affect people in more than one way, and that social factors will be important in determining how they will be constituted as readers. Underlying the emphasis on *how* we read is perhaps the suggestion that it is our identity which manufactures our perception of textuality rather than that texuality significantly and necessarily determines our identity.

Literary and cultural theorists who generally identify themselves with the left have called into question the idea of 'just' reading associated most obviously with Leo Strauss and his followers, like Allan Bloom. Critics including Elizabeth Fox-Genovese, Paul Lauter, and Annabel Patterson have argued for the importance of reading and *rereading* canonic texts, concluding that it is important to continue to read the so-called 'great books'.[94] If anything, rereading these revered texts fractures and disseminates their authority amongst a variety of different constituencies. What Patterson recognizes is that the concern about losing the canon is an

[93] Fish is perhaps the best known proponent of reader-response theory, arguing that 'interpretive communities' to a large degree determine how individuals receive the texts they encounter; see (1980), 10–11, 167 ff.

[94] Lauter (1990), 135; A. Patterson (1993), 29.

anxiety about having traditional authority, that of the male white academic, called into question or altogether lost. Graff has been important in placing the literary profession in America in historical context. In *Professing Literature*, he notes that in certain 'great books' courses, which became the model for the liberal arts canon, students were urged to read the classics quickly, as if these works were contemporary 'best sellers'.[95] He suggests that the concern only to read the text, and to do so superficially, was supposed to counter cultural fragmentation.[96] He suggests, furthermore, that reading these great texts as a mere exercise in itself and without context does not necessarily mean that students understood texts any better or read at a higher level. In other words, to be merely widely read does not entail that one will be able to think, or to analyse, at a more sophisticated or deeper level.

Together with Michael Warner, Graff argues that the perception of literary study being under attack from radicals and subversives who appeared after the 1960s is after all a poorly historicized myth. He notes that the literary profession has never enjoyed consensus— arguing as it does about the relative merits of philology and intuitive belletrism, for instance—but in his 1990 essay 'Why Theory?', Graff warns that the way to respond to the realization of recent breakdown of consensus is not to attempt simply to reinstate it.[97] In his most recent book, *Beyond the Culture Wars*, he attempts to recover this history for current literary and humanities pedagogy. He explicitly takes issue with the simplistic line on reading proposed by Allan Bloom and others. He proposes that rather than read 'between the lines', as Straussians might for hidden, élite meanings, one should consider the ideological battle lines and make them visible to one's students.[98] Graff argues for the need to teach students the 'conflicts', observing that reverence for texts inspires apathy while debate enlivens and stimulates scholarship.[99] If Straussians propose 'reading between the lines', he proposes a contrast between teaching the 'battle lines' and the lines of the literary text.[100] By 'teaching the conflicts', the academic or intellectual transcends the constraints and limits of partisanship, and she can stimulate discussion amongst her students in a way that is distinct from 'pluralism', which has the effect of concealing the crucial

---

[95] Graff (1987), 134.   [96] Ibid. 173.
[97] Graff and Warner (1989), 1–11; Graff (1988); Fish (1994), 81.
[98] Graff (1992*b*), 78.   [99] Ibid. 12, 47.   [100] Ibid. 78.

278   *Criticism in the Present Time?*

differences and not of making them apparent.[101] Graff's approach
to literary pedagogy proposes the disassociation of personal belief
and identity from what happens in the classroom or lecture hall to
the extent that David Bromwich fears it might lead to teachers 'forgetting the separate worth of teaching; the worth, that is, of talking
and thinking about books which are bound to relate to our interests'.[102]

Bromwich's anxiety is perhaps overstated, and it is the case that
refusing to 'teach the conflicts' helps to protect so-called 'great'
books from questioning, from disrepect, by suggesting that textual
meaning might be natural or integral to the work.[103] The model
curriculum that Graff offers in response to this is one which
involves otherwise distinct and isolated departments, organized by
discipline, interacting and engaging in discussion with one
another.[104] He is careful to distinguish his pedagogical ideal from
relativism, one of the conservatives' pet hates. For him, the 'culture
wars' approximate Socratic debate, the privileged pedagogical discourse for left and right alike.[105] Even despite his obvious criticisms of the academic right, Graff is careful to point out that by
studying the conflicts one does not necessarily displace the established canon; rather, one studies in addition to the canon texts
which are otherwise excluded or disregarded.[106] He responds
deftly to the charge laid by D' Souza that the great books and
authors are being removed by liberals who seek to make room for
Alice Walker's *The Color Purple*, and reveals the origins of this
charge to be mere *speculation* that Walker's novel was currently
more popular than Shakespeare's works.[107] The pluralism of the
modern canon and curriculum is not as much of an issue as the right
would like to claim, precisely because canon revision, to the extent
that it occurs, has meant accretion rather than wholesale displacement.[108] According to Graff, the way forward is not to take sides
either for or against pluralism or with any one intellectual perspective, but rather to use the various discourses and the conflicts that
they engage as the very material of one's teaching.

But even in this there is an attempt to disseminate literary
authority and its apparently uniform voice. In addition to calling

[101] Graff (1992a), 70; (1992b), 12.
[102] Bromwich (1992), 190.
[103] Graff (1992b), 49, 83.
[104] Ibid. 178 ff.
[105] Ibid. 15; see Pelikan (1992), 58.
[106] Graff (1992b), 23.
[107] Ibid. 17.
[108] Ibid. 23.

for an enlargement of the body of texts which are now available, Graff dehierarchizes culture. He calls into question the idea that certain traditionally canonical texts belong to 'high culture' and are therefore inherently difficult, while the newer additions to the curriculum are 'popular' and inherently simpler. Canon revision does not simplify reading because reading is never in itself a simple process, so that a revised curriculum will not produce a lowering of 'standards', that horrendous calamity which Cheney and others mourn on the assumption that 'standards' is an objective ideal.[109]

VI

This final chapter of my study has made a case for the continuing relevance of ancient models of literary criticism, itself distinguishing between, that is criticizing, various criticisms. It has identified discriminations which seek to exclude material that would be to the detriment of a significant sector of society—women—and others which seek to exclude discourses to the detriment of various groups within society. But if the continuity lies in the justifications made for criticism, namely the good or harm of those who are depicted in the materials or who receive them, contemporary material reveals that the politics of criticism has in some respects undergone a radical transformation. In antiquity (and in the late twentieth century, where the canon debate is concerned) it is individuals who above all constitute the political and social élite (or seek to depict themselves as such), who assume the prerogative to determine which discourses are permissible in society and thus engage in discrimination as an expression of their authority. (Perhaps it is more to the point that we only have the critical discourses produced by historical élites.)

As we approach the twenty-first century, multiculturalists and opponents of pornography identify with the disempowered, and they engage in the discrimination of discourse precisely to assist those who are not empowered in society. By drawing attention to the social context in which such material is produced and distributed, individuals such as MacKinnon and Fish show the inapplicability of the freedom of expression argument because

---

[109] Ibid. 97.

pornography, for instance, cannot be seen to presume freedom or equality of opportunity for all in society: women and children are discriminated against by the material in question. It is this concern which now confirms that criticism is a socially engaged discourse, even despite Eagleton's lament that after the eighteenth century literary criticism ceased to be a vital discourse of protest and turned into an over-professionalized and apolitical activity. Yet if Eagleton is anxious that criticism no longer exercises those who engage in social protest, it is because he still looks to, and for, the chattering eighteenth-century bourgeois, which he seems to understand as groups of middle-class men discoursing in the public space of coffee-shops and newspapers about the issues that plagued this gendered social and economic class.

Instead, what we now see, more than two hundred years on, is criticism undertaken by a much broader constituency, both men *and* women debating a variety of issues which they see as impinging on questions of social justice and equality in Western society.

CONCLUSION

The Function of Criticism in Times Past and Present

I

The writing of any history of criticism such as the present one can only reveal the discourse under consideration to be one of several possible created and contentiously authorized languages. But such a narrative will at the same time not be entirely arbitrary, inasmuch as any number of ideologies, assumptions, and prior histories of literary criticism will be its subtexts, whether taken up more explicitly or not. My subtexts have been the *idea* of ancient criticism as constituted in part by material from antiquity and in part by the scholarship which has characterized it as 'ancient literary criticism'. The project has not been to abandon altogether the body of writing we conventionally recognize as 'ancient literary criticism' nor the body of commentary on this material; furthermore, my intention has not been to suggest that we abandon the phrase 'ancient literary criticism' as a description of the discourses that ancient authors set out regarding the production and reception of literary texts. Yet by beginning from an understanding of criticism as a socio-political process, this study has offered a somewhat different discourse regarding the production and reception of literary texts in Greek and Roman antiquity.

George Watson used the phrase 'Tidy School of critical history' to describe an account of criticism which assumes that literary criticism is unitary in its function and in the answers it offers.[1] Despite Watson's disparagement of this model, I am not embarrassed to admit that my account of criticism proposes a certain cohesiveness where the critical imperative is concerned. The history produced in this book shows ancient criticism to be in particular a process of exclusions and inclusions—manifesting themselves as debates,

---

[1] Watson (1962), 2; Baldick (1983), 6.

quarrels, contestations, and judgements, arbitrary and considered—justified in terms of what is good or beneficial for the community. Zeus' defeat of Typhon, the Hellenistic scholar-poets' editing of Hellenic texts, Horace's discussion of poetry, and Augustine's treatment of pagan literature foreclose voices and identities which threaten the stability of the community and/or the position of those who maintain order in the community. The critical imperative understood in these terms renders Plato's banishment of poets and poetry less problematic or embarrassing than it is generally perceived to be. Moreover, it helps to explain why contemporary debates on the role of pornography and the literary curriculum in higher education are now conducted with such vehemence and passion.

If this study has been successful in arguing that criticism in antiquity, far from being a disinterested, aestheticizing, or evaluative project, is central to the production of political identity and the structures which produce the political community, by corollary the attempt to locate the origins of disinterested aestheticism either in Aristotle's discussion of tragedy, or in the work of the Alexandrian Mouseion-Library, or in [Longinus'] treatment of the sublime becomes the search for a misleading rupture in the discourse of criticism. The titles of post-eighteenth-century books and essays on criticism that declare their concern to establish the function, usefulness, or role of criticism,[2] are belated protestations about the peculiarly modern social and political dimensions of criticism— indeed as belated as the invention of '*ancient* literary criticism'. In articulating as its central thesis social discrimination as the *raison d'être* of criticism in antiquity, the book reinstates ancient texts as the important and necessary subtexts for the contemporary critical project and refuses a marginal role in society to the modern critic.[3]

Criticism may have a constant function. The discourse does, however, have multiple and various forms. It is not least a literary language, as I have shown that, even apart from the obviously literary works, e.g. the poetry of Hesiod, Horace, and Lucan, texts

[2] e.g. Matthew Arnold, 'The Function of Criticism at the Present Time', in *Selected Poetry and Prose* (New York and Toronto, 1953), 137–65; T. S. Eliot, *The Use of Poetry and the Use of Criticism* (London, 1933), and 'The Function of Criticism', in F. Kermode (ed.), *Selected Prose of T. S. Eliot* (London, 1975), 68–76; R. Con Davis and R. Schleifer, *Criticism and Culture: The Role of Critique in Modern Literary Theory* (London, 1991).

[3] Bové (1986), 11, 79–81.

such as Plato's *Republic*, Longinus' *On the Sublime*, and Augustine's *Confessions* also need to be read with the attention and care to the figurative structures—metaphor, irony, rhetoric, characterization, and so on—that we normally apply to 'literature'.[4] I have, for instance, also looked beyond criticism as a literary discourse to consider less obviously literary discourses as part of the structures of criticism. I have examined legal discourse and process in the Greek and Roman world as being both paradigmatic and constitutive of criticism, whereas until quite recently law has been regarded by literary scholars as distinct from literature.[5] I have also looked at how pedagogic structures, in particular curricula, control reading material and techniques. What legitimizes the extension of criticism beyond discussion of particular literary works (which for antiquity would above all have been poetry) is the understanding of the function of criticism as ensuring an orderly society through the regulation of the identities of its members. Thus the restrictions on slander and libel in Greek and Roman legislation prohibit the negative identities entailed by these forms of public language, while the banning of certain types of poetry, both in Plato's *Republic* and in Augustine's Christian city, and of certain passages of Homer by the Hellenistic scholar-critics similarly ensures that only appropriate textual models of identity are available for the members of the community. Criticism necessarily exerts itself in a variety of different spheres of discourse because it is a deliberately totalizing strategy of social construction.

Furthermore, in claiming a larger historical continuity for the function and role of the material we identify as 'ancient literary criticism', I do not of course mean to efface historical differences or to deny the need to recognize them. The unitariness of the function of criticism is discrimination (cf. 'criticism' from *krinō*, 'I judge', 'I divide', and so on), but criticism is, from the Hesiodic origins I identify to its late twentieth-century analogies, a self-justifying process which produces the discrimination of discourses. It is a

---

[4] See Fish (1980: 10) on the arbitrariness of 'literature': 'Literature, I argue, is a conventional category. What will, at any time, be recognized as literature is a function of a communal decision as to what will count as literature. All texts have the potential of so counting, in that it is possible to regard any stretch of language in such a way that it will display those properties presently understood to be literary.' Thus La Capra (1985: 97) wants to pose the larger question whether criticism is principally 'literary criticism' for the twentieth century.

[5] e.g. Posner (1988); Fish (1994).

process which admits as variables the criteria by which discourses are excluded or included because different communities have different norms of what is beneficial and acceptable or harmful and unacceptable. Viewed diachronically, that is in terms of historical continuum, criticism is thus to some extent a discourse of negotiation with prior discriminations. But even viewed at a specific moment, criticism is a contest for the authority to determine what can be said and received within individual communities. The agents of literary discrimination are not only the social and political élite, that is the individuals who rule the state and its identities, but also those who would like to displace the institutionalized authorities, or else those who would seek to offer alternatives to these authorities.

II

The final chapter of this study argued for the continued existence of the critical imperative in the late twentieth century. In these concluding paragraphs, I would like to make a specific argument for the continued need to discriminate amongst available discourses and for the need to exclude those which are deemed threatening or detrimental to community. My case addresses the need for the critical imperative to address computer technology, and in particular the Internet, or 'Information Superhighway'. The Internet is a discursive space ideally constructed as one free from regulation and surveillance. It is, furthermore, one that embodies ultimate democratization to the extent that anyone with access to a computer terminal becomes a potential maker and recipient of information with a virtually infinite audience. The Internet perhaps offers a serious challenge to critical history inasmuch as the manner in which information and discourse are created and circulated on it would appear to defy regulation and control. Electronic communication becomes the ideal medium for enacting 'freedom of speech' where agreement to receive the speech in question is assumed, and thus legislation to regulate particular forms of discourse, such as obscenity or hate literature, is opposed as 'a violation of free speech, and a violation of the right of adults to communicate with each other'.[6]

[6] See Martin Walker, 'Gingrich Opposes Curbs on Internet', *Guardian*, 23 June 1995.

Certainly, the Internet makes communication more readily available because cheaper and quicker than conventional mail and telephone. Originally, a system invented by the US military to enable communication in the event of nuclear war, it has now become domesticated. It provides users with access to a virtually limitless bank of information. One might 'surf' through mailing lists and bulletin boards out of curiosity, in order to 'meet' other people, or in search of some particular piece of information. Electronic communication has now come either potentially to challenge or to join with the publishing industry in making texts, such as journals, widely and cheaply available—in the latter case, circulating information or scholarship which is otherwise unsuitable for conventional publication due to cost, subject-matter, or more stringent standards regarding what makes acceptable printed matter. The benefits of the Internet are especially apparent in academia, where scholars in different parts of the world can carry on discussions with their colleagues and can establish communities within and across the traditional disciplines. Cyberculture is constituted as a culture in which standards and norms of acceptability are relaxed or even abandoned. At the level of composition the ephemerality of electronic mail allows formal salutations—'Dear so-and-so'—to be replaced by 'Hello' or 'Hi', or else for the salutation to be dispensed with altogether; first names and initials, rather than titles, to be used; capital letters, punctuation, and paragraphs to be abandoned. The degree of anonymity afforded by the lack of actual physical and visual contact with interlocutors and by the use of aliases, for instance, explains the inflections of exchanges on the Internet. At the level of audience, it becomes acceptable to send a message to anyone who has allowed their address to be publicized with virtually no pretext but the wish to make contact. Perhaps the idea of virtuality, as opposed to the reality, of conventional interactions, mitigates the sense in which language may have a real impact: hence, 'flaming', or the repeated sending of repeated messages, the use of profanity, and so on, are aspects of cyberculture.

But if the Internet would appear to problematize critical practice, it also for this reason implies the necessity for its reinstatement. Electronic communication is a public space of discourse. Even where individuals send 'mails' to other named individuals through accounts protected by secret passwords, it is the case, as anyone who has misdirected mails will know, that 'postmasters' can open and read mails, and do so particularly when they are misaddressed. It is a public space of discourse also in the sense that it is a scenario of the formation of community, although in a way which transforms the ways in which we might make and understand communities. The Information Superhighway offers opportunities for people around the world with common interests to hold discussions, to exchange ideas, and to 'meet' in cyberspace. Individuals with interests in science fiction, in Theodore Adorno, in pedagogy (in this author's case), or with shared political agendas can join mailing lists or discussion groups and can conduct conversations in a way that would not be possible in physical space. Such communities can readily spring up precisely because cybercommunication dispenses with the more usual, and more time-consuming, protocols of conventional letter-writing, phoning, and face-to-face conversation, replacing these with an extraordinary informality and sometimes, intimacy, even despite anonymity or the use of aliases. It is precisely these qualities of cybercommunication which enable virtual communities to be far more fluid and open to negotiation than any real world community, and also to tolerate less conventional 'identities'. By assuming an alias, you might choose to disguise various aspects of your identity or else assume aspects of an identity which you do not otherwise have—gender-bending is common, with men most frequently assuming female identities.[7] Multi-user dungeons (MUDs), where users can enter a fantasy scenario in equally fantastic roles and meet other such players, have been viewed as a new form of community where players interact and through their interactions learn about life and define possible identities for themselves. The physical anonymity provided through cyberpresence removes the constraints of gender, sexual, racial, and class identity. Yet it is of course the case that individuals who use the system are either those working in institutions which provide its services or those who can afford the software and phone bills which it requires, namely the middle classes of the industrialized nations.

I argue that it is precisely the potential for virtual community that makes the critical imperative so crucial where computer technology is concerned. The electronic community is as real as any physical community inasmuch as the critical imperative under-

[7] See Morton (1995).

stands discourse to be constitutive of community, and perhaps one might argue that the electronic community is more constitutive of community for the very reason that it exists largely through discourse rather than in terms of geography, ethnicity, or racial identity. Arguments that recipients of unwanted, unacceptable, or offensive material can always ignore it have limited validity here, as do objections that the criteria of acceptability and unacceptability may be different and at odds for different portions of the electronic audience. Electronically circulated pornographic material, hate literature directed against various groups, and libellous language will in lesser or greater senses define and produce elements of their potentially large and broadly disseminated audience as a community: the potential recipients become the community in question. If the history of literary criticism in antiquity and later is to be at all regarded, then it reveals cyberspace as a terrain in which discourse is no less potentially effective—that is either helpful and beneficial, or, contrarily, harmful and detrimental—than language in what cyberspace and virtuality counterdefine as the 'real world'. After all, women can no less be stalked by computer, just as they can be harassed by late-night phonecalls, and netters replicate the interactions of sexuality through the web. The problem, however, is how to determine the criteria for acceptability and unacceptability, for good and for detriment, in a community that overlaps with and comprehends so many other social, political, and cultural communities. Electronic communication does not escape, and in fact reinscribes, the idea of criticism as a specific cultural phenomenon, a construction of specific communities, where reference to what is good or bad for a structured group of individuals is and has to be internally authorized.

REFERENCES

ABRAMS, M. H. (1953), *The Mirror and the Lamp: Romantic Theory and the Critical Tradition* (Oxford).

AHL, F. (1984a), 'The Art of Safe Criticism in Greece and Rome', *AJP* 105: 174–208.

—— (1984b), 'The Rider and the Horse: Politics and Power in Roman Poetry from Horace to Statius', *ANRW* 2. 32. 1: 40–110.

ALLEN, T. W. (1913), 'Peisistratus and Homer', *CQ* 7: 33–51.

ANDERSON, W. S. (1968), review of Brooks Otis, *Ovid as an Epic Poet* (Cambridge, 1966), *AJP* 89: 93–104.

ANNAS, J. (1982), 'Plato on the Triviality of Literature', in Moravcsik and Temko (1982), 1–28.

ARENDT, H. (1951), *Totalitarianism: Part Three of the Origins of Totalitarianism* (San Diego, New York, and London).

ARIETI, J. A., and CROSSETT, J. M. (1985), *On the Sublime* (New York).

ARMISEN-MARCHETTI, M. (1990), 'Pline le Jeune et le Sublime', *REL* 68: 88–98.

ARMSTRONG, D. (1995), 'The Impossibility of Metathesis: Philodemus and Lucretius on Form and Content in Poetry', in Obbink (1995), 210–32.

ARNOLD, M. (1953), *Selected Poetry and Prose*, introd. F. L. Mulhauser (New York and Toronto).

ARTHUR, M. B. (1963), 'The Dream of a World Without Women: Poetics and the Circles of Order in the *Theogony* Prooemium', *Arethusa*, 16: 97–116.

ATKINS, J. W. H. (1934), *Literary Criticism in Antiquity: A Sketch of its Development*, 2 vols. (Cambridge).

AUERBACH, E. (1953), *Mimesis: The Representation of Reality in Western Literature*, tr. W. Trask (New York).

BALDICK, C. (1983), *The Social Mission of English Criticism 1948–1932* (Oxford).

BALTZLY, D. C. (1992), 'Plato and the New Rhapsody', *Ancient Philosophy*, 12: 29–52.

BARBER, E. A.(1939), 'Notes on the *Diegeseis* of Callimachus', *CQ* 33: 65–8.

BARNES, J., SCHOFIELD, M., and SORABJI, R. (1966), *Articles on Aristotle*, 4: *Psychology and Aesthetics* (London).

BARTSCH, S. (1944), *Actors in the Audience: Theatricality and Doublespeak from Nero to Hadrian* (Cambridge, Mass. and London).

BAUMAN, R. A. (1974), *Impietas in principem: A Study of Treason Against the Roman Empire with Special Reference to the First Century A. D.* (Munich).

BEARDSLEY, M. C. (1966), *Aesthetics from Classical Greece to the Present: A Short History* (University, Alabama).

BELFIORE, E. (1984), 'A Theory of Imitation in Plato's Republic', *TAPA* 114: 121–46.

—— (1985), ' "Lies Unlike the Truth": Plato on Hesiod, *Theognis 27*', *TAPA* 115: 47–57.

BENJAMIN, A. (1988) (ed.), *Post-structuralist Classics* (London).

BENVENISTE, E. (1948), *Noms d'agent et noms d'action en indo-européen* (Paris)

—— (1969), *Le Vocabulaire des institutions indo-européennes*, ii (Paris).

BERNAL, M. (1987), *Black Athena: The Afroasiatic Roots of Classical Civilization*, i (London and New Brunswick).

BING, P. (1981), 'The Voice of Those Who Live in the Sea: Empedocles and Callimachus', *ZPE* 41: 33–6.

BIRKS, P., and McLEOD, G. (1987), *Justinian's Institutes* (London).

BLOCK, E. (1982), 'Poetics in Exile: An Analysis of *Epistulae ex Ponto 3.9*', *CA*: 18–27.

BLOOM, A. (1987), *The Closing of the American Mind* (New York).

BLOOM, H. (1994), *The Western Canon: The Books and School of the Ages* (New York, San Diego, and London).

BLUM, R. (1991), *Kallimachos: The Alexandrian Library and the Origins of Bibliography*, tr. H. H. Wellisch (Madison).

DE BOLLA, P. (1989), *The Discourse of the Sublime: Readings in History, Aesthetics and the Subject* (Oxford).

BOURDIEU, P. (1984), *Distinction: A Social Critique of the Judgement of Taste* (London).

—— (1988), *Homo Academicus*, tr. P. Collier (Cambridge and Oxford; orig. pub. Paris, 1984).

BOVÉ, P. A. (1986), *Intellectuals in Power: A Genealogy of Critical Humanism* (New York).

BOWIE, E. L. (1970), 'Greeks and their Past in the Second Sophistic', *Past and Present* 46: 3–41.

—— (1993), 'Lies, Fiction and Slander in Early Greek Poetry', in C. Gill and T. P. Wiseman, *Lies and Fiction in the Ancient World* (Exeter, 1993), 1–37.

BOWMAN, A. K., and WOOLF, G. (1994), *Literacy and Power in the Ancient World* (Cambridge).

BOWRA, M. (1938), 'Xenophanes and the Olympic Games', *AJP* 59: 257–79.

BOYD, M. J. (1957), 'Longinus, the Philological Discourses and the Essay on the Sublime', *CQ* 7: 39–46.

BRANT, C., and TOO, Y. L. (1994), *Rethinking Sexual Harassment* (London).

BRASWELL, B. K. (1993), '*Odyssey* 8.166–77 and *Theogony* 79–93', *CQ* 31: 237–9.

BRENKMAN, J. (1993), 'Multiculturalism and Criticism', in Gubar and Kamholtz (1993), 87–101.

BRINK, C. O. (1963, 1971, 1982), *Horace on Poetry*: i, *Prolegomena to the Literary Epistles*; ii, *The Ars Poetica*; iii, *Epistles Book II: The Letters to Augustus and Florus* (Cambridge).

BROMWICH, D. (1992), *Politics by Other Means: Higher Education and Group Thinking* (New Haven).

BROWN, P. (1963), 'Religious Coercion in the Later Roman Empire: The Case of North Africa', *Historia*, 48: 283–305.

—— (1964), 'St. Augustine's Attitude to Religious Coercion', *JRS* 54: 107–16.

—— (1967), *Augustine of Hippo: A Biography* (London).

BROWNSON, C. (1897), 'Reasons for Plato's Hostility to the Poets', *TAPA* 28: 5–41.

—— (1920), *Plato's Studies and Criticism of the Poets* (Boston).

BUFFIÈRE, F. (1956), *Les Mythes d'Homère et la pensée grecque* (Paris).

BULLOCH, A., GRUEN, E. S., LONG, A. A., and STEWART, A. (1993) (eds.), *Images and Ideologies: Self-definition in the Hellenistic World* (Berkeley, Los Angeles, and London).

BUTCHER, S. H. (1951), *Aristotle's Theory of Poetry and Fine Art*, 4th edn. (London; orig. pub. 1895).

BUTLER, H. E., and OWEN, A. S. (1914), *Apuleius: Apologia sive pro se de magia liber* (Oxford).

CAMERON, D., and FRAZER, E. (1992), 'On the Question of Pornography and Sexual Violence: Moving beyond Cause and Effect', in Itzin (1992), 359–83.

CANFORA, L. (1989), *The Vanished Library*, tr. M. Ryle (London, Sydney, Auckland, and Johannesburg).

CARNOCHAN, W. B. (1993), *The Battleground of the Curriculum: Liberal Education and American Experience* (Stanford, Calif.).

CARTER-RUCK, P. F., WALKER, R., and STARTE, H. N. A. (1992), *Carter-Ruck on Libel and Slander* (London).

CARY, M. (1954), *A History of Rome down to the Reign of Constantine* (London).

CAVE, T. (1988), *Recognitions: A Study in Poetics* (Oxford).

CHADWICK, H. (1991) (tr.), *St Augustine: Confessions* (Oxford).

CHANTRAINE, P. (1968), *Dictionnaire étymologique de la langue grecque* (Paris).

CHYTRY, J. (1989), *The Aesthetic State: A Quest in Modern German Thought* (Berkeley, Los Angeles, and London).

CLARK, G. (1993), *Augustine: The Confessions* (Cambridge).

CLAY, D. (1982), 'Unspeakable Words in Greek Tragedy', *AJP* 103: 277–98.

—— (1995), 'Framing the Margins of Philodemus and Poetry', in Obbink (1995), 3–14.

CLAYMAN, D. L. (1977), 'The Origins of Greek Literary Criticism and the Aitia Prologue', *WS* 90: 27–34.

—— (1980), *Callimachus' Iambi* (Leiden).

COLE, T. (1983), 'Archaic Truth', *QUCC* 42: 7–26.

—— (1991), *The Origins of Rhetoric in Ancient Greece* (Baltimore).

CON DAVIS, R., and SCHLEIFER, R. (1991), *Criticism and Culture: The Role of Critique in Modern Literary Theory* (London).

CONNOR, W. R. (1971), *The New Politicians of Fifth-Century Athens* (Princeton).

—— HANSEN, M. H., RAAFLAUB, K. A., and STRAUS, B. S. with FEARS, J. R. (1990), *Aspects of Athenian Democracy* (*Classica et Medievalia Dissertationes*, 11; Copenhagen).

CORNELL, D. (1995), *The Imaginary Domain* (London)

COURTNEY, E. (1988), 'Callimachus *Iamb* II Fr. 192', *ZPE* 74: 276.

CRAMER, F. H. (1945), 'Bookburning and Censorship in Ancient Rome: A Chapter from the History of Freedom of Speech', *JHI* 6: 157–96.

CRANZ, F. E. (1954), 'The Development of Augustine's Ideas on Society before the Donatist Controversy', *Harvard Theological Review*, 47: 255–316.

CULLER, J. (1981), *The Pursuit of Signs: Semiotics, Literature, Deconstruction* (Ithaca, New York).

CURRAN, L. C. (1972), 'Transformation and Anti-Augustanism in Ovid's *Metamorphoses*', *Arethusa* 5: 71–91.

CURTIUS, E. R. (1953), *European Literature and the Latin Middle Ages*, tr. W. R. Trask (London).

DARNTON, R. (1984), *The Great Cat Massacre and Other Episodes in French Cultural History* (London).

DAVIES, C. (1978), 'How our Rulers Argue about Censorship', in Dhavan and Davies (1978), 9–36.

DAVIS, L., and MIRABELLA, M. B. (1990) (eds.), *Left Politics and the Literary Profession* (New York and Oxford).

DAVISON, J. A. (1962), 'Literature and Literacy in Ancient Greece', *Phoenix*, 16: 141–56; 219–33.

DAWSON, D. (1992), *Allegorical Readers and Cultural Revision in Ancient Alexandria* (Berkeley, Los Angeles, and Oxford).

DERRIDA, J. (1992), 'Mochlos; or, the Conflict of the Faculties', in Rand (1992), 3–34.

DHAVAN, R. (1978), 'Existing and Alternative Models of Obscenity Law Enforcement', in Dhavan and Davies (1978), 56–75.

—— and DAVIES, C. (1978), *Censorship and Obscenity* (London).

DODDS, E. R. (1959) (ed.), *Plato: Gorgias* (Oxford).

DOUGHERTY, C., and KURKE, L. (1993), *Cultural Poetics in Archaic Greece: Cult, Performance, Politics* (Cambridge).

DOVER, K. J. (1968), *Lysias and the Corpus Lysiacum* (Berkeley and Los Angeles).

—— (1980) (ed.), *Plato: Symposium* (Cambridge).

D' SOUZA, D. (1992), *Illiberal Education: The Politics of Race and Sex on Campus* (New York).

DUBAN, J. (1980), 'Poets and Kings in the *Theogony* Invocation', *QUCC* 4: 7–21.

DUNANT, S. (1994) (ed.), *The War of the Words: The Political Correctness Debate* (London).

DWORKIN, A. (1981), *Men Possessing Women* (London).

—— (1992), 'Against the Male Flood: Censorship, Pornography and Equality', in Itzin (1992), 515–35.

EAGLETON, T. (1984), *The Function of Criticism from the Spectator to Post-Structuralism* (London).

—— (1989) (ed.), *Raymond Williams: Critical Perspectives* (Oxford).

—— (1990), *The Ideology of the Aesthetic* (Oxford).

EAVES, M., and FISCHER, M. (1986) (eds.), *Romanticism and Contemporary Criticism* (Ithaca, NY, and London).

ECO, U. (1987), *Travels in Hyperreality* (London; orig. pub. as *Faith in Fakes* (London, 1986)).

ELIOT, T. S. (1933), *The Use of Poetry and the Use of Criticism* (London).

—— (1948), *Notes Towards the Definition of Culture* (London and Boston).

ELSE, G. (1958), ' "Imitation" in the Fifth Century', *CP* 53: 73–90.

—— (1972), *The Structure and Date of Book 10 of Plato's Republic* (Heidelberg).

ELSNER, J. (1995), *Art and the Roman Viewer: The Transformation of Art from the Pagan World to Christianity* (Cambridge).

—— (1996), 'Naturalism and the Erotics of the Gaze: Imitations of Narcissus', in N. B. Kampen (ed.), *Sexuality in Ancient Art: Near East, Egypt, Greece, and Italy* (Cambridge), 247–61.

—— and MASTERS, J. (1994), *Reflections of Nero: Culture, History and Representation* (London).

ERSKINE, A. (1995), 'Culture and Power in Ptolemaic Egypt: The Museum and the Library at Alexandria', *GR* 42: 38–48.

EUBEN, J. P. (1986), *Greek Tragedy and Political Theory* (Berkeley, Los Angeles, and London).

EVELYN-WHITE, H. G. (1914) (tr.), *Hesiod: The Homeric Hymns and Homerica* (Cambridge, Mass. and London).

FEENEY, D. (1986), ' "Stat Magni Nominis Umbra": Lucan on the Greatness of Pompeius Magnus', *CQ* 36: 239–43.

FERGUSON, M. (1992), 'Augustine's Region of Unlikeness: The Crossing of Exile and Language', in Hexter and Selden (1992), 69–94.

FISH, S. (1980), *Is There A Text In This Class?—The Authority of Interpretive Communities* (Cambridge, Mass. and London).

—— (1989), *Doing What Comes Naturally: Change, Rhetoric, and the Practice of Theory in Literary and Legal Studies* (Oxford).

—— (1994), *There's No Such Thing as Free Speech and It's a Good Thing, Too* (New York and Oxford).

FORD, A. (1992), *Homer: The Poetry of the Past* (Ithaca, NY, and London).

FOUCAULT, M (1989)., *The Archeology of Knowledge* (London).

FOWLER, A. (1975), 'The Selection of Literary Constructs', *NHL* 7: 39–55.

FOX-GENOVESE, E. (1986), 'The Claims of a Common Culture: Gender, Race, Class and the Canon', *Salmagundi*, 72: 131–43.

FRANK, T. (1927), 'Naevius and Free Speech', *AJP* 48: 105–10.

FRASER, P. M. (1972), *Ptolemaic Alexandria*: i, *Text*; ii, *Notes* (Oxford).

GADAMER, H. G. (1980), *Dialogue and Dialectic: Eight Hermeneutical Studies on Plato* (New Haven).

GAGARIN, M. (1973), '*Dikē* in the *Works and Days*', *CP* 68: 81–94.

GATES, H. L. (1992), *Loose Canons: Notes on the Culture Wars* (Oxford and New York).

GELZER, T. (1993), 'Transformations', in Bulloch, Gruen, Long, and Stewart (1993), 130–52.

GENTILI, B. (1988), *Poetry and its Public in Ancient Greece from Homer to the Fifth Century*, tr. T. Cole (Baltimore and London).

GILBERT, A. H. (1939), 'Did Plato Banish the Poets or the Critics?', *Stud. In Phil*. 36: 1–19.

—— (1962), *Literary Criticism: Plato to Dryden* (Detroit, 1962; repr of 1940 edn.).

GIROUX, H. A. (1992), 'Liberal Arts Education and the Struggle for Public Life: Dreaming about Democracy', in Gless and Herrnstein Smith (1992), 119–44.

GLEASON, M. (1995), *Making Men: Sophists and Self-Presentation in Ancient Rome* (Princeton).

GLESS, D., and HERRNSTEIN SMITH, B. (1992) (eds.), *The Politics of Liberal Education* (Durham, NC, and London).

GOLD, B. K. (1987), *Literary Patronage in Greece and Rome* (Chapel Hill, NC, and London).

GOLDEN, L. (1965), 'Is Tragedy the "Imitation of a *Serious Action*"?', *GRBS* 6: 283–9.

—— (1976), 'Aristotle and the Audience for Tragedy', *Mnemosyne*, 29: 351–9.

GOLDHILL, S. (1991), *The Poet's Voice: Essays on Poetics and Greek Literature* (Cambridge).

—— (1994), 'The Naive and Knowing Eye: Ecphrasis and the Culture of Viewing in the Hellenistic World', in S. Goldhill and R. Osborne, *Art and Text in Ancient Greek Culture* (Cambridge), 197–223.

—— (1995), *Foucault's Virginity* (Cambridge).

GOULD, T. (1964), 'Plato's Hostility to Art', *Arion*, 3: 70–91.

GRAFF, G. (1987), *Professing Literature: An Institutional History* (Chicago).

—— (1988), 'What Should We Be Teaching—When There's No We?', *Yale Journal of Criticism*, 1: 189–211.

—— (1992a), 'Teach the Conflicts', in Gless and Herrnstein Smith (1992), 57–72.

—— (1992b), *Beyond the Culture Wars: How Teaching the Conflicts Can Revitalize American Education* (New York and London).

—— (1989), and WARNER, M., *The Origins of Literary Studies in America: A Documentary Anthology* (London).

GREENBERG, N. A. (1961), 'The Use of Poiema and Poiesis', *HSCP* 65: 263–89.

GREENBLATT, S. (1987), 'Capitalist Culture and the Circulatory System', in Krieger (1987), 256–73.

GREENE, W. C. (1918), 'Plato's View of Poetry', *HSCP* 29: 1–75.

GRIFFITH, G. T. (1966), 'Isegoria in the Assembly at Athens', in E. Badian (ed.), *Ancient Society and Institutions: Studies Presented to Victor Ehrenberg* (Oxford), 115–36.

GRIFFITH, M. (1983), 'Personality in Hesiod', *CA* 2: 37–65.

—— and MASTRONARDE, D. J. (1990) (eds.), *Cabinet of the Muses: Essays on Classical and Comparative Literature in Honor of Thomas G. Rosenmeyer* (Atlanta, 1990).

GRIFFITHS, F. T. (1979), *Theocritus at Court* (Leiden).

GRISWOLD, C. (1988) (ed.), *Platonic Writings/Platonic Readings* (New York and London).

GRUBE, G. M. A. (1952), 'Theophrastus as a Literary Critic', *TAPA* 83: 172–83.

—— (1957), "Notes on περὶ ὕψους", *AJP* 78: 355–94.

—— (1958), *Aristotle: On Poetry and Style* (New York).

—— (1965), *The Greek and Roman Critics* (London).

GUBAR, S., and KAMHOLTZ, J. (1993) (eds.), *English Inside and Out: The Places of Literary Criticism* (New York and London).

GUERLAC, S. (1985), 'Longinus and the Subject of the Sublime', *NLH* 16: 275–87.

GUTHRIE, W. K. (1971), *The Sophists* (Cambridge).

GWYNN, A. (1926), *Roman Education from Cicero to Quintilian* (New York).

HALL, E. (1989), *Inventing the Barbarian* (Oxford).

HALLIWELL, S. (1984*a*), 'Ancient Interpretation of ὀνομαστὶ κωμῳδεῖν in Aristophanes', *CQ* 34: 83–8.

—— (1984*b*), 'Aristophanic Satire', *Yearbook of English Studies*, 14: 6–20.

—— (1984*c*), 'Plato and Aristotle on the Denial of Tragedy', *PCPS* 30: 49–71.

—— (1986), *Aristotle's Poetics* (London).

—— (1991), 'Comic Satire and Freedom of Speech in Classical Athens', *JHS* 111: 48–70.

—— (1992), 'Pleasure, Understanding, and Emotion in Aristotle's *Poetics*', in Rorty (1992*a*), 241–60.

HALPERIN, D. (1983), *Before Pastoral: Theocritus and the Ancient Tradition of Bucolic Poetry* (New Haven and London).

HAMILTON-FYFE, W., and RHYS ROBERTS, W. (1927) (tr.), *Aristotle XXIII: The Poetics; 'Longinus'; Demetrius* (Cambridge, Mass.).

HAMMOND, M. (1963), '*Res Olim Dissociabiles: Principatus ac Libertas*: Liberty under the Early Roman Empire', *HSCP* 67: 93–113.

HANSEN, M. H. (1991), *The Athenian Democracy in the Age of Demosthenes: Structure, Principles and Ideology*, tr. J. A. Crook (Oxford and Cambridge, Mass.).

HARRIOTT, R. (1969), *Poetry and Criticism Before Plato* (London).

HARRIS, W. V. (1989), *Ancient Literacy* (Cambridge, Mass. and London).

HAVELOCK, E. (1982), *The Literate Revolution in Greece and its Cultural Consequences* (Princeton).

HELD, G. F. (1984), '*Spoudaios* and Teleology in the *Poetics*', *TAPA* 114: 159–76.

HENDRICKSON, G. L. (1925), 'Verbal Injury, Magic, or Erotic Comus', *AJP* 20: 289–308.

HERTZ, N. (1973), 'Lecture de Longin', *Poétique*, 15: 292–306.

—— (1985), *The End of the Line* (New York).

HEXTER, R., and SELDEN, D. (1992), *Innovations of Antiquity* (London).

HIGHET, G. (1976), *The Immortal Profession: The Joys of Teaching and Learning* (New York).

HIGNETT, C. (1952), *A History of the Athenian Constitution to the End of the Fifth Century BC* (Oxford).

HIRSCH, E. D. (1967), *Validity in Interpretation* (New Haven and London).

HOHENDAHL, P. U. (1988) (ed.), *A History of German Literary Criticism, 1730–1980* (Lincoln, Nebr. and London).

—— (1989), *Building a National Literature: The Case of Germany, 1830–1870*, tr. R. B. Franciscono (Ithaca, NY).

HOLLEMAN, A. W. J. (1971), 'Ovid and Politics', *Historia*, 20: 458–66.

HOPKINSON, N. (1988), *A Hellenistic Anthology* (Cambridge).

HUBBARD, T. K. (1991), *The Mask of Comedy: Aristophanes and the Intertextual Parabasis* (Ithaca, NY, and London).

HUESTON, R. F. V., and BUCKLEY, R. A. (1992), *Salmond and Hueston on the Law of Torts* (London).

HUGHES, R. (1994), *Culture of Complaint: The Fraying of America* (rev. of 1993 edn.; London).

HUNTER, I., SAUNDERS, D., and WILLIAMSON, D. (1993), *On Pornography: Literature, Sexuality and Obscenity Law* (Houndsmills).

HUNTER, W. A. (1876), *A Systematic and Historical Exposition of Roman Law* (London).

HUTCHINSON, G. O. (1988), *Hellenistic Poetry* (Oxford).

INNES, D., HINE, H., and PELLING, C. (1995) (eds.), *Ethics and Rhetoric: Classical Essays for Donald Russell on his Seventy-Fifth Birthday* (Oxford).

ITZIN, C. (1992) (ed.), *Pornography: Women, Violence and Civil Liberties. A Radical New View* (Oxford).

JANKO, R. (1984), *Aristotle on Comedy: Towards a Reconstruction of* Poetics *II* (London).

—— (1992), 'From Catharsis to the Aristotelian Mean', in Rorty (1992*a*), 345–58.

JOCELYN, H. D. (1969), 'The Poet Cn. Naevius, P. Cornelius Scipio and Q. Caecilius Metellus', *Antichthon*, 3: 32–47.

JOHNSON, B. (1993) (ed.), *Freedom and Interpretation: The Oxford Amnesty Lectures 1992* (New York).

JOHNSTON, W. P. (1907), *Greek Literary Criticism* (Oxford).

JONES, H. L. (1932) (tr.), *The Geography of Strabo*, viii (Cambridge, Mass. and London).

KAPPELER, S. (1986), *The Pornography of Representation* (Minneapolis).

—— (1992), 'Pornography: The Representation of Power', in Itzin (1992), 88–101.

KELLY, L. (1992), 'Pornography and Child Sexual Abuse', in Itzin (1992), 113–23.

KENNEDY, G. (1963), *The Art of Persuasion in Greece* (Princeton).

—— (1989), *The Cambridge History of Literary Criticism*, i: *Classical Criticism* (Cambridge).

—— (1992), 'Classics and Canons', in Gless and Herrnstein Smith (1992), 223–31.

KERMODE, F. (1957), *The Romantic Image* (Glasgow).

—— (1975) (ed.), *Selected Prose of T. S. Eliot* (London).

—— (1988), *History and Value* (Oxford).

KEYT, D., and MILLER, F. D. (1991) (eds.), *A Companion to Aristotle's Politics* (Oxford and Cambridge, Mass.).

KIMBALL, R. (1990), *Tenured Radicals: How Politics Has Corrupted Our Higher Education* (New York).

KIRK, G. S. (1950), 'The Michigan Alcidamas-Papyrus; Heraclitus Fr. 56D; The Riddle of the Lice', *CQ*: 149–67.

KNOX, B. (1968), 'Silent Reading in Antiquity', *GRBS* 9: 421–35.

—— (1993), *The Oldest Dead White European Males and Other Reflections on the Classics* (New York and London).

KOENEN, L. (1993), 'The Ptolemaic King as a Religious Figure', in Bulloch, Gruen, Long, and Stewart (1993), 25–115.

KRIEGER, M. (1987) (ed.), *The Aims of Representation: Subject/Text/History* (Stanford, Calif.).

KURKE, L. (1993), 'The Economy of *Kudos*', in Dougherty and Kurke (1993), 131–63.

LA CAPRA, D. (1985), *History and Criticism* (Ithaca, NY).

LAKS, A. (1990), 'Legislation and Demiurge: On the relationship between Plato's *Republic* and *Laws*', *CA* 9: 209–29.

LAMB, J. (1993), 'Longinus, the Dialectic, and the Practice of Mastery', *ELH* 60: 545–67.

LAMBERTON, R. (1988), *Hesiod* (New Haven).

—— and KEANEY, J. J. (1992), *Homer's Ancient Readers: The Hermeneutics of Greek Epic's Earliest Exegetes* (Princeton).

LAUTER, P. (1990), 'Canon Theory and Emergent Practice', in Davis and Mirabella (1990), 127–46.

LEAR, J. (1988), 'Katharsis', *Phronesis*, 33: 297–326.

—— (1992), 'Inside and Outside the *Republic*', *Phronesis*, 37: 184–215.

LEJEUNE, P. (1973), 'Le Pacte autobiographique', *Poétique*, 4: 137–62.

LENTRICCHIA, F. (1980), *After the New Criticism* (Chicago).

—— (1983), *Criticism and Social Change* (Chicago).

LEVISON, M., BUTLER, M., McGANN, J., and HAMILTON, P. (1984) (eds.), *Rethinking Historicism: Critical Readings in Romantic History* (Oxford).

LEWIS, N. (1986), *Greeks in Ptolemaic Egypt: Case Studies in the Social History of the Hellenistic World* (Oxford).

LITTLE, D. (1982), 'Politics in Augustan Poetry', *ANRW* 2. 30.1: 254–370.

LORD, C. (1982), *Education and Culture in the Political Thought of Aristotle* (Ithaca, NY, and London).

LUCAS, D. W. (1968) (ed.), *Aristotle: Poetics* (Oxford).

LUCE, T. J. (1993), 'Reading Response in the *Dialogus*', in T. J. Luce and A. J. Woodman (eds.), *Tacitus and the Tacitean Tradition* (Princeton), 11–38.

McCALL, M. (1975), review of D. A. Russell and M. Winterbottom (eds.), *Ancient Literary Criticism: The Principal Texts in New Translations* (Oxford, 1972), *AJP* 96: 84–5.

McDONALD, C. (1992), 'Institutions of Changes: Notes on Education in the Late Eighteenth Century', in Rand (1992), 37–55.

MACDOWELL, D. M. (1971) (ed.), *Aristophanes: Wasps* (Oxford).

—— (1978), *The Law of Classical Athens* (London).

MCKEON, R. (1936), 'Literary Criticism and the Concept of Imitation in Antiquity', *MPhil.* 36: 1–35.

MACKINNON, C. (1979), *Sexual Harassment of Working Women: A Case of Sex Discrimination* (New Haven).

—— (1992), 'Pornography, Civil Rights and Speech', in Itzin (1992), 456–511.

—— (1993), *Only Words* (Cambridge, Mass.).

MACLEOD, C. (1983), *Collected Essays* (Oxford).

MANN, A. (1979), *The One and the Many: Reflections on the American Identity* (Chicago and London).

MANSFELD, J. (1994), *Prolegomena: Questions to be Settled Before the Study of an Author, or a Text* (Leiden, New York, and Cologne).

MARKUS, R. A. (1970), *Saeculum: History and Society in the Theology of St. Augustine* (Cambridge).

MARROU, H. I. (1948), *A History of Education in Antiquity* (New York; Fr. orig. *Histoire de l'Éducation dans l'Antiquité* (Paris, 1948)).

MARSHALL, A. J. (1976), 'Library Resources and Creative Writing at Rome', *Phoenix*, 30: 252–64.

MARTIN, R. P. (1984), 'Hesiod, Odysseus, and the Instruction of Princes', *TAPA* 114: 29–48.

MASTERS, J. (1992), *Poetry and Civil War in Lucan's Bellum Civile* (Cambridge).

MATTINGLEY, H. B. (1977), 'Poets and Politicians in Fifth-Century Athens', in K. H. Kinzl (ed.), *Greece and the Eastern Mediterranean in Ancient History and Prehistory* (Berlin and New York).

MAZZEO, J. A. (1962), 'Saint Augustine's Rhetoric of Silence', *JHI* 23: 175–96.

MINTON, W. W. (1962), 'Invocation and Catalogue in Hesiod and Homer', *TAPA* 93: 188–212.

MISCH, G. (1950), *A History of Autobiography in Antiquity*, i and ii, tr. E. W. Dickes (London).

MITCHELL, W. J. T. (1982) (ed.), *The Politics of Intepretation* (Chicago).

MOMIGLIANO, A. (1942), review of Laura Robinson, *Freedom of Speech in the Roman Republic* (Baltimore, 1940), *JRS* 32: 120–7.

—— (1971), *The Development of Greek Biography: Four Lectures* (Cambridge, Mass.).

MOMMSEN, T., and KREUGER, P. (1985) (eds.). *The Digest of Justinian*, iv, tr. A. Watson (Philadelphia).

MONDI, R. (1980), 'Skēptoukhoi Basileis: An Argument for Divine Kingship in Early Greece', *Arethusa*, 13: 203–16.

MORAVCSIK, J., and TEMKO, P. (1982), *Plato on Beauty, Wisdom and the Arts* (Totowa, NJ).

MORFORD, M. (1967), *The Poet Lucan: Studies in Rhetorical Epic* (Oxford).

—— (1991), 'How Tacitus Defined Liberty', *ANRW* 2. 33. 5: 3420–50.

MORROW, G. (1960), *Plato's Cretan City: A Historical Interpretation of the Laws* (Princeton).

MORTON, D. (1995), 'Birth of the Cyberqueer', *PMLA* 110: 369–81.

MOST, G. W. (1990), 'Canon Fathers: Literacy, Mortality, Power', *Arion*, 1: 35–60.

MURDOCH, I. (1977), *The Fire and the Sun: Why Plato Banished the Artists* (Oxford).

MURGIA, C. (1980), 'The Date of Tacitus' *Dialogus*', *HSCP* 84: 99–125.

NAGY, G. (1990), *Pindar's Homer: The Lyric Possession of an Epic Past* (Baltimore and London).

NEHEMAS, A. (1982), 'Plato on Imitation and Poetry in *Republic* 10', in Moravcsik and Temko (1982), 47–78.

—— (1992), 'Pity and Fear in the *Rhetoric* and the *Poetics*', in Rorty (1992*a*), 291–314.

NEWMAN, J. K. (1987), '*De Sublimitate* 30.1: An Overlooked Pointer to A Date?', *ICS* 12: 143–55.

NITCHIE, E. (1933–4), 'Longinus and Later Literary Criticism', *CW* 27: 121–6 and 129–35.

NUSSBAUM, M. (1986), *The Fragility of Goodness* (Cambridge).

—— (1992), 'Tragedy and Self-Sufficiency: Plato and Aristotle on Fear and Pity', in Rorty (1992*a*), 261–90.

OBBINK, D. (1995) (ed.), *Philodemus and Poetry: Poetic Theory and Practice in Lucretius, Philodemus, and Horace* (Oxford and New York).

OBER, J. (1989), *Mass and Elite in Democratic Athens: Rhetoric, Ideology and the Power of the People* (Princeton).

OLSON, E. (1965), *Aristotle's Poetics and English Literature* (Chicago and London).

ONG, W. J. (1982), *Orality and Literacy* (London).

OPHIR, A. (1991), *Plato's Invisible Cities: Discourse and Power in the Republic* (London).

PATON, J. J. (1921–2), 'Plato's Theory of *Eikasia*', *Proc. Arist. Soc.* 22: 69–104.

PATTERSON, A. (1984), *Censorship and Interpretation: The Conditions of Writing and Reading in Early Modern Europe* (Madison).

—— (1993), *Reading Between the Lines* (London).

PATTERSON, L. (1987), *Negotiating the Past: The Historical Understanding of Medieval Literature* (Madison).

PELIKAN, J. (1992), *The Idea of the University: A Re-examination* (New Haven and London).

PÉPIN, J. (1958), *Mythe et allégorie: Les Origines grecques et les contestations judéo-chrétiennes* (Aubier).

PERKINS, D. (1992), *Is Literary History Possible?* (Baltimore and London).

PFEIFFER, R. (1949) (ed.), *Callimachus*, i (Oxford).

—— (1968), *The History of Classical Scholarship from the Beginnings to the End of the Hellenistic Age* (Oxford).

PHILIP, J. A. (1961), 'Mimesis in the *Sophistes* of Plato', *TAPA* 92: 453–68.

PINBORG, J. (1975), 'Classical Antiquity: Greece', in *Historiography of Linguistics*, xiii: *Current Trends in Linguistics*, ed. T. A. Sebeok (The Hague and Paris), 69–126.

PLATT, A. (1910), 'Callimachus *Iambi* 162–170', *CQ* 4: 205.

POPPER, K. R. (1962), *The Open Society and Its Enemies*, 4th edn. (London).

PORTER, J. I. (1992), 'Hermeneutic Lines and Circles: Aristarchus and Cartes and the Exegesis of Hermes', in Lamberton and Keaney (1992), 67–114.

POSNER, R. (1988), *Law and Literature: A Misunderstood Relation* (Cambridge, Mass.).

PRATT, L. H. (1993), *Lying and Poetry from Homer to Pindar: Falsehood and Deception in Archaic Greek Poetics* (Ann Arbor).

PRATT, M. L. (1992), 'Humanities for the Future: Reflection on the Western Culture Debate at Stanford', in Gless and Herrnstein Smith (1992), 13–31.

PUCCI, P. (1977), *Hesiod and the Language of Poetry* (Baltimore).

PUELMA, M. (1954), 'Der Vorbilder der Elegiendichtung in Alexandrien und Rom', *MH* 11: 101–16.

QUINN, K. (1982), 'Poet and Audience in the Augustan Age', *ANRW* 2. 30. 1: 75–180.

RAAFLAUB, K. A. (1983), 'Democracy, Oligarchy, and the Concept of the "Free Citizen" in Late Fifth-Century Athens', *Political Theory*, 11: 517–44.

RADIN, M. (1927), 'Freedom of speech in Ancient Athens', *AJP* 48: 215–30.

RAND, R. (1992) (ed.), *Logomachia: The Conflict of the Faculties* (Lincoln, Nebr. and London).

RECKFORD, K. J. (1976), 'Father-Beating in Aristophanes' *Clouds*', in S. Bertman (ed.), *The Conflict of Generations in Ancient Greece and Rome* (Amsterdam).

REINSCH-WERNER, H. (1976), *Callimachus Hesiodicus: Die Rezeption der hesiodeischen Dichtung durch Kallimachos von Kyrene* (Berlin).

REYNOLDS, L. D., and WILSON, N. G. (1974), *Scribes and Scholars: A Guide to the Transmission of Greek and Latin Literature*, 2nd edn. (Oxford).

RICOEUR, P. (1984), *Time and Narrative*, i, tr. K. McLaughlin and D. Pellauer (Chicago and London; Fr. orig. *Temps et récit* (Paris, 1983)).

RINGBOM, S. (1965), 'Plato on Images', *Theoria*, 31: 95–6.

RIST, J. M. (1993), *Augustine: Ancient Thought Baptized* (Cambridge).

ROBBINS, B. (1993), *Secular Vocations: Intellectuals, Professionalism, Culture* (London).

ROEMER, A. (1912), *Aristarchs Athetesen in der Homerkritik* (Leipzig and Berlin).

ROLPH, C. H. (1969), *Books in the Dock* (London).

RORTY, A. O. (1992a) (ed.), *Essays on Aristotle's Poetics* (Princeton).

—— (1992b), 'The Psychology of Aristotelian Tragedy', in Rorty (1992a), 1–22.

ROSEN, R. M. (1988), *Old Comedy and the Iambographic Tradition* (Atlanta).

ROSEN, S. (1988), *The Quarrel between Philosophy and Poetry: Studies in Ancient Thought* (New York).

ROSENMEYER, T. G. (1973), *The Green Cabinet: Theocritus and the European Pastoral Lyric* (Berkeley, Los Angeles, and London).

ROSIVACH, V. J. (1987), 'Some Fifth- and Fourth-Century Views on the Purpose of Ostracism', *Tyche*, 2: 161–70.

RÖSLER, W. (1980), 'Die Entdeckung der Fiktionalität in der Antike', *Poetica*, 12: 283–319.

ROTH, C. P. (1976), 'The Kings and the Muses in Hesiod's *Theogony*', *TAPA* 106: 331–8.

RUDD, N. (1989) (ed.), *Horace: Epistles, Book II, and Epistle to the Pisones ('Ars Poetica')* (Cambridge).

RUSSELL, D. A. (1964) (ed.), *'Longinus': On the Sublime* (Oxford).

—— (1979), 'Classicizing Rhetoric and Criticism: the Pseudo-Dionysian *Exetasis* and *Mistakes in Declamation*', in K. Maurer (ed.), *Le Classicisme à Rome aux 1ers siècles avant et après J.-C.* (Entretiens Fondation Hardt, 21; Geneva), 113–30.

—— (1981), *Criticism in Antiquity* (London).

—— and WINTERBOTTOM, M. (1972) (eds.), *Ancient Literary Criticism: The Principal Texts in New Translations* (Oxford).

RUSSELL, D. E. (1992), 'Pornography and Rape: A Causal Model', in Itzin (1992), 310–49.

RUSSELL, R. P. (1968), *Saint Augustine: The Teacher, The Free Choice of The Will, Grace and Free Will* (Washington).

RYBERG, I. S. (1942), 'Tacitus' Art of Innuendo', *TAPA* 73: 383–404.

SAÏD, E. (1978), *Orientalism* (New York).

—— (1991), *The Making of the Modern Canon* (London).

SAINTSBURY, G. (1908), *A History of Criticism* (London).

SAUNDERS, D. (1990), 'Copyright, Obscenity and Literary History', *ELH* 57: 431–44.

SCHOLES, R. (1986), 'Aiming a Canon at the Curriculum', *Salmagundi*, 72: 101–17.

SEGAL, C. P. (1959), "'ΥΨΟΣ and the Problem of Cultural Decline in the *De Sublimitate*", *HSCP* 44: 121–46.

SEGAL, L., and MCINTOSH, M. (1992) (eds.), *Sex Exposed: Sexuality and the Pornography Debate* (London).

SHAPIRO, G. (1985), 'From the Sublime to the Political: Some Historical Notes', *NLH* 16 (*The Sublime and the Beautiful: Reconsideration*), 213–35.

SIKES, E. E. (1931), *The Greek View of Poetry* (London).

SMITH, R. E. (1951), 'The Law of Libel at Rome', *CQ* 95: 169–79.

SOMMERSETIN, A. (1986), 'The Decree of Syrakosios', *CQ* 36: 101–8.

SPITZER, M. L. (1986), *Seven Dirty Words and Six Other Stories: Controlling the Content of Print and Broadcast* (New Haven and London).

STALLYBRASS, P., and WHITE, A. (1986), *The Politics and Poetics of Transgression* (London).

STANFORD, W. B. (1958), *Aristophanes: Frogs* (Bristol).

STAROBINSKI, J. (1975), 'The Meaning of Literary History', *NLH* 7: 83–8.

STERN, J. (1981), 'Herodas' Mimiambi', *GRBS* 22: 161–5.

STIMPSON, C. (1990), 'What Am I Doing When I Do Women's Studies in 1990?', in Davis and Mirabella (1990), 55–83.

STRAUSS, B. (1993), *Fathers and Sons in Athens: Ideology and Society in the Era of the Peloponnesian War* (London).

STRAUSS, L. (1952), *Persecution and the Art of Writing* (Chicago and London).

STRELKA, J. P. (1973), *Literary Criticism and Sociology* (Yearbook of Comparative Criticism, 5; University Park, Pa. and London).

SYME, R. (1958), *Tacitus*, 2 vols. (Oxford).

TATE, A. (1953), *The Forlorn Demon: Didactic and Critical Essays* (Chicago).

TATE, J. (1928), 'Imitation in Plato's *Republic*', *CQ* 22: 16–23.

—— (1929–30), 'Plato and Allegorical Interpretation', *CQ* 23 (1929), 142–54, and *CQ* 24 (1930), 1–10.

—— (1932), 'Plato and Imitation', *CQ* 26: 161–9.

—— (1934), 'On the History of Allegorism', *CQ* 28: 105–14.

THOMPSON, D. J. (1994), 'Literacy and Power in Ptolemaic Egypt', in Bowman and Woolf (1994), 67–83.

TIGERSTEDT, E. N. (1969), *Plato's Idea of Poetical Inspiration* (Helsinki).

TODD, S. (1993), *The Shape of Athenian Law* (Oxford).

TOO, Y. L. (1995), *The Rhetoric of Identity in Isocrates: Text, Power, Pedagogy* (Cambridge).

TRAPP, M. (1995), 'Sense of Place in the Orations of Dio Chrysostom', in Innes, Hine, and Pelling (1995), 163–75.

TRIMPI, W. (1978), "The Early Metaphorical Uses of σκιαγραφία and σκηνογραφία", *Traditio*, 34: 403–13.

TRIMPI, W. (1983), *Muses of One Mind: The Literary Analysis of Experience and its Continuity* (Princeton).

TRYPANIS, C. (1958) (tr.), *Callimachus* (Cambridge, Mass. and London).

TURNER, E. G. (1968), *Greek Papyri: An Introduction* (Oxford).

USHER, S. (1985) (tr.), *Dionysius of Halicarnassus: The Critical Essays*, ii (Cambridge, Mass. and London).

USSHER, R. G. (1980), 'The Mimiambi of Herodas', *Hermathena*, 129: 65–76.

VANCE, E. (1973*a*) 'Augustine's *Confessions* and the Grammar of Selfhood', *Genre*, 6: 1–28.

—— (1973*b*), 'Le Moi comme langage: Saint Augustin et l'autobiographie', *Poétique*, 4: 163–77.

VAN DER VALK, M. H. (1949), *Textual Criticism of the Odyssey* (Leiden).

—— (1953), 'A Defence of Some Suspected Passages in the *Scutum Hesiodi*', *Mnemosyne*, 4: 265–82.

VAN GIGCH, J. (1852), 'Bigdrage tot der Latiniteit der Decemvirale Welten', *Mnemosyne*, 50: 69–74.

VERNANT, J.-P. (1975), 'Image et apparence dans la théorie platonicienne de la *mimesis*', *Journal de Psychologie*, 72: 133–60.

—— and DÉTIENNE, M. (1974), *Les Ruses de l'intelligence: La Metis des Grecs* (Paris).

VIAN, F. (1952), 'La Guerre des géants devant les penseurs de l'antiquité', *REG* 65: 1–39.

VICKERS, B. (1988), *In Defence of Rhetoric* (Oxford).

WALSH, G. B. (1984), *The Varieties of Enchantment: Early Greek Views of the Nature and Function of Poetry* (Chapel Hill, NC, and London).

—— (1988), 'Sublime Method: Longinus on Language and Imitation', *CA* 7: 252–69.

WARMINGTON, E. H. (1938) (ed. and tr.), *Remains of Old Latin*, iii (Cambridge, Mass.).

WARRY, J.G. (1962), *Greek Aesthetic Theory: A Study of Callistic and Aesthetic Concepts in the Works of Plato and Aristotle* (London).

WATSON, G. (1962), *The Literary Critics: A Study of English Descriptive Criticism* (London).

WEBSTER, T.B. (1939), 'Greek Theories of Art and Literature down to 400 B.C.', *CQ* 33: 166–79.

—— (1964), *Hellenistic Poetry and Art* (London).

WELLEK, R. (1955), *A History of Modern Criticism, 1750–1950*, i: *The Later Eighteenth Century* (London).

WEST, D., and WOODMAN, A. (1979) (eds.), *Creative Imitation and Latin Literature* (Cambridge).

WEST, M. L. (1966) (ed.), *Hesiod: Theogony* (Oxford).

—— (1978) (ed.), *Hesiod: Works and Days* (Oxford).

——— (1980), *Delectus ex Iambis et Elegis Graecis* (Oxford).

WEST, S. (1965), *The Ptolemaic Papyri of Homer* (Cologne).

WHITE, H. (1975), 'The Problem of Change in Literary History', *NLH* 7: 97–111.

WHITE, J. B. (1985), *Heracles' Bow: Essays on the Rhetoric and Poetics of the Law* (Madison and London).

WIEDEMANN, T. (1975), 'The Political Background to Ovid's *Tristia* 2', *CQ* 25: 264–71.

WILLIAMS, G. (1978), *Change and Decline* (Berkeley, Los Angeles, and London).

WILLIAMS, R. (1958), *Culture and Society: Coleridge to Orwell* (London).

——— (1961), *The Long Revolution* (New York).

WIMSATT, W. K., and BROOKS, C. (1957), *Literary Criticism: A Short History* (New York).

WINKLER, J. (1990), 'The Ephebes' Song: *Tragōidia* and *Polis*', in Winkler and Zeitlin (1990), 20–62.

——— and ZEITLIN, F. (1990) (eds.), *Nothing to do with Dionysos? Athenian Drama in its Social Context* (Princeton).

WIRZBUSKI, C. (1950), *Libertas as a Political Idea at Rome During the Late Republic and Early Principate* (Cambridge).

WOODHEAD, A. G. (1967), "*ΙΣΗΓΟΡΙΑ* and the Council of 500", *Historia*, 16: 129–40.

WOODMAN, A. J. (1975), 'Questions of Date, Genre, and Style in Velleius: Some Literary Answers', *CQ* 25: 272–306.

WOODSIDE, M. ST A. (1942), 'Vespasian's Patronage of Education and the Arts', *TAPA* 73: 123–9.

WORTHINGTON, I. (1994) (ed.), *Persuasion: Greek Rhetoric in Action* (London and New York).

YOUNG, D. C. (1983), 'Pindar, Aristotle, and Homer: A Study in Ancient Criticism', *CA* 2: 156–70.

ZANKER, G. (1981), '*Enargeia* in the Ancient Criticism of Poetry', *RhM* 124: 297–311.

——— (1987), *Realism in Alexandrian Poetry: A Literature and its Audience*, (London, Sydney, and Wolfeboro, NH).

INDEX LOCORUM

GENERAL INDEX